RUNAWAY BEST SELLER!

"GREAT POST, BRENT!"

"Soaring. Glorious. Breathtaking!"
---The Waukegan Register

"Plato. Aquinas. Tocqueville. Ozar."
---The Walla Walla Review

"Rhapsodic and heroic. Splendid!"
---Albuquerque Book Club

"Brilliantly conceived and written! A work of sheer genius." *---Brent Ozar*

ISBN: 978-0-692-13816-8

Book Layout & eBook Conversion by manuscript2ebook.com

Table of Contents

Foreword:
300 Blogs And Running

Why Bother Blogging?

I blog primarily because there's a Certain Kind of Person that irks me to no end.

The kind of person who:

- Withholds information (you wouldn't understand anyway)
- Mocks people for not knowing what ***they*** know (oh, you silly things)
- Uses the people they mock to validate their necessity (you'd be lost without me)

It's an ego club that I don't want to be a part of, and the kind of people who take great glee in being part of this sort of club are unfortunately all too common.

When I learn something, I immediately want everyone else to know it, too. I want it in as many hands as possible.

I don't even want to charge people for it. That's only when I have to repeat myself.

The same goes for answering questions at sites like Stack Exchange. I joke about the badge/reputation feedback mechanism a lot, but at the heart of things, I really do hope that every time my Imaginary Life Bucks go up, that it's because I've helped someone out in some way.

The more people who Know A Thing, the better.

That means problems get solved faster, problems get avoided sooner, and hopefully no one has to spend hours or days of their lives banging their head against a problem.

Braining Day

What I'd love for you to take from my writing is that learning about SQL Server is like doing a puzzle that never quite ends.

The pieces I've put together are pieces that I picked up from a long list of people who have taken the time to write and teach things over the years — they deserve all the credit, really. My pieces are pretty small in the Grand Scheme of Things, but my aim is to leave the Grand Scheme of Things a little bit more put-together than I found them. A bit less... ***Fragmented.***

Tee-hee.

You know why? I have kids. I don't want them spending a single second having to think about what a primary key is. One of my grandfathers was a book binder. I'm pretty sure he never clocked out thinking "golly and gosh, I sure do hope my kids someday know the joy of an honest day's gluing."

In the same regard, I don't want you, dear reader, having to glue all this stuff together on your own. The more pieces I put firmly in place, the less time you have to spend sniffing glue and having sticky fingers.

Not that that's a bad way to spend a weekend.

Y'all Ain't Not Nothin'

I know that as far as SQL bloggers go, I'm not extraordinary in any way. There are people who are better at writing, teaching, visualizing, and who are a heck of a lot smarter than I am.

Most of them are probably far more sober, too. Perhaps there's a connection?

Nah. Let's move on.

I really just want to be consistent. I don't want to be one of those Vanishing Bloggers. The one who checks in every 6 months with a promise to blog more and a vague update about being really busy with this or that. That is, in the words of a far more consistent writer, a lot of cockadoodie.

We're all busy. You're either writing or you're not.

If I'm writing consistently then I'm learning consistently. If I'm learning consistently then I'm putting more of those pieces we talked about together.

The more often this happens, the better.

The Big Payback

None of this would have been possible without the vision, extreme patience, and hard work of many other people.

My wife, for being very understanding about the amount of time I need to spend staring at glowing rectangles.

Brent, of course, for not firing me.

Kendra and Jeremiah for overlooking my mediocre interviewing skills.

Paul White and Joe Obbish for making fun of me until I get things (mostly) right.

And of course you, dear reader (and sometimes tolerable comment-leaver), for putting up with with my pop culture references that end in 1989.

As always, Thanks for Reading!

Erik Darling

This page got archived to Azure Stretch DB,
and it cost even more than this book.

Windowing Functions

Like a window into your data's soul, with a side of mild hallucinations. This chapter pairs well with Absinthe and a sturdy helmet.

BRENT OZAR UNLIMITED®

Indexing for Windowing Functions: WHERE vs. OVER

Life Is Messy

Demo queries have this nasty habit of being clean. Even using a pit of despair like Adventure Works or World Wide Importers, it's easy to craft demo queries that fit the scenario you need to make yourself look like a genius. Stack Overflow, in all its simplicity, makes this even easier (lucky me!) because there's nothing all that woogy or wonky to dance around.

While working with a client recently — yes, Brent lets me talk to paying customers — we found a rather tough situation. They were using Windowing functions over one group of columns to partition and order by, but the where clause was touching a totally different group of columns.

The query plan wasn't happy.

Users weren't happy.

I was still dizzy from being on a boat.

Optimal?

If you've been reading the blog for a while, you may remember this post from about two years ago. Over there, we talked about a POC index, a term popularized by Itzik Ben-Gan.

But how does that work when your query has other needs?

Let's meet our query!

```sql
DECLARE @Score INT, @rn INT

SELECT @Score = p.Score,
       @rn = ROW_NUMBER() OVER ( PARTITION BY p.OwnerUserId ORDER BY p.Score DESC, p.CreationDate DESC )
FROM   dbo.Posts AS p
WHERE  p.PostTypeId = 1
       AND p.CommunityOwnedDate IS NULL
       AND p.LastActivityDate >= '2016-01-01'
```

We have a Windowing function that partitions and orders by three columns, and a where clause that uses three other columns. If we stick a POC index on the Posts table that prioritizes performance of the Windowing function, what happens? I'm going to put the three where clause columns in the include list to avoid troubleshooting key lookups later.

```sql
CREATE UNIQUE NONCLUSTERED INDEX ix_helper ON dbo.Posts (OwnerUserId, Score DESC,
CreationDate DESC, Id) INCLUDE (PostTypeId, CommunityOwnedDate, LastActivityDate)
```

Now when I run the query, here's my plan with — you guessed it! A missing index request.

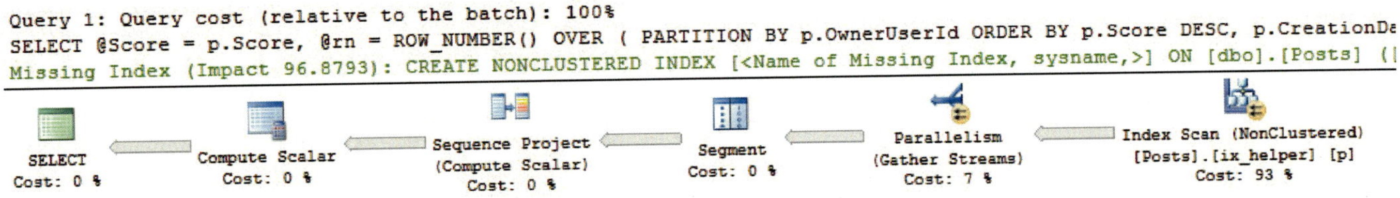

You're a wang

The missing index request is for nearly the EXACT OPPOSITE INDEX we just added. Oh boy.

```sql
/*
Missing Index Details from SQLQuery12.sql - NADAULTRA\SQL2016E.StackOverflow (sa (67))
The Query Processor estimates that implementing the following index could improve the
query cost by 96.8793%.
*/

/*
USE [StackOverflow]
GO
CREATE NONCLUSTERED INDEX [<Name of Missing Index, sysname,>]
ON [dbo].[Posts] ([CommunityOwnedDate],[PostTypeId],[LastActivityDate])
INCLUDE ([CreationDate],[OwnerUserId],[Score])
GO
*/
```

96.8%! I must be a bad DBA. I made a backwards index. I hope someone automates this soon.

Okay, so, let's create an index close in spirit to our original index. Just, y'know, backwards.

```sql
CREATE UNIQUE NONCLUSTERED INDEX ix_helper2 ON dbo.Posts (CommunityOwnedDate,
PostTypeId, LastActivityDate, Id) INCLUDE (CreationDate, OwnerUserId, Score)
```

When we re-run our query, what happens?

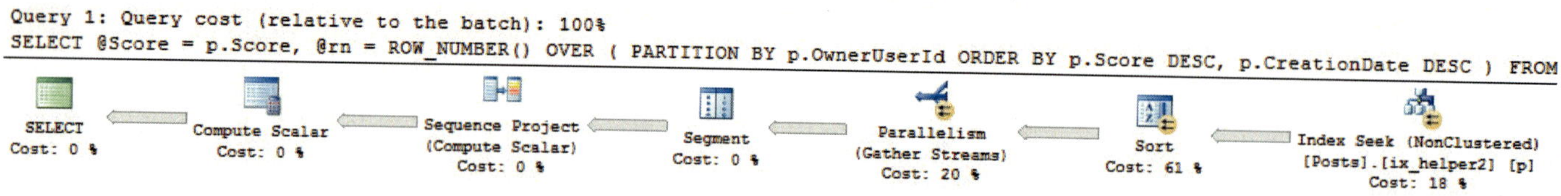

Astronaughty

Oddball

Let's pause here for a minute. Stuff like this can seem witchcrafty when it's glossed over in a blog post.

The index I created is awesome for the Windowing function, and the index that SQL registered as missing was awesome for the where clause.

When I have both indexes, SQL chooses the where-clause-awesome-index because it judges the query will be cheaper to deal with when it can easily seek and filter out rows from the key of the nonclustered index, and then pass only those rows along to the Windowing function.

Now, it can still do this with the Windowing-function-awesome-index, because the where clause columns are included, just not as efficiently as when they're key columns.

The trade-off here is a Sort operation to partition and order by for the Windowing function, but SQL says that will still be far cheaper to sort a bunch of data

Time bomb

If you're query tuning with a small amount of data, you'll take a look at these query costs, stick with the where clause awesome index, and go get extra drunk for doing a wicked good job.

Here they are back to back.

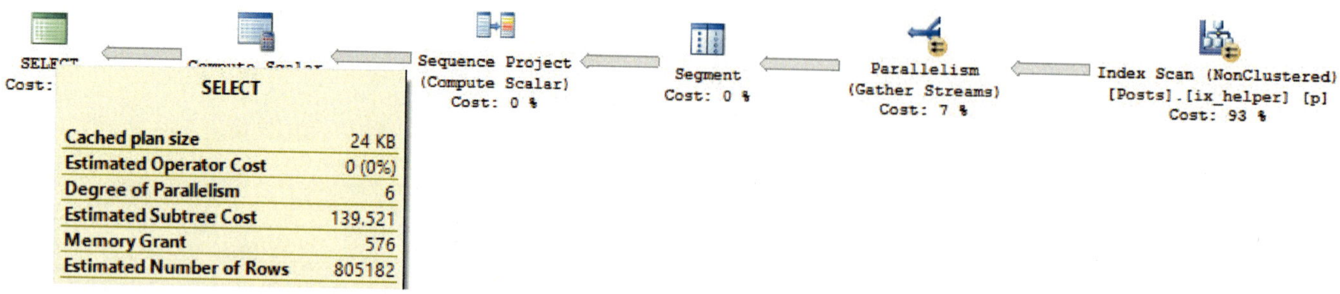

Sortless

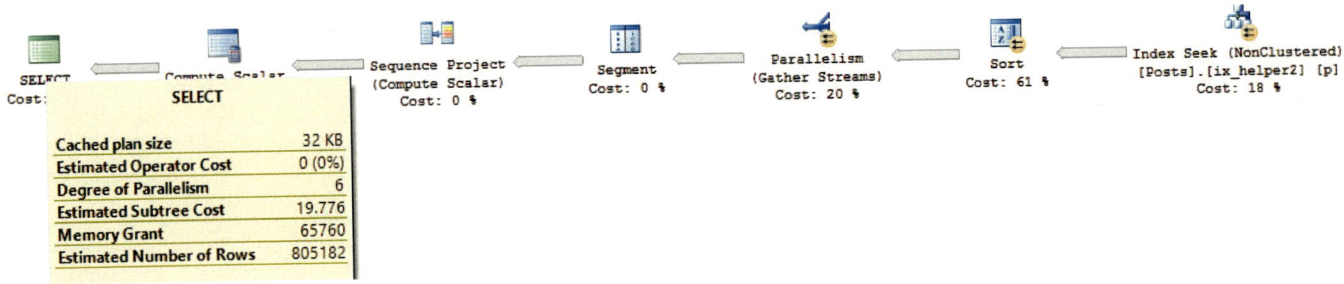

Sorta kinda

What happens when we include more data?

Going back a year further, to 2015, the costs are close to even. The Sortless plan costs about 159 query bucks, and the Sorted plan costs about 124 query bucks.

Going back to 2013, the Sortless plan now costs 181 query bucks, the Sorted plan costs 243 query bucks, and the Sort spills to disk.

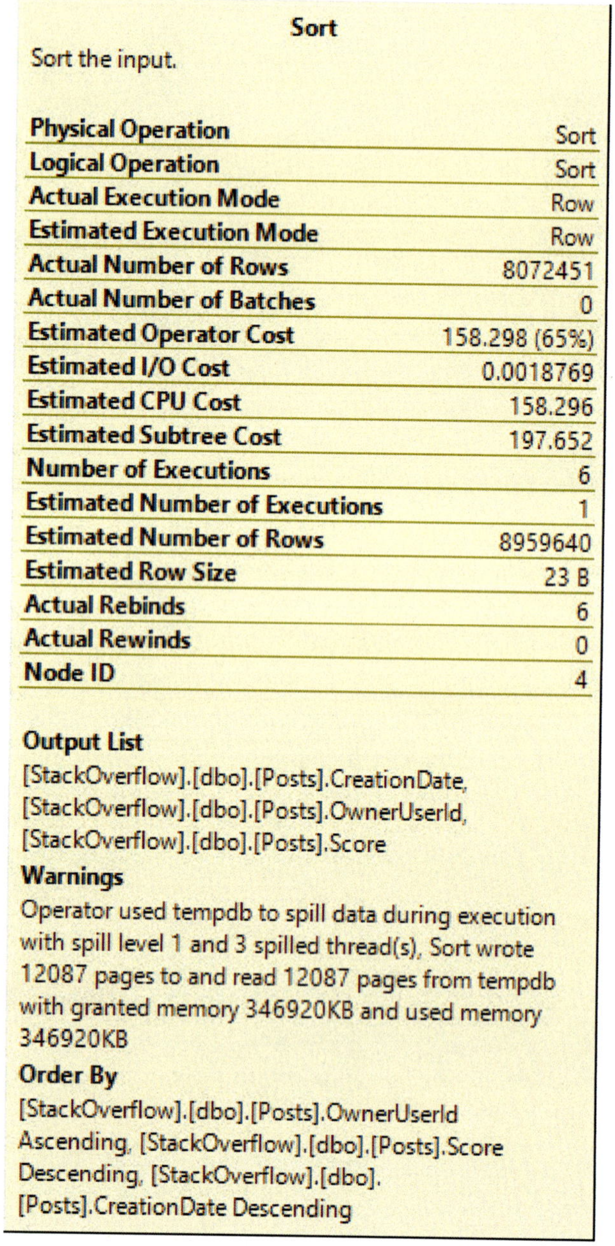

Sort

Sort the input.

Physical Operation	Sort
Logical Operation	Sort
Actual Execution Mode	Row
Estimated Execution Mode	Row
Actual Number of Rows	8072451
Actual Number of Batches	0
Estimated Operator Cost	158.298 (65%)
Estimated I/O Cost	0.0018769
Estimated CPU Cost	158.296
Estimated Subtree Cost	197.652
Number of Executions	6
Estimated Number of Executions	1
Estimated Number of Rows	8959640
Estimated Row Size	23 B
Actual Rebinds	6
Actual Rewinds	0
Node ID	4

Output List

[StackOverflow].[dbo].[Posts].CreationDate, [StackOverflow].[dbo].[Posts].OwnerUserId, [StackOverflow].[dbo].[Posts].Score

Warnings

Operator used tempdb to spill data during execution with spill level 1 and 3 spilled thread(s), Sort wrote 12087 pages to and read 12087 pages from tempdb with granted memory 346920KB and used memory 346920KB

Order By

[StackOverflow].[dbo].[Posts].OwnerUserId Ascending, [StackOverflow].[dbo].[Posts].Score Descending, [StackOverflow].[dbo].[Posts].CreationDate Descending

Little Blue Spills

So what's the point?

Missing index requests don't always have your long term health in mind when they pop up. Some may; others may just be a shot and a beer to get your query past a hangover.

If I go back and run the '2013' query with only the original index on there (the one that helps the Windowing function), there's still a missing index request, but with a lower value (75% rather than

98%). Part of this is due to how costs are estimated and where SQL expects the sort to happen (disk vs memory).

In our case, the Sort was a bit of a time bomb. At first, it didn't matter. As we included more data, it got worse. This is the kind of challenge that a lot of developers face as their app goes from a couple hundred clients to a couple thousand clients, and exactly the kind of thing our Critical Care helps with.

Thanks for reading!

Brent says: *this isn't just about missing index hints in query plans, either: it's also a great example of why you have to be a little bit careful with the missing index DMV recommendations, too. sp_BlitzIndex would report this index as missing, and you won't know which queries are asking for it (or whether they've gotten better or worse.) Every now and then, you'll add a missing index and performance will actually get worse – so you've also gotta be looking at your top resource-intensive queries via sp_BlitzCache. In this example, after you've added Clippy's index, the now-slower query would show up in sp_BlitzCache with no missing index hints, and you'd need to know how to hand-craft your own.*

Indexing for Windowing Functions

Hooray Windowing Functions

They do stuff that used to be hard to do, or took weird self-joins or correlated sub-queries with triangular joins to accomplish. That's when there's a standalone inequality predicate, usually for getting a running total.

With Windowing Functions, a lot of the code complexity and inefficiency is taken out of the picture, but they still work better if you feed them some useful indexes.

What kind of index works best?

In general, what's been termed a POC Index by Itzik Ben-Gan and documented to some extent here.

POC stands for Partition, Order, Covering. When you look at your code, you want to first index any columns you're partitioning on, then any columns you're ordering by, and then cover (with an INCLUDE) any other columns you're calling in the query.

Note that this is the optimal indexing strategy for Windowing Functions, and not necessarily for the query as a whole. Supporting other operations may lead you to design indexes differently, and that's fine.

Everyone loves a demo

Here's a quick example with a little extra something extra for the indexing witches and warlocks out there. I'm using the Stack Exchange database, which you can find out how to make your favorite new test database here.

For the links, code, and comments, go here:
https://www.brentozar.com/archive/2015/06/indexing-for-windowing-functions/

```sql
SET NOCOUNT ON

SET STATISTICS IO, TIME ON;

SELECT   p.OwnerUserId,
         p.CreationDate,
         SUM(p.ViewCount) OVER ( PARTITION BY p.OwnerUserId ORDER BY p.CreationDate ) AS TotalViews
FROM     dbo.Posts AS p
WHERE    p.PostTypeId = 1
AND      p.Score > 0
AND      p.OwnerUserId = 4653
ORDER BY p.CreationDate
OPTION ( RECOMPILE );

/*
Table 'Posts'. Scan count 5, logical reads 488907, physical reads 0, read-ahead reads 0, lob logical reads 0, lob physical reads 0, lob read-ahead reads 0.
Table 'Worktable'. Scan count 1180, logical reads 7095, physical reads 0, read-ahead reads 0, lob logical reads 0, lob physical reads 0, lob read-ahead reads 0.

 SQL Server Execution Times:
   CPU time = 2328 ms,  elapsed time = 760 ms.
*/
```

The query above is running on the Posts table which only has a Clustered Index on the Id column, that does us absolutely no good here. There are tons of access operations and logical reads. Taking a look at the plan doesn't offer much:

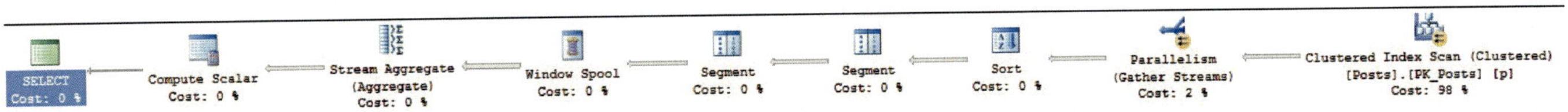

I am a plan. Love me.

Let's try a POC index to fix this up. I'm keeping ViewCount in the key because we're aggregating on it. You can sometimes get away with just using it as an INCLUDE column instead.

```sql
CREATE NONCLUSTERED INDEX IX_POC_DEMO
    ON dbo.Posts ( OwnerUserId, CreationDate, ViewCount );
```

We can note with a tone of obvious and ominous foreshadowing that creating this index on the entire table takes about 15 seconds. Insert culturally appropriate scary sound effects here.

Here's what the plan looks like running the query again:

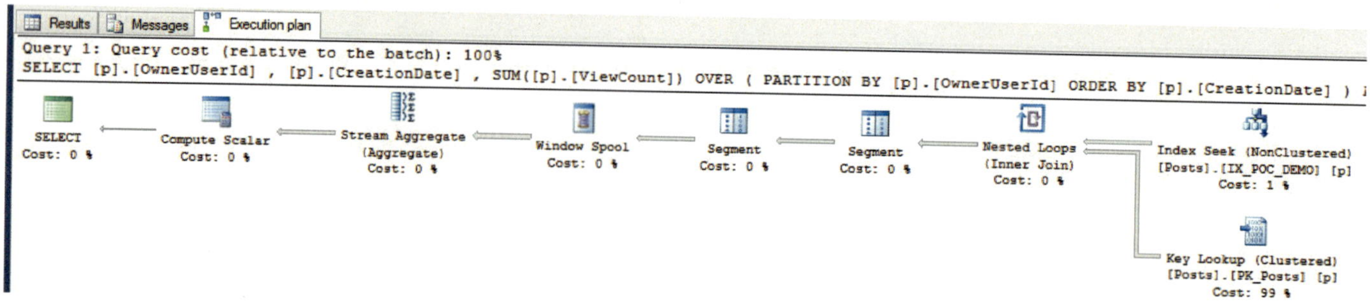

I'm a Scorpio. I like Datsuns and Winston 100s.

That key lookup is annoying.

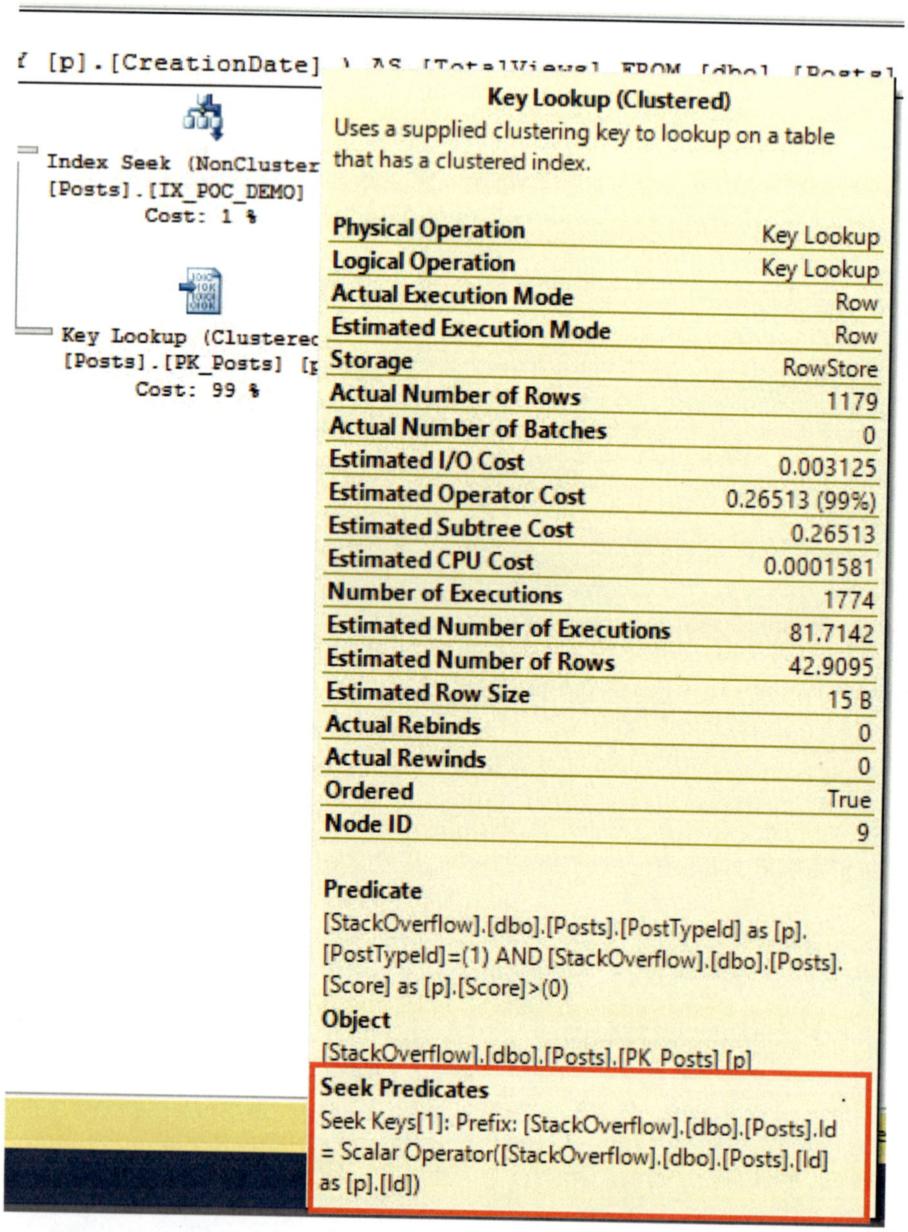

Not all key lookups are due to output columns. Some of them are predicates.

For the links, code, and comments, go here:
https://www.brentozar.com/archive/2015/06/indexing-for-windowing-functions/

We did a good job of reducing a lot of the ickiness from before:

```
/*
Table 'Worktable'. Scan count 1180, logical reads 7095, physical reads 0, read-ahead reads 0, lob logical reads 0, lob physical reads 0, lob read-ahead reads 0.
Table 'Posts'. Scan count 1, logical reads 4973, physical reads 0, read-ahead reads 0, lob logical reads 0, lob physical reads 0, lob read-ahead reads 0.

 SQL Server Execution Times:
   CPU time = 31 ms,  elapsed time = 168 ms.
*/
```

But we're not happy. Why? Because we're DBAs. Or developers. Or we just have to use computers, which are the worst things ever invented.

Behold the filtered index

```
CREATE NONCLUSTERED INDEX IX_POC_DEMO
 ON dbo.Posts ( OwnerUserId, CreationDate, ViewCount );
WHERE [PostTypeId] = 1 AND [Score] > 0
WITH (DROP_EXISTING = ON)
```

Cool. This index only takes about three seconds to create. Marinate on that.

This query is so important and predictable that we can roll this out for it. How does it look now?

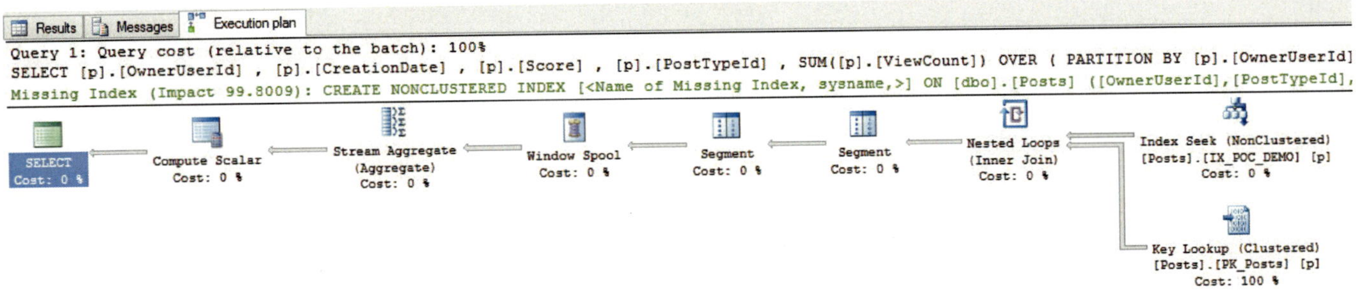

Well, but, WHY?

That key lookup is still there, and now 100% of the estimated magickal query dust cost. For those keeping track at home, this is the entirely new missing index SQL Server thinks will fix your relationship with your dad:

```
/*
USE [StackOverflow]
GO
CREATE NONCLUSTERED INDEX [<Name of Missing Index, sysname,>]
ON [dbo].[Posts] ([OwnerUserId],[PostTypeId],[Score])
INCLUDE ([CreationDate],[ViewCount])
GO
*/
```

But we took a nice chunk out of the IO and knocked a little more off the CPU, again.

```
/*
Table 'Worktable'. Scan count 1180, logical reads 7102, physical reads 0,
read-ahead reads 0, lob logical reads 0, lob physical reads 0, lob read-ahead reads 0.
Table 'Posts'. Scan count 1, logical reads 9, physical reads 0, read-ahead reads 0,
lob logical reads 0, lob physical reads 0, lob read-ahead reads 0.

 SQL Server Execution Times:
   CPU time = 0 ms,  elapsed time = 91 ms.
*/
```

What can we do here?

Include!

```
CREATE NONCLUSTERED INDEX IX_POC_DEMO
    ON dbo.Posts ( OwnerUserId, CreationDate, ViewCount )
    INCLUDE ( PostTypeId, Score )
    WHERE PostTypeId = 1
    AND   Score > 0
    WITH ( DROP_EXISTING = ON );
```

Running the query one last time, we finally get rid of that stinky lookup:

Bully for you!

And we're still at the same place for IO:

```
/*
Table 'Worktable'. Scan count 1180, logical reads 7102, physical reads 0, read-ahead reads 0, lob logical reads 0, lob physical reads 0, lob read-ahead reads 0.
Table 'Posts'. Scan count 1, logical reads 9, physical reads 0, read-ahead reads 0, lob logical reads 0, lob physical reads 0, lob read-ahead reads 0.

 SQL Server Execution Times:
   CPU time = 0 ms,  elapsed time = 90 ms.
*/
```

What did we learn? Windowing functions are really powerful T-SQL tools, but you still need to be hip to indexing to get the most out of them.

Check out our free resources on Windowing Functions here.

Jeff Moden talks at length about triangular joins here (registration required).

Window Functions and Cruel Defaults

Well, my first technical post, was about how the default index creation method is OFFLINE. If you want that sweet, sweet Enterpri$e Edition ONLINE goodness, you need to specify it. It's been a while since that one; almost six months to the day. So here's another one!

But Window Functions Are Awesome

Heck yeah they are. And how. Boy howdy. Etc. You get the point. I'm enthusiastic. What can be cruel about them? Glad you asked!

Window Functions, according to the almighty ANSI Standard, have two ways of framing data: RANGE and ROWS. Without getting into the implementation differences between the ANSI Standard and Microsoft's versions, or any performance differences between the two, there's a funny difference in how they handle aggregations when ordered by non-unique values. A simple example using the Stack Overflow database follows.

```
SELECT OwnerUserId,
 CAST(CreationDate AS DATE) AS DumbedDownDate,
 Score,
 SUM(Score) OVER ( ORDER BY CAST(CreationDate AS DATE)) AS Not_Specified,
 SUM(Score) OVER ( ORDER BY CAST(CreationDate AS DATE)RANGE UNBOUNDED PRECEDING ) AS Range_Specified,
 SUM(Score) OVER ( ORDER BY CAST(CreationDate AS DATE)ROWS UNBOUNDED PRECEDING ) AS Rows_Specified
FROM dbo.Posts
WHERE OwnerUserId = 1
AND CAST(CreationDate AS DATE) BETWEEN '2008-08-01' AND '2008-08-31'
ORDER BY CAST(CreationDate AS DATE);
```

For the month of August, Year of Our Codd 2008, we're getting a running total of the score for posts by UserId 1. Who is UserId 1? I'll never tell. But back to the syntax! In the first SUM, we're not specifying anything, for the next two we're specifying RANGE and then ROWS. Why? REASONS! And why am I casting the CreateDate column as a date? MORE REASONS!

Before you scroll down, think for a second:

If I don't specify RANGE or ROWS, which will SQL Server use?

If I left the CreateDate column as DATETIME, what eff aff difference would it make to the output?

Do you see a pattern forming here?

	OwnerUserId	DumbedDownDate	Score	Not_Specified	Range_Specified	Rows_Specified
1	1	2008-08-04	2	15	15	2
2	1	2008-08-04	8	15	15	10
3	1	2008-08-04	5	15	15	15
4	1	2008-08-10	75	90	90	90
5	1	2008-08-11	10	100	100	100
6	1	2008-08-12	4	511	511	104
7	1	2008-08-12	320	511	511	424
8	1	2008-08-12	4	511	511	428
9	1	2008-08-12	76	511	511	504
10	1	2008-08-12	7	511	511	511
11	1	2008-08-13	5	734	734	516
12	1	2008-08-13	3	734	734	519
13	1	2008-08-13	1	734	734	520
14	1	2008-08-13	214	734	734	734
15	1	2008-08-14	2	801	801	736
16	1	2008-08-14	6	801	801	742
17	1	2008-08-14	57	801	801	799
18	1	2008-08-14	2	801	801	801
19	1	2008-08-17	2	811	811	803
20	1	2008-08-17	8	811	811	811
21	1	2008-08-19	11	822	822	822
22	1	2008-08-21	77	899	899	899
23	1	2008-08-24	1	900	900	900
24	1	2008-08-25	177	1081	1081	1077
25	1	2008-08-25	4	1081	1081	1081
26	1	2008-08-27	10	1091	1091	1091
27	1	2008-08-28	11	1106	1106	1102
28	1	2008-08-28	4	1106	1106	1106

OH MY GOD IT WORKED

When we don't specify RANGE or ROWS, well, SQL Server is nice enough to pick RANGE for us. "Nice".

	OwnerUserId	DumbedDownDate	Score	Not_Specified	Range_Specified	Rows_Specified
1	1	2008-08-04	2	15	15	2
2	1	2008-08-04	8	15	15	10
3	1	2008-08-04	5	15	15	15
4	1	2008-08-10	75	90	90	90
5	1	2008-08-11	10	100	100	100
6	1	2008-08-12	4	511	511	104
7	1	2008-08-12	320	511	511	424
8	1	2008-08-12	4	511	511	428
9	1	2008-08-12	76	511	511	504
10	1	2008-08-12	7	511	511	511
11	1	2008-08-13	5	734	734	516
12	1	2008-08-13	3	734	734	519
13	1	2008-08-13	1	734	734	520
14	1	2008-08-13	214	734	734	734
15	1	2008-08-14	2	801	801	736
16	1	2008-08-14	6	801	801	742
17	1	2008-08-14	57	801	801	799
18	1	2008-08-14	2	801	801	801
19	1	2008-08-17	2	811	811	803
20	1	2008-08-17	8	811	811	811
21	1	2008-08-19	11	822	822	822
22	1	2008-08-21	77	899	899	899
23	1	2008-08-24	1	900	900	900
24	1	2008-08-25	177	1081	1081	1077
25	1	2008-08-25	4	1081	1081	1081
26	1	2008-08-27	10	1091	1091	1091
27	1	2008-08-28	11	1106	1106	1102
28	1	2008-08-28	4	1106	1106	1106

Whose fault? Default!

Deep breaths, Erik. Deep breaths.

You should also notice the difference in how each different method aggregates data. When the ordering column has duplicates, RANGE, and by extension, the default method, will SUM all the values for that group at once. When ROWS is specified as the framing method, you see the running total that most people are after.

	OwnerUserId	DumbedDownDate	Score	Not_Specified	Range_Specified	Rows_Specified
1	1	2008-08-04	2	15	15	2
2	1	2008-08-04	8	15	15	10
3	1	2008-08-04	5	15	15	15
4	1	2008-08-10	75	90	90	90
5	1	2008-08-11	10	100	100	100
6	1	2008-08-12	4	511	511	104
7	1	2008-08-12	320	511	511	424
8	1	2008-08-12	4	511	511	428
9	1	2008-08-12	76	511	511	504
10	1	2008-08-12	7	511	511	511
11	1	2008-08-13	5	734	734	516
12	1	2008-08-13	3	734	734	519
13	1	2008-08-13	1	734	734	520
14	1	2008-08-13	214	734	734	734
15	1	2008-08-14	2	801	801	736
16	1	2008-08-14	6	801	801	742
17	1	2008-08-14	57	801	801	799
18	1	2008-08-14	2	801	801	801
19	1	2008-08-17	2	811	811	803
20	1	2008-08-17	8	811	811	811
21	1	2008-08-19	11	822	822	822
22	1	2008-08-21	77	899	899	899
23	1	2008-08-24	1	900	900	900
24	1	2008-08-25	177	1081	1081	1077
25	1	2008-08-25	4	1081	1081	1081
26	1	2008-08-27	10	1091	1091	1091
27	1	2008-08-28	11	1106	1106	1102
28	1	2008-08-28	4	1106	1106	1106

Make project managers happy!

And, of course, if all the values were unique, they'd do the same thing.

```
Transact-SQL
SELECT OwnerUserId,
 CreationDate,
 Score,
 SUM(Score) OVER ( ORDER BY CreationDate ) AS Not_Specified,
 SUM(Score) OVER ( ORDER BY CreationDate RANGE UNBOUNDED PRECEDING ) AS Range_Specified,
 SUM(Score) OVER ( ORDER BY CreationDate ROWS UNBOUNDED PRECEDING ) AS Rows_Specified
FROM dbo.Posts
WHERE OwnerUserId = 1
AND CAST(CreationDate AS DATE) BETWEEN '2008-08-01' AND '2008-08-31'
ORDER BY CreationDate;
```

	OwnerUserId	CreationDate	Score	Not_Specified	Range_Specified	Rows_Specified
1	1	2008-08-04 02:45:07.717	2	2	2	2
2	1	2008-08-04 04:31:02.557	8	10	10	10
3	1	2008-08-04 08:04:41.737	5	15	15	15
4	1	2008-08-10 08:28:52.100	75	90	90	90
5	1	2008-08-11 19:23:47.160	10	100	100	100
6	1	2008-08-12 00:30:43.390	4	104	104	104
7	1	2008-08-12 04:59:35.017	320	424	424	424
8	1	2008-08-12 05:02:49.453	4	428	428	428
9	1	2008-08-12 23:13:41.470	76	504	504	504
10	1	2008-08-12 23:27:54.093	7	511	511	511
11	1	2008-08-13 01:52:36.670	5	516	516	516
12	1	2008-08-13 03:30:58.860	3	519	519	519
13	1	2008-08-13 06:14:11.197	1	520	520	520
14	1	2008-08-13 12:03:05.940	214	734	734	734
15	1	2008-08-14 03:10:22.660	2	736	736	736
16	1	2008-08-14 03:13:56.770	6	742	742	742
17	1	2008-08-14 03:17:18.153	57	799	799	799
18	1	2008-08-14 13:48:02.523	2	801	801	801
19	1	2008-08-17 02:58:18.083	2	803	803	803
20	1	2008-08-17 03:00:34.317	8	811	811	811
21	1	2008-08-19 16:51:17.103	11	822	822	822
22	1	2008-08-21 14:18:41.640	77	899	899	899
23	1	2008-08-24 23:40:09.253	1	900	900	900
24	1	2008-08-25 00:11:43.763	177	1077	1077	1077
25	1	2008-08-25 13:43:41.643	4	1081	1081	1081
26	1	2008-08-27 13:08:30.010	10	1091	1091	1091
27	1	2008-08-28 11:23:59.427	11	1102	1102	1102
28	1	2008-08-28 13:26:27.823	4	1106	1106	1106

Back for a day

Wrap. It. Up.

This one is pretty self explanatory. If you're lucky enough to be on SQL Server 2012 or greater, and you're using Window Functions to their full T-SQL potential, it's was easier to calculate running totals. Just be careful how you write your code.

If you like this sort of stuff, Check out Doug's new video series, T-SQL Level Up. There are next to zero fart jokes in it.

For the links, code, and comments, go here:
https://www.brentozar.com/archive/2015/09/window-functions-and-cruel-defaults/

Of Windowing Functions And Where Clauses

Seen One, Seen'em All

This isn't about indexing! I promise. In fact, I've dropped all my indexes for this. It's just that, well, I've seen this happen with two clients in a row, so maybe it's time to blog about it.

If you run this query, you get a fairly obvious plan.

```
WITH nonsense
    AS (    SELECT    *,
                      ROW_NUMBER() OVER ( PARTITION BY v.UserId
                                          ORDER BY v.CreationDate ) AS rn
            FROM      dbo.Votes AS v )
SELECT  *
FROM    nonsense AS n
WHERE   n.VoteTypeId = 5
AND n.rn = 1;
GO
```

Carpaccio

With no index to help us avoid Sorting, we gotta do some of that, and we need a Filter operator for our WHERE clause.

Since the results of the ROW_NUMBER aren't persisted anywhere, that's the only way to narrow the results down to just rn = 1.

But there's something else being filtered!

Filter

Restricting the set of rows based on a predicate.

Physical Operation	Filter
Logical Operation	Filter
Actual Execution Mode	Row
Estimated Execution Mode	Row
Actual Number of Rows	59228
Actual Number of Batches	0
Estimated Operator Cost	0.5294 (1%)
Estimated I/O Cost	0
Estimated CPU Cost	0.529434
Estimated Subtree Cost	77.5957
Number of Executions	12
Estimated Number of Executions	1
Estimated Number of Rows	243165
Estimated Row Size	43 B
Actual Rebinds	0
Actual Rewinds	0
Node ID	1

Predicate

[SUPERUSER].[dbo].[Votes].[VoteTypeId] as [v].[VoteTypeId]=(5) AND [Expr1001]=(1)

Output List

[SUPERUSER].[dbo].[Votes].Id, [SUPERUSER].[dbo].[Votes].PostId, [SUPERUSER].[dbo].[Votes].UserId, [SUPERUSER].[dbo].[Votes].BountyAmount, [SUPERUSER].[dbo].[Votes].VoteTypeId, [SUPERUSER].[dbo].[Votes].CreationDate, Expr1001

WHY clause

This is a perfectly SARGable predicate that we can perfectly push to the Clustered Index.

Why Doesn't That Happen Here?

Well, in this case, predicate pushdown might give you... incorrect different results.

```
WITH nonsense
    AS (    SELECT    *,
                      ROW_NUMBER() OVER ( PARTITION BY v.UserId
                                          ORDER BY v.CreationDate ) AS rn
            FROM      dbo.Votes AS v
            WHERE     v.VoteTypeId = 5 )
SELECT  *
FROM    nonsense AS n
WHERE   n.rn = 1;
GO
```

This query is logically different. I think you can see why. It may not be obvious in the results at first, but just getting a simple count gives us two slightly different results.

```
WITH nonsense
    AS (    SELECT    *,
                      ROW_NUMBER() OVER ( PARTITION BY v.UserId
                                          ORDER BY v.CreationDate ) AS rn
            FROM      dbo.Votes AS v )
SELECT  COUNT(*) AS records
FROM    nonsense AS n
WHERE   n.VoteTypeId = 5
AND n.rn = 1;
GO


WITH nonsense
    AS (    SELECT    *,
                      ROW_NUMBER() OVER ( PARTITION BY v.UserId
                                          ORDER BY v.CreationDate ) AS rn
            FROM      dbo.Votes AS v
            WHERE     v.VoteTypeId = 5 )
SELECT  COUNT(*) AS records
FROM    nonsense AS n
WHERE   n.rn = 1;
GO
```

	records
1	59222

	records
1	60064

Off by one!

I can hear a lot of you running to go fix code. Don't worry, this will be here when you get back.

When Can It Happen?

If the column that you're filtering on in the WHERE clause is in the PARTITION BY clause of your Windowing function, the predicate can be safely pushed.

```
WITH nonsense
    AS (   SELECT    *,
                     ROW_NUMBER() OVER ( PARTITION BY v.UserId, v.VoteTypeId
                                         ORDER BY v.CreationDate ) AS rn
           FROM      dbo.Votes AS v )
SELECT  *
FROM    nonsense AS n
WHERE   n.VoteTypeId = 5
AND n.rn = 1;
GO
```

This case, the plan shows us the VoteTypeId predicate being applied to the Clustered Index Scan, and the Filter only being used for the rn = 1 predicate.

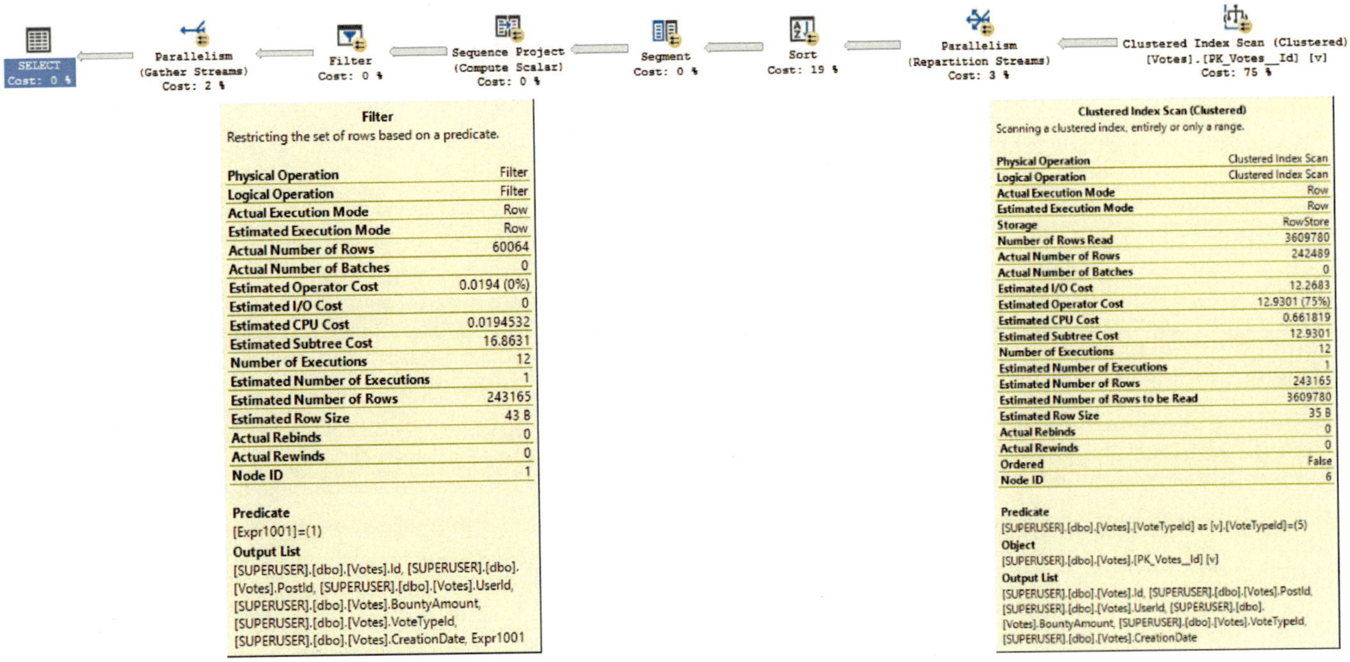

LORELEIIIIIIIIIIII

The same doesn't work if it's only in the ORDER BY of the Windowing Function.

This query is logically different from the other two, and by even more (this one only brings back 52,294 records).

It's not a drop-in replacement for one or the other, it's just an example of when a predicate like this can be pushed.

Does This Happen Anywhere Else?

Yes, it will also happen in derived tables and views.

You can work around this sort of thing with inline table valued functions, as Paul White notes in this answer on Stack Overflow.

Thanks for reading!

COULD NOT CONTINUE SCAN WITH NOLOCK
DUE TO DATA MOVEMENT

Special Indexes

Births, marriages (even in that order), and kindergarten graduations. These indexes call for the good stuff! Break out that bottle you even have to hide from yourself.

BRENT OZAR UNLIMITED®

Indexing for GROUP BY

It's not glamorous

And on your list of things that aren't going fast enough, it's probably pretty low. But you can get some pretty dramatic gains from indexes that cover columns you're performing aggregations on.

We'll take a quick walk down demo lane in a moment, using the Stack Overflow database.

Query outta nowhere!

```sql
SET NOCOUNT ON

SET STATISTICS TIME, IO ON

SELECT v.UserId, v.BountyAmount, SUM(v.BountyAmount) AS BountyTotal
FROM dbo.Votes AS v
WHERE v.BountyAmount IS NOT NULL
GROUP BY v.UserId, v.BountyAmount;
```

Looking at the plan, it's pretty easy to see what happened. Since the data is not ordered by an index (the clustered index on this table is on an Id column not referenced here), a Hash Match Aggregate was chosen, and off we went.

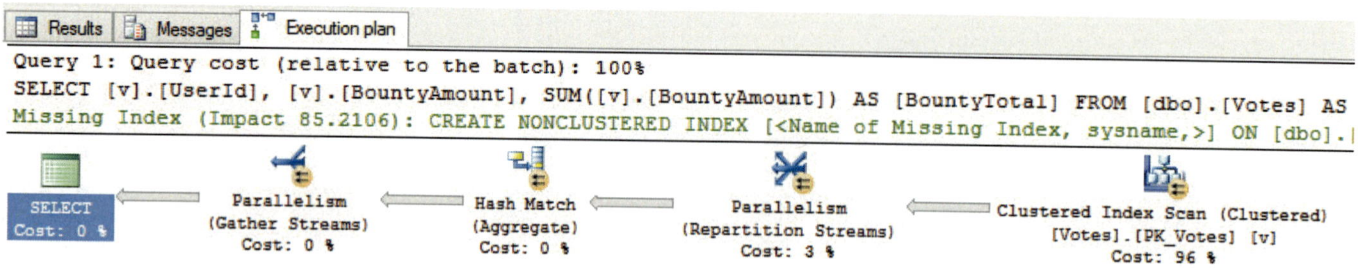

Look how much fun we're having.

Zooming in a bit on the Hash Match, this is what it's doing. It should look pretty familiar to you if you've ever seen a Hash Match used to JOIN columns. The only difference here is that the Hash table is built, scanned, and output. When used in a JOIN, a Probe is also built to match the Residual buckets, and then the results are output.

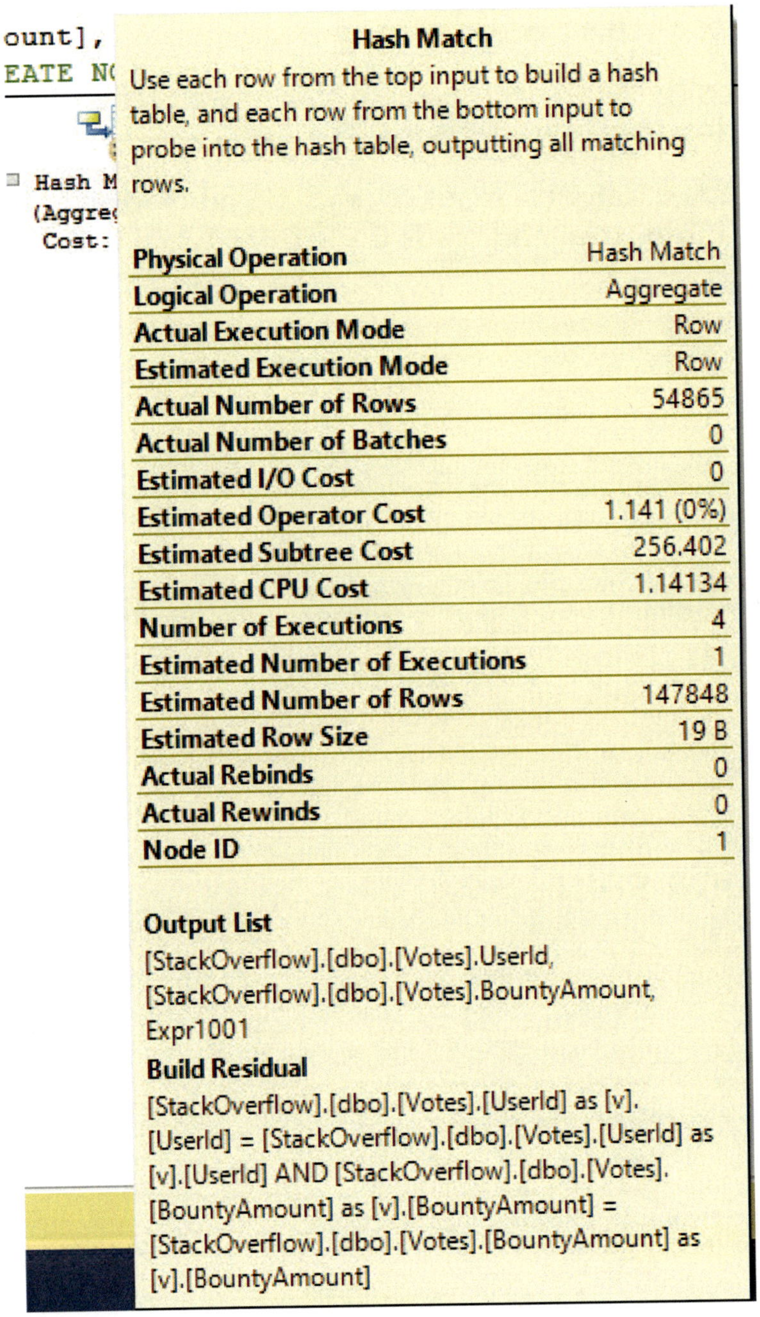

It's basically wiping its hands on its pants.

It took quite a bit of activity to do a pretty simple thing.

```
/*

Table 'Votes'. Scan count 5, logical reads 315406, physical reads 0, read-ahead reads 0, lob logical reads 0, lob physical reads 0, lob read-ahead reads 0.

Table 'Worktable'. Scan count 0, logical reads 0, physical reads 0, read-ahead reads 0, lob logical reads 0, lob physical reads 0, lob read-ahead reads 0.

Table 'Workfile'. Scan count 0, logical reads 0, physical reads 0, read-ahead reads 0, lob logical reads 0, lob physical reads 0, lob read-ahead reads 0.

SQL Server Execution Times:

CPU time = 3609 ms, elapsed time = 1136 ms.

*/
```

Since this query is simple, our index is simple.

```sql
CREATE NONCLUSTERED INDEX IX_GRPBY ON dbo.Votes ( BountyAmount, UserId );
```

I'm using the BountyAmount column in the first position because we're also filtering on it in the query. We don't really care about the SUM of all NULLs.

Taking that new index out for a spin, what do we end up with?

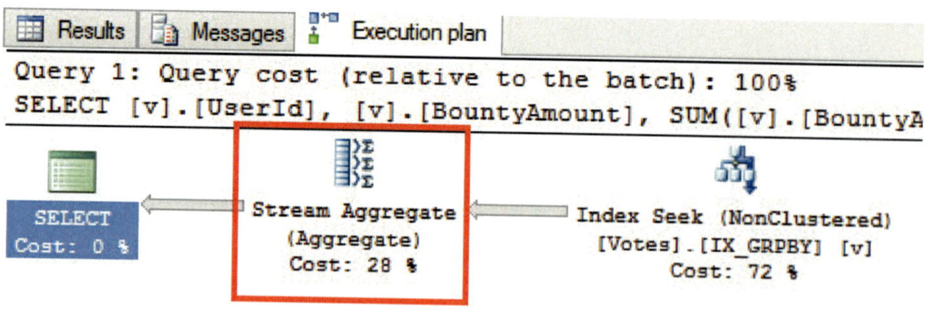

Stream Theater

For the links, code, and comments, go here: https://www.brentozar.com/archive/2015/06/indexing-for-group-by/

The Hash Match Aggregate has been replaced with a Stream Aggregate, and the Scan of the Clustered Index has been replaced with a Seek of the Non-Clustered Index. This all took significantly less work:

```
/*
Table 'Votes'. Scan count 1, logical reads 335, physical reads 0, read-ahead reads 0, lob logical reads 0, lob physical reads 0, lob read-ahead reads 0.

SQL Server Execution Times:

CPU time = 0 ms, elapsed time = 278 ms.

*/
```

Zooming in on the Stream Aggregate operator, because we gave the Hash Match so much attention. Good behavior should be rewarded.

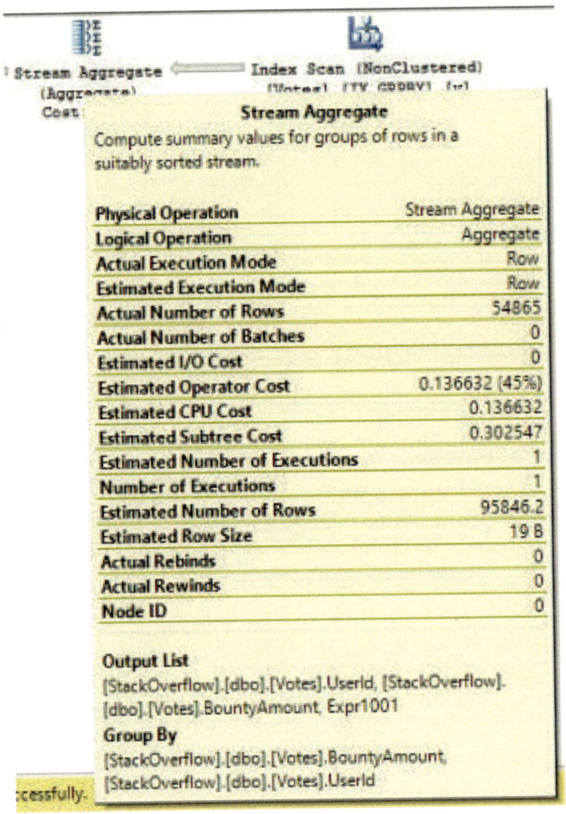

You make it look so easy, Stream Aggregate.

Filters, filters, filters

If we want to take it a step further, we can filter the index to avoid the NULLs all together.

```
Transact-SQL
CREATE NONCLUSTERED INDEX IX_GRPBY
  ON dbo.Votes ( BountyAmount, UserId )
  WHERE BountyAmount IS NOT NULL
  WITH ( DROP_EXISTING = ON );
```

This results in very slightly reduced CPU and IO. The real advantage of filtering the index here is that it takes up nearly 2 GB less space than without the filter. Collect two drinks from your SAN admin.

```
/*
Table 'Votes'. Scan count 1, logical reads 333, physical reads 0, read-ahead reads 0, lob logical reads 0, lob physical reads 0, lob read-ahead reads 0.

SQL Server Execution Times:

CPU time = 0 ms, elapsed time = 233 ms.
*/
```

And, because I knew you'd ask, I did try making the same index with the column order reversed. It was not more efficient, because it ended up doing a Scan of the Non-Clustered Index instead, which results in a bit more CPU time.

Performance Benefits of Unique Indexes

SQL server loves unique indexes

Why? Because it's lazy. Just like you. If you had to spend all day flipping pages around, you'd probably be even lazier. Thank Codd someone figured out how to make a computer do it. There's some code below, along with some screen shots, but...

TL;DR

SQL is generally pretty happy to get good information about the data it's holding onto for you. If you know something ***will*** be unique, let it know. It will make better plan choices, and certain operations will be supported more efficiently than if you make it futz around looking for repeats in unique data.

There is some impact on inserts and updates as the constraint is checked, but generally it's negligible, especially when compared to the performance gains you can get from select queries.

So, without further ado!

Q: What was the last thing the Medic said to the Heavy?

A: Demooooooooo!

We'll start off by creating four tables. Two with unique clustered indexes, and two with non-unique clustered indexes, that are half the size. I'm just going with simple joins here, since they seem like a pretty approachable subject to most people who are writing queries and creating indexes. I hope.

Transact-SQL

```
USE tempdb

/*
The drivers
*/
;WITH E1(N) AS (
    SELECT NULL UNION ALL SELECT NULL UNION ALL SELECT NULL UNION ALL
    SELECT NULL UNION ALL SELECT NULL UNION ALL SELECT NULL UNION ALL
    SELECT NULL UNION ALL SELECT NULL UNION ALL SELECT NULL UNION ALL
    SELECT NULL  ),
E2(N) AS (SELECT NULL FROM E1 a, E1 b, E1 c, E1 d, E1 e, E1 f, E1 g, E1 h, E1 i, E1 j),
Numbers AS (SELECT TOP (1000000) ROW_NUMBER() OVER (ORDER BY (SELECT NULL)) AS N FROM E2)
SELECT
ISNULL(N.N, 0) AS ID,
ISNULL(CONVERT(DATE, DATEADD(SECOND, N.N, GETDATE())),     '1900-01-01') AS OrderDate,
ISNULL(SUBSTRING(CONVERT(VARCHAR(255), NEWID()), 0, 9) , 'AAAAAAAA') AS PO
INTO UniqueCL
FROM Numbers N;

ALTER TABLE UniqueCL ADD CONSTRAINT PK_UniqueCL PRIMARY KEY CLUSTERED (ID) WITH (FILLFACTOR = 100)


;WITH E1(N) AS (
    SELECT NULL UNION ALL SELECT NULL UNION ALL SELECT NULL UNION ALL
    SELECT NULL UNION ALL SELECT NULL UNION ALL SELECT NULL UNION ALL
    SELECT NULL UNION ALL SELECT NULL UNION ALL SELECT NULL UNION ALL
    SELECT NULL  ),
E2(N) AS (SELECT NULL FROM E1 a, E1 b, E1 c, E1 d, E1 e, E1 f, E1 g, E1 h, E1 i, E1 j),
Numbers AS (SELECT TOP (1000000) ROW_NUMBER() OVER (ORDER BY (SELECT NULL)) AS N FROM E2)
SELECT
ISNULL(N.N, 0) AS ID,
ISNULL(CONVERT(DATE, DATEADD(SECOND, N.N, GETDATE())),     '1900-01-01') AS OrderDate,
ISNULL(SUBSTRING(CONVERT(VARCHAR(255), NEWID()), 0, 9) , 'AAAAAAAA') AS PO
INTO NonUniqueCL
FROM Numbers N;

CREATE CLUSTERED INDEX CLIX_NonUnique ON dbo.NonUniqueCL (ID) WITH (FILLFACTOR = 100)


/*
The joiners
*/

;WITH E1(N) AS (
    SELECT NULL UNION ALL SELECT NULL UNION ALL SELECT NULL UNION ALL
    SELECT NULL UNION ALL SELECT NULL UNION ALL SELECT NULL UNION ALL
    SELECT NULL UNION ALL SELECT NULL UNION ALL SELECT NULL UNION ALL
    SELECT NULL  ),
E2(N) AS (SELECT NULL FROM E1 a, E1 b, E1 c, E1 d, E1 e, E1 f, E1 g, E1 h, E1 i, E1 j),
Numbers AS (SELECT TOP (1000000) ROW_NUMBER() OVER (ORDER BY (SELECT NULL)) AS N FROM E2)
SELECT
ISNULL(N.N, 0) AS ID,
ISNULL(CONVERT(DATE, DATEADD(SECOND, N.N, GETDATE())),     '1900-01-01') AS OrderDate,
ISNULL(SUBSTRING(CONVERT(VARCHAR(255), NEWID()), 0, 9) , 'AAAAAAAA') AS PO
INTO UniqueJoin
FROM Numbers N
WHERE N.N < 5000001;

ALTER TABLE UniqueJoin ADD CONSTRAINT PK_UniqueJoin PRIMARY KEY CLUSTERED (ID, OrderDate)
WITH (FILLFACTOR = 100)

;WITH E1(N) AS (
    SELECT NULL UNION ALL SELECT NULL UNION ALL SELECT NULL UNION ALL
    SELECT NULL UNION ALL SELECT NULL UNION ALL SELECT NULL UNION ALL
    SELECT NULL UNION ALL SELECT NULL UNION ALL SELECT NULL UNION ALL
    SELECT NULL  ),
E2(N) AS (SELECT NULL FROM E1 a, E1 b, E1 c, E1 d, E1 e, E1 f, E1 g, E1 h, E1 i, E1 j),
Numbers AS (SELECT TOP (1000000) ROW_NUMBER() OVER (ORDER BY (SELECT NULL)) AS N FROM E2)
SELECT
ISNULL(N.N, 0) AS ID,
ISNULL(CONVERT(DATE, DATEADD(SECOND, N.N, GETDATE())),     '1900-01-01') AS OrderDate,
ISNULL(SUBSTRING(CONVERT(VARCHAR(255), NEWID()), 0, 9) , 'AAAAAAAA') AS PO
INTO NonUniqueJoin
FROM Numbers N
WHERE N.N < 5000001;

CREATE CLUSTERED INDEX CLIX_NonUnique ON dbo.NonUniqueJoin (ID, OrderDate) WITH (FILLFACTOR = 100);
```

Now that we have our setup, let's look at a couple queries. I'll be returning the results to a variable so we don't sit around waiting for SSMS to display a bunch of uselessness.

```sql
DECLARE @ID BIGINT;

SELECT   @ID = uc.ID
FROM     dbo.UniqueCL AS uc
JOIN     dbo.UniqueJoin AS uj
    ON uj.ID = uc.ID
WHERE    uc.ID % 2 = 0
ORDER BY uc.ID;

GO

DECLARE @ID BIGINT;

SELECT   @ID = nuc.ID
FROM     dbo.NonUniqueCL AS nuc
JOIN     dbo.NonUniqueJoin AS nuj
    ON nuj.ID = nuc.ID
WHERE    nuc.ID % 2 = 0
ORDER BY nuc.ID;

GO
```

What does SQL do with these?

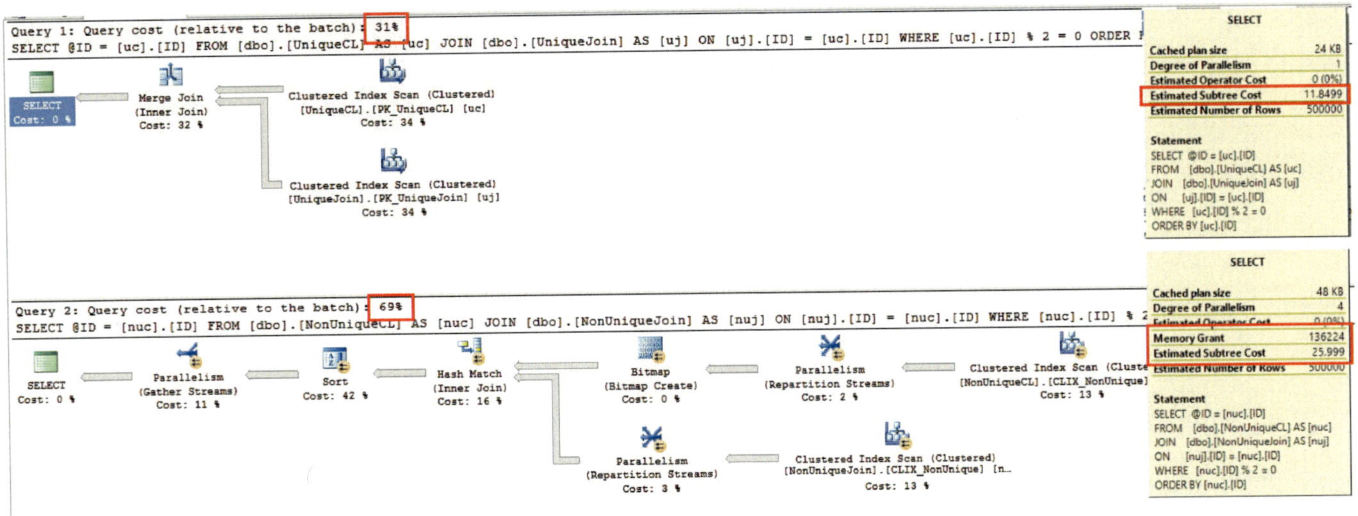

Ugly as a river dolphin, that one.

Not only does the query for the unique indexes choose a much nicer merge join, it doesn't even get considered for ~~parallelilzazation~~ going parallel. The batch cost is about 1/3, and the sort is fully supported.

The query against non-unique tables requires a sizable memory grant, to boot.

Looking at the STATISTICS TIME and IO output, there's not much difference in logical reads, but you see the non-unique index used all four cores available on my laptop (4 scans, 1 coordinator thread), and there's a worktable and workfile for the hash join. Overall CPU time is much higher, though there's only ever about 100ms difference in elapsed time over a number of consecutive runs.

```
Table 'UniqueJoin'. Scan count 1, logical reads 3969, physical reads 0,
read-ahead reads 0, lob logical reads 0, lob physical reads 0, lob read-ahead reads 0.
Table 'UniqueCL'. Scan count 1, logical reads 3968, physical reads 0, read-ahead reads 0,
lob logical reads 0, lob physical reads 0, lob read-ahead reads 0.

SQL Server Execution Times:
CPU time = 266 ms, elapsed time = 264 ms.

Table 'NonUniqueCL'. Scan count 5, logical reads 4264, physical reads 0,
read-ahead reads 0, lob logical reads 0, lob physical reads 0, lob read-ahead reads 0.
Table 'NonUniqueJoin'. Scan count 5, logical reads 4264, physical reads 0,
read-ahead reads 0, lob logical reads 0, lob physical reads 0, lob read-ahead reads 0.
Table 'Workfile'. Scan count 0, logical reads 0, physical reads 0, read-ahead
reads 0, lob logical reads 0, lob physical reads 0, lob read-ahead reads 0.
Table 'Worktable'. Scan count 0, logical reads 0, physical reads 0, read-ahead
reads 0, lob logical reads 0, lob physical reads 0, lob read-ahead reads 0.

SQL Server Execution Times:
CPU time = 1186 ms, elapsed time = 353 ms.
```

Fair fight

So, obviously going parallel threw some funk on the floor. If we force a MAXDOP of one to the non-unique query, what happens?

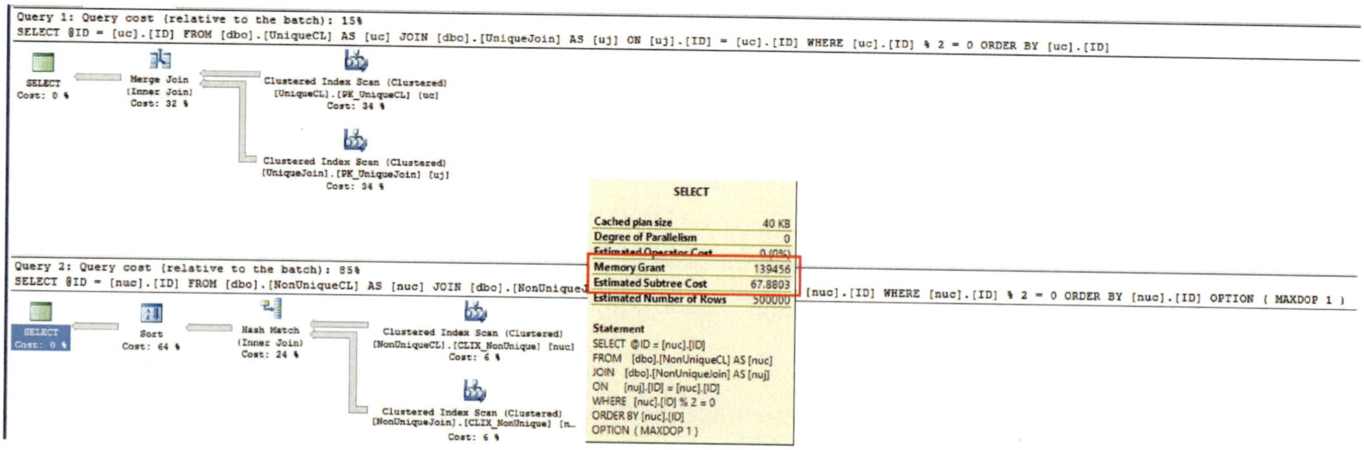

You Get Nothing! You Lose! Good Day, Sir!

Yep. Same thing, just single threaded this time. The plan looks a little nicer, sure, but now the non-unique part is up to 85% of the batch cost, from, you know, that other number. You're not gonna make me say it. This is a family-friendly blog.

Going back to TIME and IO, the only noticeable change is in CPU time for the non-unique query. Still needed a memory grant, still has an expensive sort.

```
Table 'UniqueJoin'. Scan count 1, logical reads 3969, physical reads 0, read-ahead reads 0, lob logical reads 0, lob physical reads 0, lob read-ahead reads 0.
Table 'UniqueCL'. Scan count 1, logical reads 3968, physical reads 0, read-ahead reads 0, lob logical reads 0, lob physical reads 0, lob read-ahead reads 0.

SQL Server Execution Times:
CPU time = 265 ms, elapsed time = 264 ms.

Table 'Workfile'. Scan count 0, logical reads 0, physical reads 0, read-ahead reads 0, lob logical reads 0, lob physical reads 0, lob read-ahead reads 0.
Table 'Worktable'. Scan count 0, logical reads 0, physical reads 0, read-ahead reads 0, lob logical reads 0, lob physical reads 0, lob read-ahead reads 0.
Table 'NonUniqueJoin'. Scan count 1, logical reads 4218, physical reads 0, read-ahead reads 0, lob logical reads 0, lob physical reads 0, lob read-ahead reads 0.
Table 'NonUniqueCL'. Scan count 1, logical reads 4218, physical reads 0, read-ahead reads 0, lob logical reads 0, lob physical reads 0, lob read-ahead reads 0.

SQL Server Execution Times:
CPU time = 766 ms, elapsed time = 807 ms.
```

Just one index

The nice thing is that a little uniqueness goes a long way. If we join the unique table to the non-unique join table, we end up with nearly identical plans.

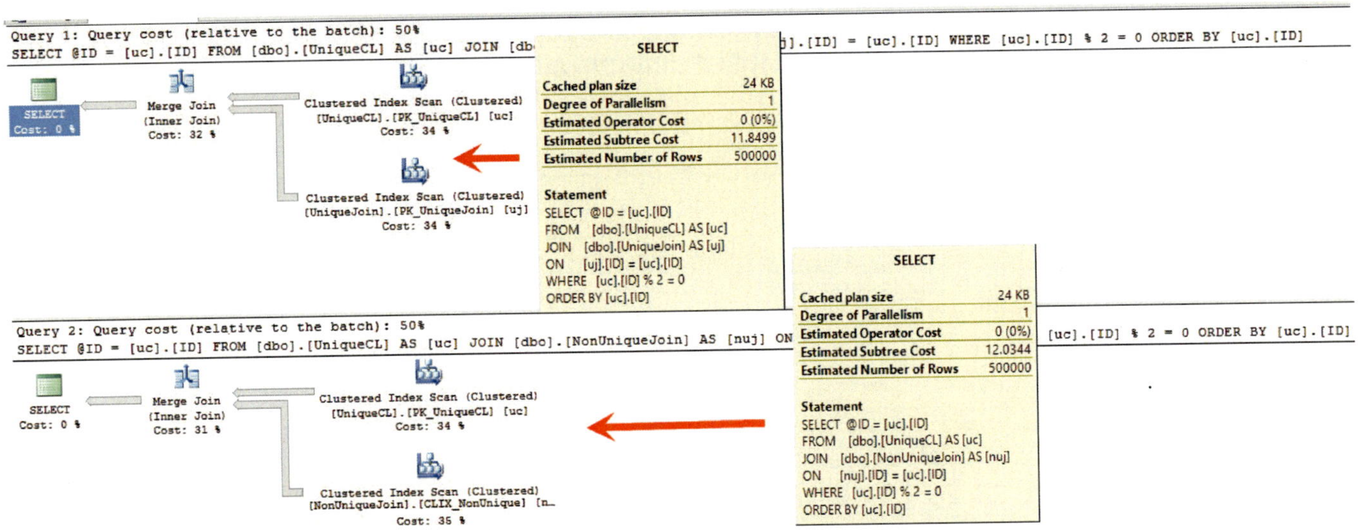

You're such a special flower.

For the links, code, and comments, go here:
https://www.brentozar.com/archive/2015/08/performance-benefits-of-unique-indexes/

```
Table 'UniqueJoin'. Scan count 1, logical reads 3969, physical reads 0, read-ahead reads 0, lob logical reads 0, lob physical reads 0, lob read-ahead reads 0.
Table 'UniqueCL'. Scan count 1, logical reads 3968, physical reads 0, read-ahead reads 0, lob logical reads 0, lob physical reads 0, lob read-ahead reads 0.

 SQL Server Execution Times:
   CPU time = 265 ms,  elapsed time = 267 ms.

Table 'NonUniqueJoin'. Scan count 1, logical reads 4218, physical reads 0, read-ahead reads 0, lob logical reads 0, lob physical reads 0, lob read-ahead reads 0.
Table 'UniqueCL'. Scan count 1, logical reads 3968, physical reads 0, read-ahead reads 0, lob logical reads 0, lob physical reads 0, lob read-ahead reads 0.

 SQL Server Execution Times:
   CPU time = 266 ms,  elapsed time = 263 ms.
```

Done and doner

So, you made it to the end. Congratulations. I hope your boss didn't walk by too many times.

By the way, the year is 2050, the Cubs still haven't won the world series, and a horrible race of extraterrestrials have taken over the Earth and are using humans as slaves to mine gold. Wait, no, that's something else.

But! Hey! Brains! You have more of them now, if any of this was enlightening to you. If you spaced out and just realized the page stopped scrolling, here's a recap:

- Unique indexes: SQL likes'em
- You will generally see better plans when the optimizer isn't concerned with duplicate values
- There's not a ton of downside to using them where possible
- Even one unique index can make a lot of difference, when joined with a non-unique index.

As an aside, this was all tested on SQL Server 2014. An exercise for Dear Reader; if you have SQL Server 2012, look at the tempdb spills that occur on the sort and hash operations for the non-unique indexes. I'm not including them here because it's a bit of a detour. It's probably not the most compelling reason to upgrade, but it's something to consider — tempdb is way less eager to write to disk these days!

Thanks for reading!

Brent says: *I always wanted proof that unique clustered indexes made for better execution plans!*

Filtered Indexes: Just Add Includes

I found a quirky thing recently

While playing with filtered indexes, I noticed something odd. By 'playing with' I mean 'calling them horrible names' and 'admiring the way other platforms implemented them'.

I sort of wrote about a similar topic in discussing indexing for windowing functions. It turns out that a recent annoyance could also be solved by putting the column my filter expression is predicated on in the included columns definition. That's the fanciest sentence I've ever written, BTW. If you want more, don't get your hopes up.

Ready for Horrible

Let's create our initial index. As usual, we're using the Stack Overflow database. We'll look at a small group of users who have a Reputation over 400k. I dunno, it's a nice number. There are like 8 of them.

```sql
CREATE UNIQUE NONCLUSTERED INDEX Users_400k_Club
 ON dbo.Users ( DisplayName, Id )
 WHERE Reputation > 400000;
```

With that in place, we'll run some queries that should make excellent use of our thoughtful and considerate index.

```sql
--Will I Nill I?
SELECT u.Id, u.DisplayName
FROM   dbo.Users AS u
WHERE  u.Reputation > 400000;

SELECT u.Id, u.DisplayName
FROM   dbo.Users AS u
WHERE  u.Reputation > 400000
AND    u.Reputation < 450000; SELECT u.Id, u.DisplayName FROM dbo.Users AS u WHERE u.Reputation > 400001;

SELECT u.Id, u.DisplayName
FROM   dbo.Users AS u
WHERE  u.Reputation > 500000;
```

If you were a betting organism, which ones would you say use our index? Money on the table, folks! Step right up!

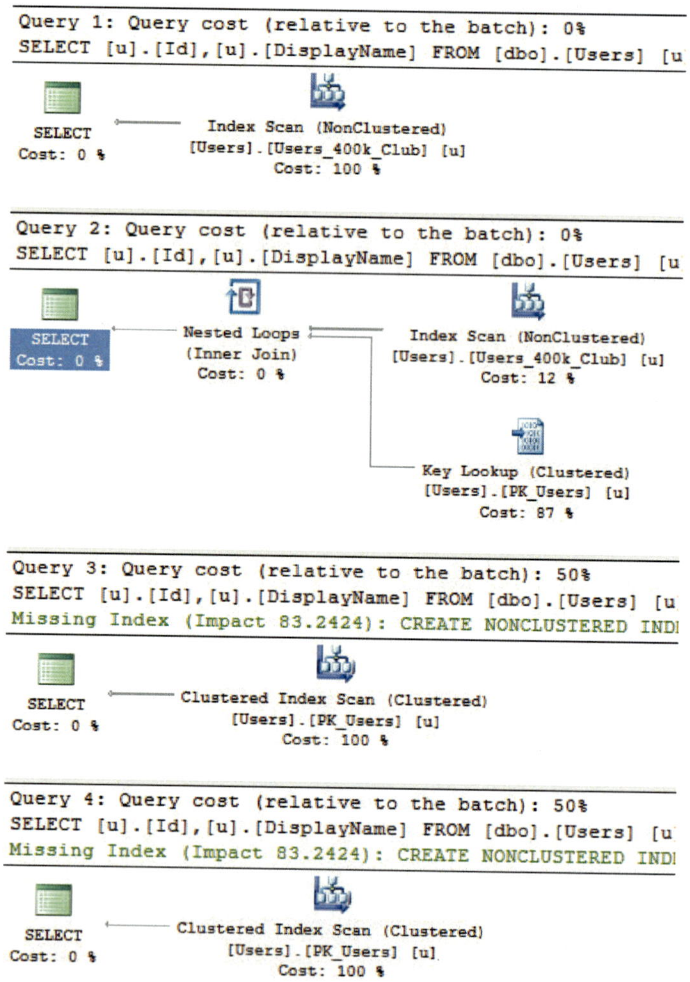

Yes, Sorta, No, No.

That didn't go well at all. Only the first query really used it. The second query needed a key lookup to figure out the less than filter, and the last two not only ignored it, but told me I need to create an index. The nerve!

Send me your money

Let's make our index better:

```
CREATE UNIQUE NONCLUSTERED INDEX Users_400k_Club
  ON dbo.Users ( DisplayName, Id )
  INCLUDE ( Reputation )
  WHERE Reputation > 400000
  WITH ( DROP_EXISTING = ON );
```

Run those queries again. You don't even have to recompile them.

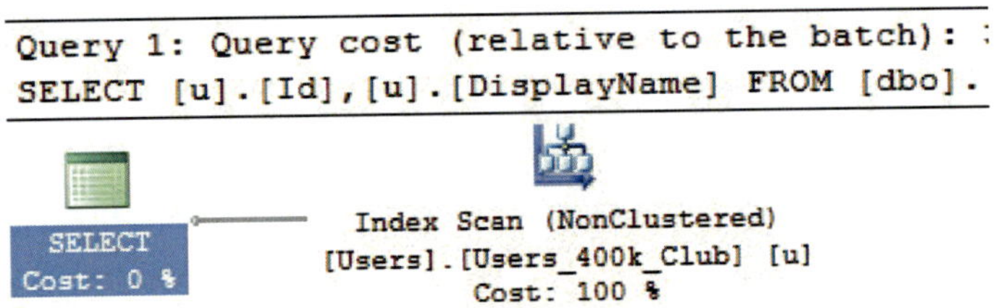

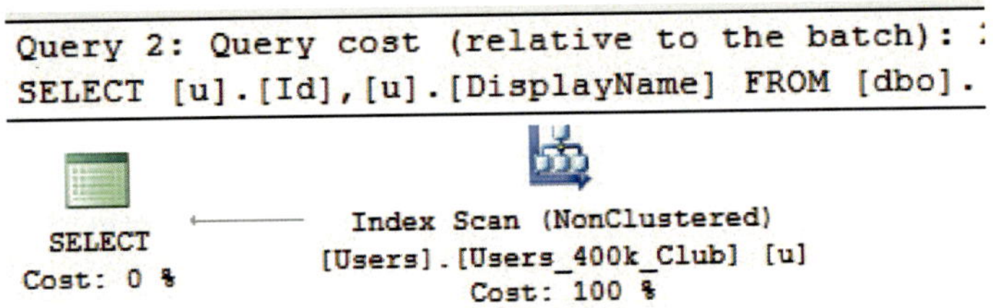

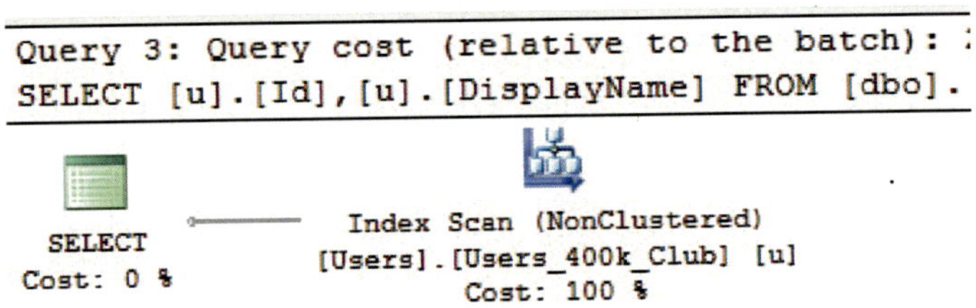

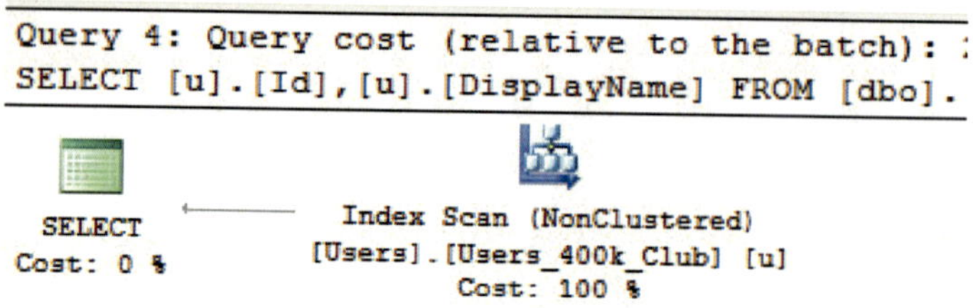

Can't you tell by the way I run every time you make eyes at me?

They all magically found a way to use our New and Improved index.

What was the point?

When I first started caring about indexes, and filtering them, I would get so mad when these precious little Bloody Mary recipes didn't get used.

I followed all the rules!

There were no errors!

But why oh why didn't SQL use my filtered indexes for even ***smaller*** subsets of the filter condition? It seemed insane to me that SQL would know the filter for the index is on (x > y), but wouldn't use them even if (z > x).

The solution was to put the filtered column in the include list. This lets SQL generate statistics on the column, and much like getting rid of the predicate key lookup, allows you to search within the filtered index subset for even more specific information.

Filtered Indexes and Variables: Less Doom and Gloom

It Is Known

That when you use filtered indexes, they get ignored when your queries are parameterized. This is a Plan Caching Thing©, of course. The simplest example is a bit column with a filtered index. If your index is on WHERE Bit = 1, it doesn't have data for WHERE Bit = 0. That index would only be suitable for one variation of the query, so caching a plan that uses an index which can't be reused for every variation isn't feasible.

There would be errors everywhere. Your users would hate you. You'd end up in a belltower, probably ordering a lot of pizza and waiting for one of those Kevin Costner movie marathons where they play everything from that real awkward stretch from 1992 to uh... oh wow, it never stopped. There are a lot of bad movies in there. Tin Cup was funny though.

Mix and Match

But on the bright side, plans can be cached if they're parameterized and the parameter isn't for the filter condition. Let's look at a quick example.

```sql
CREATE UNIQUE NONCLUSTERED INDEX
ix_helper ON dbo.Users
  (UpVotes, DownVotes, Id)
INCLUDE (DisplayName, Reputation)
  WHERE Reputation >= 400000
```

This is a pretty index, isn't it? Unique, narrow, selective filter condition. It's a winner. What could go wrong?

Well...

Just so you don't think I'm lying, here's what happens if we disobey the first rule of filtered indexes.

```
DECLARE @r INT = 400000

SELECT  u.DisplayName,
        u.Reputation,
        u.UpVotes,
        u.DownVotes
FROM    dbo.Users AS u
WHERE   u.Reputation >= @r;
```

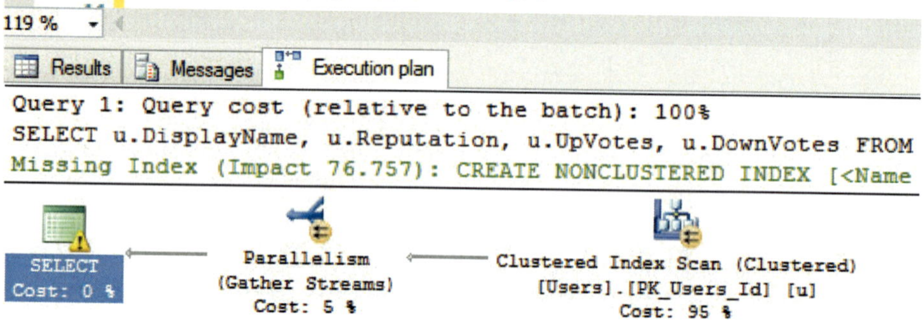

Monsters.

Clustered index scan, missing index request. The works. When offered our filtered index, the optimizer makes the same face I do when the all the scotch behind the bar starts with "Glen".

But...

Other things can be variables! Remember that our index is keyed on UpVotes, DownVotes, and Id. It would be daffy to create the index we did just to search on Reputation. So let's expand our horizons.

```sql
CREATE PROCEDURE dbo.YouBigDummy (@u INT = 15340, @d INT = 4761)
AS
BEGIN
        SELECT    u.DisplayName,
                  u.Reputation
        FROM      dbo.Users AS u
        WHERE     u.Reputation >= 400000
                  AND u.UpVotes = @u
                  AND u.DownVotes = @d;
END;

EXEC dbo.YouBigDummy
```

UpVotes and DownVotes take parameters as predicates, but Reputation is a literal value. In this case, the optimizer makes the same face I do when I find a Chateauneuf-Du-Pape I haven't had yet. Infinite joy.

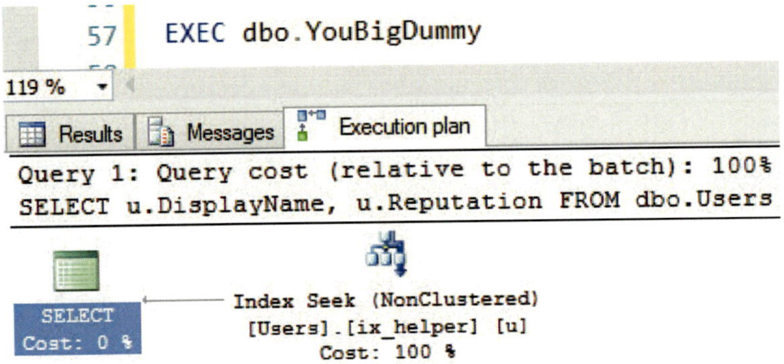

Joy, Ode To

Filtration System

While index filter conditions don't deal with parameters well, you can still use parameters for predicates in other columns. That's an important distinction to make when evaluating filtered index usage.

Thanks for reading!

Is leading an index with a BIT column always bad?

"Throughout history, slow queries are the normal condition of man. Indexes which permit this norm to be exceeded — here and there, now and then — are the work of an extremely small minority, frequently despised, often condemned, and almost always opposed by all right-thinking people who don't think bit columns are selective enough to lead index keys. Whenever this tiny minority is kept from creating indexes, or (as sometimes happens) is driven out of a SCRUM meeting, the end users then slip back into abject query performance.

This is known as "Business Intelligence."

–Bobby Q. Heinekens

Fake quotes and people aside

Let's look at a scenario where you have a BIT column that's fairly selective, and perhaps the rest of your predicates are ranged. This isn't so out of the ordinary, especially because people like to know when stuff happened and how many times it happened.

"How many lunches have I eaten today?"

"Where did that bear learn to drive?"

"Am I being slowly disassembled on a molecular level by millions of tiny black holes?"

Yes, China or Florida, and Probably!

So let's figure this out quick

For the links, code, and comments, go here:
https://www.brentozar.com/archive/2015/08/is-leading-an-index-with-a-bit-column-always-bad/

```
Transact-SQL
WITH E1(N) AS (
    SELECT NULL UNION ALL SELECT NULL UNION ALL SELECT NULL UNION ALL
    SELECT NULL UNION ALL SELECT NULL UNION ALL SELECT NULL UNION ALL
    SELECT NULL UNION ALL SELECT NULL UNION ALL SELECT NULL UNION ALL
    SELECT NULL  ),
E2(N) AS (SELECT NULL FROM E1 a, E1 b, E1 c, E1 d, E1 e, E1 f, E1 g, E1 h, E1 i, E1 j),
Numbers AS (SELECT TOP (1000000) ROW_NUMBER() OVER (ORDER BY (SELECT NULL)) AS N FROM E2)
SELECT
        IDENTITY (BIGINT, 1,1) AS ID ,
    ABS(CHECKSUM(NEWID()) / 100000000) + 1 AS CustomerID,
        ISNULL(CONVERT(DATE, DATEADD(MINUTE, -N.N, GETDATE())),      '1900-01-01') AS OrderDate ,
        CASE WHEN N.N % 19 = 0 THEN 1 ELSE 0 END AS isBit
INTO NotAshleyMadisonData
FROM    Numbers N
ORDER BY OrderDate;

ALTER TABLE NotAshleyMadisonData ADD CONSTRAINT PK_NotAshleyMadisonData PRIMARY KEY CLUSTERED
(ID) WITH (FILLFACTOR = 100);

CREATE NONCLUSTERED INDEX IX_BITFIRST ON dbo.NotAshleyMadisonData
(isBit, OrderDate);

CREATE NONCLUSTERED INDEX IX_DATEFIRST ON dbo.NotAshleyMadisonData
(OrderDate, isBit);
```

Here's one table with one million rows in it. Since it's random, if you run this on your own it may turn out a little different for you, but I'm sure you can adapt. You are, after all, wearing the largest available diaper size.

I've also gone ahead and created two indexes (neither one filtered!) to avoid the appearance of impropriety. The first one goes against the oft-chanted mantra of not leading your index with a BIT column. The other complies to your thumb-addled rules of index creation where your more unique column comes first, though not to an opposing rule to lead your index with equality predicates and then range predicates.

Only 52,631 rows out of a million have a BIT value of 1. And with the exception of the first and last date values, each date has 75 or 76 BIT = 1 columns.

If you had to do this in your head, which would you do first? Find all the BIT = 1 rows, and then only count occurrences from the desired range? Or would you Find your start and end dates and then count all the BIT = 1 values?

(Hint: it doesn't matter, you're not the query engine. Unless you're Paul White. Then maybe you are. Has anyone seen them in the same room together?)

Images of Query Plans

```sql
SELECT COUNT_BIG(*) AS Records
FROM   dbo.NotAshleyMadisonData AS namd
WHERE  namd.isBit = 1
AND    namd.OrderDate BETWEEN '2013-09-25' AND '2015-08-20'; --All dates

SELECT COUNT_BIG(*) AS Records
FROM   dbo.NotAshleyMadisonData AS namd
WHERE  namd.isBit = 1
AND    namd.OrderDate BETWEEN '2013-09-25' AND '2014-09-01'; --About half the dates

SELECT COUNT_BIG(*) AS Records
FROM   dbo.NotAshleyMadisonData AS namd
WHERE  namd.OrderDate BETWEEN '2013-09-25' AND '2014-09-01'
AND    namd.isBit = 1; -- Flipping them doesn't change anything

SELECT COUNT_BIG(*) AS Records
FROM   dbo.NotAshleyMadisonData AS namd
WHERE  namd.OrderDate = '2013-09-26' --It's not until here that the other index gets used
AND    namd.isBit = 1;
```

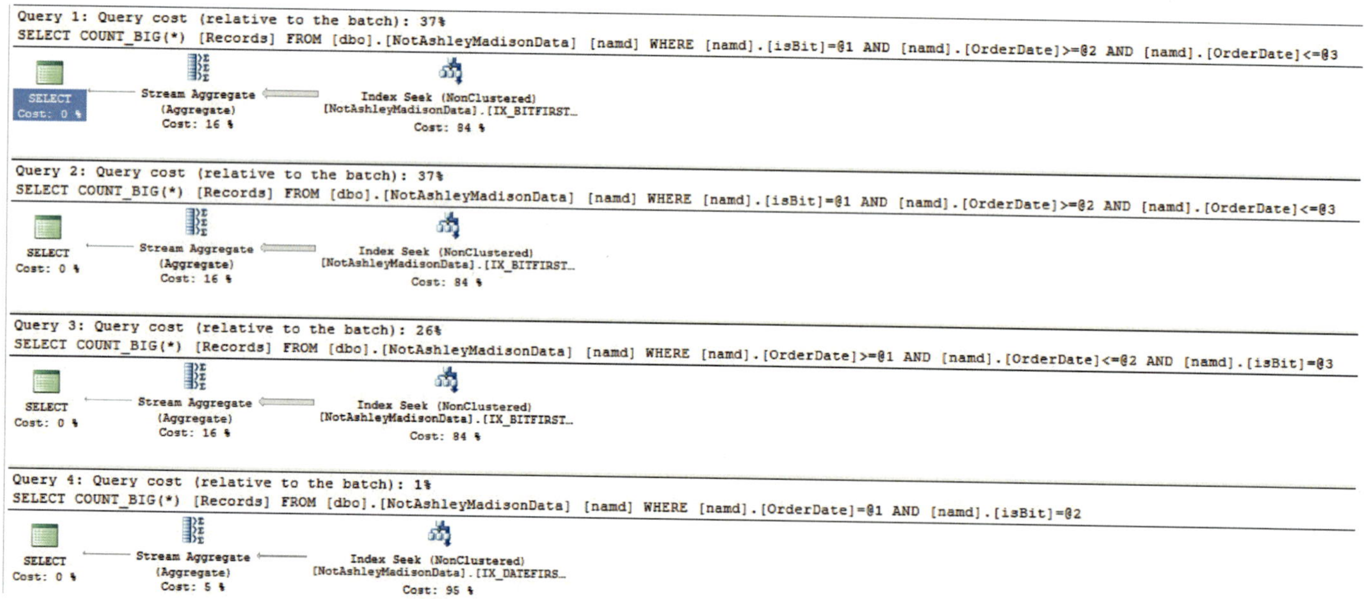

Peter Godwin will never play my birthday party.

Put on your recap cap

This is another case where knowing the data, and knowing the query patterns in your environment is important. It's easy to overlook or reject obvious things when you're bogged down by dogma.

The stamp of approval for an idea shouldn't come from blogs, forums, white papers, or hash tags. It should come from how much something helps in your environment.

Thanks for reading!

Unique Indexes and Row Modifications: Weird

Confession time

This started off with me reading a blurb in the release notes about SQL Server 2016 CTP 3.3. The blurb in question is about statistics. They're so cool! Do they get fragmented? NO! Stop trying to defragment them, you little monkey.

> *Autostats improvements in CTP 3.3*
> *Previously, statistics were automatically recalculated when the change exceeded a fixed threshold. As of CTP 3.3, we have refined the algorithm such that it is no longer a fixed threshold, but in general will be more aggressive in triggering statistics scans, resulting in more accurate query plans.*

I got unnaturally excited about this, because it sounds like the behavior of Trace Flag 2371. Anyone who has taken a bite out of a terabyte database probably knows about this one. Ever try waiting for statistics to automatically update on a billion row table? You're gonna need a crate of Snickers bars. I'm still going to write about the 2016 stuff, but I caught something weird when I was working on a way to demonstrate those thresholds. And that something was how SQL tracks modifications to unique indexes. It freaked me out for, like, days.

We're gonna need a couple tables

But they'll be slightly different. It's the only way to really show you how weird it gets inside SQL's head.

Table 1 has a clustered PK on the ID column. It has a non-unique, nonclustered index on DateFiller and TextFiller.

For the links, code, and comments, go here:
https://www.brentozar.com/archive/2016/03/unique-indexes-and-row-modifications-weird/

```sql
IF OBJECT_ID('[dbo].[Nuisance]') IS NOT NULL
    DROP TABLE dbo.Nuisance;
GO

CREATE TABLE dbo.Nuisance
     (
         ID BIGINT NOT NULL,
         DateFiller DATETIME2
             DEFAULT SYSDATETIME() NOT NULL,
         TextFiller VARCHAR(10)
             DEFAULT 'A' NOT NULL
     );

ALTER TABLE dbo.Nuisance
ADD CONSTRAINT PK_Nuisance
    PRIMARY KEY CLUSTERED ( ID );

CREATE NONCLUSTERED INDEX ix_Nuisance
    ON dbo.Nuisance ( DateFiller, TextFiller );
```

Table 2 has the same structure, but the clustered PK is on ID and DateFiller. Same nonclustered index, though.

```sql
IF OBJECT_ID('[dbo].[Nuisance2]') IS NOT NULL
   DROP TABLE [dbo].[Nuisance2];
GO

CREATE TABLE [dbo].[Nuisance2]
       (
         [ID] BIGINT NOT NULL ,
         [DateFiller] DATETIME2 DEFAULT SYSDATETIME() NOT NULL ,
         [TextFiller] VARCHAR(10) DEFAULT 'A' NOT NULL
       );

ALTER TABLE dbo.Nuisance2
ADD CONSTRAINT PK_Nuisance2
    PRIMARY KEY CLUSTERED ( ID, DateFiller );

CREATE NONCLUSTERED INDEX ix_Nuisance2
    ON dbo.Nuisance2 ( DateFiller, TextFiller );
```

All this code works, I swear. Let's drop a million rows into each.

```sql
INSERT dbo.Nuisance WITH ( TABLOCK ) ( ID, DateFiller, TextFiller )
SELECT TOP 1000000
       ROW_NUMBER() OVER ( ORDER BY ( SELECT NULL )),
       DATEADD(SECOND, sm1.message_id, SYSDATETIME()),
       SUBSTRING(sm1.text, 0, 9)
FROM   sys.messages AS sm1, sys.messages AS sm2, sys.messages AS sm3;

INSERT dbo.Nuisance2 WITH ( TABLOCK ) ( ID, DateFiller, TextFiller )
SELECT TOP 1000000
       ROW_NUMBER() OVER ( ORDER BY ( SELECT NULL )),
       DATEADD(SECOND, sm1.message_id, SYSDATETIME()),
       SUBSTRING(sm1.text, 0, 9)
FROM   sys.messages AS sm1, sys.messages AS sm2, sys.messages AS sm3;
```

Now let's take a basic look at what's going on in our indexes and statistics. We just created tables! And inserted a million rows! Each! That has to count for something, right? Here's a query to check that kind of thing.

```sql
SELECT t.name AS table_name,
 si.name AS index_name,
 si.dpages AS data_pages,
 si.rowcnt AS index_row_count,
 si.rows AS index_rows,
 ddsp.rows AS stats_rows,
 ddsp.rows_sampled AS stats_rows_sampled,
 si.rowmodctr AS index_row_modifications,
 ddsp.modification_counter AS stats_modification_counter,
 ddsp.last_updated AS last_stats_update
FROM sys.sysindexes AS si
JOIN sys.stats AS s
 ON si.id = s.object_id
 AND si.indid = s.stats_id
JOIN sys.tables AS t
 ON t.object_id = si.id
CROSS APPLY sys.dm_db_stats_properties(s.object_id, s.stats_id) AS ddsp
WHERE t.name LIKE 'Nuisance%'
ORDER BY t.name, si.indid;
```

Holy heck why don't we have any statistics? The indexes tracked our million modifications from the insert, but the statistics aren't showing us anything. They're all NULL! Right now, SQL has no idea what's going on in here.

table_name	index_name	data_pages	index_row_count	index_rows	stats_rows	stats_rows_sampled	index_row_modifications	stats_modification_counter	last_stats_update
Nuisance	PK_Nuisance	4588	1000000	1000000	NULL	NULL	1000000	NULL	NULL
Nuisance	ix_Nuisance	4202	1000000	1000000	NULL	NULL	1000000	NULL	NULL
Nuisance2	PK_Nuisance2	4588	1000000	1000000	NULL	NULL	1000000	NULL	NULL
Nuisance2	ix_Nuisance2	4202	1000000	1000000	NULL	NULL	1000000	NULL	NULL

Empty inside

At least, until it has to. If we ran a query with a WHERE clause, an initial statistics update would fire off. Hooray. SQL is lazy. We can skip all that fuss and just update manually. I want a FULLSCAN! No fullscan, no peace. Or something.

```
Transact-SQL
UPDATE STATISTICS dbo.Nuisance
 WITH FULLSCAN;

UPDATE STATISTICS dbo.Nuisance2
 WITH FULLSCAN;
```

If we go back to our DMV query, the stats columns will at least not be NULL now. It will show 1,000,000 rows sampled, and no modifications, and the last stats update column will have a date in it. Wonderful. You don't need a picture of that. Conceptualize. Channel your inner artist.

Weir it all gets whered

Let's think back to our indexes.

- Nuisance has the clustered PK on ID
- Nuisance2 has the clustered PK on ID, DateFiller
- They both have non-unique nonclustered indexes on DateFiller, TextFiller

One may posit, then, that they could let their workloads run wild and free, and that SQL would dutifully track modifications, and trigger automatic updates when necessary. This is being run on 2014, so we don't expect the dynamic threshold stuff. The rule that applies to us here, since our table is >500 rows, is that if 20% of the table + 500 rows changes, SQL will consider the statistics stale, and trigger an update the next time a query runs against the table, and uses those statistics.

But, but, but! It does not treat all modifications equally. Let's look at some examples, and then buckle in for the explanation. No TL;DR here. You must all suffer as I have suffered.

We'll start with an update of the nonclustered index on Nuisance.

```sql
UPDATE n
SET    n.DateFiller = DATEADD(MICROSECOND, 1, n.DateFiller), n.TextFiller = REPLACE(n.TextFiller, ' ', '')
FROM   dbo.Nuisance AS n
WHERE  n.ID >= 1
AND    ID <= 100000 AND n.DateFiller >= '0001-01-01'
AND    n.DateFiller <= '9999-12-31';

SELECT @@ROWCOUNT AS [Rows Modified];
```

We use @@ROWCOUNT to verify the number of rows that were updated in the query. Got it? Good. It should show you that 100,000 rows were harmed during the filming of that query. Poor rows.

Here's the execution plan for it. Since we don't have a kajillion indexes on the table, we get a narrow plan. There are some compute scalars to come up with the date adding, the replace, and the predicates in our WHERE clause. It's all in the book. You should get the book.

ACTUAL EXE-CUTIE-PIE

At this point, if you run the DMV query, you should see 100,000 modifications to the nonclustered index on Nuisance. Not enough to trigger an update, but we don't care about that in this post. It makes sense though, right? We updated 100k rows, SQL tracked 100k modifications.

What if we run the same update on Nuisance2? We still only update 100k rows, but our execution plan changes a little bit...

Split! Sort! Collapse! Fear! Fire! Foes!

And now we have TWO HUNDRED THOUSAND MODIFICATIONS?

table_name	index_name	data_pages	index_row_count	index_rows	stats_rows	stats_rows_sampled	index_row_modifications	stats_modification_counter	last_stats_update
Nuisance	PK_Nuisance	4588	1000000	1000000	1000000	1000000	2	2	2016-02-13 12:25:26.9170000
Nuisance	ix_Nuisance	4208	1000000	1000000	1000000	1000000	1100001	1100001	2016-02-13 12:25:27.2730000
Nuisance2	PK_Nuisance2	4611	1000000	1000000	1000000	1000000	200000	200000	2016-02-13 12:25:27.5600000
Nuisance2	ix_Nuisance2	4205	1000000	1000000	1000000	1000000	200000	200000	2016-02-13 12:25:27.9100000

What in the wide world of sports?

This is how SQL handles updates on columns with unique constraints, which we'll get to. But let's look at a couple other updates first!

For the links, code, and comments, go here:
https://www.brentozar.com/archive/2016/03/unique-indexes-and-row-modifications-weird/

```
UPDATE n
SET    n.ID += 1
FROM   dbo.Nuisance AS n;

SELECT @@ROWCOUNT AS [Rows Modified];
```

If we go back and update just the ID column of Nuisance, something really cool happens.

table_name	index_name	data_pages	index_row_count	index_rows	stats_rows	stats_rows_sampled	index_row_modifications	stats_modification_counter	last_stats_update
Nuisance	PK_Nuisance	4588	1000000	1000000	1000000	1000000	0	0	2016-02-13 12:25:26.9170000
Nuisance	ix_Nuisance	4205	1000000	1000000	1000000	1000000	100000	100000	2016-02-13 12:25:27.2730000
Nuisance2	PK_Nuisance2	4611	1000000	1000000	1000000	1000000	200000	200000	2016-02-13 12:25:27.5600000
Nuisance2	ix_Nuisance2	4205	1000000	1000000	1000000	1000000	200000	200000	2016-02-13 12:25:27.9100000

Two is the loneliest number

It only took two modifications to update one million rows in the clustered index. We still had to update all million rows of the nonclustered index (+1, I'm guessing, to insert the new row for ID 1,000,001).

That's because, if you've been paying attention, nonclustered indexes carry all the key columns of your clustered index. We updated the clustered index, so we had to update our nonclustered index. If we had multiple nonclustered indexes, we'd have to update them all. This is why many sane and rational people will tell you to not pick columns you're going to update for your clustered index.

If you're still looking at execution plans, you'll see the split/sort/collapse operators going into the clustered index again, but only split and sort going into the nonclustered index update.

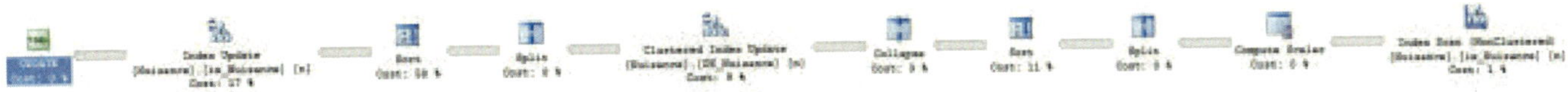

Oh, yeah. That update.

If we run the same update on Nuisance2, and check back in on the DMVs, it took a million modifications (+5 this time; due to the data distribution, there are net 5 new rows, since there are exactly five unique values in DateFiller). But at least it didn't take 2 million modifications to update it, right?

table_name	index_name	data_pages	index_row_count	index_rows	stats_rows	stats_rows_sampled	index_row_modifications	stats_modification_counter	last_stats_update
Nuisance	PK_Nuisance	4588	1000000	1000000	1000000	1000000	2	2	2016-02-13 12:25:26.9170000
Nuisance	ix_Nuisance	4208	1000000	1000000	1000000	1000000	1100001	1100001	2016-02-13 12:25:27.2730000
Nuisance2	PK_Nuisance2	4614	1000000	1000000	1000000	1000000	1200005	1200005	2016-02-13 12:25:27.5600000
Nuisance2	ix_Nuisance2	4208	1000000	1000000	1000000	1000000	1200005	1200005	2016-02-13 12:25:27.9100000

I still can't do math.

Bring it on home

Why are there such big differences in the modification counts?

For the update to the ID column of Nuisance, it only took two modifications. This is because of the split/sort/collapse operations.

Split takes the update, and, as the name implies, splits it into inserts and deletes. If you think about what it would look like to change 1 through 1,000,000 to 2 through 1,000,001, it really is only two modifications:

- Delete row 1
- Insert row 1,000,001

All the other numbers in the range already exist, in order. That's what the sort does, basically. Orders the values, and whether they need an insert or a delete to occur. The final operation, collapse, removes duplicate actions. You don't need to delete and re-insert every number.

Unfortunately, for Nuisance2, it results in doubling the modifications required. This is true for the clustered index update, where DateFiller is the second column, and the nonclustered index update, where DateFiller is the leading column.

It doesn't appear to be the data distribution, or the data type of the column that causes the double working. As things stand in this demo, there are only five unique values in DateFiller. I tried where it was all unique, I also tried it as DATE, and BIGINT, but in each scenario, SQL tracked 2x the number of modifications to each index.

Transact-SQL

```
Nuisance nonclustered index update
/*
SQL Server parse and compile time:
   CPU time = 0 ms, elapsed time = 3 ms.
Table 'Nuisance'. Scan count 1, logical reads 630970, physical reads 0,
read-ahead reads 0, lob logical reads 0, lob physical reads 0, lob read-ahead reads 0.

 SQL Server Execution Times:
   CPU time = 1062 ms,  elapsed time = 1129 ms.
*/

Nuisance2 nonclustered index update
/*
SQL Server parse and compile time:
   CPU time = 0 ms, elapsed time = 0 ms.
SQL Server parse and compile time:
   CPU time = 0 ms, elapsed time = 2 ms.
Table 'Nuisance2'. Scan count 5, logical reads 1231177, physical reads 0,
read-ahead reads 0, lob logical reads 0, lob physical reads 0, lob read-ahead reads 0.

```

```
 SQL Server Execution Times:
   CPU time = 2484 ms,  elapsed time = 2633 ms.
*/

Nuisance clustered index update
/*
SQL Server parse and compile time:
   CPU time = 0 ms, elapsed time = 0 ms.
SQL Server parse and compile time:
   CPU time = 0 ms, elapsed time = 1 ms.
Table 'Nuisance'. Scan count 1, logical reads 9191793, physical reads 0,
read-ahead reads 0, lob logical reads 0, lob physical reads 0, lob read-ahead reads 0.

 SQL Server Execution Times:
   CPU time = 20625 ms,  elapsed time = 20622 ms.
*/

Nuisance2 clustered index update
/*
SQL Server parse and compile time:
   CPU time = 0 ms, elapsed time = 0 ms.
SQL Server parse and compile time:
   CPU time = 1 ms, elapsed time = 1 ms.
Table 'Nuisance2'. Scan count 1, logical reads 12191808, physical reads 0,
read-ahead reads 0, lob logical reads 0, lob physical reads 0, lob read-ahead reads 0.

 SQL Server Execution Times:
   CPU time = 36141 ms,  elapsed time = 36434 ms.
*/
```

Takeaways

I'm all for unique indexes! I'm even okay with two column PK/clustered indexes. But be really careful when assigning constraints, and make sure you test your workload against them. While they may obviously help read queries, there's some cost to maintaining them when modifying data.

What I didn't mention this whole time, because I didn't want it to get in the way up there, was how long each update query took. So I'll leave you with the statistics time and IO results for each one.

Thanks for reading!

Brent says: *go back and read this again, because you didn't digest it the first time. Plus, trust me, the time it takes you to read is nowhere near what it took for Erik to get to the root cause on this. (We saw the play-by-play unfold in the company chat room.)*

Is there a trace flag for loneliness?

Index General

This chapter is thirsty for your every day drinker.
You know, the stuff you keep in your glove compartment.
It's a long one, so make sure the garage is well-ventilated.

BRENT OZAR UNLIMITED®

When Does Index Size Change Index Choice?

Size Matters?

One thing I hear a lot is that the optimizer will take the size of an index into account when choosing which one to use.

The tl;dr here is that it may make more of a difference when it comes to index ***width*** (think the number of columns in an index) than it does the actual size in MB or GB of the index.

You can usually observe this behavior with COUNT(*) queries.

If you have a table with a clustered index, and then a narrow(er) nonclustered index, it's generally more efficient to just get a universal count from the nonclustered index because it's less work to read.

This will likely change if you COUNT(a column not in the nonclustered index), but hey.

A column in the index is worth two key lookups.

Or something.

Queen Size

Let's skip a lot of the nonsense! For once.

If I create a modest table with 1 million rows and a couple indexes with the key columns flipped, I can get a good starting test.

For the links, code, and comments, go here:
https://www.brentozar.com/archive/2018/01/index-size-change-index-choice/

```sql
DROP TABLE IF EXISTS dbo.SizeQueen
CREATE TABLE dbo.SizeQueen
(
 id INT IDENTITY PRIMARY KEY CLUSTERED,
 order_date DATETIME NOT NULL,
 inefficiency DATETIME NOT NULL,
 INDEX ix_use_me NONCLUSTERED (order_date, inefficiency),
 INDEX ix_do_not_use_me NONCLUSTERED (inefficiency, order_date)
);

INSERT dbo.SizeQueen ( order_date, inefficiency )
SELECT TOP 1000000 x.n, x.n + 1
FROM   (   SELECT      ROW_NUMBER() OVER ( ORDER BY @@DBTS ) AS n
           FROM        sys.messages AS m
           CROSS JOIN sys.messages AS m2 ) AS x;
```

I'm only going to be running two queries. One that does a direct equality, and one that looks for a hundred year range.

```sql
SET STATISTICS TIME, IO ON

--Equality
SELECT COUNT(*) AS records
FROM dbo.SizeQueen AS sq
WHERE sq.order_date = '1980-11-04'

--Year range
SELECT COUNT(*) AS records
FROM dbo.SizeQueen AS sq
WHERE sq.order_date >= '1980-11-04'
AND sq.order_date < DATEADD(YEAR, 100, '1980-11-04')
```

To spice things up, we'll fragment the index in a way that ***may*** eventually cause problems: we'll add a bunch of empty space.

We'll do this with the magic of fill factor.

```sql
ALTER INDEX ix_use_me ON dbo.SizeQueen REBUILD WITH (FILLFACTOR = 90)
ALTER INDEX ix_use_me ON dbo.SizeQueen REBUILD WITH (FILLFACTOR = 80)
ALTER INDEX ix_use_me ON dbo.SizeQueen REBUILD WITH (FILLFACTOR = 70)
ALTER INDEX ix_use_me ON dbo.SizeQueen REBUILD WITH (FILLFACTOR = 60)
ALTER INDEX ix_use_me ON dbo.SizeQueen REBUILD WITH (FILLFACTOR = 50)
ALTER INDEX ix_use_me ON dbo.SizeQueen REBUILD WITH (FILLFACTOR = 40)
ALTER INDEX ix_use_me ON dbo.SizeQueen REBUILD WITH (FILLFACTOR = 30)
ALTER INDEX ix_use_me ON dbo.SizeQueen REBUILD WITH (FILLFACTOR = 20)
ALTER INDEX ix_use_me ON dbo.SizeQueen REBUILD WITH (FILLFACTOR = 10)
```

Pay careful attention here: we're adding 10% ***free*** space to every page in the index incrementally.

We're doing this to the index that has order_date as the first column, which is also the column that both of our queries are predicated on.

That makes this index the more efficient choice. The other nonclustered index on this table has order_date second, which means we'd essentially have to read every page — the pages with the date range we're looking for aren't guaranteed to all be together in order.

Technically they are, but the optimizer doesn't know that.

The way data is loaded, dates in the 'inefficiency' column are only one day ahead of dates in the order_date column.

```sql
SELECT TOP 10 *
FROM dbo.SizeQueen AS sq
ORDER BY sq.order_date

SELECT TOP 10 *
FROM dbo.SizeQueen AS sq
ORDER BY sq.inefficiency
```


For the links, code, and comments, go here:
https://www.brentozar.com/archive/2018/01/index-size-change-index-choice/

id	order_date	inefficiency
819	1900-01-02 00:00:00.000	1900-01-03 00:00:00.000
1	1900-01-03 00:00:00.000	1900-01-04 00:00:00.000
410	1900-01-04 00:00:00.000	1900-01-05 00:00:00.000
2864	1900-01-05 00:00:00.000	1900-01-06 00:00:00.000
2455	1900-01-06 00:00:00.000	1900-01-07 00:00:00.000
1228	1900-01-07 00:00:00.000	1900-01-08 00:00:00.000
820	1900-01-08 00:00:00.000	1900-01-09 00:00:00.000
2	1900-01-09 00:00:00.000	1900-01-10 00:00:00.000
411	1900-01-10 00:00:00.000	1900-01-11 00:00:00.000
2865	1900-01-11 00:00:00.000	1900-01-12 00:00:00.000

id	order_date	inefficiency
819	1900-01-02 00:00:00.000	1900-01-03 00:00:00.000
1	1900-01-03 00:00:00.000	1900-01-04 00:00:00.000
410	1900-01-04 00:00:00.000	1900-01-05 00:00:00.000
2864	1900-01-05 00:00:00.000	1900-01-06 00:00:00.000
2455	1900-01-06 00:00:00.000	1900-01-07 00:00:00.000
1228	1900-01-07 00:00:00.000	1900-01-08 00:00:00.000
820	1900-01-08 00:00:00.000	1900-01-09 00:00:00.000
2	1900-01-09 00:00:00.000	1900-01-10 00:00:00.000
411	1900-01-10 00:00:00.000	1900-01-11 00:00:00.000
2865	1900-01-11 00:00:00.000	1900-01-12 00:00:00.000

Complicated Game

Ocean Motion

So what happens when we lower fill factor and run the equality query?

- The nonclustered index with order_date first ***always*** gets picked. Even when I set fill factor to 1, meaning 99% of the page is empty.
- The query never really does any more work, either. Every run takes 3ms, and does between 3-5 logical reads.

The range query is a bit more interesting. By more interesting, I mean that something finally changed.

But I had to drop fill factor down to 2% before the optimizer picked the other index.

Wanna see why?

Tag Team

The first one chooses the less efficient index, with order_date second.

The second query is forced to use the other index where order_date is first, but where fill factor is set to 2%.

```
--Query 1
SELECT COUNT(*) AS records
FROM dbo.SizeQueen AS sq --This uses the other index on its own
WHERE sq.order_date >= '1980-11-04'
AND sq.order_date < DATEADD(YEAR, 100, '1980-11-04')

--Query 2
SELECT COUNT(*) AS records
FROM dbo.SizeQueen AS sq WITH (INDEX = ix_use_me) --Index forced
WHERE sq.order_date >= '1980-11-04'
AND sq.order_date < DATEADD(YEAR, 100, '1980-11-04')
```

With the less efficient index at 100% fill factor, meaning every single page is full of data, here's what we get from stats time and IO.

```
Table 'SizeQueen'. Scan count 1, logical reads 4990, physical reads 0, read-ahead reads 0,
lob logical reads 0, lob physical reads 0, lob read-ahead reads 0.

 SQL Server Execution Times:
   CPU time = 93 ms,  elapsed time = 94 ms.
```

About 5000 reads, and about 100ms of CPU time.

The forced index query gives us this:

```
Table 'SizeQueen'. Scan count 1, logical reads 5259, physical reads 0, read-ahead reads 0,
lob logical reads 0, lob physical reads 0, lob read-ahead reads 0.

 SQL Server Execution Times:
   CPU time = 0 ms,  elapsed time = 6 ms.
```

So, about 270 more logical reads, but no CPU time.

Huh.

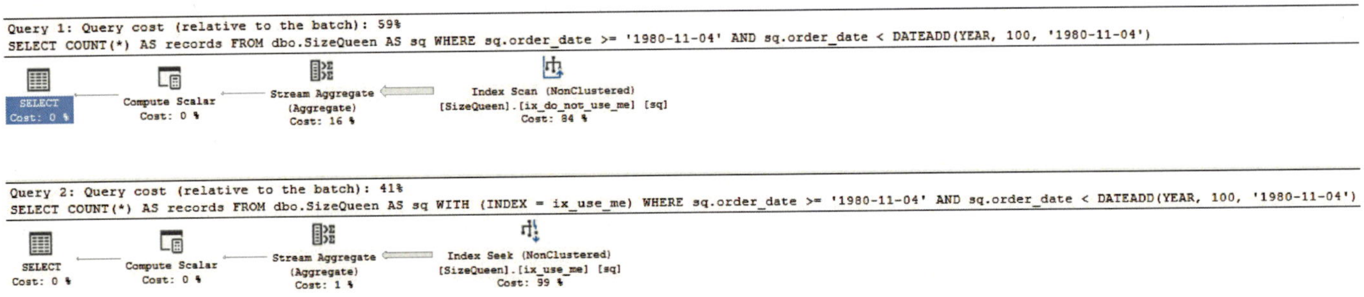

Oddballs

No, not that

I don't care much about the batch cost here, or 100ms of CPU time. That's trivial in nearly every scenario outside of, like, anime gif rendering, where every nonsecond counts.

I'm looking at those reads.

It took the 'good' index being 98% free space for the number of reads to surpass a 100% full index with the key columns switched.

Now, 5000 reads isn't much. If we do 5000 reads every million rows, and our table gets up to 100 million rows, we'll do 500,000 reads.

If we have the wrong index.

With the right indexes in place, fragmentation becomes much less of a concern.

Thanks for reading!

For the links, code, and comments, go here:
https://www.brentozar.com/archive/2018/01/index-size-change-index-choice/

Does index fill factor affect fragmentation?

Everybody wants to know about index fragmentation

It is an inescapable vortex of malaise and confusion. Like that swamp in The Neverending Story that killed the horse. Sorry if you haven't seen that movie. The horse wasn't that cool, anyway.

Neither is index fragmentation, but it's not worth losing sleep over. Or a horse.

I see a lot of people messing with the fill factor of their indexes. Sometimes you gotta. If you use GUIDs for a clustering key, for example. If you don't lower fill factor from 100, you're going to spend a lot of time splitting pages when you insert records. GUIDs are hard to run out of, but they're even harder to put in order.

Setting fill factor under 100 tells SQL to leave free space on index pages at the leaf level for new records to be add to. If you don't, and a record needs to be added to a page, it will do about a 50/50 split to two other pages.

When does it hurt?

Like most things, not at first. To prove it, let's rebuild an index at different fill factors, and insert some fragmentation information into a table. It's pretty easy. Create a table, rebuild the index, insert record to table. I could have done this in a loop, but I'm kind of lazy today.

For the links, code, and comments, go here:
https://www.brentozar.com/archive/2015/12/does-index-fill-factor-affect-fragmentation/

```sql
CREATE TABLE dbo.[FillFactor]
    (
        TableName NVARCHAR(128) NULL,
        IndexName sysname NULL,
        index_type_desc NVARCHAR(60) NULL,
        avg_fragmentation_in_percent FLOAT NULL,
        page_count BIGINT NULL,
        fill_factor TINYINT NOT NULL
    ) ON [PRIMARY];
GO

INSERT dbo.[FillFactor] (
                              TableName,
                              IndexName,
                              index_type_desc,
                              avg_fragmentation_in_percent,
                              page_count,
                              fill_factor
                         )
SELECT OBJECT_NAME(ddips.object_id) AS TableName,
       i.name AS IndexName,
       ddips.index_type_desc,
       ddips.avg_fragmentation_in_percent,
       ddips.page_count,
       i.fill_factor
FROM   sys.dm_db_index_physical_stats(DB_ID(N'StackOverflow'),
OBJECT_ID('dbo.Votes'), NULL, NULL, 'LIMITED') AS ddips
JOIN   sys.tables AS t
    ON t.object_id = ddips.object_id
JOIN   sys.indexes AS i
    ON  i.object_id = ddips.object_id
    AND i.index_id = ddips.index_id;

ALTER INDEX PK_Votes ON dbo.Votes REBUILD WITH ( FILLFACTOR = 100 );
ALTER INDEX PK_Votes ON dbo.Votes REBUILD WITH ( FILLFACTOR = 80 );
ALTER INDEX PK_Votes ON dbo.Votes REBUILD WITH ( FILLFACTOR = 60 );
ALTER INDEX PK_Votes ON dbo.Votes REBUILD WITH ( FILLFACTOR = 40 );
ALTER INDEX PK_Votes ON dbo.Votes REBUILD WITH ( FILLFACTOR = 20 );

SELECT   ff.TableName, ff.IndexName, ff.index_type_desc,
ff.avg_fragmentation_in_percent, ff.page_count, ff.fill_factor
FROM     dbo.[FillFactor] AS ff
ORDER BY ff.fill_factor DESC;
```

Put on your thinking cap. Fragmentation percent doesn't budge. Granted, we rebuilt the index, so that's expected. But look at page counts. Every time we reduce fill factor, page count gets higher. Why does that matter? Each page is 8kb. The more pages are in your index, the more you're reading from disk into memory. The lower your fill factor, the more blank space you're reading from disk into memory. You could be wasting a lot of unnecessary space both on disk and in memory by lowering fill factor.

TableName	IndexName	index_type_desc	avg_fragmentation_in_percent	page_count	fill_factor
Votes	PK_Votes	CLUSTERED INDEX	0.01	308527	100
Votes	PK_Votes	CLUSTERED INDEX	0.01	384336	80
Votes	PK_Votes	CLUSTERED INDEX	0.01	509535	60
Votes	PK_Votes	CLUSTERED INDEX	0.01	764302	40
Votes	PK_Votes	CLUSTERED INDEX	0.01	1528602	20

Space Age Love Song is probably the best Flock of Seagulls song, just so you know.

Let's do math!

Because everyone loves math. Let's take page count, multiply it by 8, and then divide it by 1024 twice to get the size of each index in GB.

```
SELECT    ff.TableName,
          ff.IndexName,
          ff.index_type_desc,
          ff.avg_fragmentation_in_percent,
          ff.page_count,
          ff.fill_factor,
          ( ff.page_count * 8. ) / 1024. / 1024. AS SizeGB
FROM      dbo.[FillFactor] AS ff
ORDER BY ff.fill_factor DESC;
```

Even reducing this to 80 takes up about an extra 600MB. That can really add up. Granted, disk and memory are cheap, but they're not infinite. Especially if you're on Standard Edition.

TableName	IndexName	index_type_desc	avg_fragmentation_in_percent	page_count	fill_factor	SizeGB
Votes	PK_Votes	CLUSTERED INDEX	0.01	308527	100	2.35387420605
Votes	PK_Votes	CLUSTERED INDEX	0.01	384336	80	2.93225097656
Votes	PK_Votes	CLUSTERED INDEX	0.01	509535	60	3.88744354199
Votes	PK_Votes	CLUSTERED INDEX	0.01	764302	40	5.83116149902
Votes	PK_Votes	CLUSTERED INDEX	0.01	1528602	20	11.66230773925

Ack! Numbers!

It's in everything

It's not just queries that reading extra pages can slow down. DBCC CHECKDB, backups, and index and statistics maintenance all have to deal with all those pages. Lowering fill factor without good reason puts you in the same boat as index fragmentation does, except regular maintenance won't "fix" the problem.

You can run sp_BlitzIndex® to help you find indexes that have fill factor set to under 100.

Why Not Just Create Statistics?

Here at Brent Ozar Unlimited

We have a proud tradition of not blaming index fragmentation for everything. There are points you should deal with it, but they're probably not 5% and 30% and 1000 pages. But that's not what this blog post is about. I'm hoping to clarify why we're more interested in up to date statistics, and also why statistics outside of indexes aren't really the most helpful thing. If they were, we'd all just create statistics and every query would magically blaze from select to offset without a care in the world.

Statistics: It's What's Inside That Counts

Statistics are what SQL Server uses to figure out how many rows to expect from accessing a data structure. You can do some things that fundamentally break this, like using functions in joins or where clauses, using local variables or optimize for unknown, using table variables without recompile hints, and a sniffed parameter can just allow SQL to run a query without guessing at all. It already guessed once. No tag backs. As you may imagine, this is important information for SQL to have for running your queries optimally.

Indexes: Pride and Vanity

Indexes of the nonclustered variety contain subsets of your table or view's data. Clustered ones are your table or view data ordered by the clustering key(s). Focusing on the nonclustered variety, they're the "and the [band name]" to your clustered index's "[lead singer name]", and they're great for providing SQL with a more appropriate data structure for your query.

If you don't need to select all the columns, and you do need to filter, join, order by, or aggregate a column not in the key of the clustered index, nonclustered indexes get a solo after the chorus. Give the drummer some.

For the links, code, and comments, go here:
https://www.brentozar.com/archive/2016/07/not-just-create-statistics/

Nonclustered indexes will, under normal circumstances, get a statistics object created with rolling density information for the key columns going left to right, and a histogram on only the leftmost column.

All Density	Average Length	Columns
3.752261E-07	4	OwnerUserId
3.395366E-08	12	OwnerUserId, CreationDate
3.38987E-08	16	OwnerUserId, CreationDate, Id

Histogram Steps

RANGE_HI_KEY	RANGE_ROWS	EQ_ROWS	DISTINCT_RANGE_ROWS	AVG_RANGE_ROWS
-1	0	11028	0	1
0	0	249265	0	1
1583	140867	7647	1155	121.9628
4279	177929	4327	1784	99.73598
6309	103162	14560	1184	87.13007
10397	194680	3121	1909	101.9801
13302	154459	8457	1343	115.0104
17034	191347	15602	1568	122.0325
19068	80477	14174	870	92.5023
22656	146238	32915	1492	98.01475
27535	162379	5140	1885	86.14271
34088	189960	6334	2229	85.22208
37213	85541	7681	951	89.94848
42139	114652	2807	1527	75.08317
47773	122421	3208	1772	69.08634
65863	439576	6786	5606	78.41171
70604	113238	4789	1435	78.9115
76337	103080	5392	1683	61.24777
85371	182822	5749	2774	65.90555
88656	70540	2885	1002	70.3992
95810	125819	6348	2086	60.31591
100297	80868	15265	1444	56.00277

I AM I SAID

With that out of the way

Why do we care more about statistics being updated than indexes being fragmented? Largely, because reading pages with some empty space from a fragmented index is oh-so-very-rarely the root cause of a performance issue. Especially if those pages are already in memory. Out of date statistics can allow SQL to continue to make some really bad guesses, and keep giving you a lousy execution plan no matter which way you tune your query.

The bigger your table gets, the worse the problem gets. Prior to 2016, if you don't turn on Trace Flag 2371, about 20% of your table's rows need to change before an automatic statistics update kicks in. For a 100 million row table, this can be a long ways off. Poor cardinality estimates here can really sink you. Rebuilding indexes for a 100 million row table is a B-U-M-M-E-R.

Log Shipping? Mirroring? Availability Group? Good luck with that.

Crappy server? Low memory? Slow disk? Dead man walking.

You may ultimately spend more time and expend more server resources defragmenting indexes than your queries will spend reading extra pages from fragmented indexes. Rebuilding or reorganizing large indexes can be a special kind of brutal.

For the links, code, and comments, go here:
https://www.brentozar.com/archive/2016/07/not-just-create-statistics/

Consider the process

Read a bunch of index pages with sys.dm_db_index_physical_stats to figure out if there's fragmentation, reorganize or rebuild based on feedback.

- Reorganize is online but single threaded and can take FOREVER on big tables, especially if you're compacting LOBs.
- Rebuild is offline and single threaded in Standard, online and potentially parallel in Enterprise, but you better hope you're patched up so you don't corrupt anything.

Is that worth it? Every night? For every index on every table in every user database? Only if you can prove it.

The one upside to Rebuilding is that it also updates statistics with a full scan. Think about this the next time you say something like "rebuilding the index fixed the problem", you may have an epiphany on the way.

Wait for it.

Wait for it.

Wait for it.

Statistics with no indexes

SQL Server doesn't make easy work of getting information about your Statistics, or finding out which statistics get used. Even at the query level, you have to use a spate of Trace Flags to find out what gets loaded and looked at. Cached plans don't fare much better.

No wonder everyone cares about indexes and their fragmentation. Microsoft has made information about them easy and abundant, while Statistics are kept hidden in the basement next to piles of soft bones and a bowl of hot blood.

Head rush moment: SQL may use information from histograms outside of the index it chooses for cardinality estimation.

Back to earth: If you just create a bunch of statistics instead of indexes, you're (at best) using your Clustered Index for everything (which is still bad), or you're using a HEAP for everything (which is usually worse). You're still generally better off creating good indexes for your workload. They'll get statistics objects created and associated with them, and if SQL thinks another column is interesting, it will create a single column statistics object for it, as long as you haven't turned off auto create stats.

Sure, you can put on your black cloak and goat mask and create some multi-column or filtered statistics, but in the words of a wise man (Doug), you end up with more stats to maintain and understanding query behavior gets more difficult.

Filtered statistics suffer from a problem where they don't automatically update based on the filtered row count, but rather the table row count. Imagine you have a 100 million row table, and your filtered index is on 1 million rows. All million of those rows might change, but the statistics on that index won't. 1 million is not 20% of 100 million. You'll have to update the statistics manually, or rebuild the filtered index.

Multi-column statistics are hardly a replacement for a multi-column index, and it's not like you get an enhanced histogram that includes the second column. It's just like a normal histogram. All you get is the density information for the columns you throw in there. Boo hiss.

Moral of the story (B-B-B-B-B-B-BENNY WITHOUT THE JETS)

Indexes are a really important factor for performance, but index fragmentation very rarely is. Statistics are super helpful when they're not out of date, and getting them up to date is much easier on your server's nerves. Though not perfect, I'd rather take my chances here. Updating statistics can also cause a bad execution plan to get flushed out of the cache. On their own they can sometimes help queries, but you should only end up here after you've really tuned your indexes.

Unless you can establish a metric that makes nightly index defragmentation worthwhile, don't jump to it as the default. Try just updating statistics. You may find that nothing at all changes, and you now have many extra hours a night to do maintenance. Like run DBCC CHECKDB. If you think index fragmentation is a performance problem, try corruption sometime. That's not what Brent meant when he said "the fastest query is one you never make."

Thanks for reading!

Can Indexes My Query Doesn't Use Help My Query?

This came up during Office Hours

And I love questions like this, because they reveal some interesting underpinnings of how the cardinality estimator works. It was something along the lines of "I have a slow query, and when I add an index the query goes faster even though it doesn't use the index I created."

We can see an example of this with unique indexes and constraints, but another possibility is that the created index had better statistical information via the histogram. When you add an index, you get Fresh Hot Stats, whereas the index you were using could be many modifications behind current for various reasons. If you have a big table and don't hit auto-update thresholds often, if you're not manually updating statistics somehow, or if you're running into ascending key weirdness. These are all sane potential reasons. One insane potential reason is if you have autocreate stats turned off, and the index you create is on a column that didn't have a statistics object associated with it. But you'd see plan warnings about operators not having associated statistics.

Again, we're going to focus on how ADDING an index your query doesn't use can help. I found out the hard way that both unique indexes and constraints can cease being helpful to cardinality estimation when their statistics get out of date.

One Million Rows!

Here's some setup script. You love setup script.

Transact-SQL

```
USE tempdb

CREATE TABLE dbo.t1 (col1 INT NOT NULL, col2 INT NOT NULL, col3 VARCHAR(8000) NOT NULL)

CREATE CLUSTERED INDEX cx_t1_col1 ON dbo.t1 (col1)

INSERT dbo.t1 WITH (TABLOCK) ( col1, col2, col3 )
SELECT TOP 1000000
    x.rn, x.rn, x.text
  FROM
  (
    SELECT ROW_NUMBER() OVER (ORDER BY (SELECT NULL)) rn, m.text
    FROM sys.messages AS m
    CROSS JOIN sys.messages AS m2
  ) AS x
```

I know, I know. What kind of lunatic creates a non-unique clustered index? Well, actually, a lot of you. Even after I told you how great they are! It's a good thing I have the emotional fortitude of a week old banana.

So, table. Table needs a query. Let's find a love connection.

```sql
SELECT *
FROM dbo.t1 AS t
WHERE 1=1
AND t.col1 >= 1 AND t.col1 < 10001
```

Now, this is BY NO MEANS the worst estimate I've ever seen. It's pretty close, but it's weird that it's still not right, because we literally just filled this table up with delicious and nutritious rows.

Clustered Index Seek (Clustered)

Scanning a particular range of rows from a clustered index.

Physical Operation	Clustered Index Seek
Logical Operation	Clustered Index Seek
Actual Execution Mode	Row
Estimated Execution Mode	Row
Storage	RowStore
Number of Rows Read	10000
Actual Number of Rows	10000
Actual Number of Batches	0
Estimated I/O Cost	0.0705324
Estimated Operator Cost	0.0806891 (100%)
Estimated Subtree Cost	0.0806891
Estimated CPU Cost	0.0101567
Number of Executions	1
Estimated Number of Executions	1
Estimated Number of Rows	9090.63
Estimated Row Size	4019 B
Actual Rebinds	0
Actual Rewinds	0
Ordered	True
Node ID	0

Object

[tempdb].[dbo].[t1].[cx_t1_col1] [t]

Output List

[tempdb].[dbo].[t1].col1, [tempdb].[dbo].[t1].col2, [tempdb].[dbo].[t1].col3

Seek Predicates

Seek Keys[1]: Start: [tempdb].[dbo].[t1].col1 >= Scalar Operator((1)), End: [tempdb].[dbo].[t1].col1 < Scalar Operator((10001))

Mostly there.

But we can pretend

Let's say this rugged old table has been around since SQL Server 2005, and is chock full of customer data. Let's pretend that being 90% right is still too wrong. We're allowed to create an index! I bet one on just the column the clustered index is on would help.

```sql
CREATE NONCLUSTERED INDEX ix_partytime ON dbo.t1 (col1)
```

And now, magically, if we run that exact same query...

Clustered Index Seek (Clustered)

Scanning a particular range of rows from a clustered index.

Physical Operation	Clustered Index Seek
Logical Operation	Clustered Index Seek
Actual Execution Mode	Row
Estimated Execution Mode	Row
Storage	RowStore
Number of Rows Read	10000
Actual Number of Rows	10000
Actual Number of Batches	0
Estimated I/O Cost	0.0771991
Estimated Operator Cost	0.0883561 (100%)
Estimated Subtree Cost	0.0883561
Estimated CPU Cost	0.011157
Number of Executions	1
Estimated Number of Executions	1
Estimated Number of Rows	10000
Estimated Row Size	4019 B
Actual Rebinds	0
Actual Rewinds	0
Ordered	True
Node ID	0

Object

[tempdb].[dbo].[t1].[cx_t1_col1] [t]

Output List

[tempdb].[dbo].[t1].col1, [tempdb].[dbo].[t1].col2, [tempdb].[dbo].[t1].col3

Seek Predicates

Seek Keys[1]: Start: [tempdb].[dbo].[t1].col1 >= Scalar Operator((1)), End: [tempdb].[dbo].[t1].col1 < Scalar Operator((10001))

At least 10% of all percentages are numbers.

And yes

If you drop the index and re-run the query, the estimate goes back to 9090.63. Of course, in our case, we could have just updated statistics, but that may not be the obvious solution all the time. Given a choice, I'd much rather update stats than create a fresh index just to update stats. Which is basically what rebuilding indexes is. Heh. Anyway, I hope this helps.

Thanks for reading!

Crappy Missing Index Requests

When you're tuning queries

It's sort of a relief when the first time you get your hands on it, you get the plan and there's a missing index request. Even if it's not a super high-value one, something in there is crying for help. Where there's smoke, there's a bingo parlor.

But does adding missing indexes from requests always make things better?

The question goes for any tool, whether it's DTA, or the missing index DMVs, or your own wild speculation. Testing is important.

Not all requests are helpful

In fact, some of them can be harmful. Let's look at a recent example from the Orders database. After running for a while, I noticed the UpdateShipped stored procedure was asking for an index. And not just any index, but one that would reduce query costs by 98.5003%. That's incredible. That's amazing. Do you take DBA Express cards?

```
CREATE NONCLUSTERED INDEX [<Name of Missing Index, sysname,>]
ON [dbo].[Orders] ([ShipDate],[OrderDate])
```

The code in question is the part where the update actually happens.

```
UPDATE o
 SET o.ShipDate = DATEADD(HOUR, 24, o.OrderDate)
FROM dbo.Orders as o
WHERE o.ShipDate IS NULL
AND o.OrderDate >= DATEADD(DAY, DATEDIFF(DAY, 0, @MinOrderDate), '19000101')
AND o.OrderDate <= DATEADD(DAY, DATEDIFF(DAY, 0, @MinOrderDate), '23:59:59')
```

The index that it's currently using is very thoughtful. Extra thoughtful. Maybe the most thoughtful index I've ever created for free. Though somewhat forgetfully named.

```sql
CREATE UNIQUE NONCLUSTERED INDEX ix_Orders_OD_SD ON dbo.Orders (OrderDate, ID)
INCLUDE (ShipDate) WHERE (ShipDate IS NULL)
```

What about the query plan?

Aside from some baked-in problems, it's pretty normal. It has a cost of 2829 query bucks. Pretty high! Like I said, baked in problems.

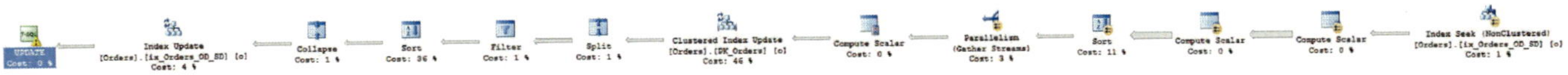

El Stinko

The baked in problems are an exercise for you, dear reader.

So what happens to it when we add the missing index?

```sql
CREATE NONCLUSTERED INDEX Crappy ON dbo.Orders (ShipDate, OrderDate)
```

It's crappy! The query doesn't even use it, but we do now have to update it. ShipDate is in the index, ShipDate is being updated. We have to update the index, like, now. Duh. This query now has a cost of 6792 query bucks. That's the opposite of a reduction, and a far cry from the 98 point some-odd percent reduction the missing index DMV promised us.

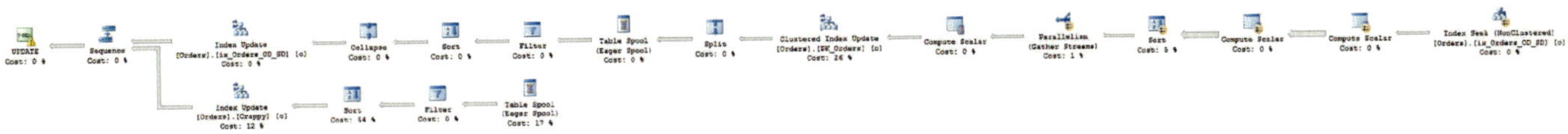

Totally crappy

If we go a step further. Or farther? You tell me. We can add an index hint to force the matter, and of course, forcing the matter makes matters worse. And that matters. The forced index query has a crappy cost of 6837 query bucks. This is why our cost based estimator does not choose this plan on its own.

Most crappiest

See?

UPDATE

Cached plan size	96 KB
Degree of Parallelism	6
Estimated Operator Cost	0 (0%)
Estimated Subtree Cost	6837.43
Memory Grant	2781216
Estimated Number of Rows	30274800

Statement

UPDATE o
SET o.ShipDate = DATEADD(HOUR, 24, o.OrderDate)
FROM dbo.Orders as o WITH (INDEX = Crappy)
WHERE o.ShipDate IS NULL
AND o.OrderDate >= DATEADD(DAY, DATEDIFF(DAY, 0, @MinOrderDate), '19000101')
AND o.OrderDate <= DATEADD(DAY, DATEDIFF(DAY, 0, @MinOrderDate), '23:59:59')

Warnings

The query memory grant detected "ExcessiveGrant", which may impact the reliability. Grant size: Initial 2781216 KB, Final 2781216 KB, Used 896 KB.

Legacy of Frugality

Lies And DMV Lies

When running sp_BlitzIndex, we often recommend testing out any index with an estimated benefit of >1mm per day. But that's the key word: testing. A missing index request that gets added and causes harm will rarely harm the query that's asking for it. I got pretty lucky here in demoland with an example. Usually you have to add the index, make sure it doesn't hurt the query you're adding it for, and then do regression testing on other queries in play. This includes modification queries.

Thanks for reading!

Clustered Index key columns in Nonclustered Indexes

Clustered indexes are fundamental

And I'm not just saying that because Kendra is my spiritual adviser!

They are not ~a copy~ of the table, they are the table, ordered by the column(s) you choose as the key. It could be one. It could be a few. It could be a GUID! But that's for another time. A long time from now. When I've raised an army, in accordance with ancient prophecy.

What I'd like to focus on is another oft-neglected consideration when indexing:

Columns in the clustering key will be in all of your nonclustered indexes

"How do you know?"

"Can I join your army?"

"Why does it do that?"

You may be asking yourself all of those questions. I'll answer one of them with a demo, and one of them with "no".

D-D-D-DEMO FACE

```
USE tempdb;

IF OBJECT_ID('tempdb..ClusterKeyColumnsTest') IS NOT NULL
DROP TABLE tempdb..ClusterKeyColumnsTest

;WITH E1(N) AS (
    SELECT NULL UNION ALL SELECT NULL UNION ALL SELECT NULL UNION ALL
    SELECT NULL UNION ALL SELECT NULL UNION ALL SELECT NULL UNION ALL
    SELECT NULL UNION ALL SELECT NULL UNION ALL SELECT NULL UNION ALL
    SELECT NULL  ),
E2(N) AS (SELECT NULL FROM E1 a, E1 b, E1 c, E1 d, E1 e, E1 f, E1 g, E1 h,
E1 i, E1 j),
Numbers AS (SELECT TOP (10000) ROW_NUMBER() OVER (ORDER BY (SELECT NULL))
AS N FROM E2)
SELECT
        IDENTITY (BIGINT, 1,1) AS ID ,
        ISNULL(CONVERT(DATE, DATEADD(HOUR, -N.N, GETDATE()    )),
        '1900-01-01') AS OrderDate ,
        ISNULL(CONVERT(DATE, DATEADD(HOUR, -N.N, GETDATE() + 1)),
        '1900-01-01') AS ProcessDate ,
        ISNULL(CONVERT(DATE, DATEADD(HOUR, -N.N, GETDATE() + 3)),
        '1900-01-01') AS ShipDate ,
        REPLICATE(CAST(NEWID() AS NVARCHAR(MAX)), CEILING(RAND() * 10))
        AS DumbGUID
INTO ClusterKeyColumnsTest
FROM    Numbers N
ORDER BY N.N DESC;

ALTER TABLE ClusterKeyColumnsTest ADD CONSTRAINT PK_ClusterKeyColumnsTest
PRIMARY KEY CLUSTERED (ID) WITH (FILLFACTOR = 100);

CREATE NONCLUSTERED INDEX IX_ALLDATES ON dbo.ClusterKeyColumnsTest
(OrderDate, ProcessDate, ShipDate) WITH (FILLFACTOR = 100);
```

That code will create a pretty rudimentary table of random data. It was between 3-4 GB on my system.

You can see a Clustered Index was created on the ID column, and a Nonclustered Index was created on the three date columns. The DumbGUID column was, of course, neglected as a key column in both. Poor GUID.

Running these queries, the Nonclustered Index on the date columns will be used, because SQL does this smart thing where it takes page count into consideration when choosing an index to use.

For the links, code, and comments, go here:
https://www.brentozar.com/archive/2015/08/clustered-index-key-columns-in-nonclustered-indexes/

```sql
SELECT ckct.ID
FROM   dbo.ClusterKeyColumnsTest AS ckct;

SELECT ckct.ID
FROM   dbo.ClusterKeyColumnsTest AS ckct
WHERE  ckct.OrderDate = '2014-12-18';

SELECT ckct.ID, ckct.DumbGUID
FROM   dbo.ClusterKeyColumnsTest AS ckct
WHERE  ckct.OrderDate = '2014-12-18';
```

Notice that the only time a Key Lookup was needed is for the last query, where we also select the DumbGUID column. You'd think it would be needed in all three, since the ID column isn't explicitly named in the key or as an include in the Nonclustered Index.

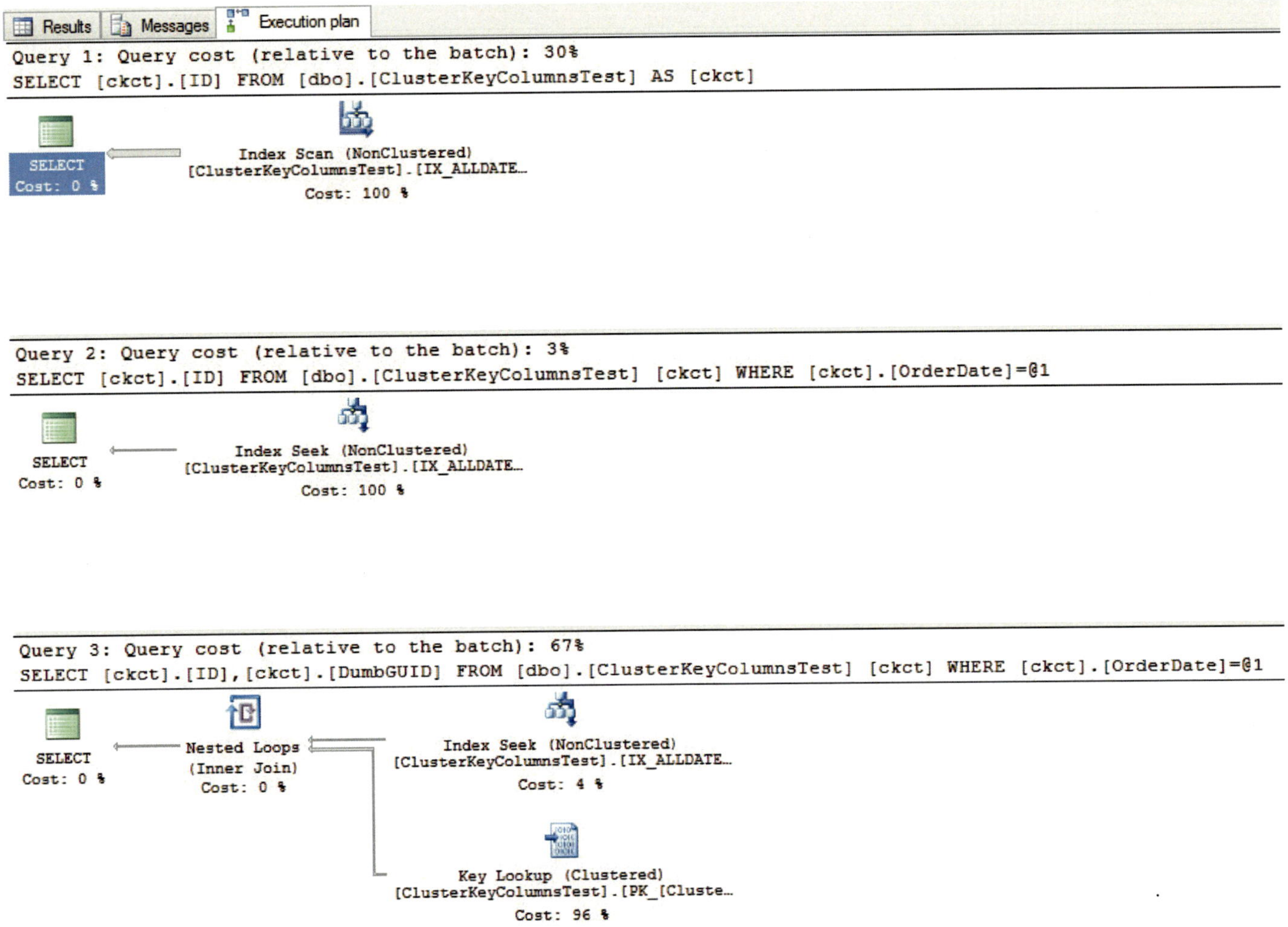

Key Lookups really are really expensive and you should really fix them. Really.

sp_BlitzIndex® to the rescue

If you find yourself trying to figure out indexes, Kendra's sp_BlitzIndex® stored procedure is invaluable. It can do this cool thing where it shows you SECRET columns!

Since I've already ruined the surprise, let's look at the indexes on our test table.

```sql
EXEC dbo.sp_BlitzIndex
    @DatabaseName = N'tempdb' ,
    @SchemaName = N'dbo' ,
    @TableName = N'ClusterKeyColumnsTest'
```

Here's the output. The detail it gives you on index columns and datatypes is really awesome. You can see the ID column is part of the Nonclustered Index, even though it isn't named in the definition.

Results | Messages | Execution plan

	Details: schema.table.index(indexid)	Definition: [Property] ColumnName {datatype maxbytes}	Secret Columns
1	Database [tempdb] as of 2015-07-14 14:38 (sp_BlitzIn...	http://BrentOzar.com/BlitzIndex	Thanks from the Brent Ozar Unlimited(TM) team. ...
2	dbo.ClusterKeyColumnsTest.PK_[ClusterKeyColumnsT...	[CX] [PK] [1 KEY] ID {bigint 8}	
3	dbo.ClusterKeyColumnsTest.IX_ALLDATES (2)	[3 KEYS] OrderDate {date 3}, ProcessDate {date 3}, ShipDate {date 3}	[1 KEY] ID {bigint 8}

Ooh, shapes!

One step beyond

Run the code to drop and recreate our test table, but this time add these indexes below instead of the original ones.

```sql
ALTER TABLE ClusterKeyColumnsTest
ADD CONSTRAINT [PK_[ClusterKeyColumnsTest]
    PRIMARY KEY CLUSTERED ( ID, OrderDate )
    WITH ( FILLFACTOR = 100 );

CREATE NONCLUSTERED INDEX IX_ALLDATES
    ON dbo.ClusterKeyColumnsTest ( ProcessDate, ShipDate )
    INCLUDE ( DumbGUID )
    WITH ( FILLFACTOR = 100 );
```

Running the same three queries as before, our plans change only slightly. The Key Lookup is gone, and the statement cost per batch has evened out.

For the links, code, and comments, go here:
https://www.brentozar.com/archive/2015/08/clustered-index-key-columns-in-nonclustered-indexes/

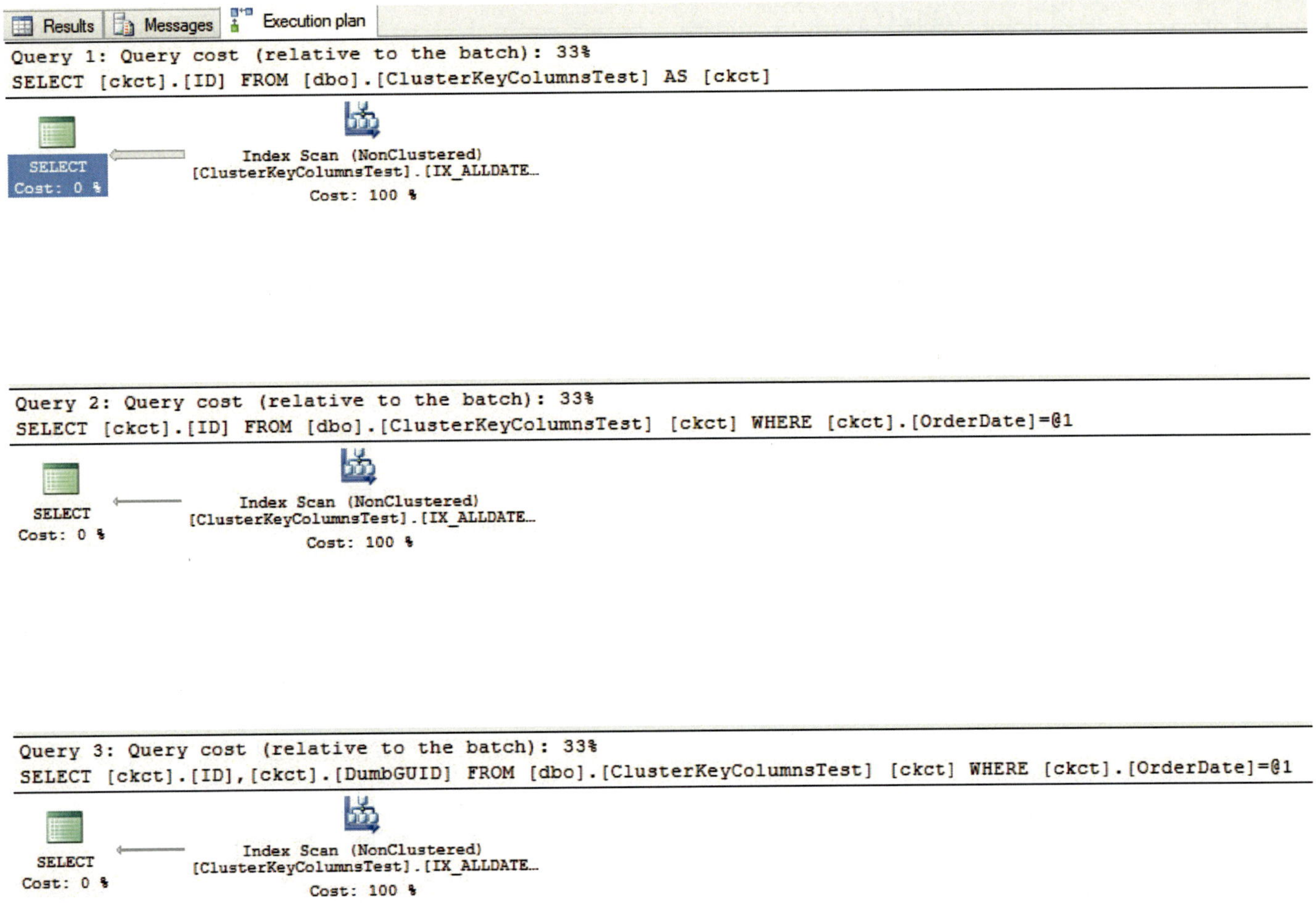

You too can be a hero by getting rid of Key Lookups.

But notice that, for the second query, where we're searching on the OrderDate column, we're still scanning the Nonclustered Index.

We moved that out of the Nonclustered Index and used it as part of the Clustering Key the second time around. What gives?

Running sp_BlitzIndex® the same as before, OrderDate is now a secret column in the Nonclustered Index.

	Details: schema.table.index(indexid)	Definition: [Property] ColumnName {datatype maxbytes}	Secret Columns
1	Database [tempdb] as of 2015-07-14 14:48 (sp_BlitzIn...	http://BrentOzar.com/BlitzIndex	Thanks from the Brent Ozar Unlimited(TM) tea...
2	dbo.ClusterKeyColumnsTest.PK_[ClusterKeyColumnsT...	[CX] [PK] [2 KEYS] ID {bigint 8}, OrderDate {date 3}	
3	dbo.ClusterKeyColumnsTest.IX_ALLDATES (2)	[2 KEYS] ProcessDate {date 3}, ShipDate {date 3} [1 INCLUDE] DumbGUID {varchar 8000}	[2 KEYS] ID {bigint 8}, OrderDate {date 3}

Fun Boy Three does the best version of Our Lips are Sealed, BTW.

Did we learn anything?

Sure did!

1. SQL 'hides' the columns from the Key of the Clustered Index in Nonclustered Indexes
2. Since those columns are part of the index, you don't need to include them in the definition
3. Secret columns in Nonclustered Indexes can be used to avoid keylookups AND satisfy WHERE clause searches!

Well, at least until all indexes are ColumnStore Indexes.

Kendra says: *One of the most common questions I get is whether there's a penalty or downside if you list the columns from the clustered index in your nonclustered index. You can stop worrying: there's no penalty.*

For the links, code, and comments, go here:
https://www.brentozar.com/archive/2015/08/clustered-index-key-columns-in-nonclustered-indexes/

Missing Index Impact and Join Type

Just Another Way

No matter how you delve into missing index requests — whether it's the plan level, DMV analysis, or (forgive me for saying it), DTA, the requests will generally be the same.

They'll prioritize equality predicates, the columns may or not may be in the right order, the columns may or may not be in the right part of the index, and the impact...

Oh, that impact.

It's all just a cry for help, anyway.

Like a teenager watching anime and buying intricate parasols.

Salted Grains

If I run these three queries with different join types:

```sql
SELECT b.UserId, b.Name, b.Date, p.CreationDate
FROM dbo.Badges AS b
JOIN dbo.Posts AS p
ON b.UserId = p.OwnerUserId
WHERE b.Date = '20170101'
OPTION(LOOP JOIN, MAXDOP 1, RECOMPILE)

SELECT b.UserId, b.Name, b.Date, p.CreationDate
FROM dbo.Badges AS b
JOIN dbo.Posts AS p
ON b.UserId = p.OwnerUserId
WHERE b.Date = '20170101'
OPTION(MERGE JOIN, MAXDOP 1, RECOMPILE)

SELECT b.UserId, b.Name, b.Date, p.CreationDate
FROM dbo.Badges AS b
JOIN dbo.Posts AS p
ON b.UserId = p.OwnerUserId
WHERE b.Date = '20170101'
OPTION(HASH JOIN, MAXDOP 1, RECOMPILE)
```

They're all going to ask for the same missing index:

```sql
USE [StackOverflow]
GO
CREATE NONCLUSTERED INDEX [<Name of Missing Index, sysname,>]
ON [dbo].[Badges] ([Date])
INCLUDE ([Name],[UserId])
```

Kinda weird already, that a join column is an INCLUDE, but hey.

What's even weirder is that they have diminishing estimated impacts based on join type.

- Loop: 99.1954%
- Merge: 42.7795%
- Hash: 28.7901%

It gets a bit stranger if I force parallelism!

```sql
SELECT b.UserId, b.Name, b.Date, p.CreationDate
FROM dbo.Badges AS b
JOIN dbo.Posts AS p
ON b.UserId = p.OwnerUserId
WHERE b.Date = '20170101'
OPTION(LOOP JOIN, USE HINT('ENABLE_PARALLEL_PLAN_PREFERENCE'), RECOMPILE)

SELECT b.UserId, b.Name, b.Date, p.CreationDate
FROM dbo.Badges AS b
JOIN dbo.Posts AS p
ON b.UserId = p.OwnerUserId
WHERE b.Date = '20170101'
OPTION(MERGE JOIN, USE HINT('ENABLE_PARALLEL_PLAN_PREFERENCE'), RECOMPILE)

SELECT b.UserId, b.Name, b.Date, p.CreationDate
FROM dbo.Badges AS b
JOIN dbo.Posts AS p
ON b.UserId = p.OwnerUserId
WHERE b.Date = '20170101'
OPTION(HASH JOIN, USE HINT('ENABLE_PARALLEL_PLAN_PREFERENCE'), RECOMPILE)
```

Now the estimated impacts look like this:

- Loop: 98.9569%
- Merge: 29.1982%
- Hash: 44.2455%

The Hash and Merge join impacts have just about changed places.

The funny thing is...

I totally agree.

As far as indexes go, that's a crappy index for the Merge and Hash Join plans. But no better one is being offered, not even sneakily.

For the nested loops plans, it's super easy to grab the UserIds for that date, and dig into the Posts table for just those.

For the merge join plans, it's less helpful. While it's nice that we can easily filter the date predicate, we still have to order our data for the merge join. There are further complications in the parallel version.

For the hash join plans, it's a similar situation. We need to create a hash table on UserId. It being in the leaf of an index on Date doesn't help us much, or rather as much as it would if it were in the key.

In short, both the merge and hash join plans have cost-increasing operators thrown into the mix that the index as requested just wouldn't help.

Thanks for reading!

***Brent says:** in the Mastering Index Tuning class, these types of examples are why I tell students that you should look at one-key-column index suggestions carefully. In most cases, SQL Server really needs one (or more) of the included fields to be in the key. The hard part is figuring out which one(s) without looking at the execution plans.*

This blank page is brought to you by a bad SAN firmware update.

Computed Columns

Sometimes life just doesn't add up.
Sometimes you gotta do the adding yourself.
This chapter pairs well with the juice that gets the noggin' joggin' -- reader's choice!

BRENT OZAR
UNLIMITED®

Computed Columns: Reversing Data For Easier Searching

During Training

We were talking about computed columns, and one of our students mentioned that he uses computed columns that run the REVERSE() function on a column for easier back-searching.

What's back-searching? It's a word I just made up.

The easiest example to think about and demo is Social Security Numbers.

One security requirement is often to give the last four.

Obviously running this for a search WHERE ssn LIKE '%0000' would perform badly over large data sets.

Now, if you only ever needed the last four, you could easily just use SUBSTRING or RIGHT to pull out the last four.

If you wanted to give people the ability to expand their search further, REVERSE becomes more valuable.

For the links, code, and comments, go here:
https://www.brentozar.com/archive/2018/01/computed-columns-reversing-data-easier-searching/

Oh, a demo

You must have said please.

Let's mock up some dummy data.

```
Transact-SQL
USE tempdb;

DROP TABLE IF EXISTS dbo.AllYourPersonalInformation;

CREATE TABLE dbo.AllYourPersonalInformation
(
    id INT IDENTITY(1, 1) PRIMARY KEY CLUSTERED,
    fname VARCHAR(10),
    lname VARCHAR(20),
    ssn VARCHAR(11)
);

INSERT INTO dbo.AllYourPersonalInformation WITH ( TABLOCK )
                ( fname, lname, ssn )
SELECT      TOP ( 1000000 )
            'Does',
            'Notmatter',
              RIGHT('000'  + CONVERT(VARCHAR(11), ABS(CHECKSUM( NEWID() )) ), 3) + '-'
            + RIGHT('00'   + CONVERT(VARCHAR(11), ABS(CHECKSUM( NEWID() )) ), 2) + '-'
            + RIGHT('0000' + CONVERT(VARCHAR(11), ABS(CHECKSUM( NEWID() )) ), 4)
FROM        (SELECT 1 AS n FROM sys.messages AS m CROSS JOIN sys.messages AS m2) AS x;

CREATE INDEX ix_ssn ON dbo.AllYourPersonalInformation (ssn);
```

We should have 1 million rows of randomly generated (and unfortunately not terribly unique) data.

If we run this query, we get a query plan that scans the index on ssn and reads every row. This is the ~bad~ kind of index scan.

```
Transact-SQL
SELECT COUNT(*) AS records
FROM dbo.AllYourPersonalInformation AS aypi
WHERE aypi.ssn LIKE '%9156'
```

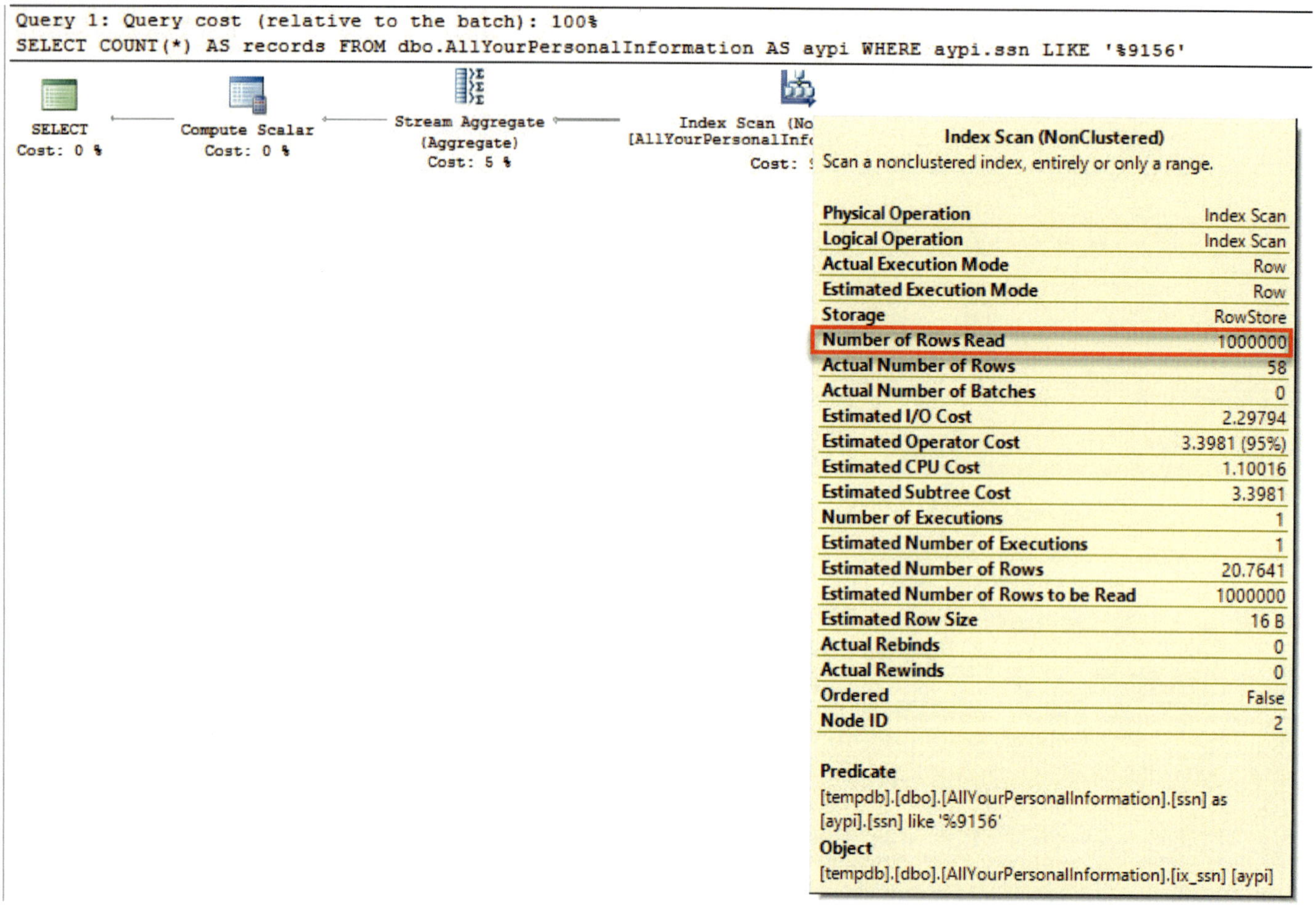

Ouch

Let's add that reverse column and index it. We don't have to persist it.

```
ALTER TABLE dbo.AllYourPersonalInformation
ADD reversi AS REVERSE(ssn);

CREATE NONCLUSTERED INDEX ix_reversi ON dbo.AllYourPersonalInformation (reversi);
```

Now we can run queries like this — without even directly referencing our reversed column — and get the desired index seeks.

```sql
SELECT COUNT(*) AS records
FROM dbo.AllYourPersonalInformation AS aypi
WHERE REVERSE(aypi.ssn) LIKE REVERSE('%9156')

SELECT COUNT(*) AS records
FROM dbo.AllYourPersonalInformation AS aypi
WHERE REVERSE(aypi.ssn) LIKE REVERSE('%90-9156')

SELECT COUNT(*) AS records
FROM dbo.AllYourPersonalInformation AS aypi
WHERE REVERSE(aypi.ssn) LIKE REVERSE('%082-90-9156')
```

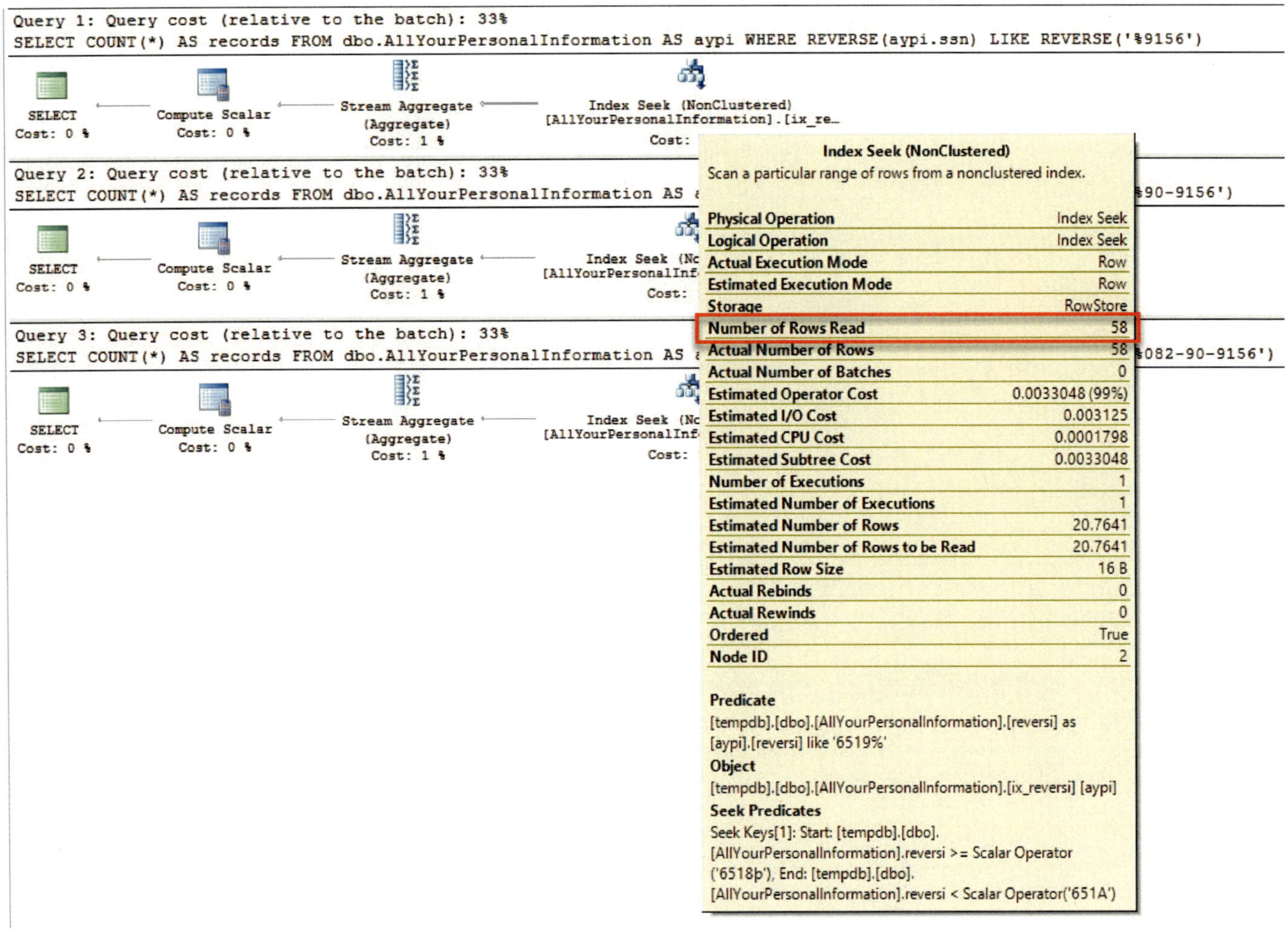

(Hot 97 air horn)

What I thought was cool

Was that the REVERSE on the LIKE predicate put the wildcard on the correct side. That's usually the kind of thing that I hope works, but doesn't.

Thanks, whoever wrote that!

And thank YOU for reading!

Computed Columns and Cardinality Estimates

:thinking_face:

When most people think about computed columns, they don't think about cardinality estimates.

Heck, I'm not sure most people think about cardinality estimates. At all. Ever.

One of the few people who has ever responded to my emails does, and I didn't even have to threaten him.

Do you think about computed columns?

If you're here, you might just be thinking about lunch, avoiding jail time, or how much you hate Access.

But seriously, they're great for a lot of things. Just don't put functions in them.

One thing they can help with, without you needing to persist or index them, is cardinality estimates.

Demo Block

If I run this query:

```sql
SELECT  COUNT(*) AS records
FROM    dbo.Users AS u
JOIN    dbo.Posts AS p
    ON p.OwnerUserId = u.Id
WHERE   u.UpVotes + u.DownVotes = 0
        AND p.Score >= 5;
```

I get this plan:

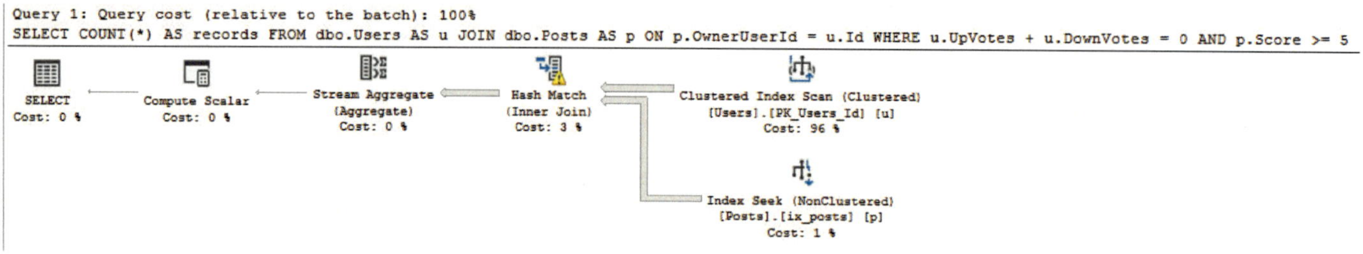

Dead wrong

The first thing that jumps out to most people is the warning on the Hash Join — indeed, it's grail overfloweth.

Hash Match

Use each row from the top input to build a hash table, and each row from the bottom input to probe into the hash table, outputting all matching rows.

Physical Operation	Hash Match
Logical Operation	Inner Join
Actual Execution Mode	Row
Estimated Execution Mode	Row
Actual Number of Rows	10413
Actual Number of Batches	0
Estimated Operator Cost	1.355908 (3%)
Estimated I/O Cost	0
Estimated CPU Cost	0.994168
Estimated Subtree Cost	41.4276
Number of Executions	1
Estimated Number of Executions	1
Estimated Number of Rows	35931.4
Estimated Row Size	9 B
Actual Rebinds	0
Actual Rewinds	0
Node ID	2

Warnings
Operator used tempdb to spill data during execution with spill level 1 and 1 spilled thread(s), Hash wrote 880 pages to and read 880 pages from tempdb with granted memory 6784KB and used memory 6728KB

Hash Keys Probe
[SUPERUSER].[dbo].[Posts].OwnerUserId

Probe Residual
[SUPERUSER].[dbo].[Users].[Id] as [u].[Id]=[SUPERUSER].[dbo].[Posts].[OwnerUserId] as [p].[OwnerUserId]

Choosing poorly

For the links, code, and comments, go here:
https://www.brentozar.com/archive/2018/02/computed-columns-cardinality-estimates/

The root cause of this bad guess is from the Users table. Our WHERE clause is just awful. How on earth would SQL Server know how many Upvotes + Downvotes = 0? In fact, it's guess is just plan goofy.

Clustered Index Scan (Clustered)

Scanning a clustered index, entirely or only a range.

Physical Operation	Clustered Index Scan
Logical Operation	Clustered Index Scan
Actual Execution Mode	Row
Estimated Execution Mode	Row
Storage	RowStore
Number of Rows Read	623700
Actual Number of Rows	492220
Actual Number of Batches	0
Estimated I/O Cost	39.1179
Estimated Operator Cost	39.8042 (96%)
Estimated CPU Cost	0.686227
Estimated Subtree Cost	39.8042
Number of Executions	1
Estimated Number of Executions	1
Estimated Number of Rows	22193.8
Estimated Number of Rows to be Read	623700
Estimated Row Size	19 B
Actual Rebinds	0
Actual Rewinds	0
Ordered	False
Node ID	4

Predicate

([SUPERUSER].[dbo].[Users].[UpVotes] as [u].[UpVotes]+ [SUPERUSER].[dbo].[Users].[DownVotes] as [u].[DownVotes])=(0)

Object

[SUPERUSER].[dbo].[Users].[PK_Users_Id] [u]

Output List

[SUPERUSER].[dbo].[Users].Id

[Boos Internally]

The guess is off by about 470k rows. If your concern is with cardinality estimates, you may try the Advanced Dead End known as multi-column statistics.

```
CREATE STATISTICS users_upv_dv ON dbo.Users (UpVotes, DownVotes) WITH FULLSCAN;
```

But that doesn't help!

You might even try Advanced-Advanced Dead End known as filtered multi-column statistics.

```
CREATE STATISTICS users_upv_dv ON dbo.Users (UpVotes, DownVotes)
WHERE UpVotes = 0 AND DownVotes = 0 WITH FULLSCAN;
```

And that still won't help.

Even if you RECOMPILE. Even if you free the proc cache. Even if you rebuild indexes. Even if you restart SQL.

Magically, I can add this computed column:

```
ALTER TABLE dbo.Users ADD UpvotesPlusDownvotes AS UpVotes + DownVotes;
```

I'm not persisting it, and I'm not even indexing it. But my plan changes! Kind of.

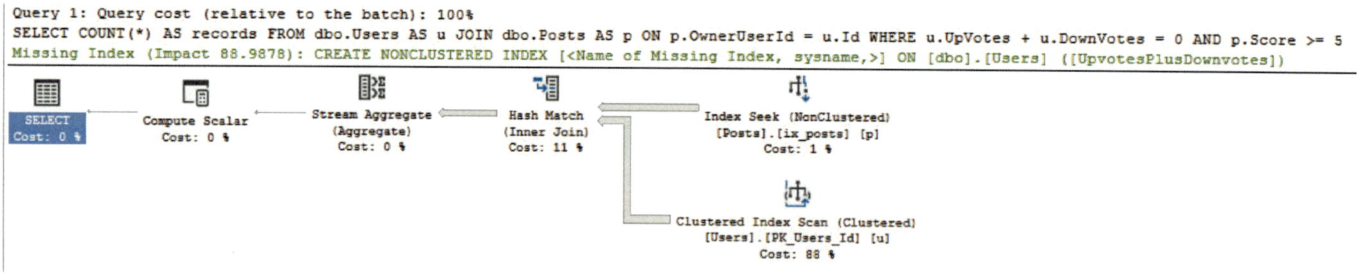

Have you seen me?

The Hash Join is no longer spilling!

Before you go accusing me of taking advantage of Batch Mode Memory Grant Feedback — I'm not using any cOLU MNstor3 indexes in here. Everything is plain old row mode.

It's just a result of the cardinality estimate improving.

For the links, code, and comments, go here:
https://www.brentozar.com/archive/2018/02/computed-columns-cardinality-estimates/

Clustered Index Scan (Clustered)

Scanning a clustered index, entirely or only a range.

Physical Operation	Clustered Index Scan
Logical Operation	Clustered Index Scan
Actual Execution Mode	Row
Estimated Execution Mode	Row
Storage	RowStore
Number of Rows Read	623700
Actual Number of Rows	492220
Actual Number of Batches	0
Estimated I/O Cost	39.1179
Estimated Operator Cost	39.8042 (88%)
Estimated CPU Cost	0.686227
Estimated Subtree Cost	39.8042
Number of Executions	1
Estimated Number of Executions	1
Estimated Number of Rows	486817
Estimated Number of Rows to be Read	623700
Estimated Row Size	19 B
Actual Rebinds	0
Actual Rewinds	0
Ordered	False
Node ID	6

Predicate

([SUPERUSER].[dbo].[Users].[UpVotes] as [u].[UpVotes]+
[SUPERUSER].[dbo].[Users].[DownVotes] as [u].[DownVotes])=(0)

Object

[SUPERUSER].[dbo].[Users].[PK_Users_Id] [u]

Output List

[SUPERUSER].[dbo].[Users].Id

Crazy Eddie

The much improved cardinality estimate leads the optimizer to ask for a larger memory grant.

SELECT

Cached plan size	40 KB
Estimated Operator Cost	0 (0%)
Degree of Parallelism	1
Estimated Subtree Cost	45.1826
Memory Grant	21944
Estimated Number of Rows	1

Statement

```
SELECT  COUNT(*) AS records
FROM    dbo.Users AS u
JOIN    dbo.Posts AS p
   ON p.OwnerUserId = u.Id
WHERE   u.UpVotes + u.DownVotes = 0
      AND p.Score >= 5
```

Oh, you did that.

Rather than a small, crappy memory grant (for this query).

SELECT

Cached plan size	40 KB
Estimated Operator Cost	0 (0%)
Degree of Parallelism	1
Estimated Subtree Cost	41.4491
Memory Grant	6784
Estimated Number of Rows	1

Statement

```
SELECT  COUNT(*) AS records
FROM    dbo.Users AS u
JOIN    dbo.Posts AS p
   ON p.OwnerUserId = u.Id
WHERE   u.UpVotes + u.DownVotes = 0
      AND p.Score >= 5
```

Don't like you.

Is this as good as it gets?

Obviously not. We could make some other changes to improve things, but I think this is pretty cool.

We didn't have to change our query, even, for the optimizer to make this adjustment.

If you've got this kind of stuff in your queries, a computed column might be a good way to improve performance.

Thanks for reading!

For a good time, call Adam Machanic 214-748-3647

Query Plan

We're finally not drinking alone. The optimizer has been drinking for years. In fact, it's got quite a head start. Time to play catch up. Liquor is quicker, so grab those shot glasses.

BRENT OZAR UNLIMITED®

Logical Query Processing

You can't do that on management studio

Recently, while working with a client, I did something in a query that they were mystified by. I didn't think much of it, but I thought it might be useful to you, dear readers, as well. Along with an explanation.

Here's a sample query that takes advantage of the same type of trick, but with a few extra bats and worms added in to illustrate a larger point.

```
SELECT   TOP 100
         b.Name, b.UserId, COUNT_BIG(*) AS Coconuts
FROM     dbo.Badges AS b
WHERE    b.Date >= '2014-01-01 00:00:00.003'
GROUP BY b.Name, b.UserId
HAVING   COUNT_BIG(*) > 100
ORDER BY Coconuts DESC;
```

Can you dig it?

What I did was order by the alias of the COUNT_BIG(*) column, Coconuts.

What they didn't understand was why that's legal, but filtering on that alias wouldn't be legal. A more familiar scenario might be using ROW_NUMBER(); you can ORDER BY it, but not filter on it in the WHERE clause to limit result sets to the TOP N per set. You would have to get an intermediate result in a CTE or temp table and then filter.

When SQL goes to figure out what to do with all this, it doesn't look at it in the order you typed it. It's a bit more like this:

> 8\. SELECT
> 9\. DISTINCT
> 11\. TOP
> 1\. FROM
> 2\. ON
> 3\. JOIN
> 4\. WHERE
> 5\. GROUP BY
> 6\. WITH CUBE/ROLLUP
> 7\. HAVING
> 10\. ORDER BY
> 12\. OFFSET/FETCH

To make that a easier to read:

> 1. FROM
> 2. ON
> 3. JOIN
> 4. WHERE
> 5. GROUP BY
> 6. WITH CUBE/ROLLUP
> 7. HAVING
> 8. SELECT
> 9. DISTINCT
> 10. ORDER BY
> 11. TOP
> 12. OFFSET/FETCH

And that's how babies get made

Since the ORDER BY is processed after the SELECT list, ORDER BY can use a column aliased there. You can't do that in the WHERE clause because it gets processed before SQL does its fancy footwork to get you some stuff to look at.

Here are some examples of what happens when you try to move the alias to different parts of the query.

Using it in the HAVING filter:

```sql
SELECT   TOP 100
         b.Name, b.UserId, COUNT_BIG(*) AS Coconuts
FROM     dbo.Badges AS b
WHERE    b.Date >= '2014-01-01 00:00:00.003'
GROUP BY b.Name, b.UserId
HAVING   Coconuts > 100
ORDER BY Coconuts DESC;
```

And again using it in the WHERE clause:

```sql
SELECT TOP 100
 b.Name, b.UserId, COUNT_BIG(*) AS Coconuts
FROM dbo.Badges AS b
WHERE b.Date >= '2014-01-01 00:00:00.003'
AND Coconuts > 100
GROUP BY b.Name, b.UserId
ORDER BY Coconuts DESC;
```

Both result in the same error, give or take a line number. Coconuts is not reference-able at either of these points.

> Msg 207, Level 16, State 1, Line 33
>
> Invalid column name 'Coconuts'.

CTEs, Inline Views, and What They Do

By now, you have probably heard of CTEs

And you may have even heard them referred to as Inline Views. Really, an Inline View can be any type of derived table. It's very easy to illustrate when one may turn into a performance problem with CTEs, if you aren't careful.

A lot of people think that when you call a CTE, the results are somehow persisted in a magical happy place and the underlying query just hangs back admiring the output as it sails into the upper deck.

Take the following example, which serves no real purpose.

```sql
WITH t1
    AS ( SELECT u.Id FROM dbo.Users AS u WHERE u.Id = 1 )
SELECT *
FROM   t1;
```

It has a perfectly reasonable execution plan, and will lead a happy life.

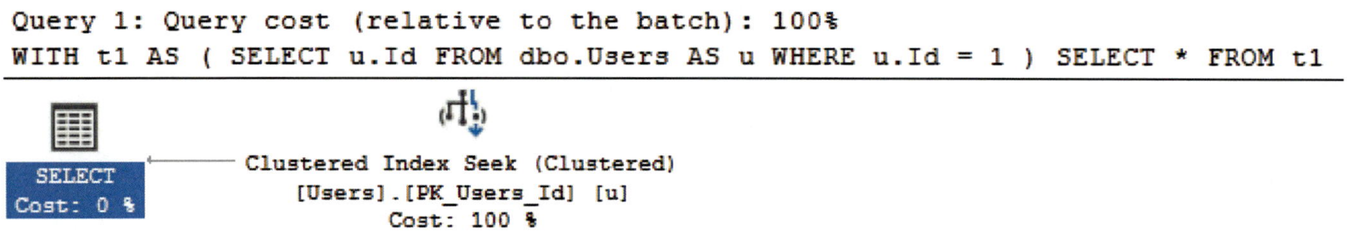

I am from the future

Now, let's join that to itself.

```sql
WITH t1
    AS ( SELECT u.Id FROM dbo.Users AS u WHERE u.Id = 1 )
SELECT *
FROM   t1
JOIN   t1 AS t2
    ON t2.Id = t1.Id;
```

Doesn't get much easier than that. But what happened with the plan?

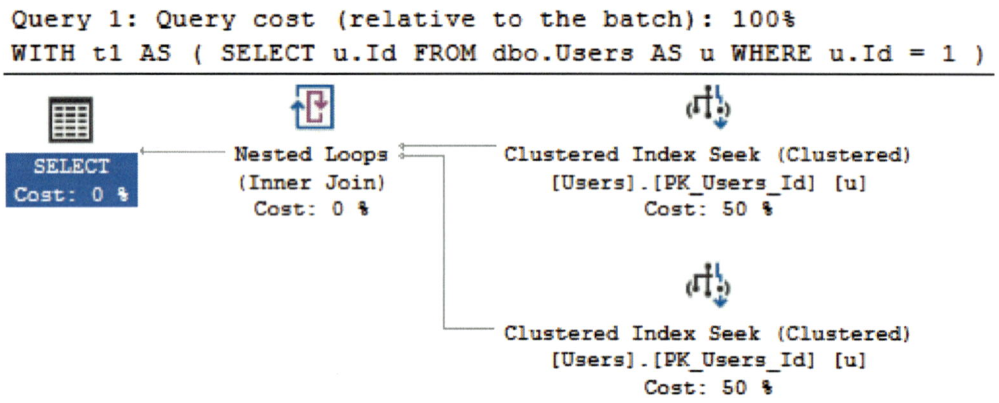

SPOOKY

Huh. That's a whole other index operation. So just like when you join to a view, the view has to be executed and returned. In fact, if you keep throwing joins that reference the original CTE, you'll keep getting more index operations.

```sql
WITH t1
    AS ( SELECT u.Id FROM dbo.Users AS u WHERE u.Id = 1 )
SELECT *
FROM   t1
JOIN   t1 AS t2
    ON t2.Id = t1.Id
JOIN   t1 AS t3
    ON t3.Id = t1.Id;
```

Did someone say they wanted another index operation? Because I thought I heard that.

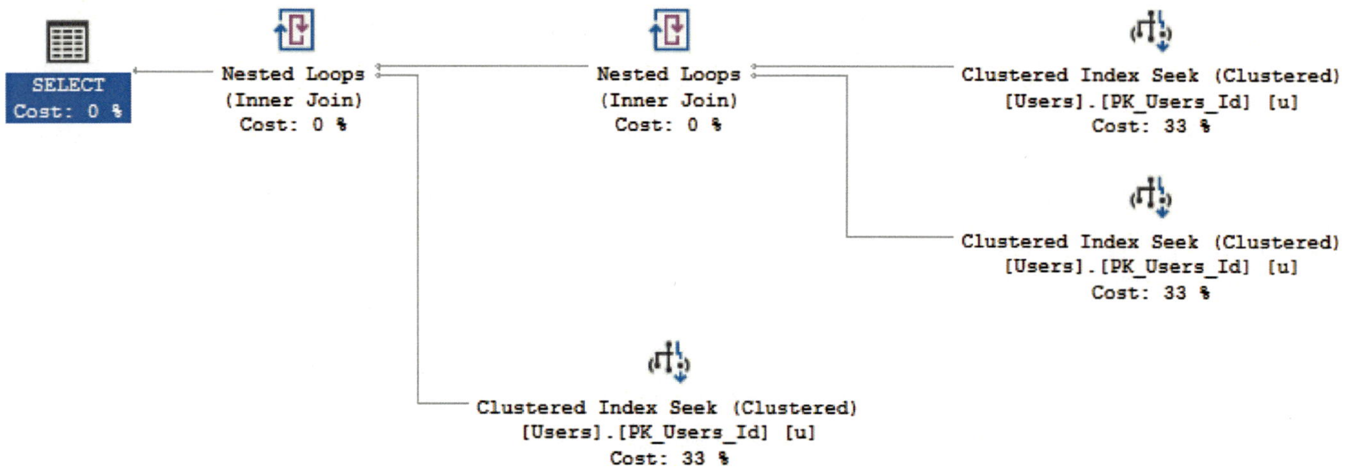

TEH TRES

To sum things up, CTEs are a great base

From which you can reference and filter on items in the select list that you otherwise wouldn't be able to (think windowing functions), but every time you reference a CTE, they get executed. The fewer times you have to hit a larger base set, and the fewer reads you do, the better. If you find yourself referencing CTEs more than once or twice, you should consider a temp or persisted table instead, with the proper indexes.

I Most Certainly Do Have A Join Predicate

FREAK OUT

You wrote a query. You joined tables.

You have the right ON clause.

You have the right WHERE clause.

But the query plan has a problem!

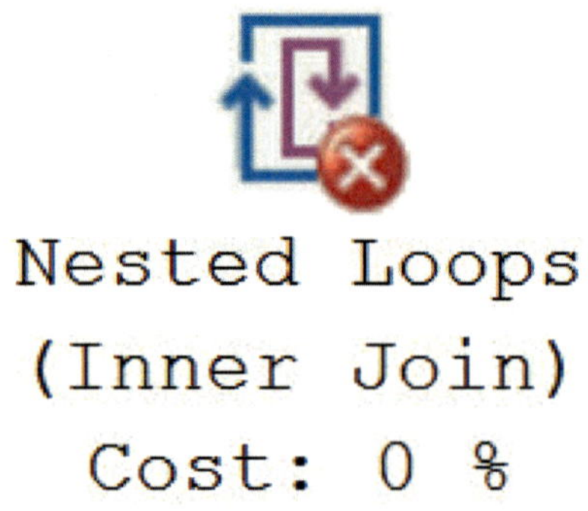

BugBurg

How Could This Happen To Me?

Oh, relax. You're not crazy. You just assumed the worst.

Like me whenever I feel pain near my liver.

Call the mortician.

For a query like this, the optimizer can play some tricks.

```sql
SELECT TOP 10 p.OwnerUserId, c.Id
FROM dbo.Posts AS p
JOIN dbo.Comments AS c
ON p.OwnerUserId = c.UserId
WHERE p.OwnerUserId = 22656
```

One of our join columns is in the where clause, too.

That means our plan looks like this!

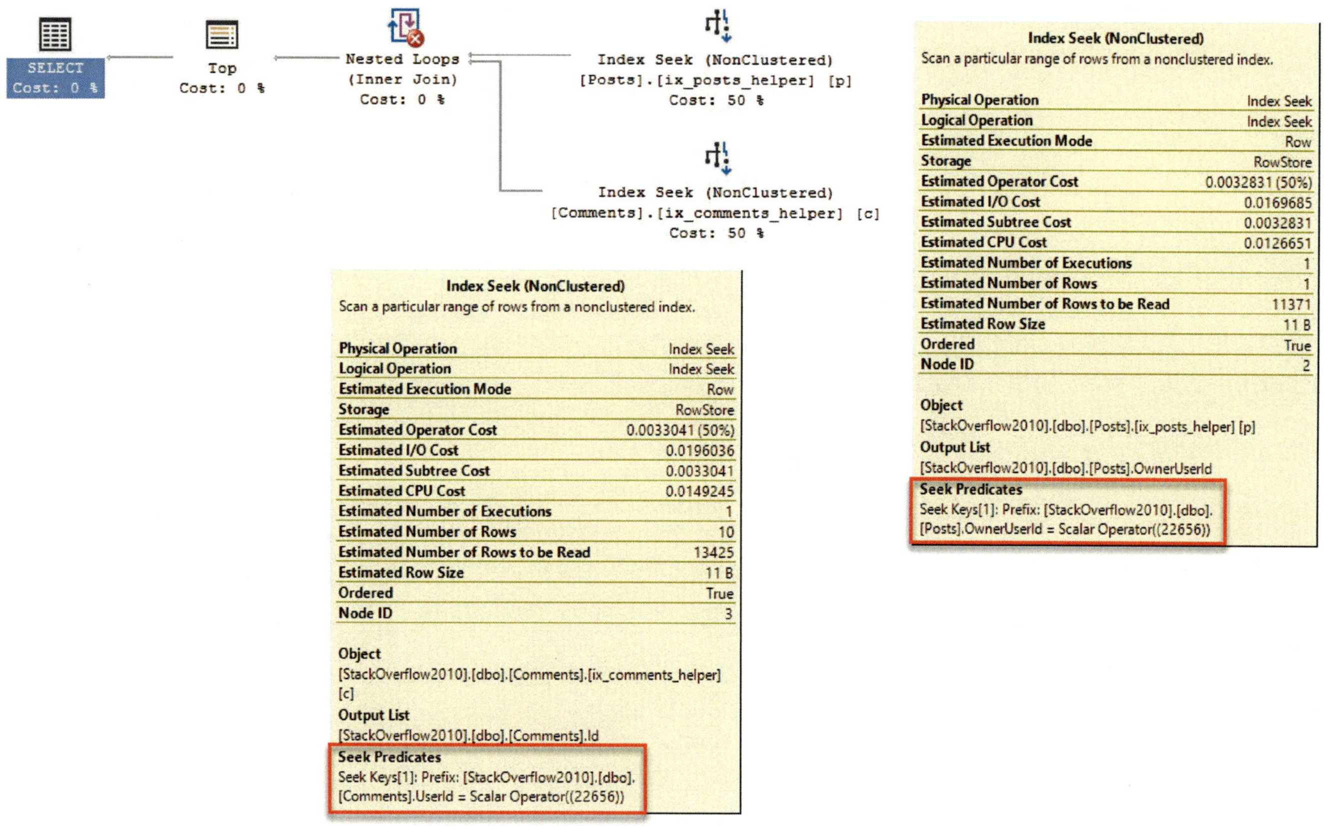

Lemons!

You see, when the optimizer looks at the join and the where, it knows that if it pushes the predicate to the two index seeks, whatever values come out will match.

I don't think it even needs the join at that point, but hey.

It certainly doesn't need the warning.

Thanks for reading!

***Brent says:** Erik's like that dying replicant at the end of Blade Runner. He's seen things you people wouldn't believe. Also, he has superhuman strength.*

The Many Mysteries of Merge Joins

Not A Single Picture Of A Zipper

There are some interesting things about Merge Joins, and Merge Join plans that I figured I'd blog about.

Merge joins have at least one interesting attribute, and may add some weird stuff to your query plans.

It's not that I think they're bad, but they can be tricky.

Lots of people see a Merge Join and are somewhere between grateful (that it's not a Hash Join) and curious (as to why it's not Nested Loops).

Oh, you exotic Merge Join.

E pluribus unum

In a "good" Merge Join, the join operator in the query plan will have the Many to Many: False attribute.

The optimizer knows this because the Primary Key on Id (though a unique index or constraint offers similar assurances) is distinct for each value in the Users table.

Having one unique input give you a one to many Merge Join.

For the links, code, and comments, go here:
https://www.brentozar.com/archive/2018/04/many-mysteries-merge-joins/

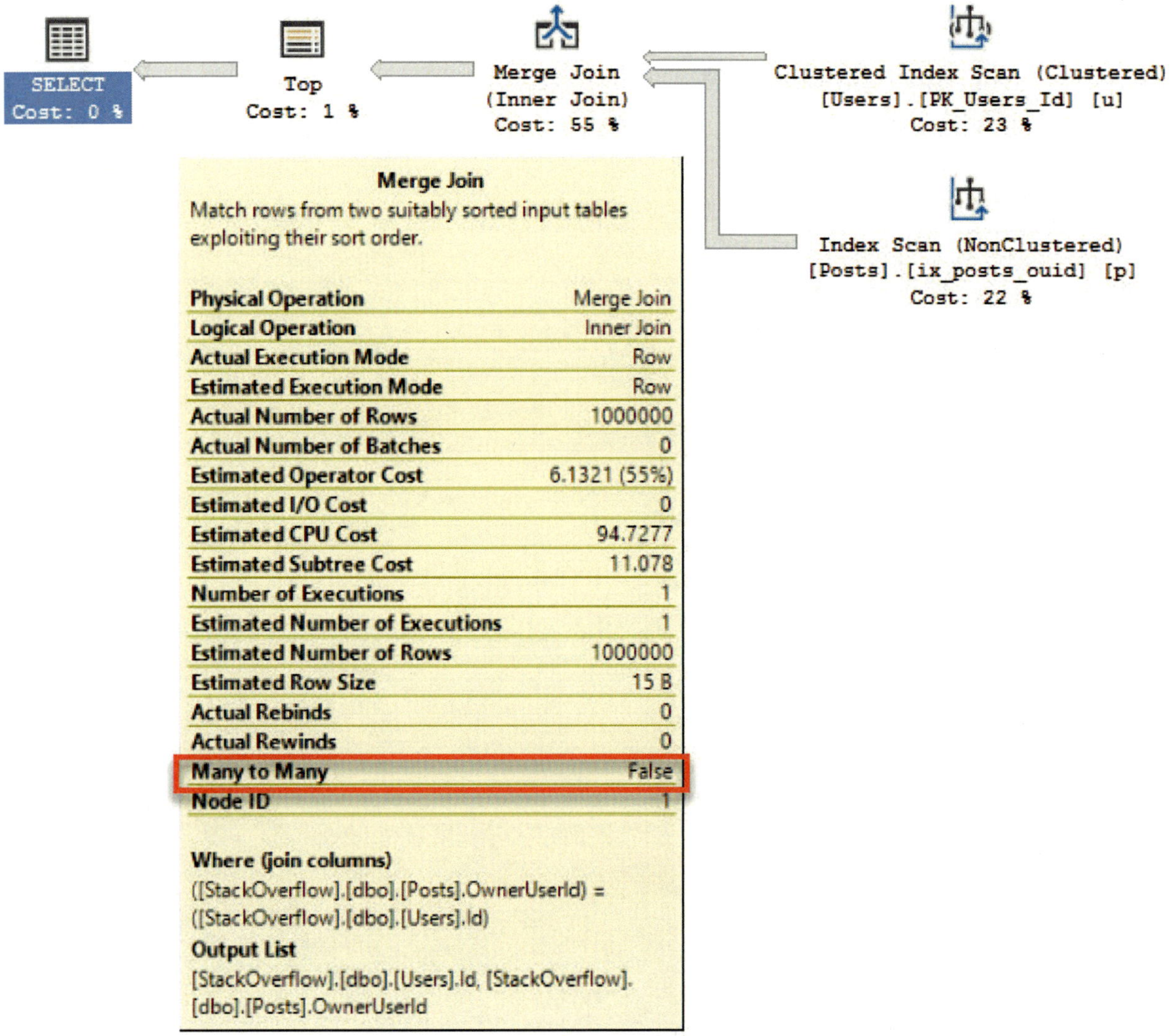

Simple as a pimple

The statistics TIME and IO profile for this query is about like so:

```
Table 'Posts'. Scan count 1, logical reads 2282, physical reads 0, read-ahead reads 0,
lob logical reads 0, lob physical reads 0, lob read-ahead reads 0.
Table 'Users'. Scan count 1, logical reads 417, physical reads 0, read-ahead reads 0,
lob logical reads 0, lob physical reads 0, lob read-ahead reads 0.

 SQL Server Execution Times:
   CPU time = 329 ms,  elapsed time = 333 ms.
```

Not too shabby for one meeeeeeeeeeeeeeeeeeeellion rows.

E pluribus pluribus

In a "bad" Merge Join, that attribute will be True.

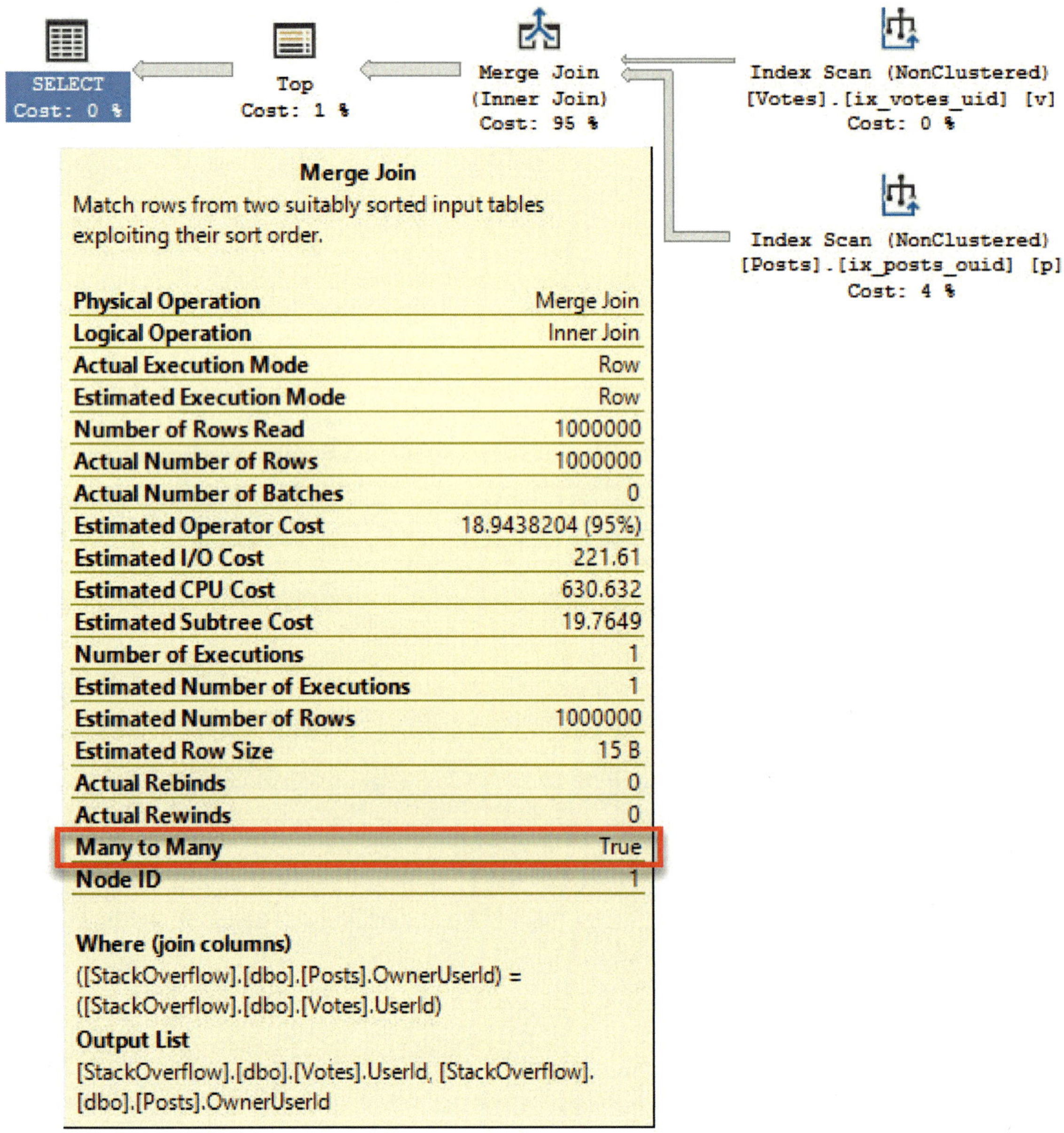

Hamburger Lady

Why does this happen, and why is it bad?

It happens when there are, or may be duplicates on both sides of the results.

Internally, the Merge Join will spin up a work table (similar to how a Hash Join operates), and work out the duplicate situation.

The stats TIME and IO profile of this plan looks like so:

For the links, code, and comments, go here:
https://www.brentozar.com/archive/2018/04/many-mysteries-merge-joins/

```
Table 'Worktable'. Scan count 1, logical reads 28836, physical reads 0, read-ahead reads 0,
lob logical reads 0, lob physical reads 0, lob read-ahead reads 0.
Table 'Posts'. Scan count 1, logical reads 38, physical reads 0, read-ahead reads 0,
lob logical reads 0, lob physical reads 0, lob read-ahead reads 0.
Table 'Votes'. Scan count 1, logical reads 5, physical reads 1, read-ahead reads 464,
lob logical reads 0, lob physical reads 0, lob read-ahead reads 0.

 SQL Server Execution Times:
   CPU time = 343 ms,  elapsed time = 366 ms.
```

If we were to, say, choose that serial Merge Join plan in the compilation of a stored procedure that became the victim of parameter sniffing, we could run into trouble.

```
Table 'Worktable'. Scan count 505697, logical reads 67579461, physical reads 0, read-ahead reads 0,
lob logical reads 0, lob physical reads 0, lob read-ahead reads 0.
Table 'Posts'. Scan count 1, logical reads 62710, physical reads 0, read-ahead reads 55333,
lob logical reads 0, lob physical reads 0, lob read-ahead reads 0.
Table 'Votes'. Scan count 1, logical reads 15112, physical reads 0, read-ahead reads 14640,
lob logical reads 0, lob physical reads 0, lob read-ahead reads 0.

 SQL Server Execution Times:
   CPU time = 459079 ms,  elapsed time = 459432 ms.
```

Yes, that is seven minutes and forty seconds. A little over half of one metric cigarette break.

Head to head, the large merge (many to many) is costed higher than the smaller merge (one to many). But you won't see that in a parameter sniffing situation.

You'll only see the lower costed Merge Join version of the plan.

The optimizer will sometimes to try protect itself from such hi jinks.

Aggregation Ruling The Nation

In some cases, the optimizer may inject an aggregation into one side of the join ahead of time to distinctify the data. It doesn't need to do both — we only need one distinct input for the many to many attribute to be false.

I haven't seen a situation where both inputs get aggregated merely to support the Merge Join, but it might happen if you ask for other aggregations on the join column.

It can use a Stream Aggregate, which would generally make more sense, since both the Stream Aggregate and the Merge join require sorted data.

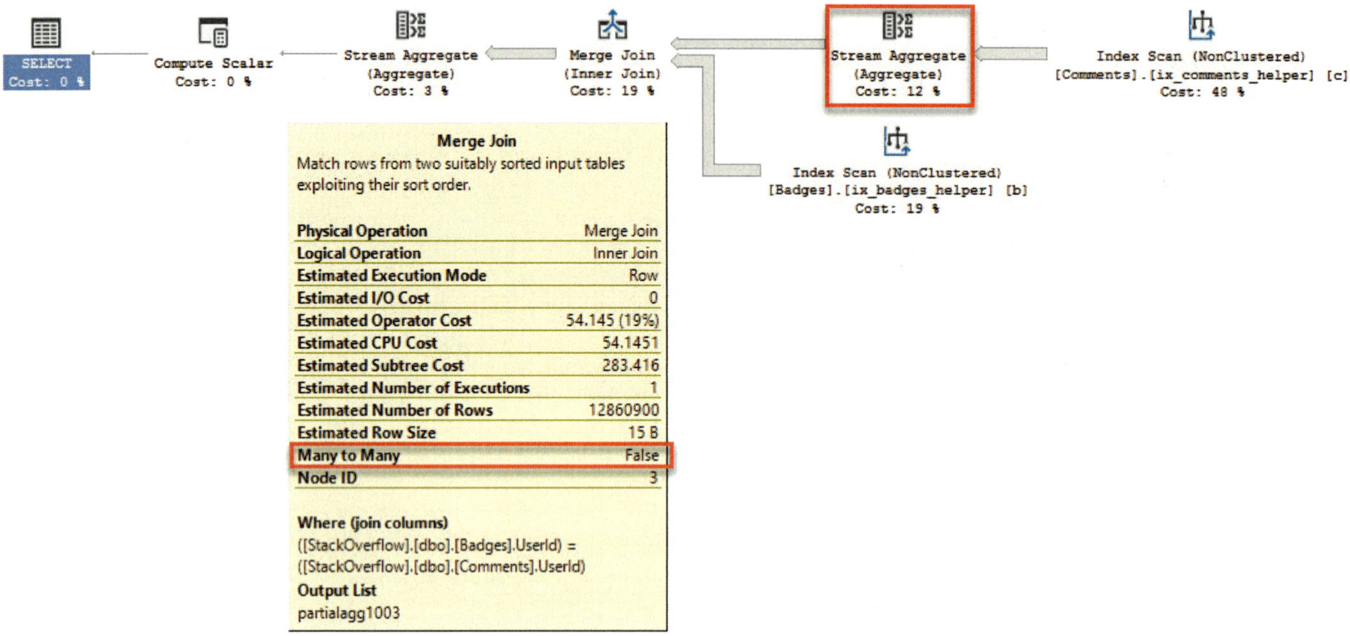

Sense and Sensibility

Under less reasonable circumstances, you may get a Hash Match Aggregate. This plan has the additional misfortune of needing to re-order the data for the Merge Join. Teehee.

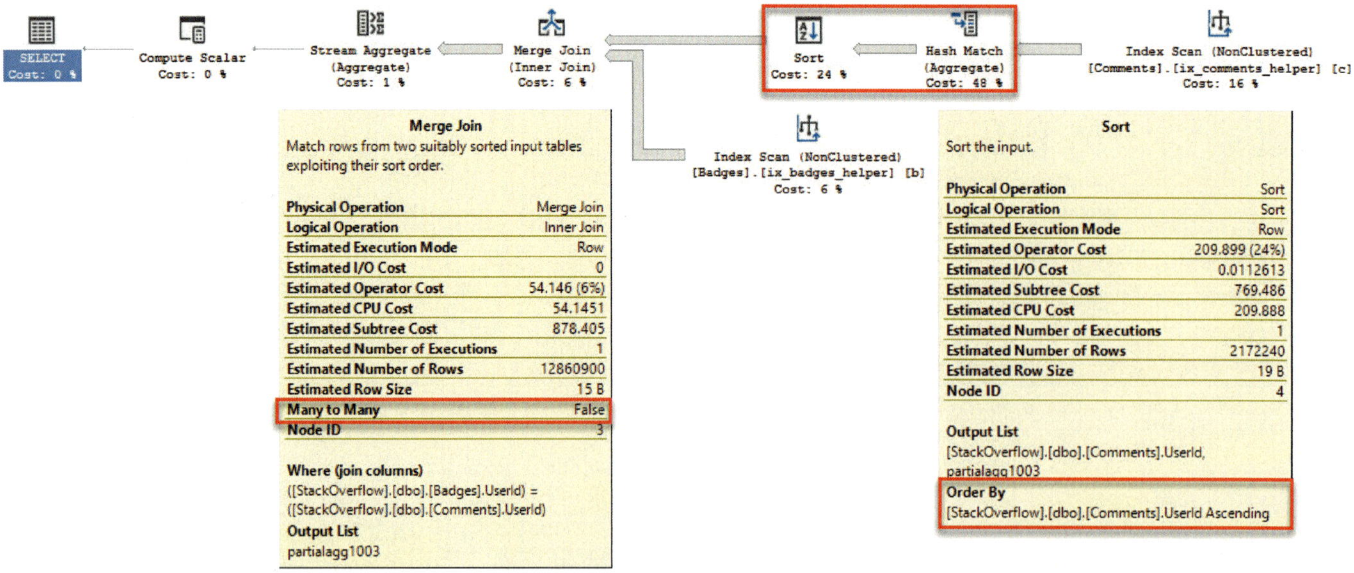

Hash Gang

For the links, code, and comments, go here:
https://www.brentozar.com/archive/2018/04/many-mysteries-merge-joins/

If you see this, something has truly gone wrong in your life. This query was heavily under the hint-fluence.

A Sort Is A Sort

Much more common is seeing a Sort injected into a plan to support one or more downstream operators that require sorted input (Merge Joins, Stream Aggregates, Windowing Functions).

For instance, a query like this:

```sql
WITH Votes
    AS (    SELECT    v.UserId,
                      ROW_NUMBER() OVER ( PARTITION BY v.UserId
                                          ORDER BY v.Id ) AS rn
            FROM      dbo.Votes AS v )
SELECT  COUNT(*) AS records
FROM    dbo.Posts AS p
JOIN    Votes AS v
    ON p.OwnerUserId = v.UserId
WHERE   v.rn = 1;
```

May give you a plan like this:

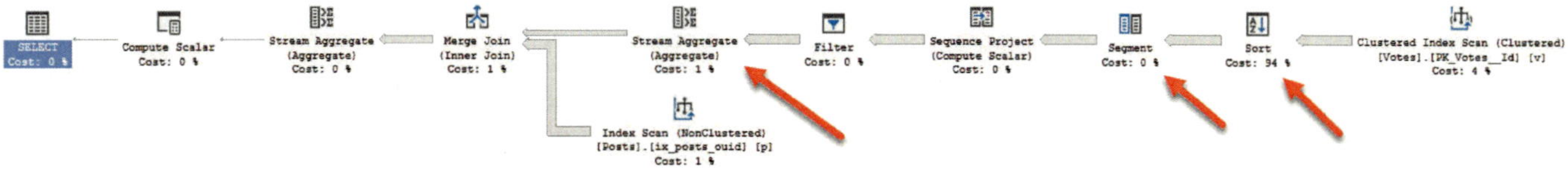

Sort early, Sort often

In this case, the Sort happens early on to support the Window Function. It also aids the Stream Aggregate, but whatever. Once data is sorted, the optimizer tends to not un-sort it.

The Sort in the next example will be needed with no index on, or where the join column is not the leading column in the index (there's an If here, which we'll get to).

If this is my index on the Votes table, data is sorted by PostId, and then UserId

```sql
CREATE INDEX ix_votes_uid ON dbo.Votes (PostId, UserId);
```

When my query is just a simple join, like this:

```
FROM     dbo.Votes AS v
JOIN     dbo.Posts AS p
    ON v.UserId = p.OwnerUserId
ORDER BY p.OwnerUserId;
```

My query plan will look like this, with a big honkin' Sort in it:

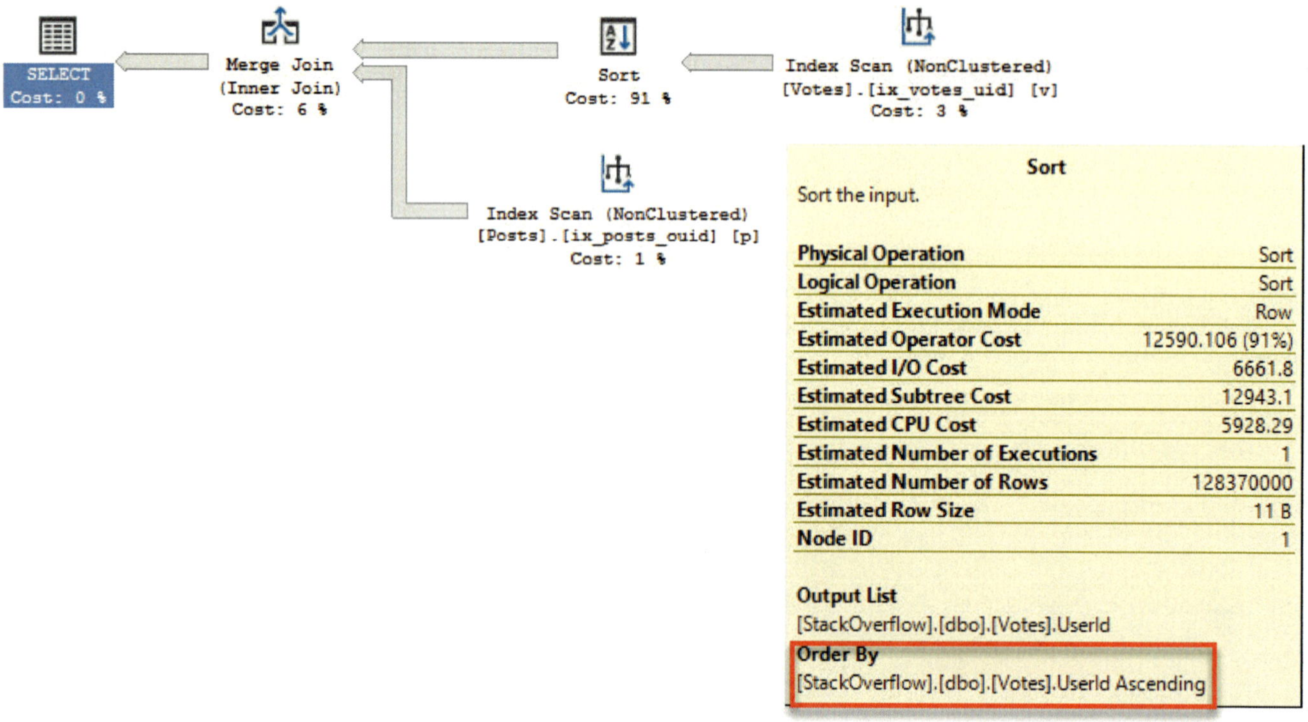

Is kill

On the other hand, if my query looks like this:

```
FROM     dbo.Votes AS v
JOIN     dbo.Posts AS p
    ON v.UserId = p.OwnerUserId
WHERE v.PostId = 11227809
ORDER BY p.OwnerUserId
```

My WHERE clause filters the leading column to a single PostId (one Post can be voted on by many Users), the UserId column will already be sorted for that single PostId value.

We won't need to physically sort data coming out of that.

For the links, code, and comments, go here:
https://www.brentozar.com/archive/2018/04/many-mysteries-merge-joins/

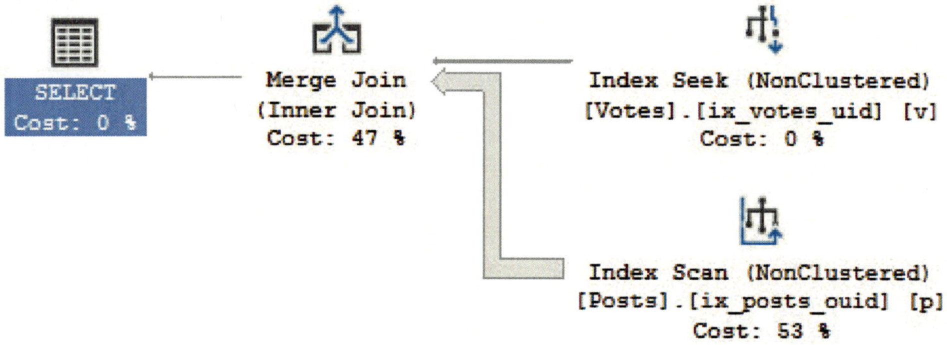

Like mustard

Out In The Street, They Call It Merge Join

I hope you learned some stuff that you can use when troubleshooting, or trying to understand a Merge Join plan.

This is one of many places that the optimizer may inject a Sort into a plan that you didn't ask for.

Thanks for reading!

ZIPPER FREE!

Hash Join Memory Grant Factors

Buskets

Much like Sorts, Hash Joins require some amount of memory to operate efficiently — without spilling, or spilling too much.

And to a similar degree, the number of rows and columns passed to the Hashing operator matter where the memory grant is concerned. This doesn't mean Hashing is bad, but you may need to take some extra steps when tuning queries that use them.

The reasons are pretty obvious when you think about the context of a Hash operation, whether it's a join or aggregation.

1. All rows from the build side have to arrive at the operator (in parallel plans, usually after a bitmap filter)
2. The hashing function gets applied to join or grouping columns
3. In a join, the hashed values from the build side probe hashed values from the outer side
4. In some cases, the actual values need to be checked as a residual

During all that nonsense, all the columns that you SELECT get dragged along for the ride.

Here's a quick example!

This query doesn't return any rows, because Jon Skeet hadn't hit 1 million rep in the data dump I'm using (Stack Overflow 2010).

Transact-SQL

```
/*Returns nothing*/
SELECT u.DisplayName
FROM   dbo.Users AS u
JOIN   dbo.Posts AS p
    ON u.Id = p.OwnerUserId
WHERE  u.Reputation >= 1000000;
```

Despite that, the memory asks for about 7 MB of memory to run. This seems to be the lowest memory grant I could get the optimizer to ask for

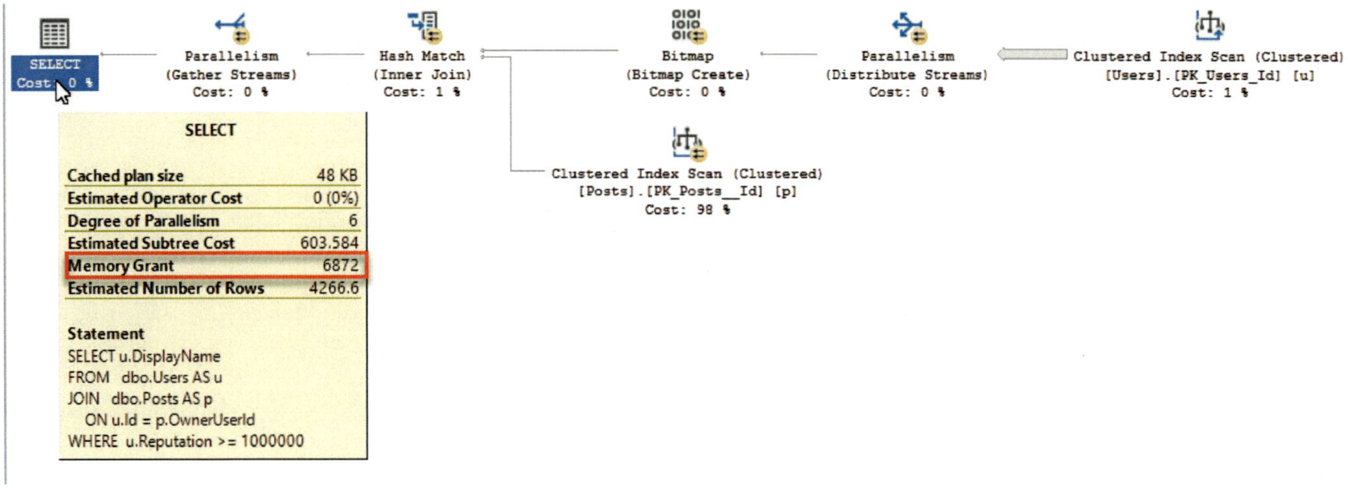

Hashtastic

If we drop the Reputation filter down a bit so some rows get returned, the memory grant stays the same.

```
SELECT u.DisplayName
FROM   dbo.Users AS u
JOIN   dbo.Posts AS p
    ON u.Id = p.OwnerUserId
WHERE  u.Reputation >= 500000;
```

That's why I'm calling 7MB the "base" grant here — that, and if I drop the Reputation filter lower to allow more people in, the grant will go up.

```
SELECT u.DisplayName
FROM   dbo.Users AS u
JOIN   dbo.Posts AS p
    ON u.Id = p.OwnerUserId
WHERE  u.Reputation >= 400000;
```

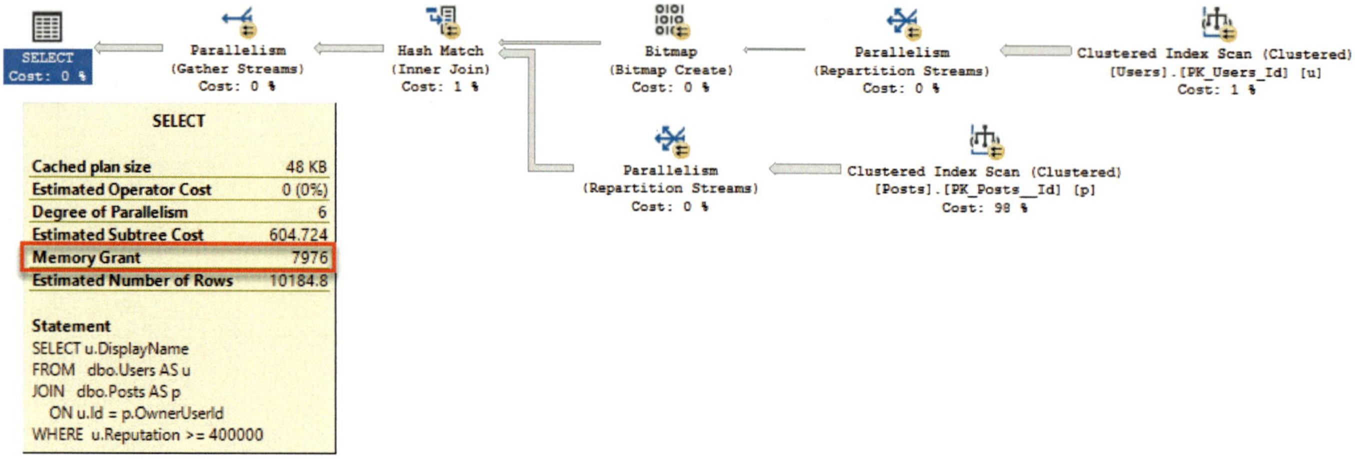

Creepin and creepin and creepin

But we can also get a grant higher than the base by requesting more columns.

```
Transact-SQL
SELECT u.DisplayName, p.Title
FROM   dbo.Users AS u
JOIN   dbo.Posts AS p
    ON u.Id = p.OwnerUserId
WHERE  u.Reputation >= 500000;
```

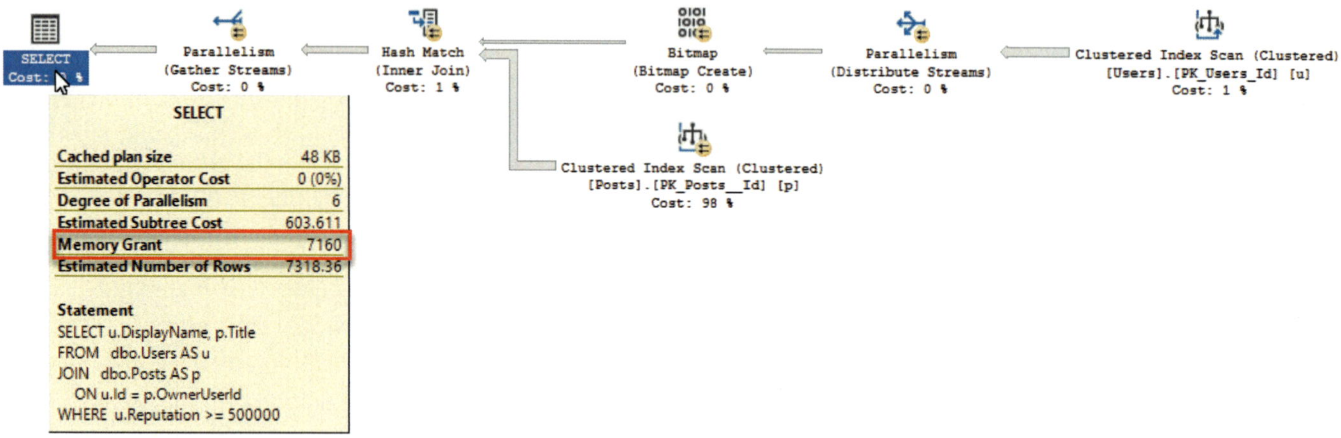

ARF ARF

This is more easily accomplished by selecting string data. Again, just like with Sorts, we don't need to actually sort ***by*** string data for the memory grant to go up. We just need to make it pass through a memory consuming operator.

Thanks for reading!

Brent says: *you remember how, in the beginning of your career, some old crusty DBA told you to avoid SELECT *? Turns out they were right.*

For the links, code, and comments, go here:
https://www.brentozar.com/archive/2018/03/hash-join-memory-grant-factors/

Why sp_prepare Isn't as "Good" as sp_executesql for Performance

sp_prepare For Mediocre

You may remember me from movies like Optimize for... Mediocre? and Why You're Tuning Stored Procedures Wrong (the Problem with Local Variables)!

Great posts, Kendra!

Following the same theme, we found this issue while looking at queries issued from JDBC. Specifically, the prepared statement class seems to cause queries to hit the density vector rather than the histogram for cardinality estimation.

Puddin'

Let's create an index to make our query's work easy!

```
CREATE INDEX ix_whatever ON dbo.Users (Reputation) INCLUDE (DisplayName);
```

Now, to mimic the behavior of a JDBC query:

```sql
DECLARE @out INT;
EXEC sys.sp_prepare @out OUTPUT,
                    N'@r INT',
                    N'SELECT COUNT(DisplayName) as records
                      FROM dbo.Users AS u
                      WHERE u.Reputation = @r;',
                       1;

EXEC sys.sp_execute @out, 1;

EXEC sys.sp_execute @out, 2;

EXEC sys.sp_execute @out, 6;

EXEC sys.sp_execute @out, 10;

EXEC sys.sp_unprepare @out;
GO
```

The query plans for all of these have something in common. They have the exact same estimate!

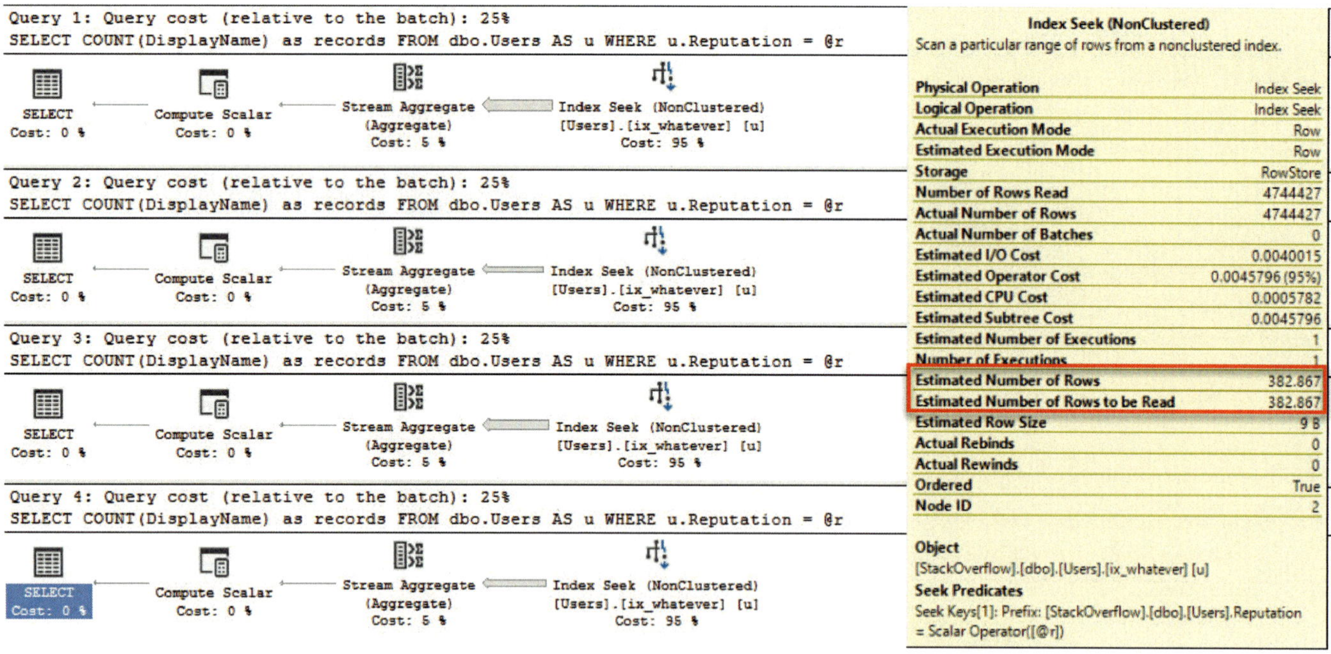

Ze Bad Guess

You might be saying to yourself that the first parameter is sniffed, and you'd be wrong.

That estimate exactly matches the density vector estimate that I'd get with a local variable or optimize for unknown: SELECT (7250739 * 5.280389E-05)

For the links, code, and comments, go here:
https://www.brentozar.com/archive/2018/03/sp_prepare-isnt-good-sp_executesql-performance/

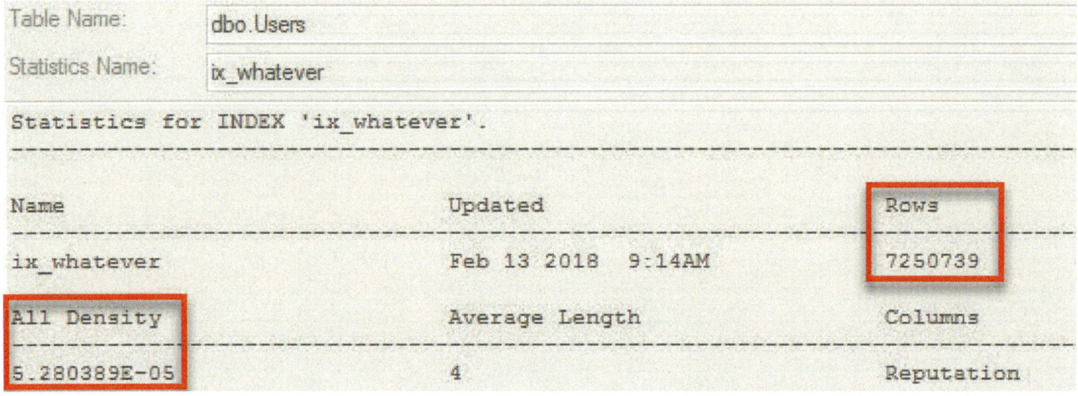

Cruddy

You can validate things a bit by adding a recompile hint to the demo code.

```
DECLARE @out INT;
EXEC sys.sp_prepare @out OUTPUT,
                    N'@r INT',
                    N'SELECT COUNT(DisplayName) as records
                      FROM dbo.Users AS u
                      WHERE u.Reputation = @r
                      OPTION(RECOMPILE);',
                      1;

EXEC sys.sp_execute @out, 1;

EXEC sys.sp_execute @out, 2;

EXEC sys.sp_execute @out, 6;

EXEC sys.sp_execute @out, 10;

EXEC sys.sp_unprepare @out;
GO
```

The plans for all of the recompiled queries get different estimates, and no estimate matches the 382 estimate we saw from the first round.

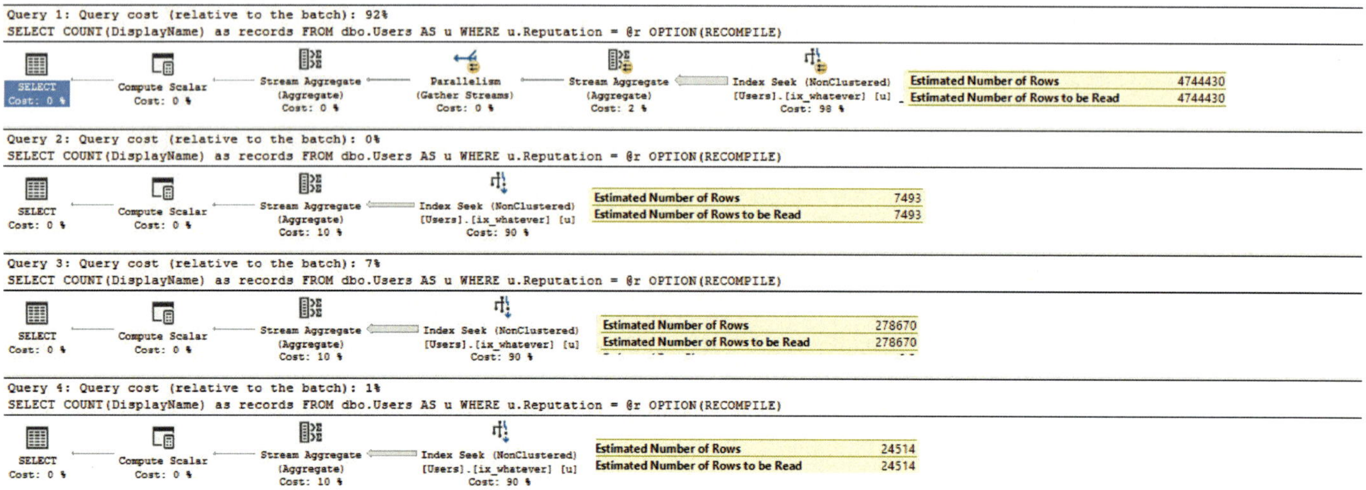

BIG MONEY

Am I saying you should recompile all of your queries to get around this?

No, of course not. Query compilation isn't what you should be spending your SQL Server licensing money on.

You may want to not use JDBC anymore, but...

How Is sp_executesql Different?

Well, sp_executesql "sniffs" parameters.

```sql
DECLARE @sql NVARCHAR(MAX ) = N''
SET @sql += N'SELECT COUNT(DisplayName) as records
                      FROM dbo.Users AS u
                      WHERE u.Reputation = @r;'

EXEC sys.sp_executesql @sql, N'@r INT', 1;

EXEC sys.sp_executesql @sql, N'@r INT', 2;

EXEC sys.sp_executesql @sql, N'@r INT', 6;

EXEC sys.sp_executesql @sql, N'@r INT', 10;
GO
```

If I run my demo queries in this order, the plan for Reputation = 1 gets cached and reused by all the other calls.

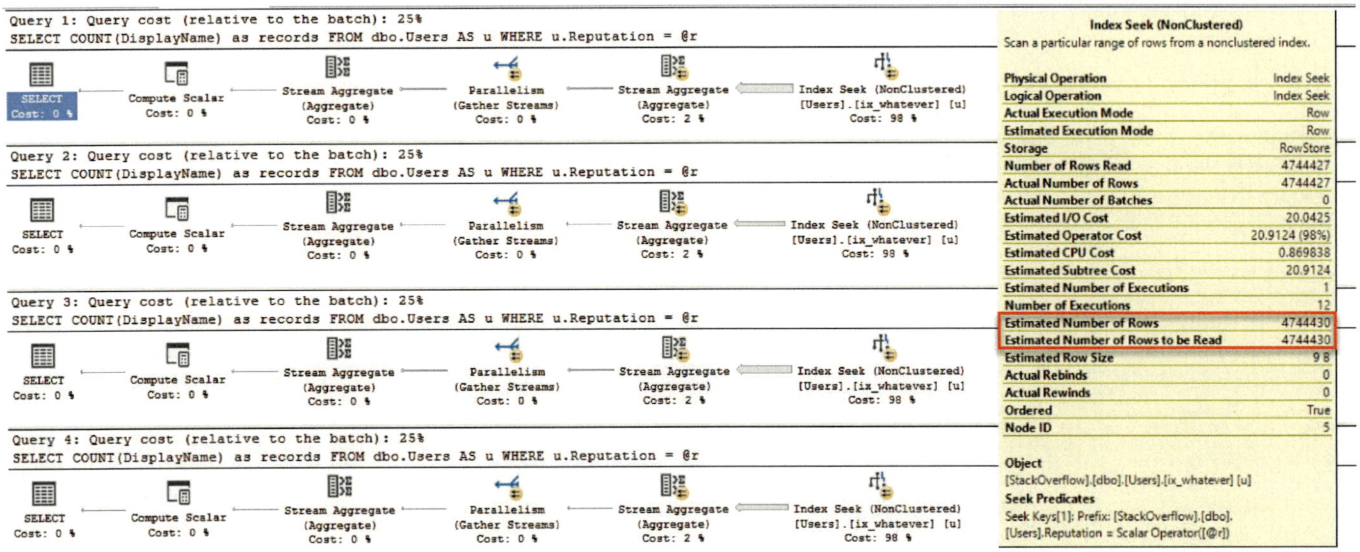

Sniff sniff pass

If I change the order so Reputation = 2 runs first, the plans change (after clearing the plan out of the cache, of course).

Now they all reuse that plan:

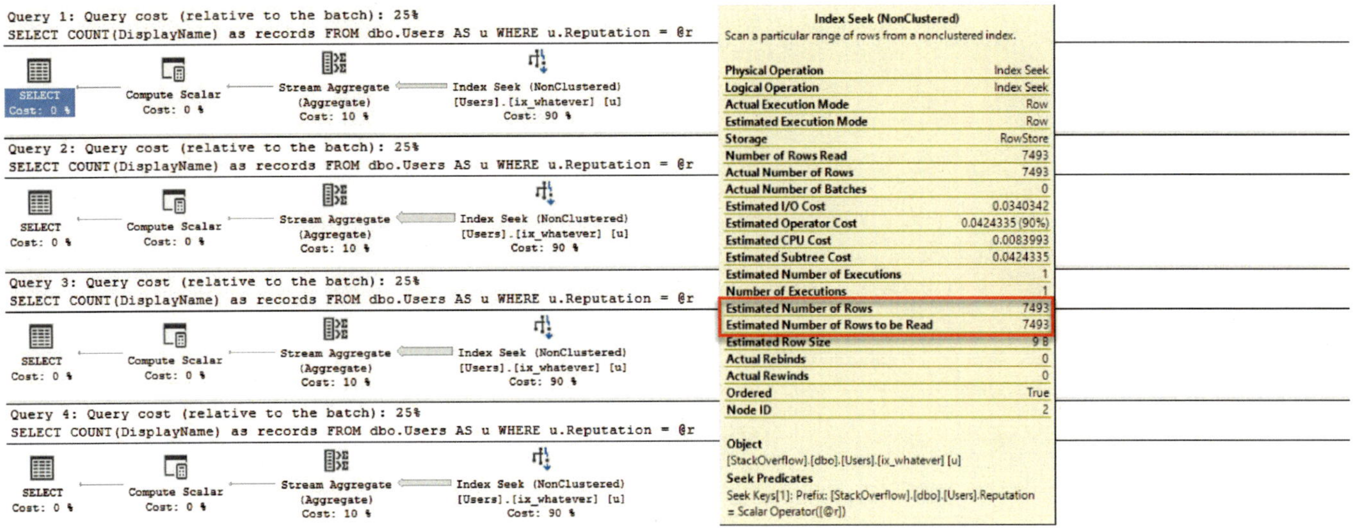

Look at you then

Why Is One better?

I put together this handy chart!

"Feature"	sp_executesql	sp_prepare
Accurate cardinality estimates	Yes, for the sniffed parameter	No, uses density estimate
Stable execution plan	Yes, until a recompile	Yes, but maybe not a good one
Good for small amounts of data	Yes	
Good for highly skewed data	Sometimes, if you get a Goldilocks plan	Maybe, until you query the highly skewed part
Can call victim to parameter sniffing	Yes, and this can suck	No, but density estimate can be bad anyway
Can't I just stick a recompile hint on it?	Yes, but this can backfire spectacularly if you need to compile a complicated query plan each time it runs	

IT'S ONLY A PICTURE

I'm not smart enough to get a formatted table like this into a web page.

I'm a bad DBA.

Thanks for reading!

UPDATE:

The admirable and honorable Joseph Gooch notes in the comments that you can configure this with the jTDS JDBC driver:

> prepareSQL (default – 3 for SQL Server, 1 for Sybase)This parameter specifies the mechanism used for Prepared Statements.
>
> | Value | Description |
> |---|---|
> | 0 | SQL is sent to the server each time without any preparation, literals are inserted in the SQL (slower) |
> | 1 | Temporary stored procedures are created for each unique SQL statement and parameter combination (faster) |
> | 2 | sp_executesql is used (fast) |
> | 3 | sp_prepare and sp_cursorprepare are used in conjunction with sp_execute and sp_cursorexecute (faster, SQL Server only) |

Though I'm not too thrilled that sp_prepare is called "faster".

And! That similar options are available in the 6.1.6 preview of the Microsoft JDBC drivers.

Query Plans: Trivial Optimization vs Simple Parameterization

Facemaking

You know when you think you know something, and the obviousness of it makes you all the more confident that you know it?

That's usually the first sign that there's a giant gotcha waiting for you.

And that's what happened to me over the weekend.

The setup

I answered a question.

And after I answered it, I got to thinking... Would partitioning help? After all, smart people agree. Partitioning is ColumnStore's friend.

So I started looking at it a little bit more differenter.

First, I had to set up a partitioning function and scheme. I used dynamic SQL to create the function because no way in Hades am I typing numbers from 1-999.

```
USE tempdb

DROP TABLE IF EXISTS dbo.t1 --2016+ only

CREATE TABLE t1 (Id INT NOT NULL, Amount INT NOT NULL)

--TRUNCATE TABLE t1

SET NOCOUNT ON
SET STATISTICS TIME, IO OFF

DECLARE @sql NVARCHAR(MAX) = N'', @i INT = 0, @lf NCHAR(4) = NCHAR(13) + NCHAR(10)
  SET @sql = N'CREATE PARTITION FUNCTION Pfunc (INT) AS RANGE RIGHT FOR VALUES ('
    WHILE @i < 1000
    BEGIN
      SET @sql += @lf + '(' + CAST(@i AS NVARCHAR) + N')' + N','
      SET @i += 1
    END
  SET @sql += @lf + '(' + CAST(@i AS NVARCHAR) + N')' +  + N');';
    EXEC sp_executesql @sql;
    PRINT @sql
GO

--I don't have a ton of filegroups, I just want everything on Primary
CREATE PARTITION SCHEME Pyramid
    AS PARTITION Pfunc
    ALL TO  ( [PRIMARY] );
```

Next, I loaded in a billion rows.

Yes, a billion.

And you know, it turns out generating a billion rows at once is terribly slow. So I wrote an awful loop to insert 1 million rows 1000 times.

Transact-SQL

```
DECLARE @c INT = 0
DECLARE @msg NVARCHAR(1000) = N''

WHILE @c < 1000

BEGIN

;WITH T (N)
AS ( SELECT X.N
     FROM (
      VALUES (NULL), (NULL), (NULL),
             (NULL), (NULL), (NULL),
             (NULL), (NULL), (NULL),
             (NULL), (NULL), (NULL) ) AS X (N)
           ), NUMS (N) AS (
            SELECT TOP ( 1000000 )
                   ROW_NUMBER() OVER ( ORDER BY ( SELECT NULL )) AS N
            FROM   T AS T1, T AS T2, T AS T3,
                   T AS T4, T AS T5, T AS T6,
                   T AS T7, T AS T8, T AS T9,
                   T AS T10,T AS T11,T AS T12)
INSERT dbo.t1 WITH ( TABLOCK ) (
    Id, Amount )
SELECT NUMS.N % 999 AS Id, NUMS.N % 9999 AS Amount
FROM   NUMS;

SET @c += 1

SET @msg = 'Insert loop: ' + CONVERT(NVARCHAR(5), @c) + '.'
RAISERROR(@msg, 0, 1) WITH NOWAIT

END
```

Then, you know, I needed some indexes.

Lemme be straight with you here: don't create the indexes first. After about the 4th loop, things grind to a halt.

This is why other smart people will tell you the fastest way to load data is into a HEAP.

Lemme be straight with you about something else: I couldn't figure out how to just create the ColumnStore index on the partitioned table. I had to create a regular clustered index, and then the ColumnStore index over it with DROP_EXISTING.

```sql
CREATE CLUSTERED INDEX CX_WOAHMAMA ON dbo.t1 (Id) WITH (DATA_COMPRESSION = PAGE) ON Pyramid (Id)
GO

CREATE CLUSTERED COLUMNSTORE INDEX CX_WOAHMAMA ON dbo.t1 WITH (DROP_EXISTING = ON) ON Pyramid (Id)
GO
```

So there I had it, my beautiful, billion-row table.

Partitioned, ColumnStore-d.

What could go wrong?

Plantastic

Let's look at one query with a few variations.

```sql
SELECT COUNT(*) AS [Records], SUM(CONVERT(BIGINT, t.Amount)) AS [Total]
FROM   dbo.t1 AS t
WHERE  t.Id > 0
       AND t.Id < 3;
```

The plan for it is alright. It's fairly straightforward and the query finishes in about 170ms.

We can see from the graphical execution plan that it's been Simple Parameterized. SQL Server does this to make plan caching more efficient.

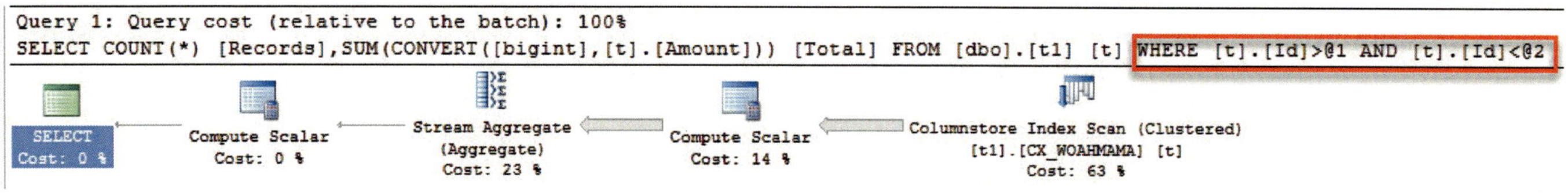

GOLD STARS FOR EVERYONE

With parameters in place rather than literals, the plan is accessible to more queries using the same predicate logic on the Id column.

We can also see the plan is Trivial. If you're following along, hit F4 while the SELECT operator is highlighted in the query plan , and a Properties pane should open up magically on the right side of the screen.

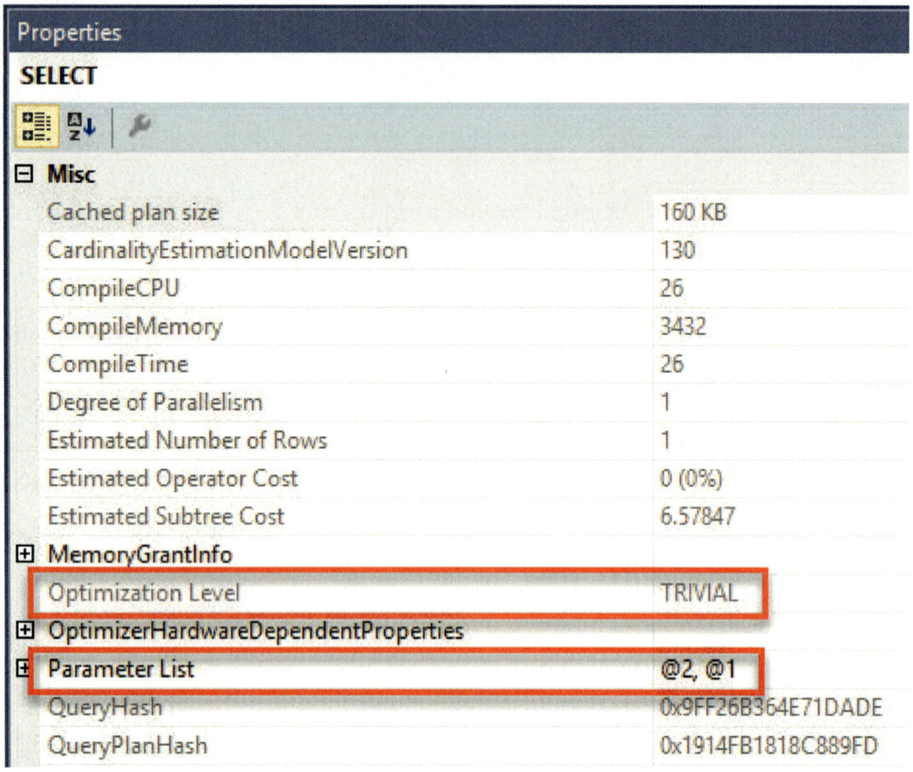

Pallies

Well, I can change that! I know a trick! I learned it from Paul White!

If I add 1 = 1 somewhere in my WHERE clause, I can get around Simple Parameterization and the Trivial plan.

Right?

```sql
SELECT COUNT(*) AS [Records], SUM(CONVERT(BIGINT, t.Amount)) AS [Total]
FROM   dbo.t1 AS t
WHERE  t.Id > 0
       AND t.Id < 3
       AND 1 = 1;
```

Heh heh heh, that'll show you.

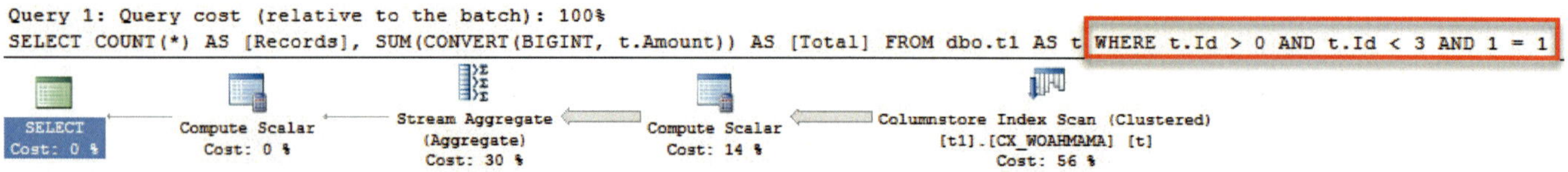

Stringy

For the links, code, and comments, go here:
https://www.brentozar.com/archive/2017/06/query-plans-trivial-optimization-vs-simple-parameterization/

Oh but, no. The plan is still trivial, and it still runs in about 172ms.

Properties

SELECT

Misc	
Cached plan size	72 KB
CardinalityEstimationModelVersion	130
CompileCPU	10
CompileMemory	1960
CompileTime	10
Degree of Parallelism	1
Estimated Number of Rows	1
Estimated Operator Cost	0 (0%)
Estimated Subtree Cost	4.96994
MemoryGrantInfo	
Optimization Level	TRIVIAL
OptimizerHardwareDependentProperties	
QueryHash	0x9FF26B364E71DADE
QueryPlanHash	0x1914FB1818C889FD

D.R.A.T.

So how do you beat the trivial plan?

You use yet another trick from Paul White.

> Dear Paul,
>
> Thanks.
>
> — The rest of us

If you stick a goofy subquery in, the optimizer will regard it with contempt and suspicion, and give it a full pat down.

```sql
SELECT COUNT(*) AS [Records], SUM(CONVERT(BIGINT, t.Amount)) AS [Total]
FROM   dbo.t1 AS t
WHERE  t.Id > 0
       AND t.Id < 3
       AND 1 = (SELECT 1);
```

Here's the plan for this query.

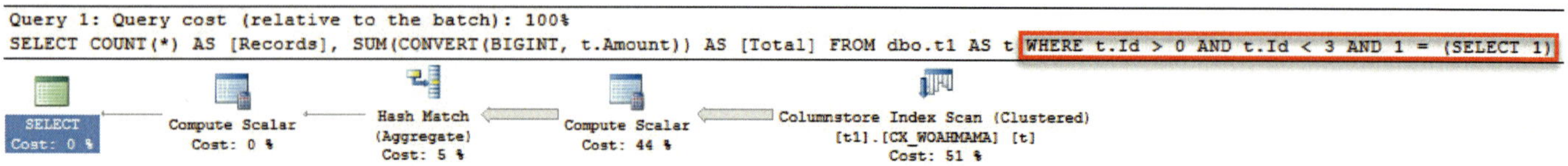

Still not Simple!

And, amazingly, it gets FULL optimization.

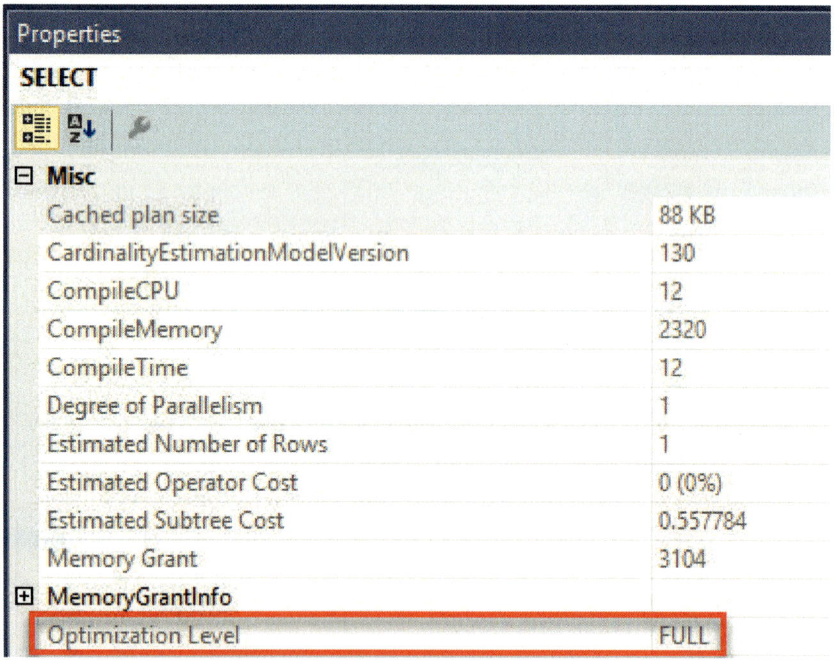

Full of what, exactly?

Why is this better?

Astute observers may have picked up that the plan changed a little bit. Earlier plans that got Trivial optimization used a Stream Aggregate operator, where the Full optimization plan uses a Hash Match Aggregate.

What's the deal with that?

For the links, code, and comments, go here:
https://www.brentozar.com/archive/2017/06/query-plans-trivial-optimization-vs-simple-parameterization/

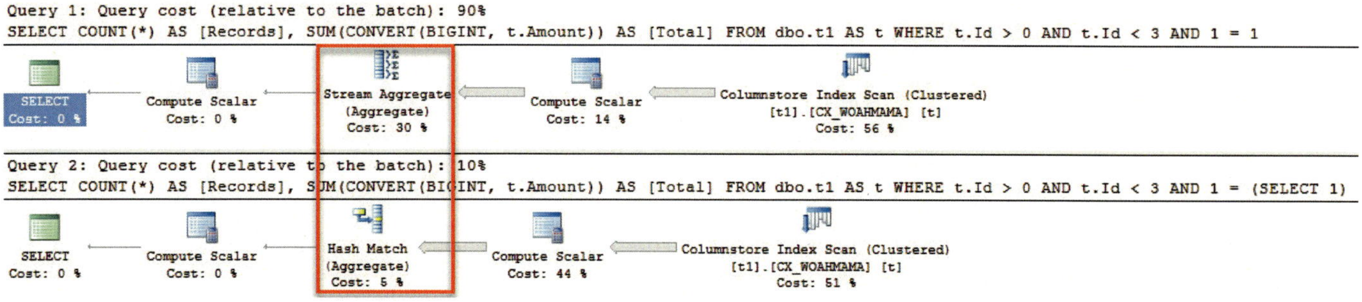

Aggregatin'

To make matters more interesting, the Full optimization query finishes in 11ms.

That's down from 172ms for the Trivial plan.

What else was different?

There's a really important difference in the two plans.

The Trivial plan was run in RowStore execution mode. This is the enemy of ColumnStore indexes.

It's essentially using them the old fashioned way.

Columnstore Index Scan (Clustered)

Scan a columnstore index, entirely or only a range.

Physical Operation	Columnstore Index Scan
Logical Operation	Clustered Index Scan
Actual Join Type	AdaptiveJoin
Actual Execution Mode	Row
Estimated Execution Mode	Row
Storage	ColumnStore

Voices carry

The plan that gets Full optimization runs in Batch execution mode, and this makes everyone very happy.

Columnstore Index Scan (Clustered)
Scan a columnstore index, entirely or only a range.

Physical Operation	Columnstore Index Scan
Logical Operation	Clustered Index Scan
Actual Join Type	AdaptiveJoin
Actual Execution Mode	Batch
Estimated Execution Mode	Batch
Storage	ColumnStore

CAUGHT

This is why sp_BlitzCache will warn you about both Trivial plans, and ColumnStore indexes being executed in RowStore mode.

Database	Cost	Query Text	Query Type	Warnings
tempdb	6.57847	SELECT COUNT(*) [Records],SUM(CONVERT([bigint],[t]...	Statement	Trivial Plans, Plan created last 4hrs, ColumnStore Row Mode

Because that's why.

Thanks for reading!

For the links, code, and comments, go here:
https://www.brentozar.com/archive/2017/06/query-plans-trivial-optimization-vs-simple-parameterization/

SARGable

SARGable. A word that sounds like drunk talk, but means expressing your queries clearly. This chapter pairs well with any clear liquor. Gin, vodka, moonshine, or that bottle of whiskey that's so old it's sun-bleached.

BRENT OZAR
UNLIMITED®

Optional Parameters and Missing Index Requests

That's when it all gets blown away

At one point or another in everyone's SQL-querying career, they end up writing a query that goes something like this:

```
Transact-SQL
SELECT something
FROM stuff
WHERE (@thing1 is NULL or whatever = @thing1)
AND ...
```

These are often called optional parameters, and if you spend any time looking at queries, this will make you shudder for many reasons. Poor cardinality estimates, full scans, etc.

One thing that often gets overlooked is that queries constructed like this don't register missing index requests.

As usual, using the Stack Overflow database for a demo.

```
SELECT COUNT(*) AS [Records]
FROM   dbo.Users AS u
WHERE  u.DisplayName = 'Jon Skeet'
       AND u.Reputation  = 849122;
GO
```

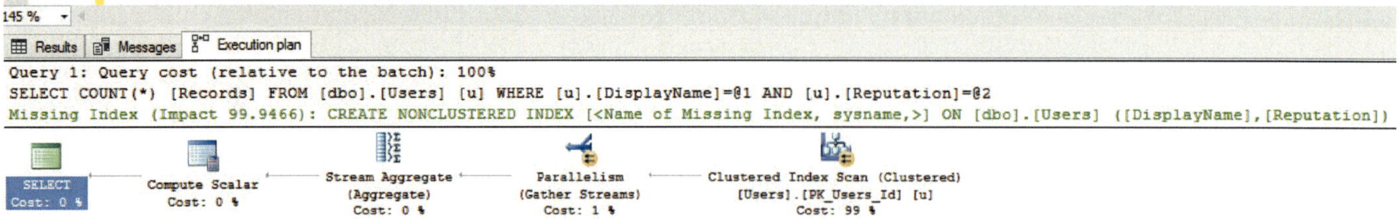

Askance

With literal values, the optimizer goes into index matching mode, finds nothing helpful, and tells you all about it. The missing index request is pretty predictable, on DisplayName and Reputation. Makes sense so far, right?

What about with NULL variables?

```sql
DECLARE @DisplayName NVARCHAR(40), @Reputation INT;

SELECT COUNT(*) AS [Records]
FROM   dbo.Users AS u
WHERE  (@DisplayName IS NULL
        OR u.DisplayName = @DisplayName )
       AND (@Reputation IS NULL
            OR u.Reputation = @Reputation);
GO
```

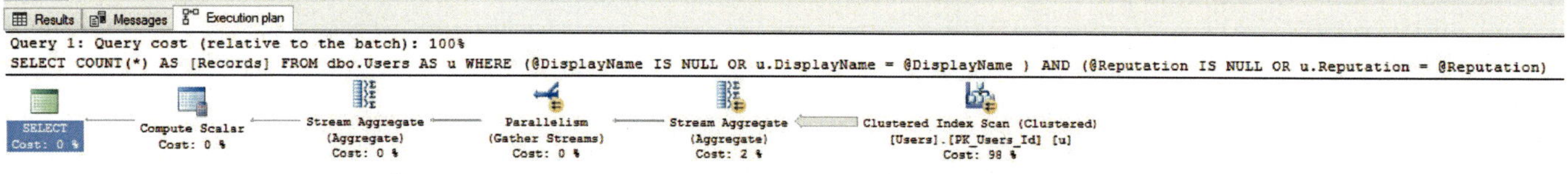

Kiss your missing index request goodbye

You may blame the NULLs, but it's not their fault.

```sql
DECLARE @DisplayName NVARCHAR(40) = 'Jon Skeet', @Reputation INT = 849122;

SELECT COUNT(*) AS [Records]
FROM   dbo.Users AS u
WHERE  (@DisplayName IS NULL
        OR u.DisplayName = @DisplayName )
       AND (@Reputation IS NULL
            OR u.Reputation  = @Reputation);
GO
```

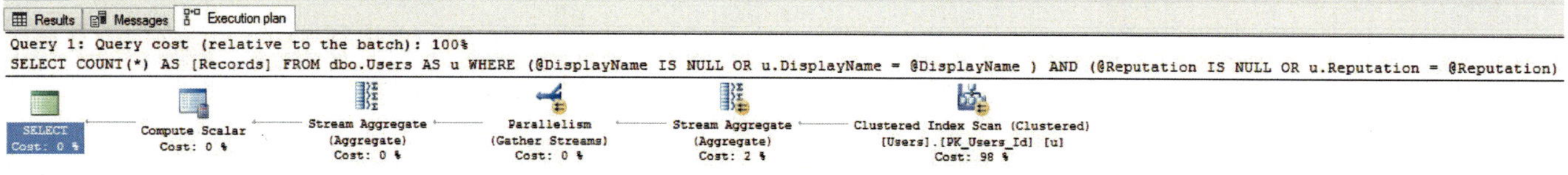

Milli VaNULLi

What about with a RECOMPILE hint? Someone on the internet told me that if I use RECOMPILE I'll get an optimal plan.

```sql
DECLARE @DisplayName NVARCHAR(40), @Reputation INT;

SELECT COUNT(*) AS [Records]
FROM   dbo.Users AS u
WHERE  (@DisplayName IS NULL
        OR u.DisplayName = @DisplayName )
       AND (@Reputation IS NULL
            OR u.Reputation = @Reputation)
OPTION(RECOMPILE);
GO
```

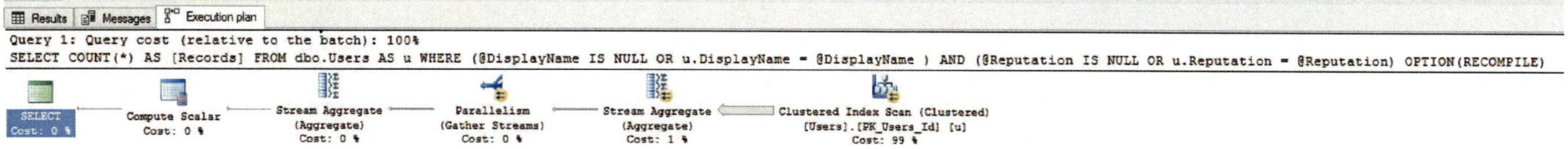

Like Crest on plaque

Someone on the internet was, well, not wrong, but not right either. By most standards, you'll get an optimal plan. But still no missing index request.

Using a stored procedure doesn't help with that, either (unless you recompile, but that may not be ideal for other reasons).

```
CREATE PROCEDURE dbo.OptionalParameters (@DisplayName NVARCHAR(40) = 'Jon Skeet', @Reputation INT = 849122)
AS

BEGIN

SELECT COUNT(*) AS [Records]
FROM   dbo.Users AS u
WHERE  (@DisplayName IS NULL
            OR u.DisplayName = @DisplayName )
        AND (@Reputation IS NULL
                OR u.Reputation  = @Reputation);

END

EXEC dbo.OptionalParameters @DisplayName = 'Jon Skeet', @Reputation = 849122
```

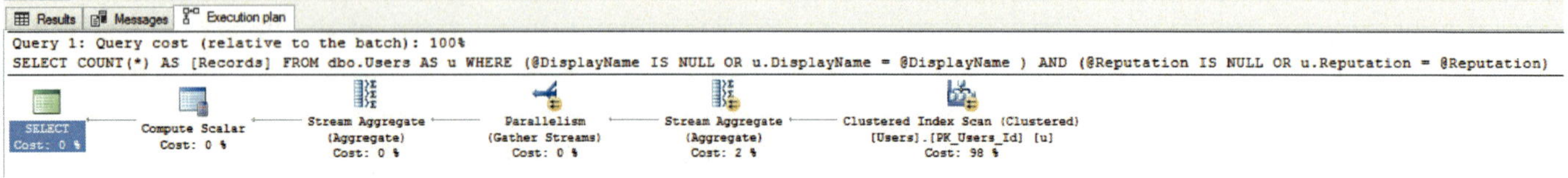

Swamp of Sadness

Big Deal?

If we add an index with the correct definition, all of those queries will use it as written.

```
CREATE INDEX ix_helper ON dbo.Users (DisplayName, Reputation);
GO
```

That's not exactly the problem. Nor is the missing index request being missing a direct affront to anyone who has been tuning queries for more than 30 seconds. It's obvious what a ***good enough index*** would be for ***this query***.

What could be very misleading is if you're using the DMVs to round up missing index requests, you're unfamiliar with the overall schema and current index design, or if the optional parameter searches are part of a larger query where the index usage patterns being sub optimal aren't apparent.

The bottom line on this type of search is that it's not SARGable. Like using functions and other icky-messies across joins and where clauses, it will prevent missing index requests from popping up. And while missing index requests aren't perfect, they are a valuable workload analysis tool, especially to beginners.

Thanks for reading!

Brent says: *This is such a good example of why you need at least 3 tuning passes for performance tuning: run sp_BlitzIndex looking for obvious index improvements, then run sp_BlitzCache to tune the queries that are still slow, then after tuning them, run sp_BlitzIndex one more time to catch the new missing index requests.*

MAX Data Types Do WHAT?

Users are horrible, I know

You can just never rely on them to pass in reasonable search strings. When you write stored procedures to retrieve information for them, it's really tempting to define all your string variables as MAX length. As long as the actual data type, N/VARCHAR matches, you're cool, right? Avoid that pesky implicit conversion and live another day.

Well, not really. Let's test it out. We'll be using StackOverflow, and hitting the Users table. We have a column, DisplayName, that's an NVARCHAR(40), which sets us up well enough to demo.

My Favorite Martian

There's a user with the handle Eggs McLaren, which cracks me up. It reminds me of this old Red Stripe commercial. I use him for all my demos, even though he doesn't really exist.

AboutMe
<p>This is a puppet test account I use to validate "regular user" stuff on the site</p> <p>-- <a href="http://stackoverflow.com/users/1/jeff-atwood" rel="nofollow">Jeff Atwood</a>

Well played, Jeff.

So what happens when we go looking for Eggs?

```sql
DECLARE @DisplayName NVARCHAR(MAX) = 'Eggs McLaren'

SELECT *
FROM dbo.Users AS u
WHERE u.DisplayName = @DisplayName
GO
```

We get the correct results, but the execution plan has some bad news for us.

For the links, code, and comments, go here:
https://www.brentozar.com/archive/2016/10/max-data-types/

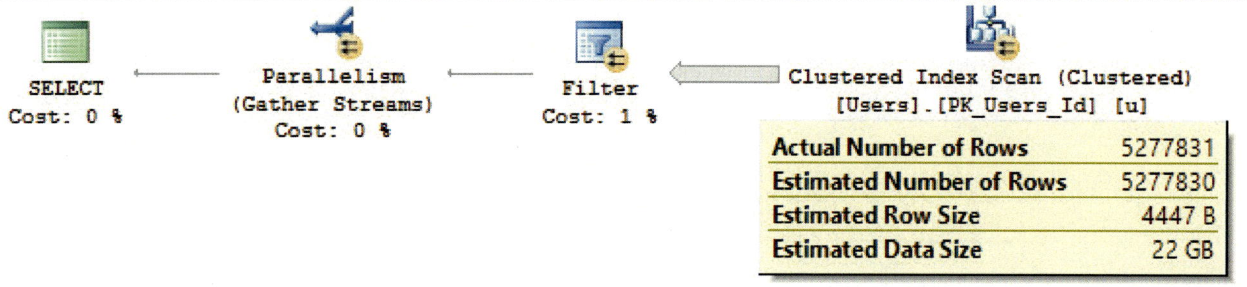

I prefer my queries unfiltered.

In short, we read everything in the clustered index. This could be mitigated with a smaller index, sure, but you'd still read all 5.2 million rows of it, and pass them into a filter operator. I'm using the clustered index here to highlight why this can be extra bad. We read and passed 22 GB of data into that filter operator, just to get one row out.

Why is this bad, and when is it different?

SQL Server makes many good and successful attempts at something called predicate pushdown, or predicate pushing. This is where certain filter conditions are applied directly to the data access operation. It can sometimes prevent reading all the rows in a table, depending on index structure and if you're searching on an equality vs. a range, or something else.

What it's really good for is limiting data movement. When rows are filtered at access time, you avoid needing to pass them all to a separate operator in order to reduce them to the rows you're actually interested in. Fun for you! Be extra cautious of filter operators happening really late in your execution plans.

Even adjusting the variable type to NVARCHAR(4000) gets us there. If your users need to pass in search strings longer than 4000 characters, you have some serious thinking to do.

Transact-SQL

```
DECLARE @DisplayName NVARCHAR(4000) = 'Eggs McLaren'

SELECT *
FROM dbo.Users AS u
WHERE u.DisplayName = @DisplayName
GO
```

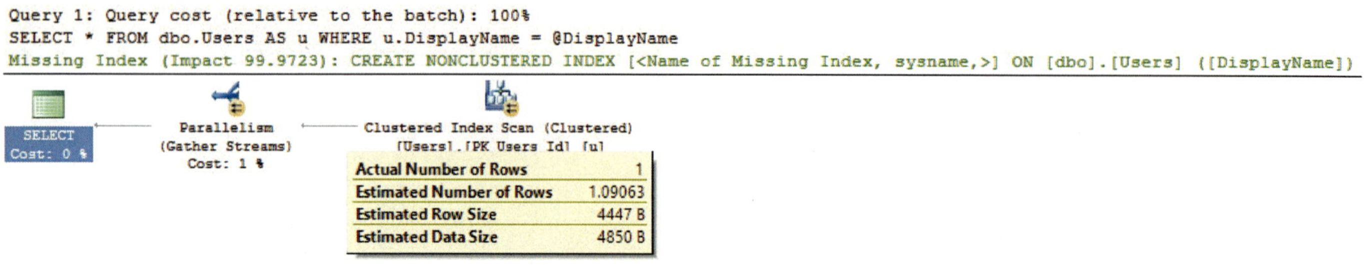

And a missing index request. What a peach.

Rather than 22 GB, we're looking at passing 4850 bytes to the next operator. This seems much more optimal to me. Next up is figuring out which columns we actually need, so we're not running SELECT * every time.

That's another bummer.

Thanks for reading!

Date Math In The WHERE Clause

Oh, THAT SARGability

I realize that not everyone has a Full Metal Pocket Protector, and that we can't all spend our days plunging the depths of query and index tuning to eek out every CPU cycle and I/O operation from our servers. I mean, I don't even do that. Most of the time I'm just happy to get the right result back!

I kid, I kid.

For those of you out there that have never heard the word before, go watch this. You'll thank me later. Much later.

What does that have to do with me?

It has to do with you, because you're still formatting your WHERE clause poorly. You're still putting expressions around columns and comparing that output to a value, or another expression.

Huh?

Think about times when you've done something like First_Name + ' ' + Last_Name = 'Meat Tuperello', or even worse, when you've totally broken a date into YEAR(), MONTH(), and DAY() and compared them all to values.

Yes, you. Yes, that's bad.

More Common

Sometimes people forget that DATEADD exists. They go right to DATEDIFF, because it sounds like it makes more sense.

What's the difference between these two dates? Can I go home now? I'm so hungry. No one takes the Esperantan money you pay me with, Mr. Ozar.

But this can get you into a lot of trouble, especially if you're either dealing with a lot of data, or if the WHERE clause is part of a more complicated series of JOINs. Not only does it not make efficient use of any indexes, but it can really screw up cardinality estimation for other operations. What does this peril look like?

```sql
SELECT COUNT(*)
FROM dbo.SalesOrders AS so
WHERE DATEDIFF(DAY, CONVERT(DATE, so.OrderDate), GETUTCDATE()) = 55
```

Looks good to me

Of course it does. That's why you're reading this blog. You have questionable taste. There are some problems with this, though.

Index Scan (NonClustered)

Scan a nonclustered index, entirely or only a range.

Physical Operation	Index Scan
Logical Operation	Index Scan
Actual Execution Mode	Row
Estimated Execution Mode	Row
Storage	RowStore
Number of Rows Read	10000
Actual Number of Rows	5003
Actual Number of Batches	0
Estimated I/O Cost	0.0305324
Estimated Operator Cost	0.0416894 (90%)
Estimated Subtree Cost	0.0416894
Estimated CPU Cost	0.011157
Number of Executions	1
Estimated Number of Executions	1
Estimated Number of Rows	5005.13
Estimated Row Size	15 B
Actual Rebinds	0
Actual Rewinds	0
Ordered	False
Node ID	2

Predicate
datediff(day,CONVERT_IMPLICIT(datetimeoffset(7),CONVERT(date,[RebuildVsReorg].[dbo].[SalesOrders].[OrderDate] as [so].[OrderDate],0),0),CONVERT_IMPLICIT(datetimeoffset(3),getutcdate(),0))=(55)
Object
[RebuildVsReorg].[dbo].[SalesOrders].[IX_WHATEVER] [so]

Your mom.

We didn't do too bad with cardinality estimation here. The Magic Math guessed about right for our 10,000 row table. But breakthroughs in Advanced Query Plan Technology (hint: GET OFF SQL SERVER 2008R2) allow us to see that we read all 10,000 of those rows in the index, rather than just getting the 5003 rows that we actually need. Shame on us. How do we do better?

No Sets In The Champagne Room

We're going to flip things around a little bit! We're going to take the function off of the column and put it on our predicate. If you watched the video I linked to up top, you'd know why this is good. it allows the optimizer to fold the expression into the query, and push it right on down to the index access. Hooray for us. Someday we're gonna change the world.

```
Transact-SQL
SELECT COUNT(*)
FROM dbo.SalesOrders AS so
WHERE CONVERT(DATE, so.OrderDate) = DATEADD(DAY, -55, CONVERT(DATE, GETUTCDATE()))
```

Now we get a cheaper index seek, we don't read the extra 4997 rows, and the cardinality estimate is spot on. Again, it wasn't too bad in the original one, but we got off easy here.

Index Seek (NonClustered)

Scan a particular range of rows from a nonclustered index.

Physical Operation	Index Seek
Logical Operation	Index Seek
Actual Execution Mode	Row
Estimated Execution Mode	Row
Storage	RowStore
Number of Rows Read	5003
Actual Number of Rows	5003
Actual Number of Batches	0
Estimated I/O Cost	0.0171991
Estimated Operator Cost	0.0228594 (85%)
Estimated CPU Cost	0.0056603
Estimated Subtree Cost	0.0228594
Estimated Number of Executions	1
Number of Executions	1
Estimated Number of Rows	5003
Estimated Row Size	15 B
Actual Rebinds	0
Actual Rewinds	0
Ordered	True
Node ID	8

Predicate

CONVERT(date,[RebuildVsReorg].[dbo].[SalesOrders].[OrderDate] as [so].[OrderDate],0)=dateadd(day,(-55),CONVERT(date,getutcdate(),0))

Object

[RebuildVsReorg].[dbo].[SalesOrders].[IX_WHATEVER] [so]

Seek Predicates

Seek Keys[1]: Start: [RebuildVsReorg].[dbo].[SalesOrders].OrderDate > Scalar Operator([Expr1005]), End: [RebuildVsReorg].[dbo].[SalesOrders].OrderDate < Scalar Operator([Expr1006])

Just you, and nobody else but you.

Face 2 Face

If you're wondering what the plans look like side by side, here you go.

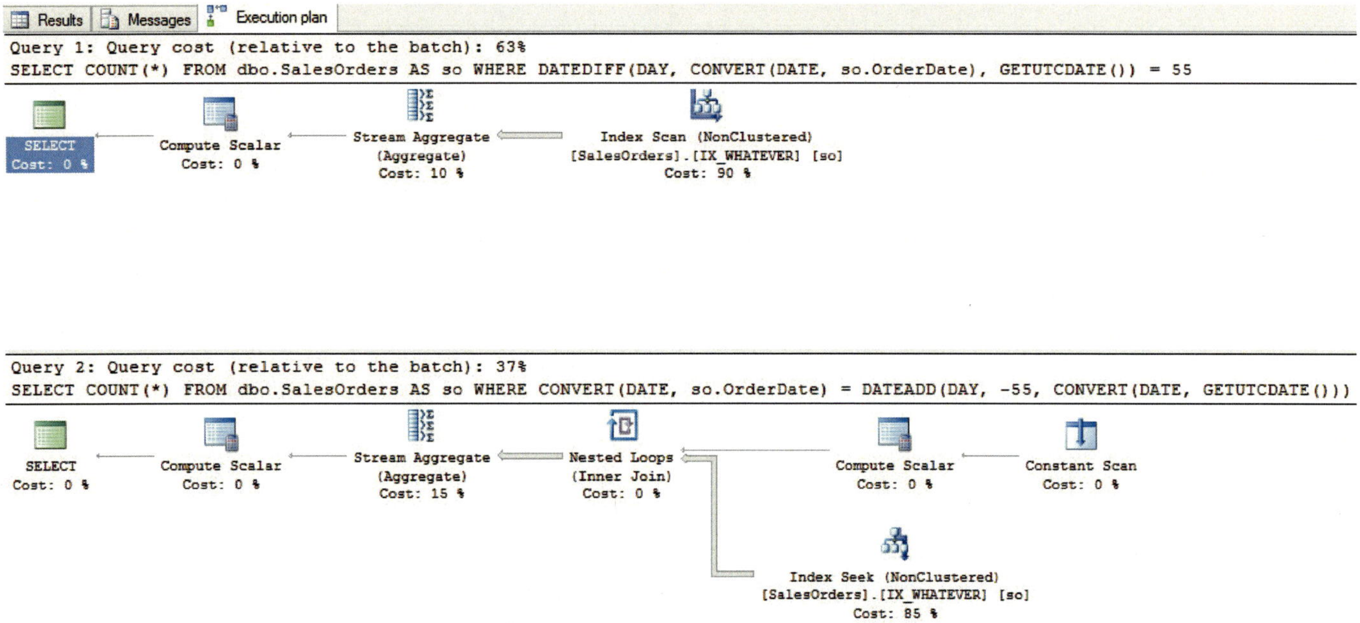

Gateway Goth

Both plans are helped by our thoughtfully named index on the OrderDate column, though the one with cheaper estimated cost is the bottom one. Yes, I know this can sometimes lie, but we're not hiding any functions in here that would throw things off horribly. If you're concerned about the Nested Loops join, don't worry too much. There is a tipping point where the Constant Scan operator is removed in favor of just index access. I didn't inflate this table to find exact row counts for that, but I've seen it at work elsewhere. And, yeah, the second query will still be cheaper even if it also scans.

Thanks for reading!

Brent says: *this is a great example of how people think SQL Server will rewrite their query in a way that makes it go faster. Yes, SQL Server could rewrite the first query to make it like the second – but it just doesn't go that extra mile for you. (And it shouldn't, you wacko – write the query right in the first place.)*

If You Can't Index It, It's Probably Not SARGable

Thumbs Rule OK?

When writing queries, it's really common to want to take shortcuts to express some logic.

I know, it "works fine", and the results are "right", and you have "more important" things to do.

But take a minute here for future you.

Just think of reading this post as a continuation of the infinite thumb-scroll that your life has become.

And Examples!

For instance, it's a lot faster for you to write `ISNULL(somecol, 0) = 0` or `YEAR(somedate) = 2018`.

In some ways it may even seem intuitive to write queries that express simple equalities like this rather than `somecol = 0 OR somecol IS NULL`.

The problem is that this isn't how indexes store, or have their data retrieved, and you can't create indexes like this:

```
CREATE INDEX ix_nope ON dbo.zilch (ISNULL(nada, 0))
```

Hence the title: If you can't index it, it's probably not SARGable.

Practically?

I've tried to point this out with functions like ISNULL and DATEDIFF.

Using the DATEDIFF example, if you write a query that does this:

```
WHERE DATEDIFF(DAY, day1, day2) = 90
```

And you've got an index like this: `CREATE INDEX ix_dates ON dbo.orders (day1, day2)`

For the links, code, and comments, go here:
https://www.brentozar.com/archive/2018/03/cant-index-probably-not-sargable/

Nothing about the index is tracking how many days apart day1 and day2 are. Nor minutes, nor hours, nor milliseconds.

It's just data ordered first by day1, then by day2. Multi-column statistics also don't track this. It's up to you to define the data points you need to retrieve for your data.

The same goes for many other built in system functions, but there's no warning sign on the doc pages that says stuff like:

- "Hey, this is only here to make presenting data easier."
- "The optimizer can't do that, Dave."
- "Only do this if you want to keep champagne flowing for consultants."

It's fairly well-documented what happens when you use these on-the-fly calculations as predicates: Nothing good.

For all the hand-wringing there is about index scans, there's equal amounts of poorly written queries that have no hope of every doing a seek.

Mass Appeal!

As development teams mature and start writing queries beyond simple selects, they may add non-SARGable constructs in other places.

CTEs, Derived Tables, and non-indexed Views are easy examples. The backing query results aren't materialized anywhere, so they're not good candidates for predicates.

For example, this query:

Transact-SQL

```
WITH your_mom
    AS (    SELECT   p.Id, COALESCE(p.ClosedDate, p.LastActivityDate) AS LastDate
            FROM     dbo.Posts AS p
            WHERE    p.CreationDate >= '20170101' )
SELECT  'your mom'
FROM    dbo.Comments AS c
JOIN    your_mom AS ym
        ON ym.Id = c.PostId
        AND  ym.LastDate >= c.CreationDate;
```

Putting the COALESCE inside the CTE doesn't magically make a new set of physical data — it's just another expression. It's really no different than if you did it directly in the WHERE clause without the CTE.

Going back to the title, you can't index a CTE or a derived table. Abstracting expressions in there doesn't persist them.

They won't be SARGable here, either.

Unawares?

If you think they're bad there, wait until you start trying to order data by expressions.

Even with a perfectly fine index thrown into the mix...

Transact-SQL

```
CREATE INDEX ix_yourmom ON dbo.Posts (ClosedDate, LastActivityDate, Id);

WITH your_mom
    AS (    SELECT    p.Id, COALESCE(p.ClosedDate, p.LastActivityDate) AS LastDate
            FROM      dbo.Posts AS p
        )
SELECT  'your mom'
FROM    dbo.Comments AS c
JOIN    your_mom AS ym
        ON ym.Id = c.PostId
        AND  ym.LastDate >= c.CreationDate
ORDER BY ym.LastDate;
```

We're forced to sort everything by hand.

Or whatever your computer uses.

Mine uses hands.

Tiny hands.

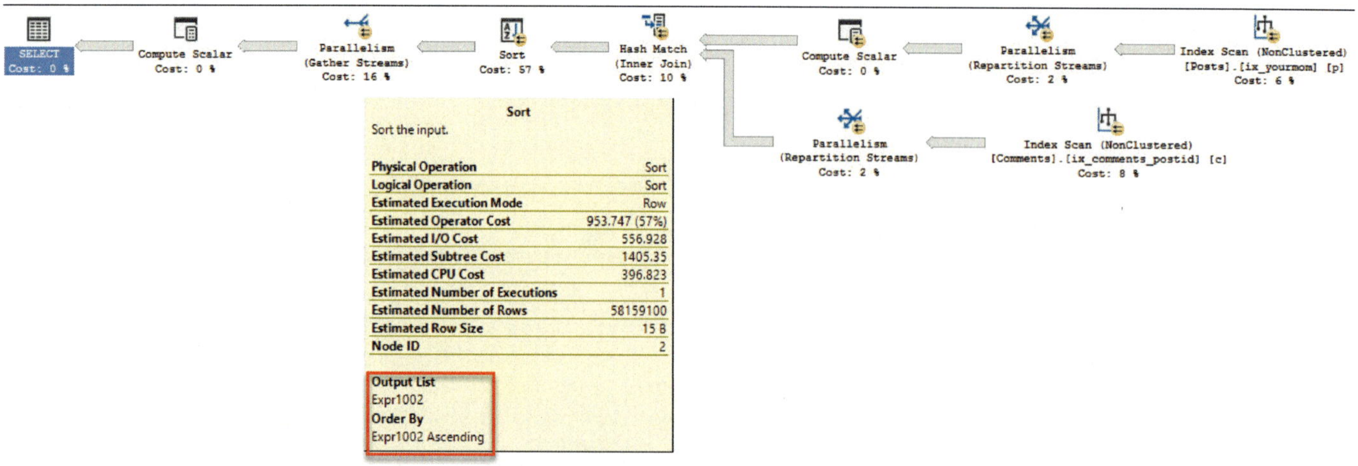

This isn't your friend

This is the kind of query that really makes your CPU fans kick in.

The kicker is that the optimizer may decide to inject a sort into your plan that you didn't ask for.

Is There An Exit?

When you're writing queries to be reliably fast, take a close look at what you're expecting the optimizer to do.

Indexes can go a long way, but they're not cure-alls. They still have to contain data the way you're trying to use the data.

If they don't, you might need to look at temp tables, computed columns, denormalizing, or lookup/junction tables to set data up the way your queries use it.

Thanks for reading!

In case of corruption, use this page to write your resume on.

Is it ever worth adding indexes to table variables?

Disclaimer

I found this totally by accident, and it even surprised me.

You can probably guess the TL;DR on this is yes, huh?

Dude, where's my table variable?

I was trying to come up with a demo for something totally different. Don't ask. Seriously. It's top secret.

Okay, so it's just embarrassing.

Anyway. I had these two queries. Which are actually the same query twice. The only difference is the table variable definition.

```sql
DECLARE @UserId TABLE (UserId INT NOT NULL)
INSERT @UserId ( UserId )
    VALUES ( 22656 )

SELECT p.OwnerUserId, COUNT(*) AS Records
FROM dbo.Posts AS p
LEFT JOIN @UserId AS ui
ON ui.UserId = p.OwnerUserId
GROUP BY p.OwnerUserId
GO


DECLARE @UserId TABLE (UserId INT NOT NULL PRIMARY KEY CLUSTERED)
INSERT @UserId ( UserId )
    VALUES ( 22656 )

SELECT p.OwnerUserId, COUNT(*) AS Records
FROM dbo.Posts AS p
LEFT JOIN @UserId AS ui
ON ui.UserId = p.OwnerUserId
GROUP BY p.OwnerUserId
GO
```

What I saw in the query plans was amazing.

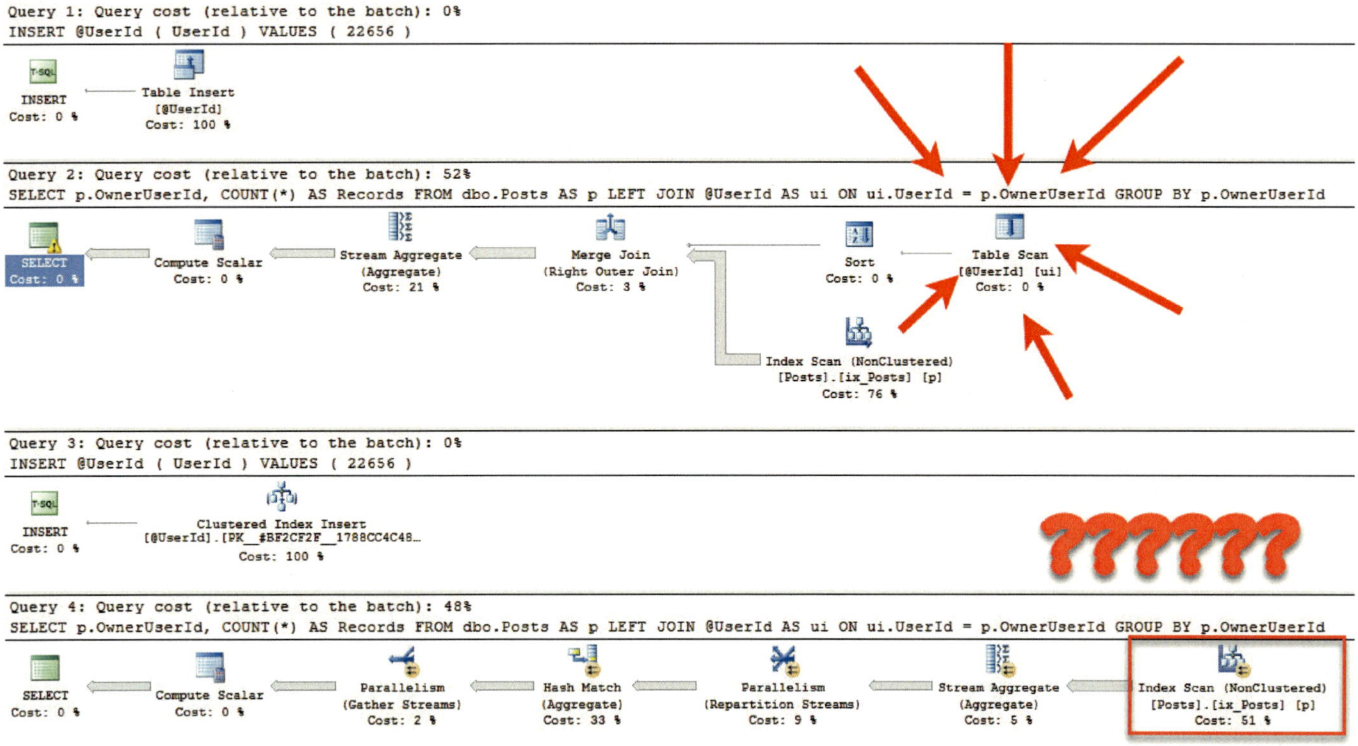

There's no table variable!

The second JOIN query had no table variable operator in it. It had been optimized away.

Well, that's pretty cool. But that doesn't seem to be anywhere in the XML. Here's a pasted plan: https://www.brentozar.com/pastetheplan/?id=H1HbqOxae

Crying Game

Since I've never seen this before with a table variable, I thought I might have stumbled on some crazy enhancement for them. But apparently it's just regular ol' join simplification.

Thanks for reading!

Brent says: *Don't feel bad if you have to read this twice to understand what was going on. It took me three times before I caught that it was a left outer join.*

How Much Can One Column Change A Query Plan? Part 1

Beyond Key Lookups

I'm going to show you two queries, and two query plans. The two queries are only different by one selected column, but the two query plans are wildly different.

Unless I've talked to you in the last few days, these may surprise you as well.

Here's the first one.

```
Transact-SQL
DECLARE @DisplayName NVARCHAR(40)

    SELECT @DisplayName = u.DisplayName
    FROM   dbo.Users AS u
    LEFT JOIN (
                  SELECT   p.OwnerUserId, COUNT_BIG(*) AS Records
                  FROM     dbo.Posts AS p
                  LEFT JOIN dbo.PostTypes AS pt
                  ON p.Id = pt.Id
                     AND pt.Id = 2
                  WHERE    p.Score >= 10
                  GROUP BY p.OwnerUserId
                  HAVING   COUNT_BIG(*) >= 10 ) AS pp
    ON pp.OwnerUserId = u.Id
    LEFT JOIN (
                  SELECT   p2.OwnerUserId, COUNT_BIG(*) AS Records
                  FROM     dbo.Posts AS p2
                  JOIN     dbo.PostLinks AS pl2
                  ON p2.Id = pl2.PostId
                     AND pl2.LinkTypeId = 1
                  WHERE    pl2.CreationDate >= '2016-01-01'
                  GROUP BY p2.OwnerUserId
                  HAVING   COUNT_BIG(*) >= 2 ) AS pl
    ON pl.OwnerUserId = u.Id
    AND pl.OwnerUserId = pp.OwnerUserId
```

```
    LEFT JOIN (
                SELECT DISTINCT p3.OwnerUserId
                FROM   dbo.Votes AS v
                JOIN   dbo.VoteTypes AS vt
                ON v.VoteTypeId = vt.Id
                   AND vt.Id = 2
                JOIN   dbo.Posts AS p3
                ON p3.Id = v.PostId ) AS pv
    ON pv.OwnerUserId = u.Id
    AND pv.OwnerUserId = p1.OwnerUserId
    LEFT JOIN (
                SELECT DISTINCT c.UserId, c.PostId
                FROM   dbo.Comments AS c
                JOIN   dbo.Users AS u2
                ON c.UserId = u2.Id
                JOIN   dbo.Posts AS p4
                ON c.PostId = p4.Id
           WHERE c.CreationDate >= '2016-01-01'
           AND c.Score >= 1) AS cc
    ON cc.UserId = pv.OwnerUserId
    AND cc.UserId = u.Id;
```

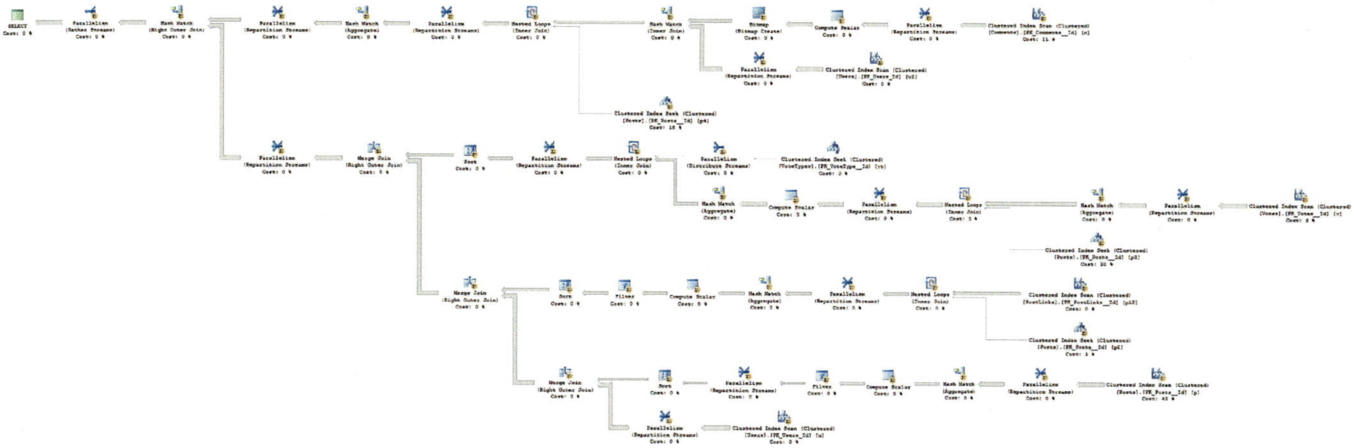

Expected?

Here's the second one.

```sql
DECLARE @DisplayName NVARCHAR(40)

    SELECT @DisplayName = u.DisplayName
    FROM   dbo.Users AS u
    LEFT JOIN (
                  SELECT   p.OwnerUserId, COUNT_BIG(*) AS Records
                  FROM     dbo.Posts AS p
                  LEFT JOIN dbo.PostTypes AS pt
                  ON p.Id = pt.Id
                     AND pt.Id = 2
                  WHERE    p.Score >= 10
                  GROUP BY p.OwnerUserId
                  HAVING   COUNT_BIG(*) >= 10 ) AS pp
    ON pp.OwnerUserId = u.Id
    LEFT JOIN (
                  SELECT   p2.OwnerUserId, COUNT_BIG(*) AS Records
                  FROM     dbo.Posts AS p2
                  JOIN     dbo.PostLinks AS pl2
                  ON p2.Id = pl2.PostId
                     AND pl2.LinkTypeId = 1
                  WHERE    pl2.CreationDate >= '2016-01-01'
                  GROUP BY p2.OwnerUserId
                  HAVING   COUNT_BIG(*) >= 2 ) AS pl
    ON pl.OwnerUserId = u.Id
    AND pl.OwnerUserId = pp.OwnerUserId
    LEFT JOIN (
                  SELECT DISTINCT p3.OwnerUserId
                  FROM   dbo.Votes AS v
                  JOIN   dbo.VoteTypes AS vt
                  ON v.VoteTypeId = vt.Id
                     AND vt.Id = 2
                  JOIN   dbo.Posts AS p3
                  ON p3.Id = v.PostId ) AS pv
    ON pv.OwnerUserId = u.Id
    AND pv.OwnerUserId = pl.OwnerUserId
    LEFT JOIN (
                  SELECT DISTINCT c.UserId--, c.PostId /*Just one column removed*/
                  FROM   dbo.Comments AS c
                  JOIN   dbo.Users AS u2
                  ON c.UserId = u2.Id
                  JOIN   dbo.Posts AS p4
                  ON c.PostId = p4.Id
            WHERE c.CreationDate >= '2016-01-01'
            AND c.Score >= 1) AS cc
    ON cc.UserId = pv.OwnerUserId
    AND cc.UserId = u.Id;
```

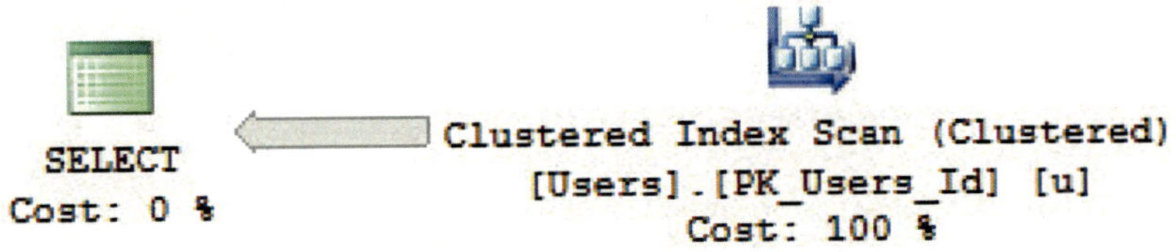

Expected?

Part 2 coming up!

In part 2, I'll discuss what happened and cite a couple of my favorite sources. In the meantime, feel free to have at it in the comments.

Unless you're someone I talked about this with in the last couple days!

Thanks for reading!

How Much Can One Column Change A Query Plan? Part 2

What happened in Part 1?

Join Elimination, naturally. Until the end. My copy of the Stack Overflow database doesn't have a single foreign key in it, anywhere.

If we go down the rabbit hole a couple steps, we end up at a very quotable place, with Rob Farley.

> 2. Duplicated rows
>
> Not necessarily duplicated completely, but certainly a row in our original table may appear multiple times in our result set, if it matches with multiple rows in the new table. Notice that this doesn't occur if the join-fields (those used in the ON clause) in the new table are known to be unique (as is the case with a Foreign-Key lookup).

When we select a distinct list from one column, or create a unique index on one column, the optimizer knows that that one column is unique and won't produce multiples of a value. I'm assured by mathematicians that even if you left join two distinct lists, it won't produce duplicates.

With more than one column involved in a DISTINCT/GROUP BY, there may be duplicates of a single value, which would change our results. There's a little more information about this over here as well.

How does that apply to us?

The results are going to be every DisplayName in the Users table, but the way our left joins are written to DISTINCT/GROUP BY the list of Ids that each produces, we know that each would only occur once.

That isn't true in the last join, where we messed with columns. That join may produce multiples of some Ids with the multi-column distinct, which means the join can't safely be eliminated. You could end up needing to show some DisplayNames more than once, in other words.

For the links, code, and comments, go here:
https://www.brentozar.com/archive/2017/09/how-much-can-one-column-change-a-query-plan-part-2/

Similarly

If I re-create all my joins by dumping them into temp tables, we get a similar effect. A difference I want to point out is that I'm not joining other temp tables to each other, like in the first query. That's why the "big" plan only has two joins. The multi-column-duplicate DISTINCT changed things up the whole tree of joins. Funny, right? Hysterical.

Transact-SQL

```
SELECT   p.OwnerUserId, COUNT_BIG(*) AS Records
INTO     #pp
FROM     dbo.Posts AS p
LEFT JOIN dbo.PostTypes AS pt
ON p.Id = pt.Id
   AND pt.Id = 2
WHERE    p.Score >= 10
GROUP BY p.OwnerUserId
HAVING   COUNT_BIG(*) >= 10;

CREATE UNIQUE CLUSTERED INDEX cx_pp ON #pp (OwnerUserId)

SELECT   p2.OwnerUserId, COUNT_BIG(*) AS Records
INTO     #pl
FROM     dbo.Posts AS p2
JOIN     dbo.PostLinks AS pl2
ON p2.Id = pl2.PostId
   AND pl2.LinkTypeId = 1
WHERE    pl2.CreationDate >= '2016-01-01'
GROUP BY p2.OwnerUserId
HAVING   COUNT_BIG(*) >= 2;

CREATE UNIQUE CLUSTERED INDEX cx_pl ON #pl (OwnerUserId)

SELECT DISTINCT p3.OwnerUserId
INTO    #pv
FROM    dbo.Votes AS v
JOIN    dbo.VoteTypes AS vt
ON v.VoteTypeId = vt.Id
   AND vt.Id = 2
JOIN    dbo.Posts AS p3
ON p3.Id = v.PostId;

CREATE UNIQUE CLUSTERED INDEX cx_pv ON #pv (OwnerUserId)

SELECT DISTINCT c.UserId, c.PostId
INTO    #cc
FROM    dbo.Comments AS c
JOIN    dbo.Users AS u2
ON c.UserId = u2.Id
```

```
JOIN   dbo.Posts AS p4
ON c.PostId = p4.Id
WHERE  c.CreationDate >= '2016-01-01'
       AND c.Score >= 1;

CREATE UNIQUE CLUSTERED INDEX cx_cc ON #cc (UserId, PostId) /*Two On One*/

SELECT DISTINCT c.UserId
INTO   #cc2
FROM   dbo.Comments AS c
JOIN   dbo.Users AS u2
ON c.UserId = u2.Id
JOIN   dbo.Posts AS p4
ON c.PostId = p4.Id
WHERE  c.CreationDate >= '2016-01-01'
       AND c.Score >= 1;

CREATE UNIQUE CLUSTERED INDEX cx_cc2 ON #cc2 (UserId) /*One On Two*/
```

Here's what happens.

Transact-SQL

```
DECLARE @DisplayName NVARCHAR(40)

  SELECT @DisplayName = u.DisplayName
  FROM   dbo.Users AS u
  LEFT JOIN #pp
  ON #pp.OwnerUserId = u.Id
  LEFT JOIN #pl
  ON #pl.OwnerUserId = u.Id
  LEFT JOIN #pv
  ON #pv.OwnerUserId = u.Id
  LEFT JOIN #cc /*Two Column*/
  ON #cc.UserId = u.Id;
GO

DECLARE @DisplayName NVARCHAR(40)

  SELECT @DisplayName = u.DisplayName
  FROM   dbo.Users AS u
  LEFT JOIN #pp
  ON #pp.OwnerUserId = u.Id
  LEFT JOIN #pl
  ON #pl.OwnerUserId = u.Id
  LEFT JOIN #pv
  ON #pv.OwnerUserId = u.Id
  LEFT JOIN #cc2 /*One Column*/
  ON #cc2.UserId = u.Id;
GO
```

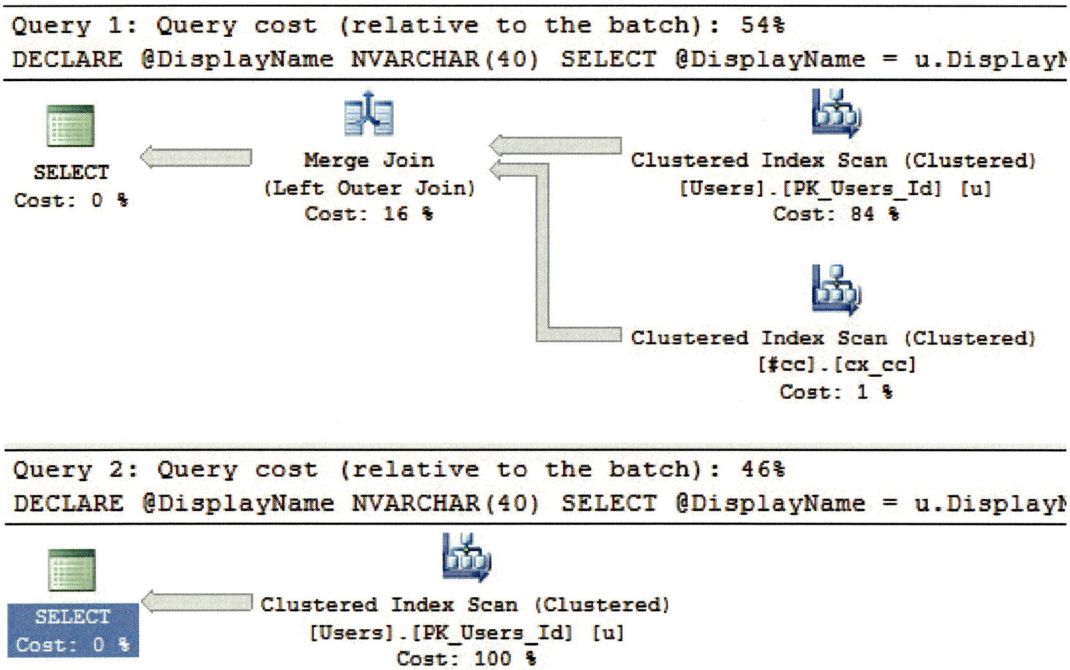

Expected?

If I go back and add in the joins, the plan changes again. The duplicate producing join has a domino effect on the other joins — now they can't be safely eliminated.

```
DECLARE @DisplayName NVARCHAR(40)

  SELECT @DisplayName = u.DisplayName
  FROM   dbo.Users AS u
  LEFT JOIN #pp
  ON #pp.OwnerUserId = u.Id
  LEFT JOIN #pl
  ON #pl.OwnerUserId = u.Id
  AND #pl.OwnerUserId = #pp.OwnerUserId
  LEFT JOIN #pv
  ON #pv.OwnerUserId = u.Id
  AND #pv.OwnerUserId = #pl.OwnerUserId
  LEFT JOIN #cc
  ON #cc.UserId = u.Id
  AND #cc.UserId = #pv.OwnerUserId;
GO
```

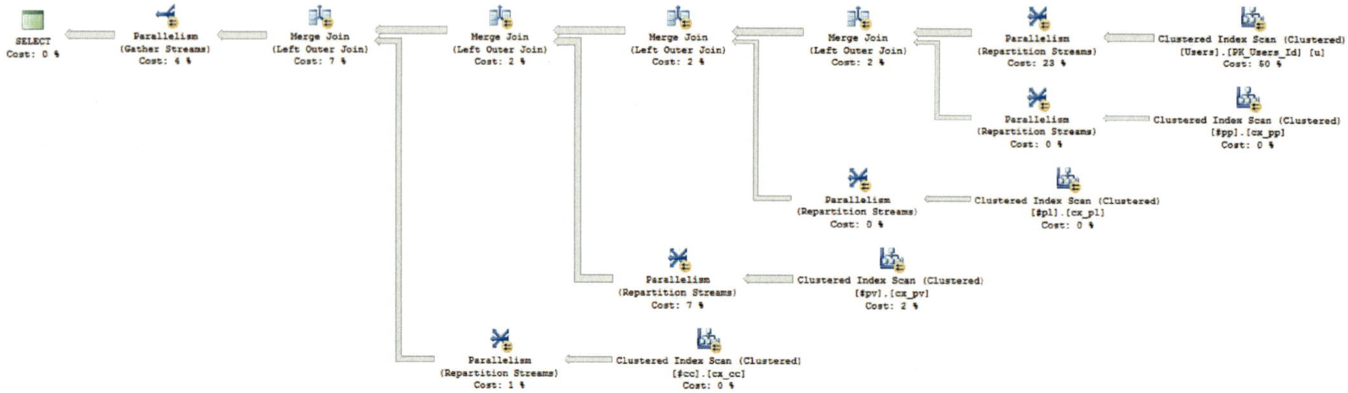

Dupes come out at night

Want a simple example?

If you'd like something a bit easier to follow along with, use this example.

```
Transact-SQL
CREATE TABLE #Example1 (Id INT NOT NULL, DanglingParticiple INT NOT NULL,
PRIMARY KEY CLUSTERED (Id))

CREATE TABLE #Example2 (Id INT NOT NULL, DanglingParticiple INT NOT NULL,
PRIMARY KEY CLUSTERED (Id, DanglingParticiple))

CREATE TABLE #Example3 (Id INT NOT NULL, DanglingParticiple INT NOT NULL,
DanglingParticiple INT NOT NULL,PRIMARY KEY CLUSTERED(Id, DanglingParticiple))

INSERT #Example1 (Id, DanglingParticiple )
VALUES ( 1, 1 )

INSERT #Example2 (Id, DanglingParticiple )
VALUES ( 1, 1 )

INSERT #Example3 (Id, DanglingParticiple )
VALUES ( 1, 1 )

SELECT e.*
FROM #Example1 AS e
LEFT JOIN #Example2 AS e2
ON e2.Id = e.Id

SELECT e.*
FROM #Example1 AS e
LEFT JOIN #Example3 AS e3
ON e3.Id = e.Id
```

Thanks for reading!

Query Performance

Faster than a speeding Bulleit, more power than a steaming Four Loco! Able to leap Tall Boys at a single bound! Nothing optimizes drinking like a beer and a shot. Time to get together with your two best friends.

BRENT OZAR UNLIMITED®

Implicit vs. Explicit Conversion

Everyone knows Implicit Conversion is bad

It can ruin SARGability, defeat index usage, and burn up your CPU like it needs some Valtrex. But what about explicit conversion? Is there any overhead? Turns out, SQL is just as happy with explicit conversion as it is with passing in the correct datatype in the first place.

Here's a short demo:

```sql
SET NOCOUNT ON;

SELECT ISNULL(x.ID, 0) AS ID, ISNULL(CAST(x.TextColumn AS VARCHAR(10)), 'A') AS TextColumn
INTO   dbo.Conversion
FROM
       (   SELECT TOP 1000000
                  ROW_NUMBER() OVER ( ORDER BY ( SELECT NULL )), REPLICATE('A',
                  ABS(CONVERT(INT, CHECKSUM(NEWID()))) % 10 + 1)
           FROM   sys.messages AS m ) AS x(ID, TextColumn);

ALTER TABLE dbo.Conversion
ADD CONSTRAINT pk_conversion_id
    PRIMARY KEY CLUSTERED ( ID );

CREATE NONCLUSTERED INDEX ix_text ON dbo.Conversion ( TextColumn );
```

One table, one million rows, two columns! Just like real life! Let's throw some queries at it. The first one will use the wrong datatype, the second one will cast the wrong datatype as the right datatype, and the third one is our control query. It uses the right datatype.

```sql
SET STATISTICS TIME, IO ON

DECLARE @txt NVARCHAR(10) = N'A', @id INT;

SELECT @id = c1.ID
FROM   dbo.Conversion AS c1
WHERE  c1.TextColumn = @txt;
GO

DECLARE @txt NVARCHAR(10) = N'A', @id INT;

SELECT @id = c1.ID
FROM   dbo.Conversion AS c1
WHERE  c1.TextColumn = CAST(@txt AS VARCHAR(10));
GO

DECLARE @txt VARCHAR(10) = 'A', @id INT;

SELECT @id = c1.ID
FROM   dbo.Conversion AS c1
WHERE  c1.TextColumn = @txt;
GO
```

The results shouldn't surprise most of you. From statistics time and I/O, the first query is El Stinko. The second two were within 1ms of each other, and the reads were always the same over every execution. Very little CPU, far fewer reads.

```sql
Query 1:
Table 'Conversion'. Scan count 1, logical reads 738, physical reads 0, read-ahead reads 0,
lob logical reads 0, lob physical reads 0, lob read-ahead reads 0.

SQL Server Execution Times:
CPU time = 47 ms,  elapsed time = 47 ms.

Query 2:
Table 'Conversion'. Scan count 1, logical reads 63, physical reads 0, read-ahead reads 0,
lob logical reads 0, lob physical reads 0, lob read-ahead reads 0.

SQL Server Execution Times:
CPU time = 0 ms, elapsed time = 4 ms.

Query 3:
Table 'Conversion'. Scan count 1, logical reads 63, physical reads 0, read-ahead reads 0,
lob logical reads 0, lob physical reads 0, lob read-ahead reads 0.

SQL Server Execution Times:
CPU time = 0 ms, elapsed time = 5 ms.
```

So there you go

Explicit conversion of parameter datatypes doesn't carry any horrible overhead. Is it easier to just pass in the correct the datatype? Yeah, probably, but you might be in a position where you can't control the parameter datatype that's incoming, but you can CAST or CONVERT it where it touches data.

Thanks for reading!

Brent says: *the key here is that we're taking an incoming NVARCHAR variable, and casting it in our query to be VARCHAR to match the table definition. This only works if you can guarantee that the app isn't going to pass in unicode – but in most situations, that's true, because the same app is also responsible for inserting/updating data in this same table, so it's already used to working with VARCHAR data. Also, just to be clear, Erik's talking about casting the variable – NOT every row in the table. That part still blows.*

A Better Way To Select Star

Mindless Self Promotion

I liked writing this blog post so much that I wrote an entire presentation on it. If you'd like to see it at GroupBy, click the link and vote.

Much has been written about this

It's probably one of the lowest hanging items a performance tuner can deal with.

Don't need all those columns?

Don't select them.

But what if you do need them?

You're left with pretty grim choices.

1. Make a really wide nonclustered index: (some key columns) include (every other column)
2. Rearrange your existing clustered index — maybe the wrong key column was chosen to begin with
3. Create a narrow nonclustered index on just the (some key columns) and then hope that by some stroke of luck, no one ever conjures up a WHERE clause that pushes the optimzer past the Key Lookup tipping point and into the clustered index scan zone

Assuming that you don't find any of those palatable: I'm 100% with you.

What if there's another way?

Query Godmother

Using the Stack Overflow database (duh) as an example, let's check out the Users table.

- dbo.Users
  - Columns
    - Id (PK, int, not null)
    - AboutMe (nvarchar(max), null)
    - Age (int, null)
    - CreationDate (datetime, not null)
    - DisplayName (nvarchar(40), not null)
    - DownVotes (int, not null)
    - EmailHash (nvarchar(40), null)
    - LastAccessDate (datetime, not null)
    - Location (nvarchar(100), null)
    - Reputation (int, not null)
    - UpVotes (int, not null)
    - Views (int, not null)
    - WebsiteUrl (nvarchar(200), null)
    - AccountId (int, null)

Not the worst, but...

There are some columns in there I'd be unhappy to index even as includes, especially AboutMe which is a MAX.

Right now, we have this query, and it has a cost of 156.8 Query Buckaroos.

Transact-SQL

```sql
SELECT u.*, p.Id AS [PostId]
FROM   dbo.Users AS u
JOIN   dbo.Posts AS p
ON p.OwnerUserId = u.Id
WHERE  u.CreationDate > '20160101'
       AND u.Reputation > 100
       AND p.PostTypeId = 1;
```

Here's the CPU and I/O profile from SET STATISTICS TIME, IO ON — I've abridged all the I/O output in the post so you don't have to read that a bunch of things did 0 reads. If it looks a little funny to you, that's why.

```
Table 'Posts'. Scan count 7, logical reads 25187
Table 'Users'. Scan count 7, logical reads 80834
Table 'Worktable'. Scan count 0, logical reads 0

SQL Server Execution Times:
CPU time = 4297 ms, elapsed time = 2324 ms.
```

The thing of it is, we created this nonclustered index

```sql
CREATE INDEX ix_Users ON dbo.Users (CreationDate, Reputation, Id);
```

But it gets no use, sort of like my willpower.

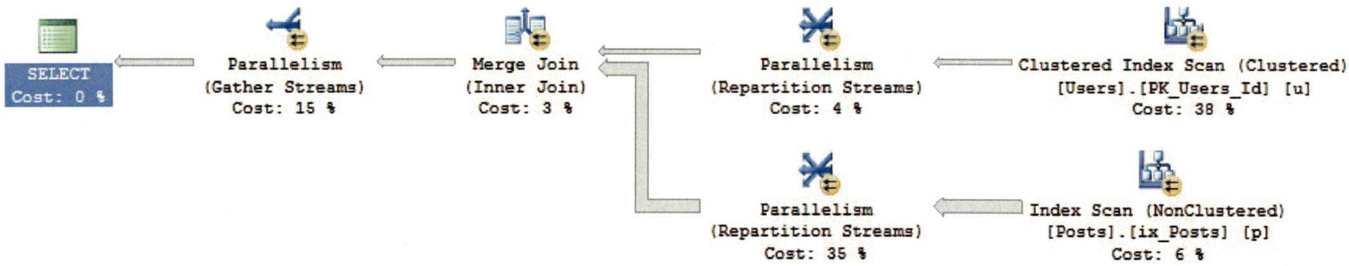

Resist temptation!

Let's pretend we care

This query only returns a couple thousand rows, so you'd think the optimizer would choose a key lookup plan.

A quick check forcing our index leaves us scratching our collective heads — this query has a 'much' higher cost, at 275.6 Query Bucks, but finishes much faster.

```sql
SELECT u.*, p.Id AS [PostId]
FROM   dbo.Users AS u WITH (INDEX = ix_Users) --Force Fed Index
JOIN   dbo.Posts AS p
ON p.OwnerUserId = u.Id
WHERE  u.CreationDate > '20160101'
       AND u.Reputation > 100
       AND p.PostTypeId = 1
```

Here's the stats output:

```
Table 'Users'. Scan count 7, logical reads 5479
Table 'Posts'. Scan count 7, logical reads 25279
Table 'Worktable'. Scan count 0, logical reads 0
Table 'Worktable'. Scan count 0, logical reads 0

SQL Server Execution Times:
CPU time = 532 ms, elapsed time = 109 ms.
```

Here's the query plan:

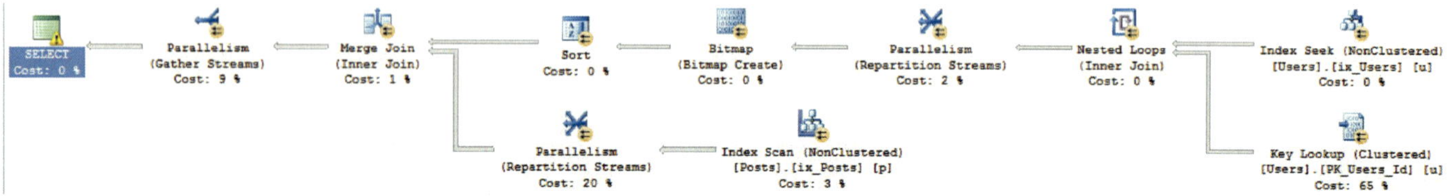

Doodles.

Recap so far: When we force our thoughtful nonclustered index, we get a more expensive plan that runs in 100 ***milliseconds*** vs 2.3 seconds.

But we hate hints

That key lookup plan might not always be awesome. Like I mentioned, this query only returns a couple thousand rows. If we expand our search, we may not want to do that key lookup a whole bunch of times. If we keep forcing the index, queries that return more rows will necessitate more key lookups, and that can really slow things down.

Key Lookup (Clustered)

Uses a supplied clustering key to lookup on a table that has a clustered index.

Physical Operation	Key Lookup
Logical Operation	Key Lookup
Actual Execution Mode	Row
Estimated Execution Mode	Row
Storage	RowStore
Number of Rows Read	1506
Actual Number of Rows	1506
Actual Number of Batches	0
Estimated Operator Cost	177.945 (65%)
Estimated I/O Cost	0.003125
Estimated CPU Cost	0.0001581
Estimated Subtree Cost	177.945
Number of Executions	1506
Estimated Number of Executions	86201.9
Estimated Number of Rows	1
Estimated Row Size	4452 B
Actual Rebinds	0
Actual Rewinds	0
Ordered	True
Node ID	9

Object

[StackOverflow].[dbo].[Users].[PK_Users_Id] [u]

Output List

[StackOverflow].[dbo].[Users].AboutMe, [StackOverflow].[dbo].[Users].Age, [StackOverflow].[dbo].[Users].DisplayName, [StackOverflow].[dbo].[Users].DownVotes, [StackOverflow].[dbo].[Users].EmailHash, [StackOverflow].[dbo].[Users].LastAccessDate, [StackOverflow].[dbo].[Users].Location, [StackOverflow].[dbo].[Users].UpVotes, [StackOverflow].[dbo].[Users].Views, [StackOverflow].[dbo].[Users].WebsiteUrl, [StackOverflow].[dbo].[Users].AccountId

Seek Predicates

Seek Keys[1]: Prefix: [StackOverflow].[dbo].[Users].Id = Scalar Operator([StackOverflow].[dbo].[Users].[Id] as [u].[Id])

Study your math, kids

Organics

So how on earth do we get the optimizer to choose our nonclustered index, have it make sense to do so, and not do row-by-row Key Lookups when it shouldn't?

One option is to use a CTE, or common table expression for those of you who have word quotas to fill.

```
Transact-SQL
WITH precheck AS (
  SELECT u.Id, p.Id AS [PostId] --Don't select much here
  FROM dbo.Users AS u
  JOIN   dbo.Posts AS p
  ON p.OwnerUserId = u.Id
  WHERE u.CreationDate > '20160101' --Filter!
  AND u.Reputation > 100 --Filter more!
  AND p.PostTypeId = 1
        )
SELECT u.*, p.PostId --Save display level column selection for the end
FROM precheck p
JOIN dbo.Users AS u
ON p.Id = u.Id;
```

How do we do? Here are the stats output results:

Table 'Users'. Scan count 7, logical reads 8340

Table 'Posts'. Scan count 7, logical reads 25279

Table 'Workfile'. Scan count 0, logical reads 0

Table 'Worktable'. Scan count 0, logical reads 0

Table 'Worktable'. Scan count 0, logical reads 0

SQL Server Execution Times:

CPU time = 577 ms, elapsed time = 109 ms.

We have very similar metrics to when we force the index with a hint. How does the plan look?

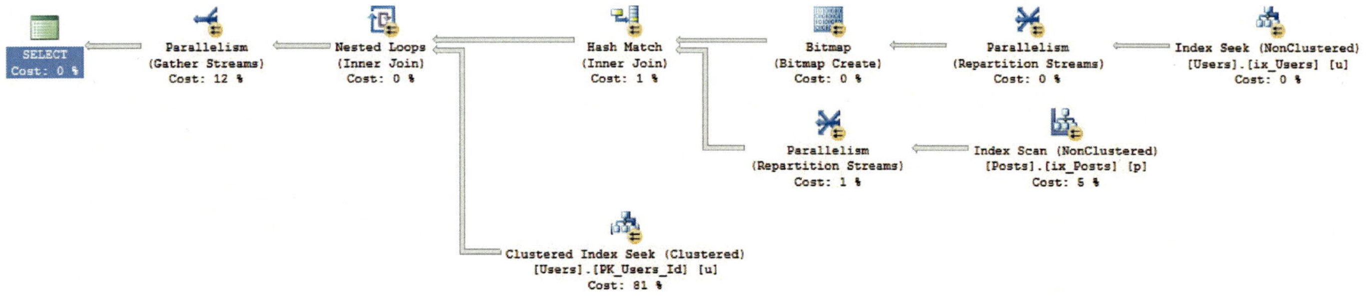

SOME

This could use some explanation, here! Why is this better?

We use two narrow nonclustered indexes to do our early joins and predicate filtering. Even though in the plan for the original query, the predicates on CreationDate and Reputation are easily pushed to the clustered index scan, they aren't key columns there. That means we read every row in the CX and filter along the way. Using the narrow nonclustered index, read far fewer pages (5.2 million rows vs 283k rows).

The results of this join are passed on and finally joined back to the clustered index on Users. This gives us our display level columns, but only for the rows we need to show you.

We're not dragging them around all throughout the query. This is a far more efficient use of, well everything.

I know what you're thinking, though. Didn't you just replace a Key Lookup with a Nested Loops Join?

YEAH I DID!

But check it out, the Nested Loops Join is a smarty pants, executes 6 times, and grabs about 407 rows per iteration. Remember our Key Lookup executed 1506 times to get 1506 rows. That's, like... One. One at a time.

Nested Loops

For each row in the top (outer) input, scan the bottom (inner) input, and output matching rows.

Physical Operation	Nested Loops
Logical Operation	Inner Join
Actual Execution Mode	Row
Estimated Execution Mode	Row
Actual Number of Rows	2440
Actual Number of Batches	0
Estimated Operator Cost	0.3174 (0%)
Estimated I/O Cost	0
Estimated CPU Cost	0.317887
Estimated Subtree Cost	171.326
Number of Executions	6
Estimated Number of Executions	1
Estimated Number of Rows	456297
Estimated Row Size	4472 B
Actual Rebinds	0
Actual Rewinds	0
Node ID	1

Output List

[StackOverflow].[dbo].[Posts].Id, [StackOverflow].[dbo].[Users].Id, [StackOverflow].[dbo].[Users].AboutMe, [StackOverflow].[dbo].[Users].Age, [StackOverflow].[dbo].[Users].CreationDate, [StackOverflow].[dbo].[Users].DisplayName, [StackOverflow].[dbo].[Users].DownVotes, [StackOverflow].[dbo].[Users].EmailHash, [StackOverflow].[dbo].[Users].LastAccessDate, [StackOverflow].[dbo].[Users].Location, [StackOverflow].[dbo].[Users].Reputation, [StackOverflow].[dbo].[Users].UpVotes, [StackOverflow].[db...

Outer References

[StackOverflow].[dbo].[Posts].OwnerUserId, Expr1006

Bully for you

This can also be extended to Cross Apply, because of course it can.

```sql
SELECT u.*, ca.PostId
FROM dbo.Users AS u
CROSS APPLY(
  SELECT
    p.Id AS [PostId]
  FROM dbo.Users AS u2
  JOIN   dbo.Posts AS p
  ON p.OwnerUserId = u2.Id
  WHERE u2.Id = u.Id
  AND u2.CreationDate > '20160101'
  AND u2.Reputation > 100
  AND p.PostTypeId = 1
) ca;
```

This results in the same plan and the same stats output. No need to rehash it all.

Different, but valid

If the logical needs of your query change, it may be simpler to express things with EXISTS, but the same basic idea works.

```sql
SELECT u.*
FROM dbo.Users AS u
WHERE EXISTS (
  SELECT
    1 AS Whatever
  FROM dbo.Users AS u2
  JOIN   dbo.Posts AS p
  ON p.OwnerUserId = u2.Id
  WHERE u2.Id = u.Id
  AND u2.CreationDate > '20160101'
  AND u2.Reputation > 100
  AND p.PostTypeId = 1
);
```

The stats output is close enough to the CTE and Cross Apply plans. The query plan is a touch different, though. A Hash Match Aggregate on the Id column is inserted after the initial join.

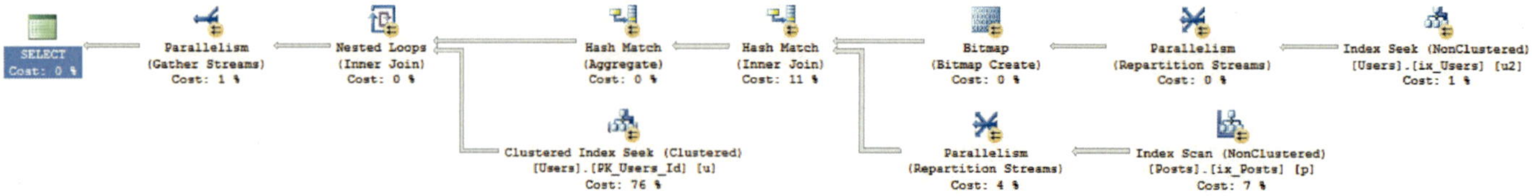

BODY ONCE TOLD ME

Shut up already

While I'm not a fan of SELECT * queries, I realize that they may be necessary sometimes. I mean, why have all those columns if you're not gonna show'em to anyone?

If you can, try to cut out unnecessary columns from queries. Richie has a good post about doing that with EF over here.

If you can't, you can always defer the pain of scanning the clustered index until you've cut results down to a more reasonable bunch of rows, and you can do it in a way where you don't have to rely on the optimizer choosing a Key Lookup plan, or forever forcing one where it might not be helpful.

Thanks for reading!

Then Why Doesn't SQL Always Seek?

Scan The Man

There seems to be a perpetual battle waged against the Index Scan.

At some point it was declared that scans were inferior to seeks, and all energy should be dedicated to eradicating them.

Much like asking why the whole plane isn't made out of the stuff the black box is made out of, you start to wonder why the Index Scan is even an operator.

Obviously, if Microsoft cared about performance, there would be no Index Scans.

Right?

Right?

I bet Postgres would never scan an index.

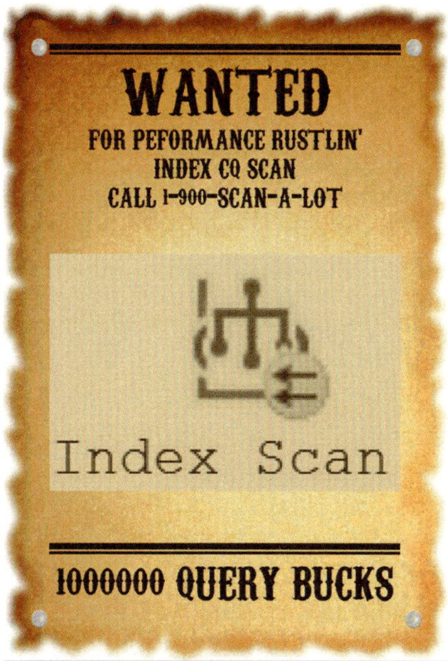

This is so dumb.

Being Practical

It should be pretty easy to prove Seek Supremacy once and for all. Then you can literally (LITERALLY!) ignore every other operator in a query plan and focus the entirety of your being on this unknown astral plane toward mocking those without the mental capacity to receive your wisdom.

About Index Scans.

Let's start with a query.

```
SELECT  COUNT(*)
FROM    dbo.Users AS u
JOIN    dbo.Posts AS p
    ON p.OwnerUserId = u.Id;
```

It has no predicates. It's just joining two tables together in total.

In the query plan, we have two scans. It's a two scan plan.

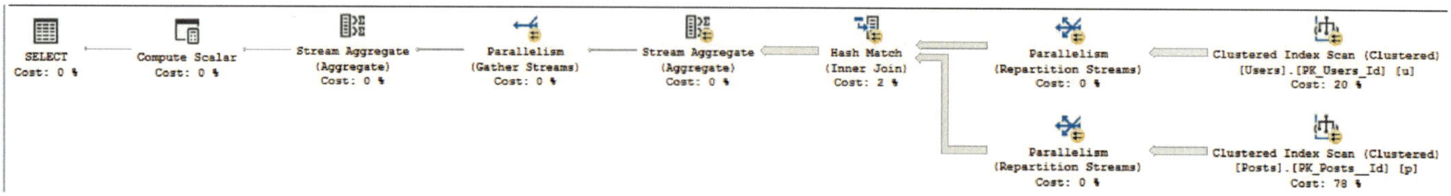

HOUR BACK GET IT?

For the Seekists out there; fear not, your moment of ascension is at hand.

```
SELECT  COUNT(*)
FROM    dbo.Users AS u WITH ( FORCESEEK )
JOIN    dbo.Posts AS p
    ON p.OwnerUserId = u.Id;
```

This plan must surely be superior.

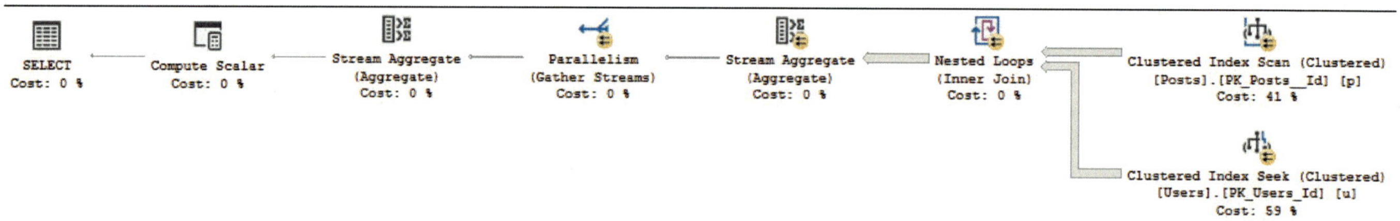

Prepare to be humbled

Not All Who Scan Are Lost

In this case, the Two Scan Plan does a bit better.

	Two Scan Plan	Seek and Scan	Difference
CPU	1375	2250	875
Reads: Users	56119	2789171	2733052
Reads: Posts	218232	218232	0

Not off to a good start.

The source of all those extra reads, and likely the extra CPU time for the seek plan is...

Well, it's in the seek.

For the links, code, and comments, go here:
https://www.brentozar.com/archive/2018/02/doesnt-sql-always-seek/

Clustered Index Seek (Clustered)

Scanning a particular range of rows from a clustered index.

Physical Operation	Clustered Index Seek
Logical Operation	Clustered Index Seek
Actual Execution Mode	Row
Estimated Execution Mode	Row
Storage	RowStore
Number of Rows Read	888157
Actual Number of Rows	888157
Actual Number of Batches	0
Estimated I/O Cost	0.003125
Estimated Operator Cost	215.325 (59%)
Estimated CPU Cost	0.0001581
Estimated Subtree Cost	215.325
Estimated Number of Executions	910733.09
Number of Executions	910733
Estimated Number of Rows	1
Estimated Number of Rows to be Read	1
Estimated Row Size	9 B
Actual Rebinds	0
Actual Rewinds	0
Ordered	True
Node ID	8

Object

[SUPERUSER].[dbo].[Users].[PK_Users_Id] [u]

Seek Predicates

Seek Keys[1]: Prefix: [SUPERUSER].[dbo].[Users].Id = Scalar Operator([SUPERUSER].[dbo].[Posts].[OwnerUserId] as [p].[OwnerUserId])

Quackin' crazy!

You can see why the optimizer chose the scan in the first place.

Hang on though, maybe we picked the wrong table to force a seek on.

```
SELECT  COUNT(*)
FROM    dbo.Users AS u
JOIN    dbo.Posts AS p WITH ( FORCESEEK )
    ON p.OwnerUserId = u.Id;
```

This must be the better choi-

```
SELECT COUNT(*)
FROM   dbo.Users AS u
JOIN   dbo.Posts AS p WITH ( FORCESEEK )
    ON p.OwnerUserId = u.Id;
```

Messages

Msg 8622, Level 16, State 1, Line 19
Query processor could not produce a query plan because of the hints defined in this query. Resubmit the query without specifying any hints and without using SET FORCEPLAN.

I need to sleep more.

Important Information

The reason we get this error here is because we don't have an index on the Posts table with OwnerUserId as a key column.

This is where most Earth Peoples start to get annoyed — they usually do have an index. In fact, if consulting has taught me anything, you have 17 of the same index with _dta_ somewhere in the name on the data you wish to seek into.

Alright then. Let's add an index.

```
CREATE INDEX ix_maybe
    ON dbo.Posts ( OwnerUserId );
```

If we re-run our query without hints, what happens?

Darn Merges and Scans

We still get two scans!

Comparing all three plans (we can force a seek on Posts now, because we have an index on OwnerUserId), the seeks still aren't doing so hot.

	Two Scan Plan	Seek Users and Scan Posts	Seek Posts and ScanUsers
CPU	312	1782	1752
Reads: Users	52964	2789171	56119
Reads: Posts	1587	1669	1990869
Scan Count: Users	1	0	7
Scan Count: Posts	1	7	623700

Hrmpf.

Now what?

Hopefully you learned that not every seek is great, and not every scan is awful.

If you're joining two tables together, often a single scan of the data is the wisest choice.

The worst part of a plan may not always be obvious, and it may not always be the method that the optimizer chooses to access data with.

Thanks for reading!

Table Valued Parameters: Unexpected Parameter Sniffing

Like Table Variables, Kinda

Jeremiah wrote about them a few years ago. I always get asked about them while poking fun at Table Variables, so I thought I'd provide some detail and a post to point people to.

There are some interesting differences between them, namely around how cardinality is estimated in different situations.

Table Valued Parameters are often used as a replacement for passing in a CSV list of "things" to then parse, usually with some God awful function. This helps by passing in the list in table-format, so you don't have to do any additional processing. TVPs don't have the exact same problems that Table Variables do, but there are some things you have to be aware of.

I'm going to go over how they're different, and how a trace flag can "help".

I know you're gonna ask: "Should I just dump the contents out to a temp table?"

And I'm gonna tell you: "That's a whole 'nother post."

What We're Testing

Since I usually care about performance (I guess. Whatever.), I want to look at them with and without indexes, like so:

```sql
CREATE TYPE dbo.YourMomsType AS TABLE (Id INT NOT NULL)
GO

CREATE TYPE dbo.YourMomsType AS TABLE (Id INT PRIMARY KEY CLUSTERED)
GO
```

Mr. Swart points out in the comments:

> The name of the primary key in your example turns out to be PK_#A954D2B_3214EC07D876E774 which gets in the way of plan forcing, a super-useful emergency technique.

```sql
CREATE TYPE dbo.YourMomsType AS TABLE (Id INT, index ix_YourMomsType unique clustered (Id) )
```

Here's the stored procedure we'll be calling:

```sql
CREATE OR ALTER PROCEDURE dbo.AmIYourMomsType (@YourMomsTypes YourMomsType READONLY)
AS
BEGIN
SET NOCOUNT ON;

    SELECT COUNT_BIG(*) AS records
    FROM dbo.Posts AS p
    JOIN @YourMomsTypes AS ymt
    ON p.OwnerUserId = ymt.Id
    WHERE p.PostTypeId = 1;

    SELECT COUNT_BIG(*) AS records
    FROM @YourMomsTypes AS ymt
    WHERE ymt.Id = 100;

    SELECT COUNT_BIG(*) AS records
    FROM @YourMomsTypes AS ymt
    WHERE ymt.Id >= 100;

    SELECT COUNT_BIG(*) AS records
    FROM @YourMomsTypes AS ymt
    WHERE ymt.Id <= 100;

    SELECT COUNT_BIG(*) AS records
    FROM @YourMomsTypes AS ymt
    WHERE ymt.Id >= 1
    AND ymt.Id <= 100;

END;
```

Now, I'm going to square with you, dear reader. I cannot write C#. If it were me in that scene from Swordfish, we'd all be dead.

Or whatever the plot line was there. Hard to tell.

I had to borrow most of my code from this post by The Only Canadian Who Answers My Emails.

Mine looks a little different, but just so it will Work On My Computer®.

And also so I can test data sets of different data sizes. I had to make the array and loop look like this:

```
                foreach (long l in new long[1])
                    for (int i = 1; i <= 100; i++)
                    {
                        dt.LoadDataRow(new object[] { l + i }, true);
                    }

OR

                foreach (long l in new long[1])
                    for (int i = 1; i <= 100000; i++)
                    {
                        dt.LoadDataRow(new object[] { l + i }, true);
                    }
```

By the end of the blog post, you'll be glad I didn't introduce much more variation in there.

Results

I have another confession to make: I used Extended Events again. It still burns a little. At least there was no PowerShell though.

First Thing: There's a fixed estimate of 100 rows for inserts

This is regardless of how many rows actually end up in there. This is the insert from the application to the TVP, so we're clear.

name	timestamp	cpu_time	dop	duration	estimated_cost	estimated_rows
query_post_execution_showplan	2018-03-07 19:42:11.1467511	661	1	661	0	100
query_post_execution_showplan	2018-03-07 19:42:02.9605973	85501	1	87977	0	100
query_post_execution_showplan	2018-03-07 19:41:54.0931422	109721	1	112291	0	100
query_post_execution_showplan	2018-03-07 19:41:49.3931636	638	1	639	0	100
query_post_execution_showplan	2018-03-07 19:41:35.9064209	380	1	380	0	100
query_post_execution_showplan	2018-03-07 19:41:21.2416809	47377	1	47377	0	100
query_post_execution_showplan	2018-03-07 19:41:05.0048498	43898	1	43899	0	100
query_post_execution_showplan	2018-03-07 19:41:00.3400253	544	1	545	0	100
query_post_execution_showplan	2018-03-07 19:34:59.7353686	683	1	683	0	100
query_post_execution_showplan	2018-03-07 19:34:49.8650338	92508	1	95502	0	100
query_post_execution_showplan	2018-03-07 19:34:33.9902028	86794	1	89058	0	100
query_post_execution_showplan	2018-03-07 19:34:29.3542050	583	1	584	0	100
query_post_execution_showplan	2018-03-07 19:34:17.1572932	349	1	349	0	100
query_post_execution_showplan	2018-03-07 19:34:02.6530311	50399	1	50400	0	100
query_post_execution_showplan	2018-03-07 19:33:47.3107176	49008	1	49011	0	100
query_post_execution_showplan	2018-03-07 19:33:42.3475464	504	1	504	0	100

Jump, jump

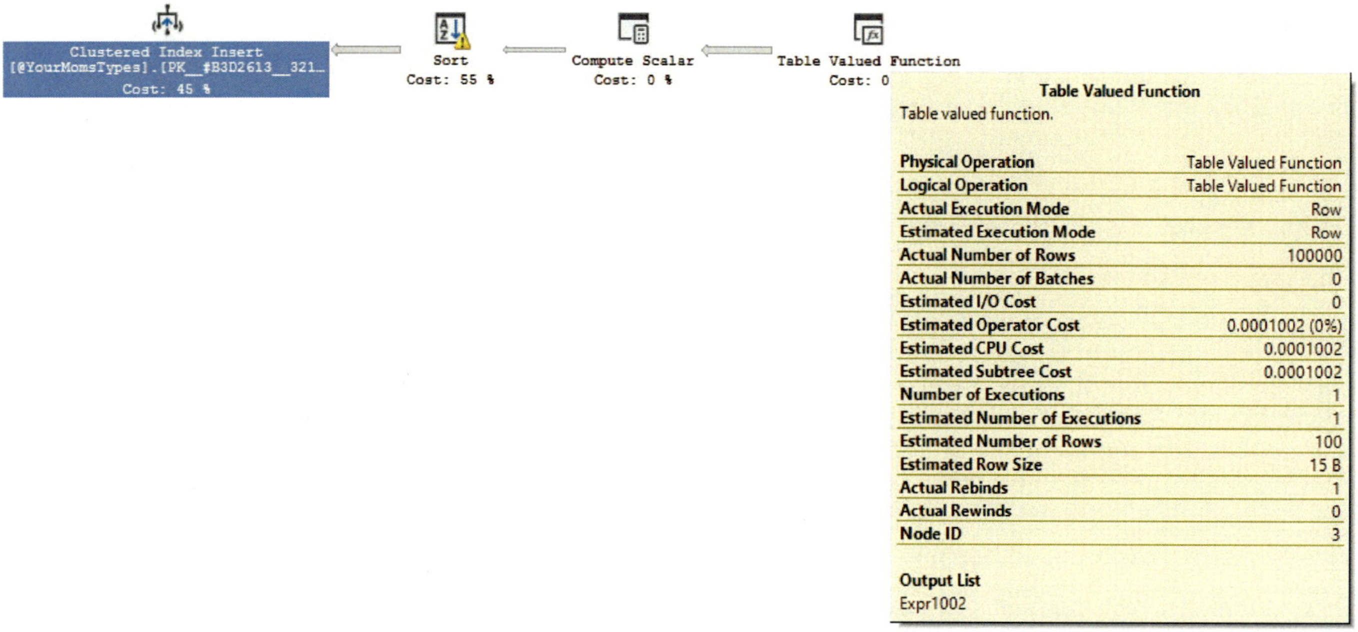

Maybe that's not so great...

Second Thing: They don't get a fixed estimate like Table Variables

Table Variables (unless you Recompile, or use a Trace Flag), will sport either a 1 or 100 row estimate, depending on which version of the Cardinality Estimator you use. The old version guesses 1 row, the new guesses 100 rows.

Table Valued Parameters get sniffed, just like... parameters! When the first plan in the cache is a 100k row TVP, we keep that number until recompilation occurs.

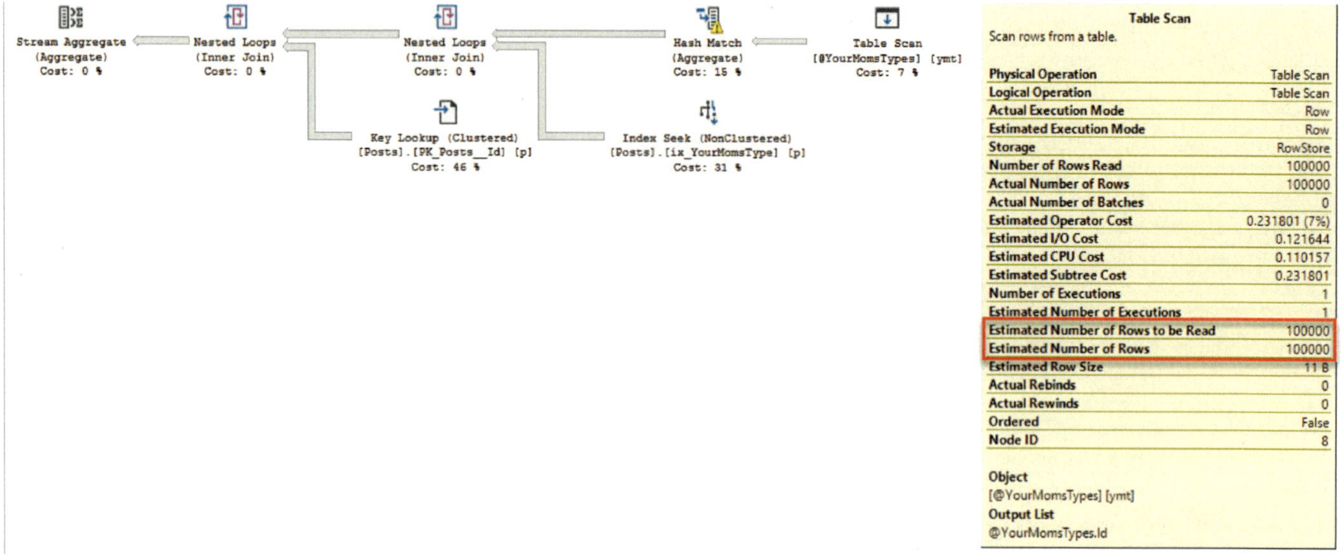

Nice guess...

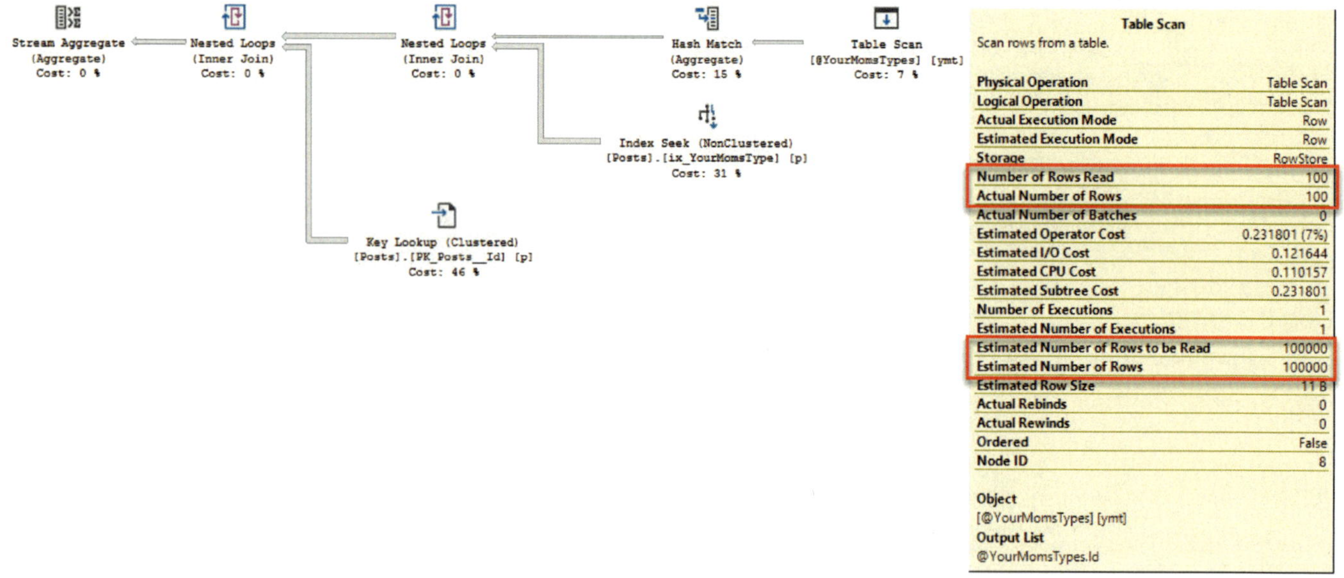

... Be a shame if something happened to it

Third Thing: Non-join cardinality estimates behave like local variables (fixed estimates)

And I am not a very good graphic artist.

For the links, code, and comments, go here:
https://www.brentozar.com/archive/2018/03/table-valued-parameters-unexpected-parameter-sniffing/

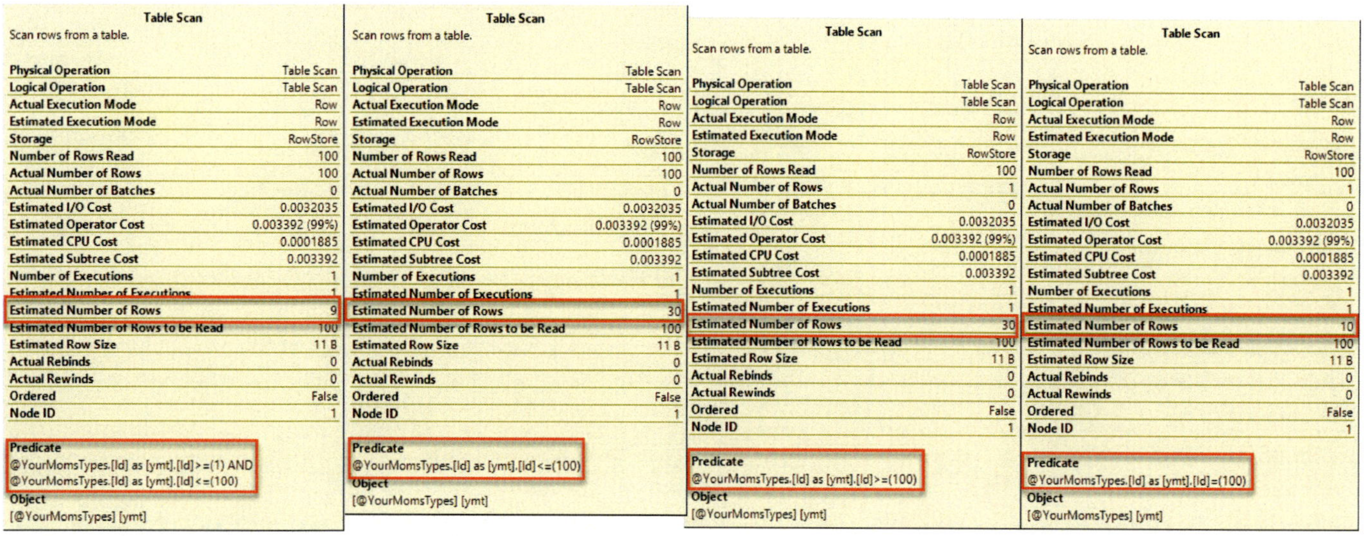

Hoowee.

Without the PK/CX, we get 10% for equality, 30% for inequality, and 9% for two inequalities.

This is detailed by Itzik Ben Gan here.

Fourth Thing: This didn't get much better with a PK/CX

The only estimate that improved was the direct equality. The rest stayed the same.

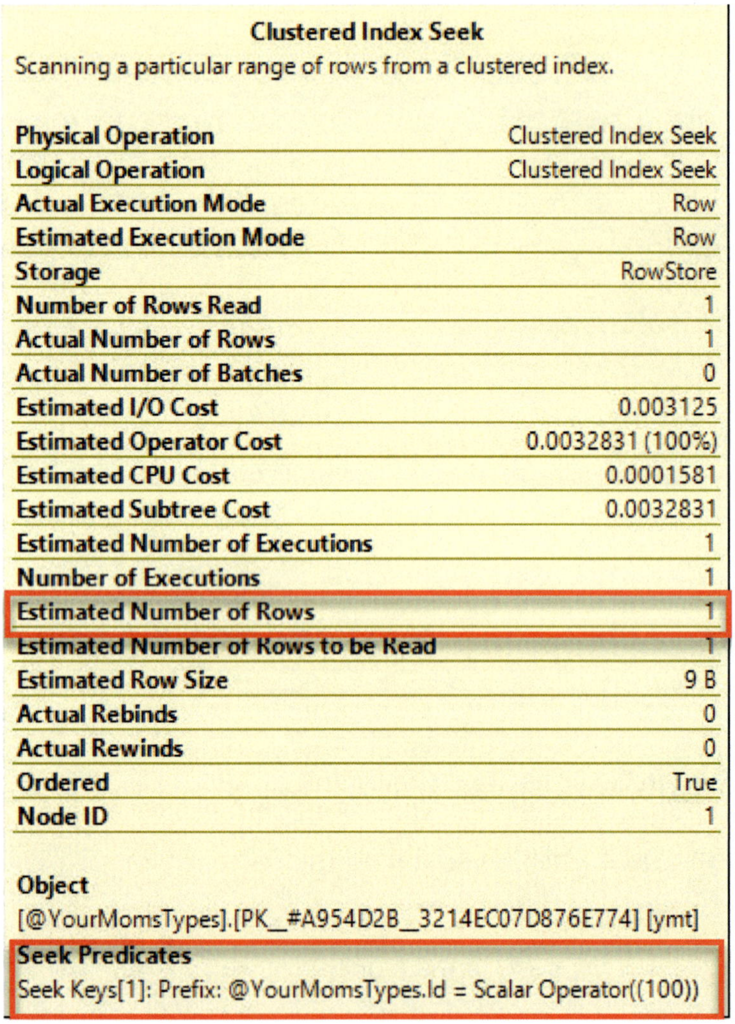

Captain Obvious, et al.

Fifth Thing: The index didn't change estimates between runs

We still got the "parameter sniffing" behavior, where whatever row count was inserted first dictated cardinality estimates until I recompiled.

Apologies, no pretty pictures here.

Sixth Thing: Trace Flag 2453 definitely did help

With or without the index, turning it on improved our cardinality estimates, but had little *ffect on standardizing capitalization of key words.

I didn't have to recompile here, because there was enough of a difference between 100 and 100,000 rows being inserted to trigger a recompilation and accurate estimate.

Pictures don't do this part justice either.

Go Away

Table Valued Parameters offer some nice improvements over Table Variables (I know, I know, there are times they're good...).

But they're also something you need to be careful with. Sniffed parameters here can cause plan quality issues just like regular parameters do.

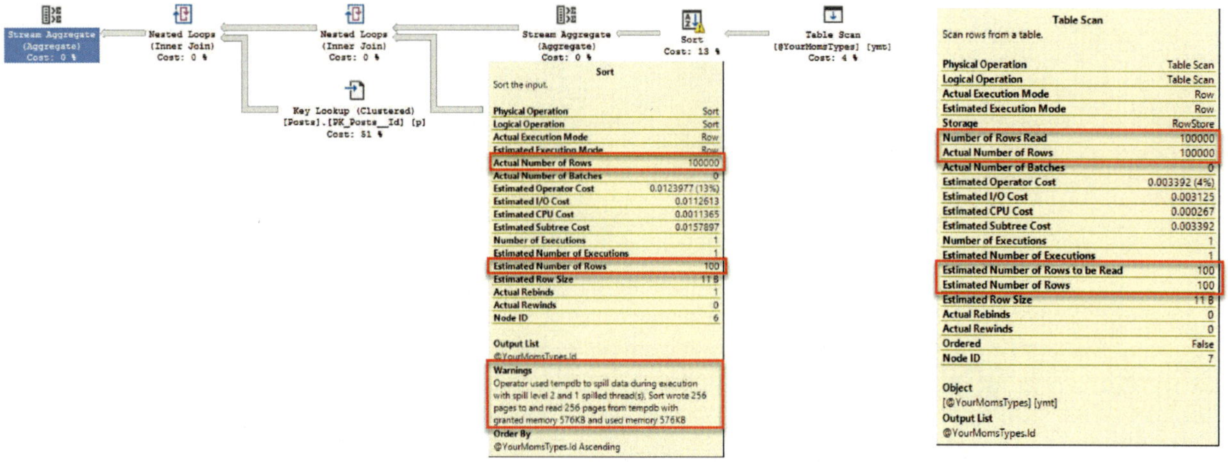

Boohoo.

In this plan, the 100 row estimate lead to a spill. To be fair, even accurate estimates can result in spills. It's just hard to fix an accurate estimate.

- The initial insert to the TVP is still serialized (just like table variables), so use caution if you're inserting a lot of rows
- There are no column level statistics, just like Table Variables, even with indexes (this leads to fixed predicate estimations)
- Trace Flag 2453 can improve estimates at the cost of recompiles
- The fixed estimate of 100 rows for each insert may not be ideal if you're inserting a lot of rows

Thanks for reading!

I just realized I forgot to thank my parents in the foreword.

Thanks, parents.

Column Store

Deep, dark, and mysterious, but loaded with the amazing.
Like most of your memories after 3pm, minus the amazing.
Close your eyes and reach deep into your liquor cabinet.
Mind those old glue traps, though.

BRENT OZAR UNLIMITED®

Key Lookups and ColumnStore Indexes

Beavis v. Butthead

I was a bit surprised that this was a possibility with ColumnStore indexes, since "keys" aren't really their strong point, but since we're now able to have both clustered ColumnStore indexes alongside row store nonclustered indexes AND nonclustered ColumnStore indexes on tables with row store clustered indexes, this kind of stuff should get a closer look.

Of course, the effects of the sometimes-maligned Key Lookup are sometimes pretty lousy.

Why dude why

You may need to mix indexes in cases where you have columns with unsupported datatypes, like MAX, or perhaps just datatypes that don't have aggregatepushdown support in ColumnStore yet. I hesitate to make a list here, since it could change in a CU, but here's what the MS doc currently says about it:

> The input and output datatype must be one of the following and must fit within 64 bits.
>
> Tiny int, int, big int, small int, bit
>
> Small money, money, decimal and numeric which has precision <= 18
>
> Small date, date, datetime, datetime2, time

Got it? Also!

> The aggregates are MIN, MAX, SUM, COUNT and COUNT(*).
>
> Aggregate operator must be on top of SCAN node or SCAN node with group by.
>
> This aggregate is not a distinct aggregate.
>
> The aggregate column is not a string column.
>
> The aggregate column is not a virtual column.

So uh, anything outside of those datatypes and aggregates can potentially inhibit optimal performance (in case you're wondering, this sentence wasn't written by a lawyer).

For the links, code, and comments, go here:
https://www.brentozar.com/archive/2017/09/key-lookups-columnstore-indexes/

D.E.M.O.

Here's how I set the tables up, finally. Remember kids: loading large volumes of data into tables with nonclustered indexes is dumb.

Don't do it.

```
USE tempdb
GO

CREATE TABLE dbo.cci
(
    Id BIGINT IDENTITY(1, 1),
    Beavis DATE,
  Butthead DATE,
    INDEX cx_whatever CLUSTERED COLUMNSTORE
);

CREATE TABLE dbo.crsi
(
    Id BIGINT IDENTITY(1, 1),
  Beavis DATE,
    Butthead DATE,
  INDEX cx_whatever CLUSTERED (Id)
);

INSERT dbo.cci WITH ( TABLOCK ) (Beavis, Butthead)
SELECT TOP 10485760 DATEADD(DAY, (x.r % 365), CONVERT(DATE, GETDATE())), DATEADD(DAY, (( x.r * -1 ) % 365), CONVERT(DATE, GETDATE()))
FROM   (    SELECT ROW_NUMBER() OVER ( ORDER BY @@ROWCOUNT ) AS r
            FROM    sys.messages AS m
            CROSS JOIN sys.messages AS m2 ) AS x;

INSERT dbo.crsi WITH (TABLOCK)(Beavis, Butthead )
SELECT c.Beavis, c.Butthead
FROM dbo.cci AS c

CREATE NONCLUSTERED INDEX ix_whatever ON dbo.cci ( Beavis )
CREATE NONCLUSTERED COLUMNSTORE INDEX ix_whatever ON dbo.crsi ( Beavis )
```

We now have the most optimal setup to get a Key Lookup plan: tables with clustered indexes and God-awful single column nonclustered indexes (okay, so there are exceptions here, but for the most part...).

Come and take it

First up, we need a date to work with. I know most of you can sympathize with that problem.

> Q: which function do DBAs have the biggest problem with in real life?
>
> A: GETDATE()

Actually, I'm told DBAs make great spouses, because you barely have to see them.

What was I saying? Date? DATE!

Date.

```
SELECT MAX(c.Beavis) AS [Cornholio]
FROM   dbo.cci AS c
WHERE  1 = (SELECT 1);
```

If you want an explanation for the 1 = (SELECT 1), head over here. Otherwise, let's write some queries.

For me, that query returns a value of 2018-08-23. The first thing I discovered is that you really have to jump through hoops to get the Key Lookup to happen. The optimizer's adversity to choosing Key Lookup plans with ColumnStore indexes is well-meaning.

With regular row store indexes, returning 28k rows out of 10,485,760 with a Key Lookup plan would be a no-brainer for the optimizer.

Hooray for index hints.

```
SELECT *
FROM dbo.cci AS c WITH (INDEX = ix_whatever) --Clustered ColumnStore, nonclustered row store index on Beavis
WHERE c.Beavis >= '2018-08-23'
AND 1 = (SELECT 1);
GO

SELECT *
FROM dbo.crsi AS c WITH (INDEX = ix_whatever) --Clustered Row Store on ID, nonclustered ColumnStore on Beavis
WHERE c.Beavis >= '2018-08-23'
AND 1 = (SELECT 1);
GO
```


For the links, code, and comments, go here:
https://www.brentozar.com/archive/2017/09/key-lookups-columnstore-indexes/

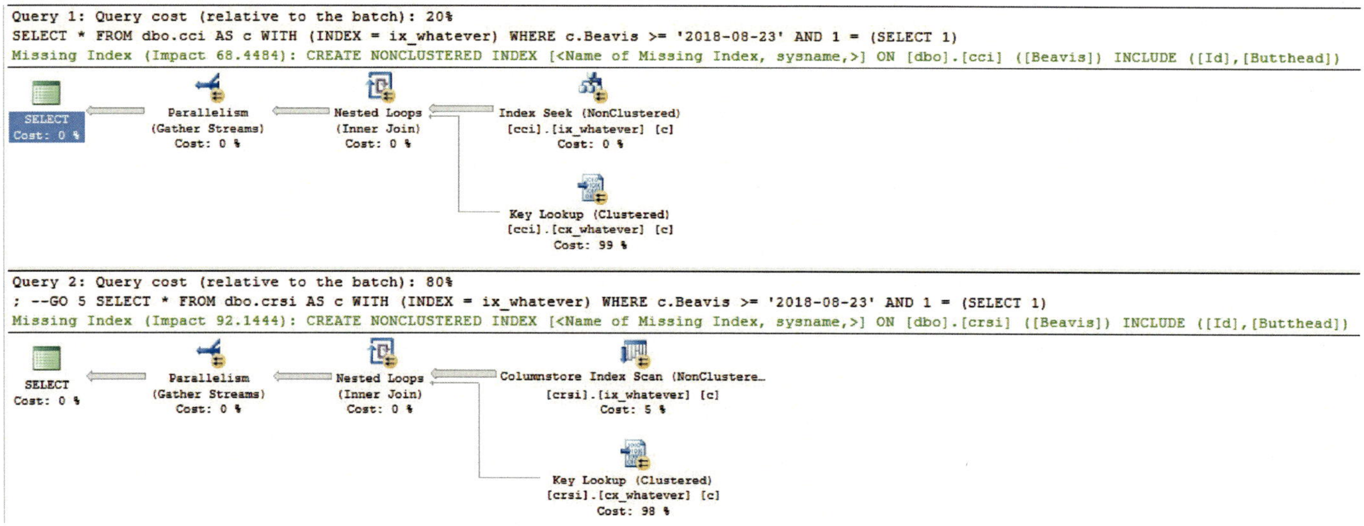

Where the wood at?

Looking at screencaps of query plans isn't too fun, is it? I stuck them on PTP for anyone interested.

And for extra credit, let's see what sp_BlitzCache says about our queries.

```
EXEC master.dbo.sp_BlitzCache @IgnoreSystemDBs = 0, @DatabaseName = 'tempdb'
```

Database	Cost	Query Text	Query Type	Warnings
tempdb	25.3987	SELECT * FROM dbo.cci AS c WITH (INDEX = ix_whatever) WHERE c.Beavis >= '2018-08-23' AND 1 = (SELECT 1)	Statement	Missing Indexes (1), Parallel, Expensive Key Lookup, Plan created last 4hrs, Forced Indexes, ColumnStore Row Mode
tempdb	102.428	SELECT * FROM dbo.crsi AS c WITH (INDEX = ix_whatever) WHERE c.Beavis >= '2018-08-23' AND 1 = (SELECT 1)	Statement	Missing Indexes (1), Parallel, Expensive Key Lookup, Unused Memory Grant, Plan created last 4hrs, Forced Indexes

Shortwide

Spellwork

It's nice when you don't have to do any work to find problems. That's why I do all the work I do on sp_BlitzCache and sp_BlitzQueryStore. I want to make your life better and easier. Let's look at some of the warnings we have for each query:

- Clustered ColumnStore: Missing Indexes (1), Parallel, Expensive Key Lookup, Plan created last 4hrs, Forced Indexes, ColumnStore Row Mode
- Clustered Row Store: Missing Indexes (1), Parallel, Expensive Key Lookup, Unused Memory Grant, Plan created last 4hrs, Forced Indexes

Without opening a plan or looking at a single tool tip or hitting f4, we know some things:

- SQL is angry about missing indexes

- We have expensive key lookups
- We're forcing indexes
- We have a ColumnStore query operating in row mode instead of Batch mode
- We have an unused memory grant
- Both plans are relatively new in the cache (duh)

But focusing on the point of the post, which we should probably do, something kind of obvious happens.

The query that uses the nonclustered ColumnStore index does a typical Key Lookup. It's able to (1) scan the ColumnStore index in Batch mode, (2) pass those rows to a Nested Loops join, and then (3) 'join' the nonclustered index to the clustered index on the clustered index key column.

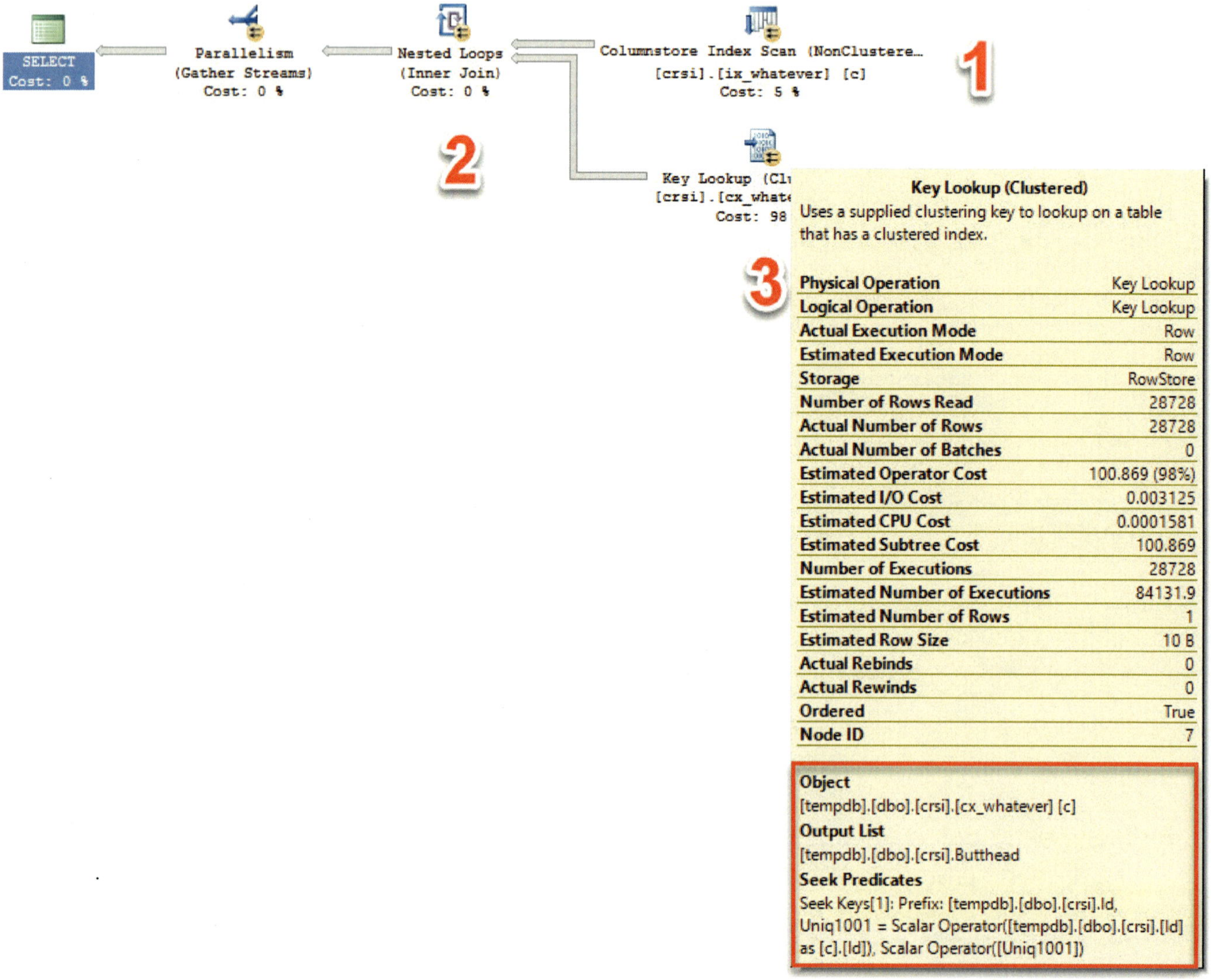

1, 2, 3, and to the 4

For the links, code, and comments, go here:
https://www.brentozar.com/archive/2017/09/key-lookups-columnstore-indexes/

But clustered ColumnStore indexes don't have key columns.

Let's look at what happens there!

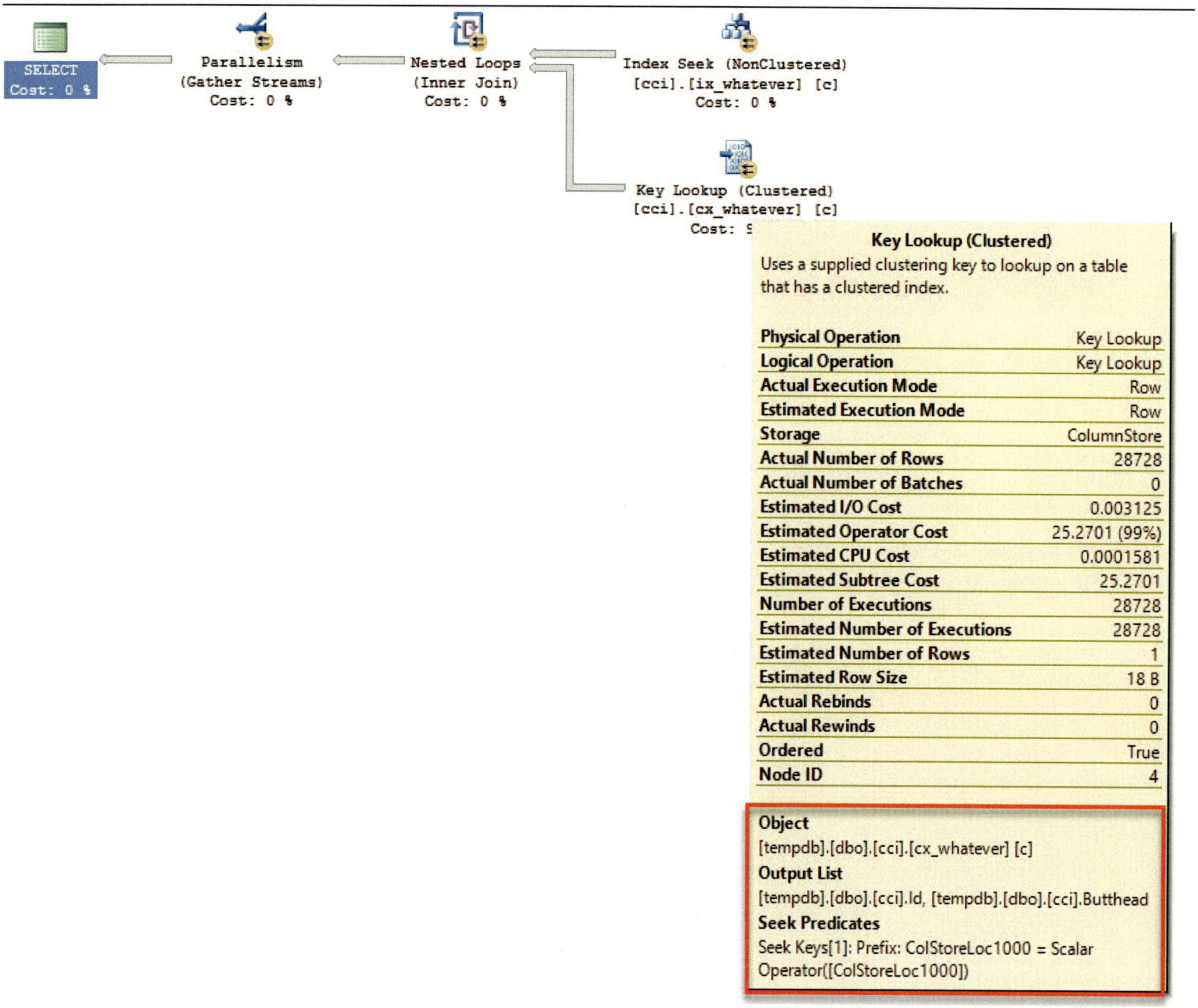

Loc Out

I'm going to assume that this is a bit like a RID Lookup in a plan using HEAPs. Without a clustered index key column, we need to rely on internal metadata to locate rows. That's what the Seek Keys[1]: Prefix: ColStoreLoc1000 = Scalar Operator([ColStoreLoc1000]) part of the Key Lookup is doing. Interesting!

Fun yet?

This isn't a knock against clustered ColumnStore indexes. The team behind them has done awesome work to make them more usable and less painful (remember back when they didn't work with Availability Group secondaries? Of course you don't!). I wrote this because I've gotten increasingly interested in ColumnStore as it becomes more powerful, and as more people start hopping on newer versions of SQL Server where they're a viable path to fixing real problems.

Thanks for reading!

ColumnStore Indexes: Rowgroup Elimination and Parameter Sniffing In Stored Procedures

Yazoo

Over on his blog, fellow Query Plan aficionado Joe Obbish has a Great Post, Brent® about query patterns that qualify for Rowgroup Elimination. This is really important to performance! It allows scans to skip over stuff it doesn't need, like skipping over the dialog in, uh... movies with really good fight scenes.

Car chases?

Soundtracks?

Soundtracks.

Fad Gadget

With Joe's permission (we're a polite people, here) I decided to pick on one of the queries that was eligible for Rowgroup Elimination and stick it in a stored procedure to see what would happen. I'm interested in a couple things.

1. Is Rowgroup Elimination considered safe with variables?
2. Will the plan change if different numbers of Rowgroups are skipped?

With those in mind, let's create a proc to test those out. Head on over to Joe's post if you want the setup scripts.

```sql
DROP PROCEDURE IF EXISTS #wonky_eye;
GO

CREATE PROCEDURE #wonky_eye
(
    @idlow BIGINT,
    @idhigh BIGINT
)
AS
    BEGIN

        SELECT  MAX(ID)
        FROM    dbo.MILLIONAIRE_CCI
        WHERE   ID BETWEEN @idlow AND @idhigh;

    END;
GO
```

With literal values, the optimizer/storage engine/unicorn toenails behind the scenes are able to figure out which Rowgroups are needed to satisfy our query.

With stored procedures, though, the first execution will cache a particular plan, and the rest of the queries will reuse that plan.

Let's test our first hypothesis! Will different passed in values result in appropriate Rowgroup Elimination?

```sql
EXEC dbo.#wonky_eye @idlow = 1, @idhigh = 1000
EXEC dbo.#wonky_eye @idlow = 1, @idhigh = 10000
EXEC dbo.#wonky_eye @idlow = 1, @idhigh = 100000
EXEC dbo.#wonky_eye @idlow = 1, @idhigh = 1000000
EXEC dbo.#wonky_eye @idlow = 1, @idhigh = 10000000
EXEC dbo.#wonky_eye @idlow = 1, @idhigh = 100000000
```

All of those queries use the exact same execution plan:

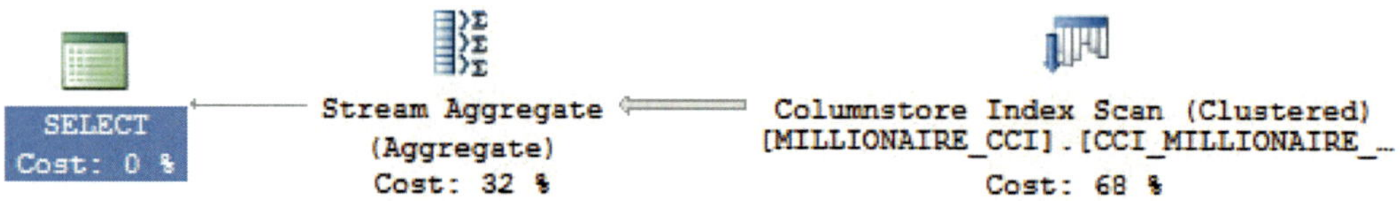

Cache Me Outside

But do they all use it as efficiently?

Well, in short, no.

Things start off okay, and to be fair, Rowgroup Elimination occurs as appropriate.

```
Table 'MILLIONAIRE_CCI'. Segment reads 1, segment skipped 99.

Table 'MILLIONAIRE_CCI'. Segment reads 1, segment skipped 99.

Table 'MILLIONAIRE_CCI'. Segment reads 1, segment skipped 99.

Table 'MILLIONAIRE_CCI'. Segment reads 1, segment skipped 99.

Table 'MILLIONAIRE_CCI'. Segment reads 10, segment skipped 90.
```

But once our high ID hits 10000000, things start to slow down.

```
SQL Server Execution Times:
  CPU time = 0 ms,  elapsed time = 0 ms.

SQL Server Execution Times:
  CPU time = 0 ms,  elapsed time = 1 ms.

SQL Server Execution Times:
  CPU time = 0 ms,  elapsed time = 5 ms.

SQL Server Execution Times:
  CPU time = 47 ms,  elapsed time = 50 ms.

SQL Server Execution Times:
  CPU time = 500 ms,  elapsed time = 492 ms.
```

And by the time we hit ID 100000000, things have melted into a fondue almost no one would want.

```
Table 'MILLIONAIRE_CCI'. Segment reads 100, segment skipped 0.

 SQL Server Execution Times:
   CPU time = 5110 ms,  elapsed time = 5095 ms.
```

Five seconds! Five! Who has that kind of time on their hands?

The performance cliff can be further exposed by incrementing IDs between 10000000 and 100000000.

While Rowgroup Elimination occurs just like before, CPU keeps on going up.

```
Transact-SQL
EXEC dbo.#wonky_eye @idlow = 1, @idhigh = 20000000
EXEC dbo.#wonky_eye @idlow = 1, @idhigh = 30000000
EXEC dbo.#wonky_eye @idlow = 1, @idhigh = 40000000
EXEC dbo.#wonky_eye @idlow = 1, @idhigh = 50000000
EXEC dbo.#wonky_eye @idlow = 1, @idhigh = 60000000
EXEC dbo.#wonky_eye @idlow = 1, @idhigh = 70000000
EXEC dbo.#wonky_eye @idlow = 1, @idhigh = 80000000
EXEC dbo.#wonky_eye @idlow = 1, @idhigh = 90000000
```

It looks like we found a potential tipping point where a different plan would be more effective.

```
Transact-SQL
SQL Server Execution Times:
  CPU time = 1000 ms,  elapsed time = 995 ms.

SQL Server Execution Times:
  CPU time = 1469 ms,  elapsed time = 1463 ms.

SQL Server Execution Times:
  CPU time = 1953 ms,  elapsed time = 1951 ms.

SQL Server Execution Times:
  CPU time = 2437 ms,  elapsed time = 2440 ms.

SQL Server Execution Times:
  CPU time = 2922 ms,  elapsed time = 2926 ms.

SQL Server Execution Times:
  CPU time = 3422 ms,  elapsed time = 3414 ms.

SQL Server Execution Times:
  CPU time = 3906 ms,  elapsed time = 3916 ms.

SQL Server Execution Times:
  CPU time = 4391 ms,  elapsed time = 4392 ms.
```

State of Confusion

So where are we? Well, we found that Rowgroup Elimination is possible in stored procedures with ColumnStore indexes, but that the cached plan doesn't change based on feedback from that elimination.

- Good news: elimination can occur with variables passed in.
- Bad news: that cached plan sticks with you like belly fat at a desk job

Remember our plan? It used a Stream Aggregate to process the MAX. Stream Aggregates are preferred for small, and/or ordered sets.

How do we know this is the wrong plan, here? How can we test it?

If we run the stored proc once the regular way, and once with a RECOMPILE hint, well...

```
EXEC dbo.#wonky_eye @idlow = 1, @idhigh = 100000000
EXEC dbo.#wonky_eye @idlow = 1, @idhigh = 100000000 WITH RECOMPILE
```

The query plans decide to be cheeky and have similar costs. You'll notice that the Hash Match plan is 51% of the cost, and the Stream Aggregate plan is 49%. The relative difference is tiny, though. The Stream Aggregate plan costs 27.8431 query bucks, and the Hash Match plan costs 28.8442 query bucks. That's a difference of 1.0011 query bucks, which is exactly the cost difference between the Stream Aggregate operator, and the Hash Match operator.

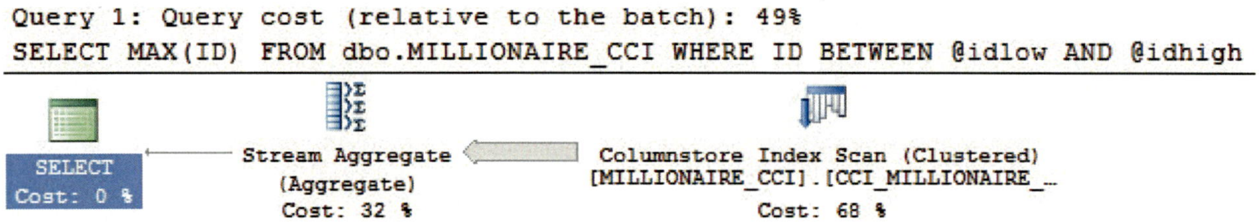

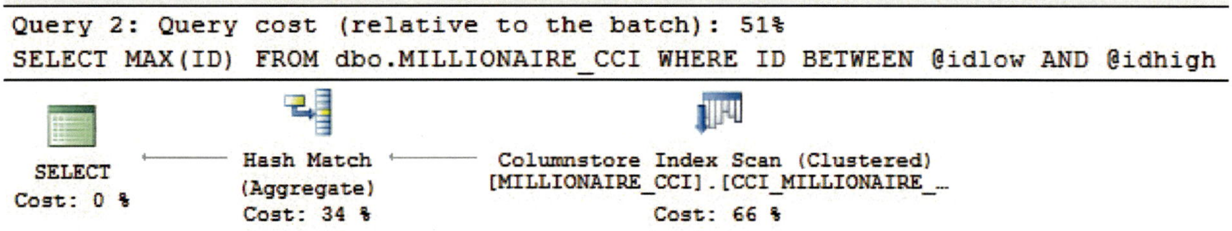

No Cache No Care

But in this case, cost is one of those awful, lying metrics. Let's look at the different execution times.

```
SQL Server Execution Times:
  CPU time = 4969 ms,  elapsed time = 4957 ms.

SQL Server Execution Times:
  CPU time = 47 ms,  elapsed time = 49 ms.
```

The plan with the RECOMPILE hint finished in 49ms. That's, like, 1000x faster. The difference of course is the Hash Match Aggregate operator replacing the Stream Aggregate operator.

So what happens if we run things in reverse order after freeing the cache?

```
EXEC dbo.#wonky_eye @idlow = 1, @idhigh = 100000000

EXEC dbo.#wonky_eye @idlow = 1, @idhigh = 1000
```

It turns out that the Hash Match Aggregate plan is just as good for the 'small' query. It has the same metrics that it did when using the Stream Aggregate plan when it ran first. In this case, there are no other differences to account for, like Key Lookups, or Parallelism.

Happy Mondays

We've come this far, so let's answer one last question: At which point will ol' crazypants choose the Hash Match plan over the Stream Aggregate plan? To answer that, we'll go back to our original test scheme, and add in recompiles so each execution gets a fresh plan.

```
EXEC dbo.#wonky_eye @idlow = 1, @idhigh = 1000 WITH RECOMPILE
EXEC dbo.#wonky_eye @idlow = 1, @idhigh = 10000 WITH RECOMPILE
EXEC dbo.#wonky_eye @idlow = 1, @idhigh = 100000 WITH RECOMPILE
EXEC dbo.#wonky_eye @idlow = 1, @idhigh = 1000000 WITH RECOMPILE
EXEC dbo.#wonky_eye @idlow = 1, @idhigh = 10000000 WITH RECOMPILE
EXEC dbo.#wonky_eye @idlow = 1, @idhigh = 100000000 WITH RECOMPILE
```

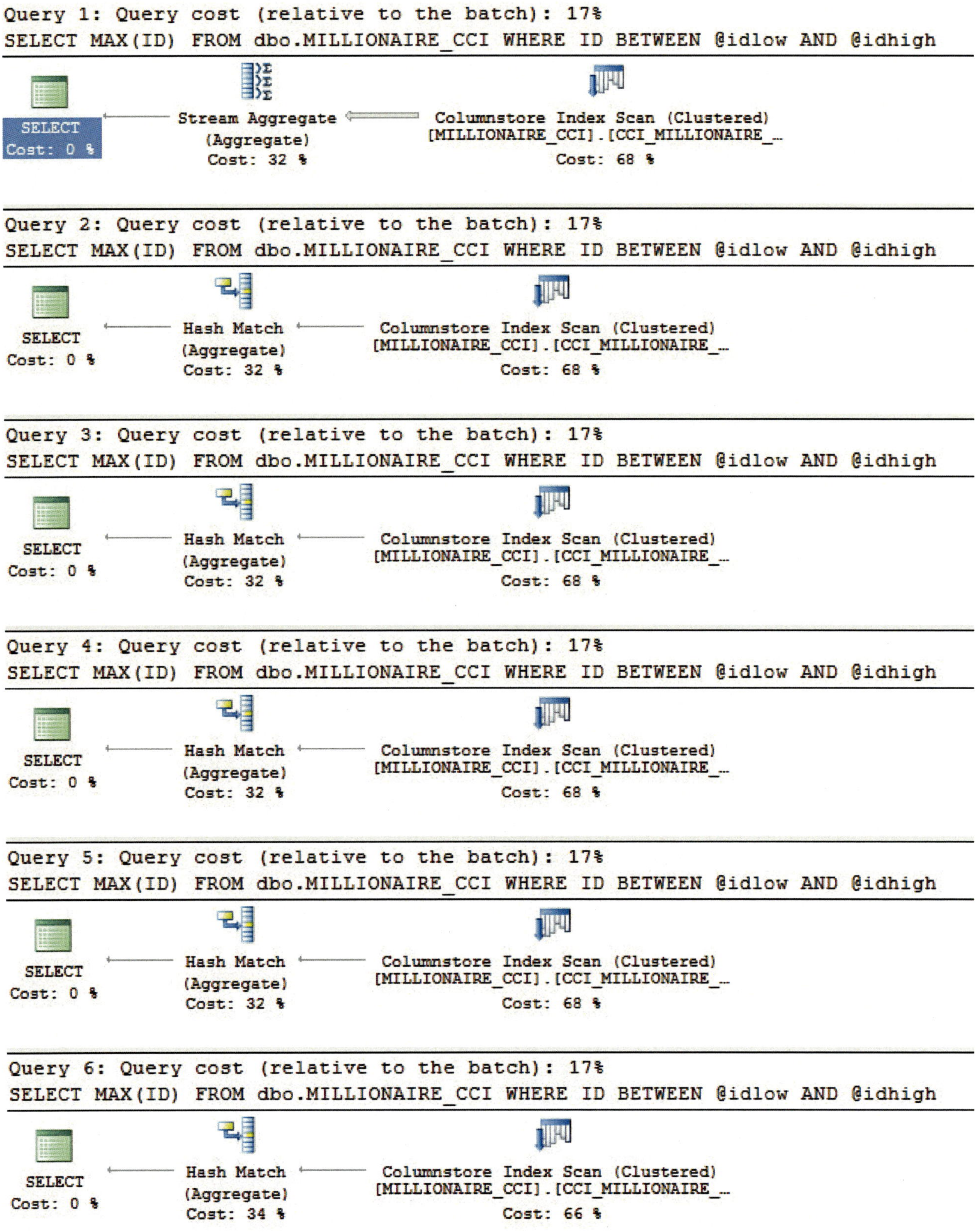

Limited Values Of Helpful

The answer is, unfortunately, pretty early on. The second query chooses the Hash Match plan, which means that, well, almost every single execution would have been better off with a different set of values passed in first, and the Hash Match plan chosen. Hmpf.

Human League

What did we learn, after all these words? Rowgroup Elimination is possible in stored procedures, but it doesn't provide any feedback to plan choice. No matter how many were eliminated or not, the plan remained the same. As eliminations decreased, performance got worse using the 'small' plan. This is textbook parameter sniffing, but with a twist.

I also tested this stuff on 2017, and there was no Adaptive magic that I could find.

Thanks for reading!

Partitioned Views

This chapter is about keeping data neat and tidy,
to keep our queries neat and tidy.
Reading this will pair well with Clase Azul,
or a martini so dry your tongue gets confused.

BRENT OZAR
UNLIMITED®

Partitioned Views: A How-To Guide

This is not about table partitioning

If you want to learn about that, there's a whole great list of links here, and the Best Blogger Alive has a tremendous post on why table partitioning won't make your queries any faster over here.

With that out of the way, let's talk about partitioned views, and then create one from a real live table in the StackOverflow database.

What is a partitioned view?

It's a view that combines the full results of a number of physical tables that are logically separated by a boundary. You can think of the boundary the same way you'd think of a partitioning key. That's right about where the similarities between table partitioning and partitioned views end.

For example, you have Table1, Table2, and Table3. All three tables are vertically compatible. Your view would look something like this.

```sql
CREATE VIEW dbo.Doodad
AS
SELECT columns...
FROM Table1
UNION ALL
SELECT columns...
FROM Table2
UNION ALL
SELECT columns...
FROM Table3

SELECT * FROM dbo.Doodad
```

Hooray. Now you have to type less.

Partitioned views don't need a scheme or a function, there's no fancy syntax to swap data in or out, and there's far less complexity in figuring out RIGHT vs LEFT boundaries, and leaving empty partitions, etc. and so forth. You're welcome.

A lot gets made out of partition level statistics and maintenance being available to table partitioning. That stuff is pretty much automatic for partitioned views, because you have no choice. It's separate tables all the way down.

How else are they different?

Each table in a partitioned view is its own little (or large) data island. Unlike partitioning, where the partitions all come together to form a logical unit. For example, if you run ALTER TABLE on a partitioned table, you alter the entire table. If you add an index to a partitioned table, it's on the entire table. In some cases, you can target a specific partition, but not all. For instance, if you wanted to apply different compression types on different partitions for some reason, you can do that.

With partitioned views, you add some flexibility in not needing to align all your indexes to the partitioning key, or alter all your partitions at once, but you also add some administrative overhead in making sure that you iterate over all of the tables taking part in your partitioned view. The underlying tables can also all have their own identity columns, if you're into that sort of thing. If you're not, you should use a Sequence here, assuming you're on 2012 or later.

Are partitioned views better?

Yes and no! The nice thing about partitioned views is that they're available in Standard Edition. You can create tables on different files and filegroups (just like with partitioning), and if you need to change the data your view covers, it's a matter of altering the view that glues all your results together.

Tables can have different columns (as long as you account for them in your view definition), which isn't true for partitioning, and you can compress or index different indexes on different partitions differently depending on the workload that hits them. Think about reporting queries that want to touch your historical data. Again, not 'aligning' all your nonclustered indexes to the partitioned view boundary doesn't necessarily hurt you here.

They do share a similar problem to regular partitioning, in that they don't necessarily make your queries better unless your predicates include the partitioning key. Sad face. It is fairly easy to get partition elimination with the correct check constraints, as long as you include a partition eliminating element in your query predicates. If your workload doesn't reliably filter on something like that, neither form of partitioning is going to help your queries go faster.

One problem I've found particularly challenging with partitioned views is getting the min/max/ average per partition the way you would with normal partitioning. There are a couple good articles about that here and here, but they don't really help with partitioned views. If anyone out there knows any tricks, leave a comment ;^}

Modifications can be tricky, too. Bulk loads will have to be directed to the tables, not the view itself. Deletes and updates may hit all the underlying tables if you're not careful with your query predicates.

Ending on a high note, the view name can obfuscate sensitive table names from them there hackers.

From the comments!

Geoff Patterson has a Connect Item about pushing Bitmap Filters through Concatenation Operators, which would be really powerful for Partitioned Views.

If this kind of thing would suit your needs, give it an upvote over here.

Enough already, what's it look like?

Download the script below. It assumes that you have a copy of the StackOverflow database with the Votes table, and that you're not a StackOverflow employee running this on the production box. Things might get weird for you.

Partitioned_View_Votes

Assuming everything runs correctly, in about a minute you should have a series of tables called Votes_20XX. How many you end up with depends on which copy of the database you have. Mine has data through 2016, so i have Votes_2008 – Votes_2016.

Each table has a PK/CX on the Id column, a constraint for the year of dates in the table on the CreationDate column, and a nonclustered index to help out some of our tester queries. You can just hit f5, and the RETURN will stop before running any of the example queries.

You should see something like this when it's done. Yay validation.

table_name	index_name	rows	index_size_mb
Votes_2008	PK_ID_2008	927932	33.38
Votes_2008	ix_Votes_2008	927932	23.45
Votes_2009	PK_ID_2009	3689979	132.52
Votes_2009	ix_Votes_2009	3689979	93.01
Votes_2010	PK_ID_2010	5536184	198.80
Votes_2010	ix_Votes_2010	5536184	139.51
Votes_2011	PK_ID_2011	9363649	336.20
Votes_2011	ix_Votes_2011	9363649	235.91
Votes_2012	PK_ID_2012	14438874	518.36
Votes_2012	ix_Votes_2012	14438874	363.73
Votes_2013	PK_ID_2013	19095319	685.49
Votes_2013	ix_Votes_2013	19095319	481.01
Votes_2014	PK_ID_2014	19514050	700.53
Votes_2014	ix_Votes_2014	19514050	491.56
Votes_2015	PK_ID_2015	22012531	790.22
Votes_2015	ix_Votes_2015	22012531	554.48
Votes_2016	PK_ID_2016	4350414	156.23
Votes_2016	ix_Votes_2016	4350414	109.66

Rows and Sizes. Important stuff.

How does query work?

It's pretty easy to see what I was talking about before. If you're not looking at CreationDate in the WHERE clause, you end up touching a lot of tables. When you use it, though, SQL is really smart about which tables it hits.

```
SELECT COUNT_BIG(*)
FROM dbo.AllVotes AS av
WHERE av.CreationDate = '2008-11-04'
```

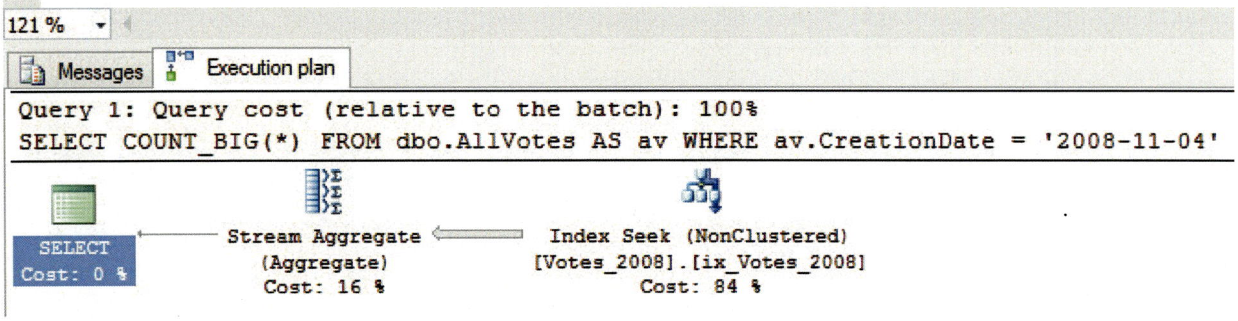

Avoidance

Ranges work pretty well too.

```
SELECT COUNT_BIG(*)
FROM dbo.AllVotes AS av
WHERE av.CreationDate >= '2008-11-04'
AND av.CreationDate <= '2009-11-04'
```

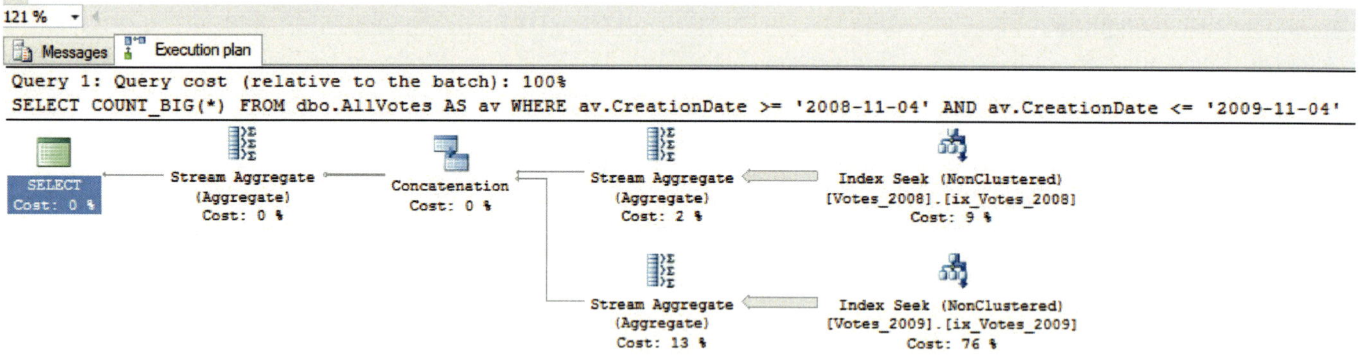

Good for you, man.

Even when they're broken up!

```
SELECT COUNT_BIG(*)
FROM dbo.AllVotes AS av
WHERE av.CreationDate >= '2008-11-04'
AND av.CreationDate <= '2009-11-04'
OR av.CreationDate >= '2016-01-01'
```

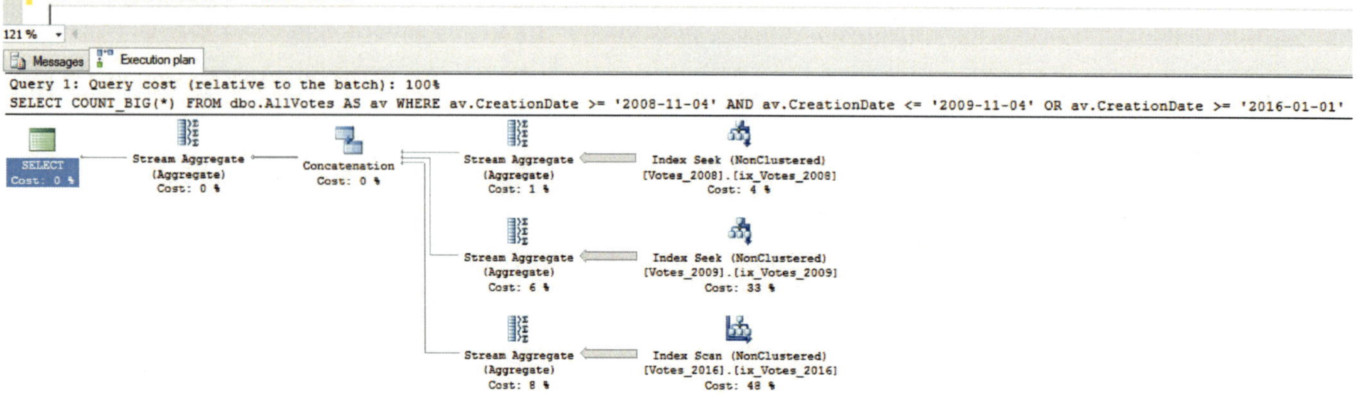

OR OR OR

For the links, code, and comments, go here:
https://www.brentozar.com/archive/2016/09/partitioned-views-guide/

But if you don't specify a date, you run into trouble.

```
SELECT COUNT_BIG(*)
FROM dbo.AllVotes AS av
WHERE av.UserId = 22656
```

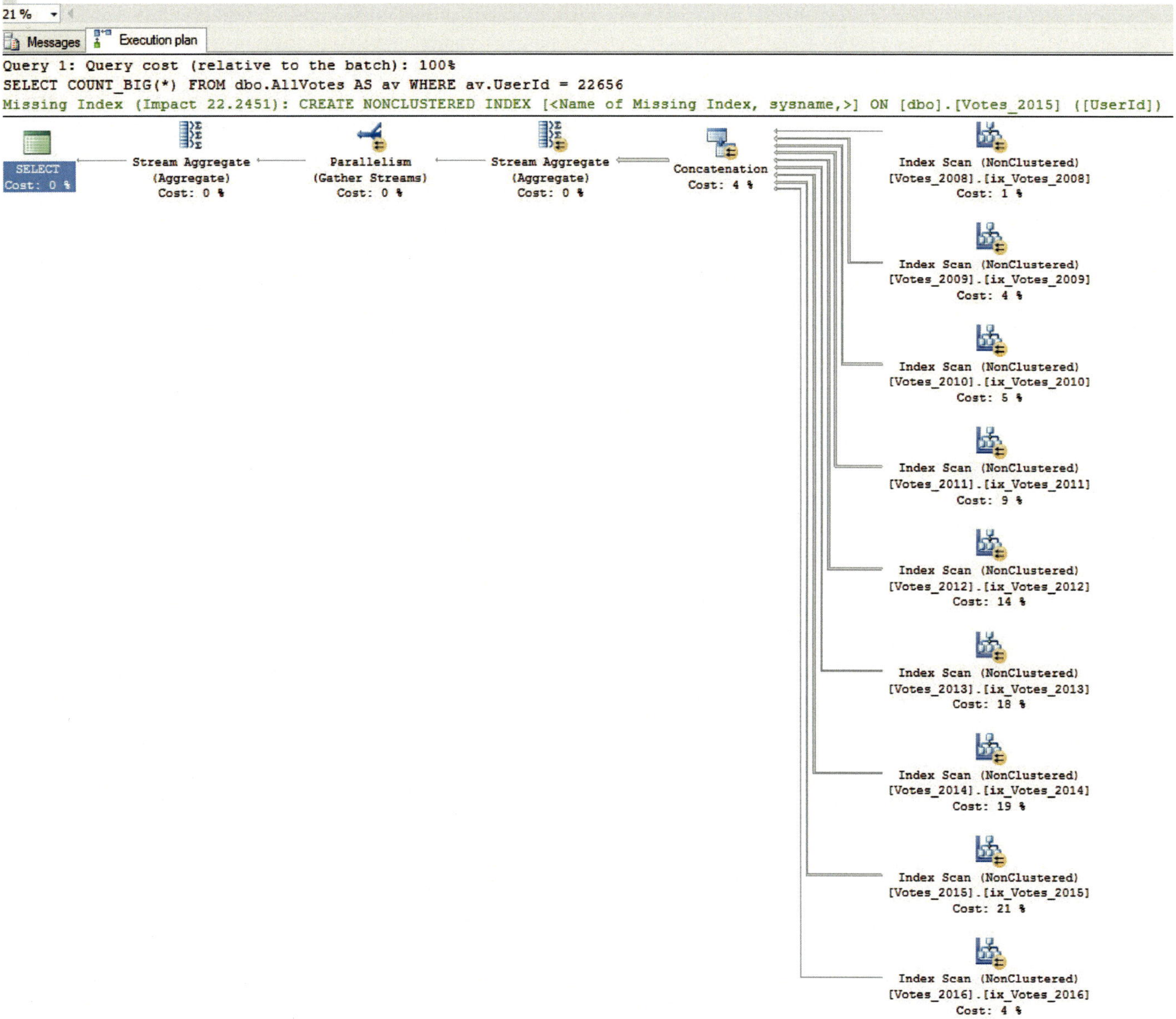

Scan every index

You'd think this would go better, but it doesn't. I mean, the MAX date would have to come from the... oh, forget it.

```
SELECT MAX(av.CreationDate)
FROM dbo.AllVotes AS av
```

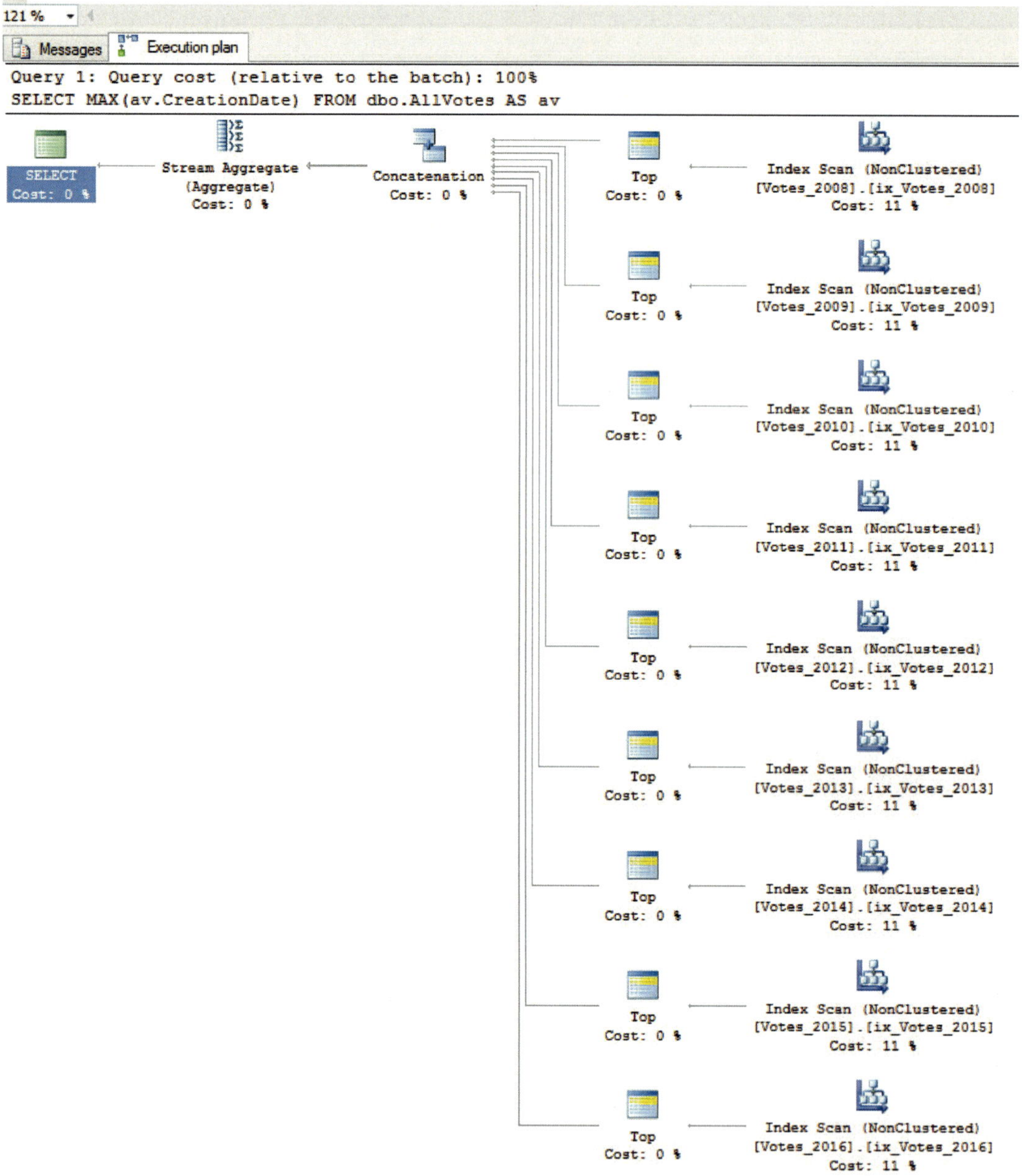

Kinda dumb.

That's all, y'all

I hope you enjoyed this, and that it helps some of you out. If you're looking to implement partitioned views, feel free to edit my script to work on your table(s). Just make sure it's on a dev server where you can test out your workload to make sure everything is compatible.

For the links, code, and comments, go here:
https://www.brentozar.com/archive/2016/09/partitioned-views-guide/

Partitioned Views, Aggregates, and Cool Query Plans

The Max for the Minimum

Paul White (obviously of course as always) has a Great Post, Brent® about Aggregates on partitioned tables.

Well, I'm not that smart or good looking, so I'll have to settle for a So-So Post about this.

There are actually quite a few similarities between the way a partitioned table and a partitioned view handle these things.

Building on previous examples with the Votes table converted into a partitioned view, let's try a couple queries out.

Selecting the global min and max give me this query plan.

```
SELECT MIN(v.CreationDate), MAX(v.CreationDate)
FROM   dbo.AllVotes AS v;
```

And I know, it looks big and mean. Because it kind of is.

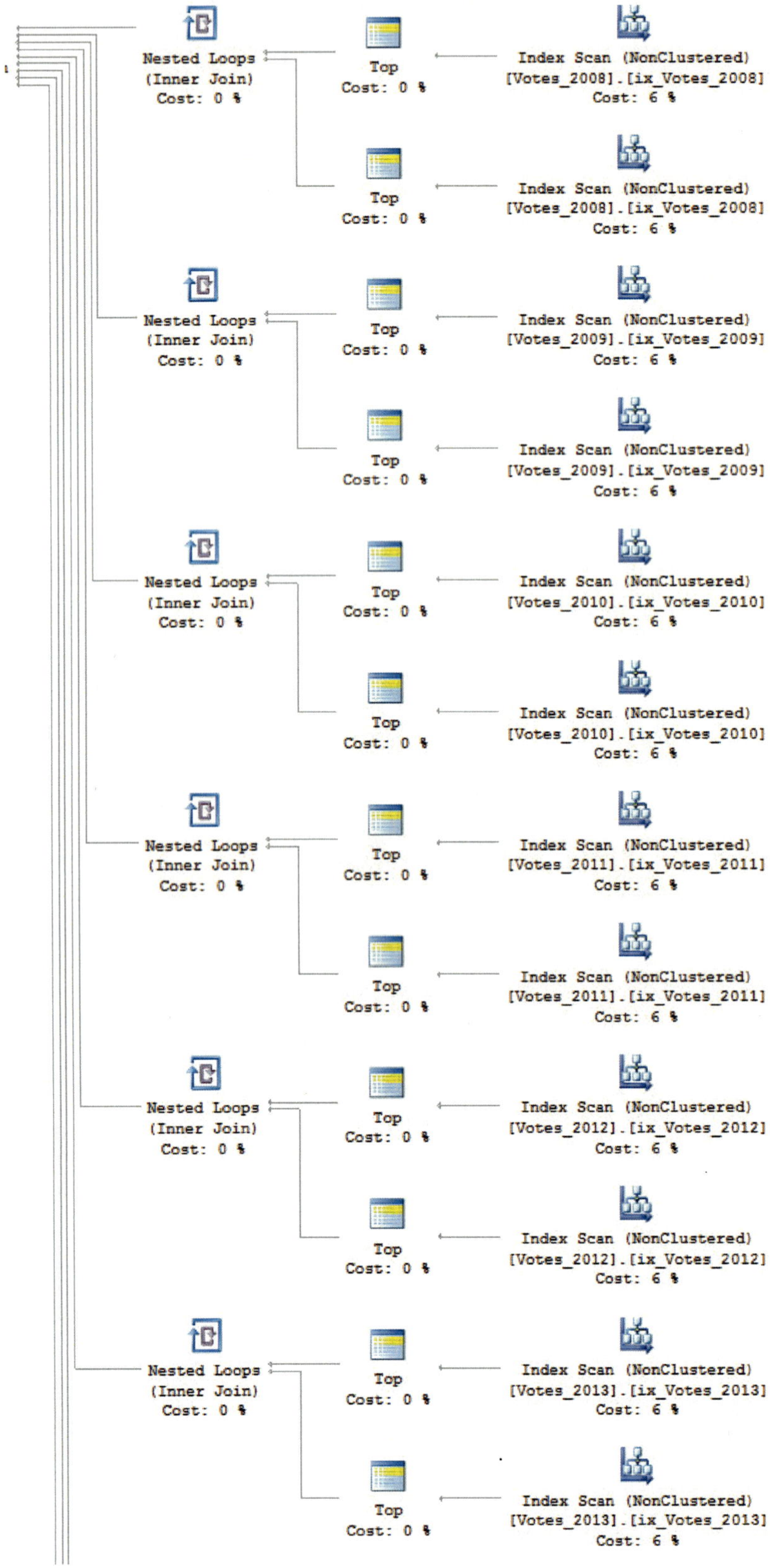

It keeps going, too.

BUT LOOK HOW LITTLE WORK IT DOES!

```
Table 'Votes_2016'. Scan count 2, logical reads 6,
Table 'Votes_2015'. Scan count 2, logical reads 6,
Table 'Votes_2014'. Scan count 2, logical reads 6,
Table 'Votes_2013'. Scan count 2, logical reads 6,
Table 'Votes_2012'. Scan count 2, logical reads 6,
Table 'Votes_2011'. Scan count 2, logical reads 6,
Table 'Votes_2010'. Scan count 2, logical reads 6,
Table 'Votes_2009'. Scan count 2, logical reads 6,
Table 'Votes_2008'. Scan count 2, logical reads 4,

 SQL Server Execution Times:
   CPU time = 0 ms,  elapsed time = 1 ms.
```

wtf I hate millennials now

Just like in Paul's post that I linked to above, each one of the top operators is a TOP 1.

For the Min, you get a forward scan, and for the Max you get a backwards scan.

That happens once per table in the partitioned view.

Easier to visualize

If we focus on a single table, it's easier to parse out.

```
SELECT MIN(v.CreationDate), MAX(v.CreationDate)
FROM   dbo.AllVotes AS v
WHERE  v.CreationDate >= '20140101'
       AND v.CreationDate < '20150101'
       AND 1 = ( SELECT 1 );
```

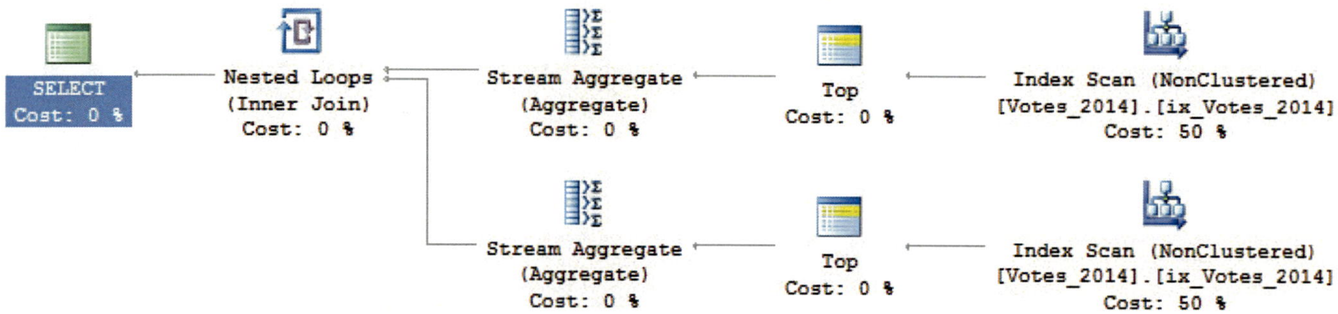

Simpleton

A lot of people may complain that there are two index accesses here, but since SQL Server doesn't have anything quite like a Skip Scan where it could hit one of the index and then jump to the other end without reading everything in between, this is much more efficient.

Thanks for reading!

Brent says: *remember, a scan doesn't mean SQL Server read the whole table, and a seek doesn't mean it only read a few rows. It's so hard to tell this stuff at a glance in execution plans, especially in estimated plans.*

Implied Predicate and Partition Elimination

>implying

Way back when, I posted about turning the Votes table in the Stack Overflow database into a Partitioned View.

While working on related demos recently, I came across something kind of cool. It works for both partitioned tables and views, assuming you've done some things right.

In this example, both versions of the table are partitioned in one year chunks on the CreationDate column.

That means when I run queries like this, neither one is eligible for partition elimination.

Why? Because the CreationDate column in the Posts table could have any range of dates at all in it, so we need to query every partition for matches.

```
SELECT COUNT(*) AS records
FROM   dbo.Votes AS v
JOIN   dbo.Posts AS p
ON p.Id = v.PostId
   AND p.CreationDate = v.CreationDate;


SELECT COUNT(*) AS records
FROM   dbo.AllVotes AS v
JOIN   dbo.Posts AS p
ON p.Id = v.PostId
   AND p.CreationDate = v.CreationDate;
```

How do we know that? Well, for the partitioned table, because all 12 partitions were scanned.

Clustered Index Scan (Clustered)

Scanning a clustered index, entirely or only a range.

Physical Operation	Clustered Index Scan
Logical Operation	Clustered Index Scan
Actual Execution Mode	Row
Estimated Execution Mode	Row
Storage	RowStore
Number of Rows Read	1496080
Actual Number of Rows	11524
Actual Number of Batches	0
Estimated I/O Cost	10.759
Estimated Operator Cost	11.3395 (49%)
Estimated Subtree Cost	11.3395
Estimated CPU Cost	0.580525
Estimated Number of Executions	1
Number of Executions	6
Estimated Number of Rows	3156940
Estimated Number of Rows to be Read	3156940
Estimated Row Size	19 B
Actual Rebinds	0
Actual Rewinds	0
Partitioned	True
Actual Partition Count	12
Ordered	False
Node ID	10

Predicate

PROBE([Bitmap1006],[SUPERUSER_Partition].[dbo].[Votes].[PostId] as [v].[PostId],[SUPERUSER_Partition].[dbo].[Votes].[CreationDate] as [v].[CreationDate])

Object

[SUPERUSER_Partition].[dbo].[Votes].[PK_Partition_CD_Id] [v]

Output List

[SUPERUSER_Partition].[dbo].[Votes].PostId,
[SUPERUSER_Partition].[dbo].[Votes].CreationDate

12! 12 years! Kinda.

For the partitioned view, well...

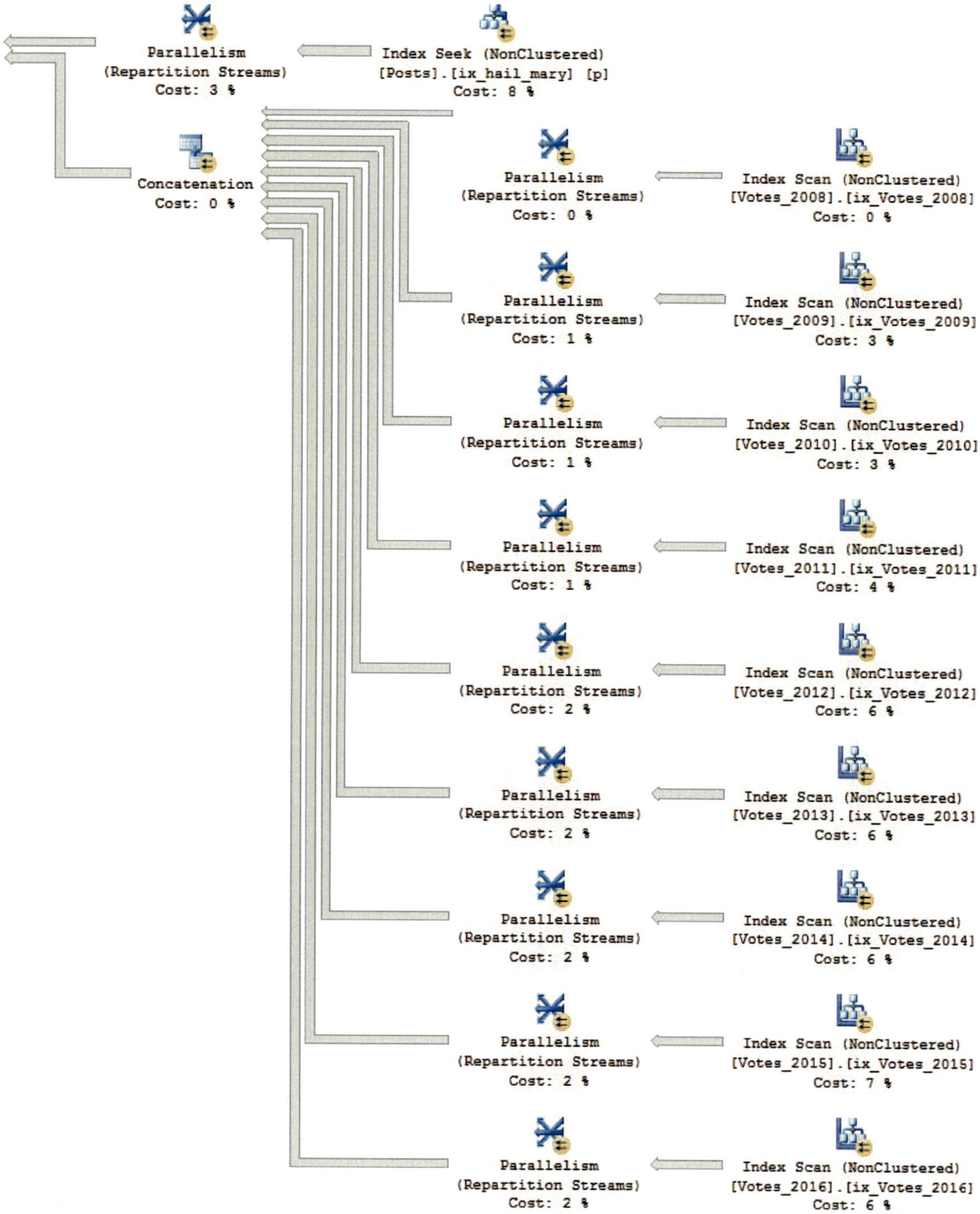

That's not cool.

I think it's obvious what's gone on here.

Eliminationist

Are you ready for the cool part?

If I add a predicate to the JOIN (or WHERE clause) for the Posts table (remember that the Votes table is partitioned, and the Posts table isn't), SQL Server is so smart, it can use that to trim the range of partitions that both queries need to access.

Transact-SQL

```
SELECT COUNT(*) AS records
FROM   dbo.Votes AS v
JOIN   dbo.Posts AS p
ON p.Id = v.PostId
    AND p.CreationDate = v.CreationDate
    AND p.CreationDate >= '20140101';


SELECT COUNT(*) AS records
FROM   dbo.AllVotes AS v
JOIN   dbo.Posts AS p
ON p.Id = v.PostId
    AND p.CreationDate = v.CreationDate
    AND p.CreationDate >= '20140101';
```

The partitioned table plan eliminates 8 partitions, and the seek predicate is converted to the Votes table.

Clustered Index Seek (Clustered)

Scanning a particular range of rows from a clustered index.

Physical Operation	Clustered Index Seek
Logical Operation	Clustered Index Seek
Actual Execution Mode	Row
Estimated Execution Mode	Row
Storage	RowStore
Number of Rows Read	1473201
Actual Number of Rows	1473201
Actual Number of Batches	0
Estimated Operator Cost	6.7281 (27%)
Estimated I/O Cost	5.08509
Estimated Subtree Cost	6.7281
Estimated CPU Cost	1.64301
Estimated Number of Executions	1
Number of Executions	1
Estimated Number of Rows	1493070
Estimated Number of Rows to be Read	1493070
Estimated Row Size	19 B
Actual Rebinds	0
Actual Rewinds	0
Partitioned	True
Actual Partition Count	4
Ordered	True
Node ID	4

Object

[SUPERUSER_Partition].[dbo].[Votes].[PK_Partition_CD_Id] [v]

Output List

[SUPERUSER_Partition].[dbo].[Votes].PostId,
[SUPERUSER_Partition].[dbo].[Votes].CreationDate

Seek Predicates

Seek Keys[1]: Start: PtnId1000 >= Scalar Operator((9)), End: PtnId1000 <= Scalar Operator((12)), Seek Keys[2]: Start: [SUPERUSER_Partition].[dbo].[Votes].CreationDate >= Scalar Operator('2014-01-01 00:00:00.000')

```
GR8
```

And the partitioned view is also smart enough to pick up on that and only scan the partitions I need.

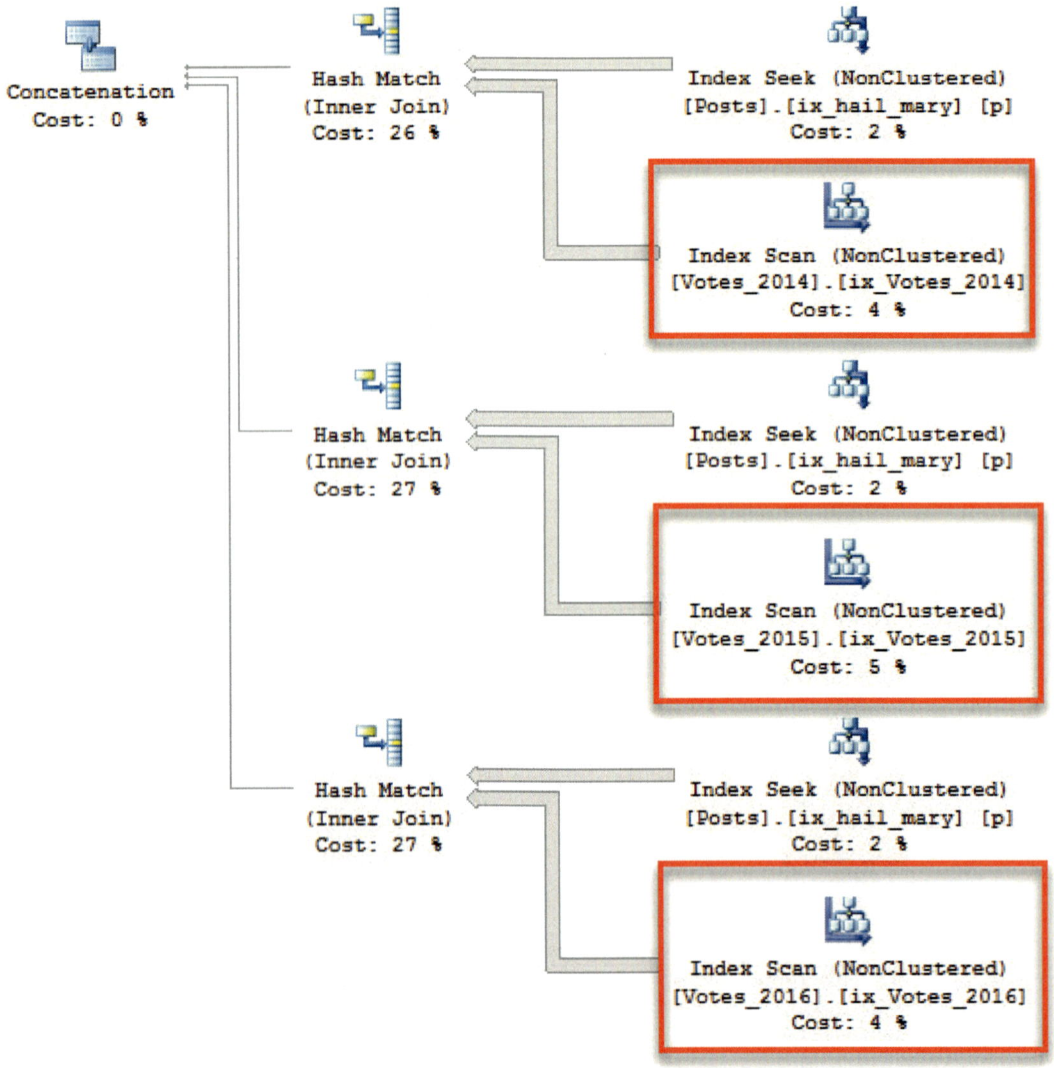

Pants: On

Expected?

Logically, it makes total sense for this to happen. The optimizer is pretty smart, so this works out.

Thanks for reading!

Serialization

This is all about what's slow and horrible. A true peek into the misery and loneliness of things that are forced to run serially. To mimic the suffering of our servers, we're going to mix gin and tequila together in a warm glass.

BRENT OZAR UNLIMITED®

Still Serial After All These Years

With each new version of SQL comes a slew of new stuff

While some changes are cosmetic, others bewildering, and the rest falling somewhere between "who cares about JSON?" and "OH MY GOD TAKE MY MONEY!", but not really my money, because I only buy developer edition. Aaron Bertrand has done a better job finding, and teaching you how to find new features than I could. Head over to his blog if you want to dive in.

What I wanted to look at was something much more near and dear to my heart: Parallelism.

(It's so special I capitalized it.)

In the past, there were a number of things that caused entire plans, or sections of plans, to be serial. Scalar UDFs are probably the first one everyone thinks of. They're bad. Really bad. They're so bad that if you define a computed column with a scalar UDF, every query that hits the table will run serially even if you don't select that column. So, like, don't do that.

What else causes perfectly parallel plan performance plotzing?

Total:

- UDFs (Scalar (but maybe not for long!), MSTVF)
- Modifying table variables

Zone:

- Backwards scan
- Recursive CTE
- TOP
- Aggregate
- Sequence
- System tables
- OUTPUT clause

Other:

- CLR functions (that perform data access)
- Dynamic cursors
- System functions

We'll just look at the items from the first two lists. The stuff in Other is there because I couldn't write a CLR function if I had Adam Machanic telling me what to type, cursors don't need any worse of a reputation, and it would take me a year of Sundays to list every internal function and test it.

I'm going to depart from my normal format a bit, and put all the code at the end. It's really just a mess of boring SELECT statements. The only thing I should say up front is that I'm leaning heavily on the use of an undocumented Trace Flag: 8649. I use it because it 'forces' parallelism by dropping the cost threshold for parallelism to 0 for each query. So if a parallel plan is possible, we'll get one. Or part of one. You get the idea.

Just, you know, don't use it in production unless you really know what you're doing. It's pretty helpful to use as a developer, **on a development server**, to figure out why queries aren't going parallel. Or why they're partially parallel.

All of this was run on 2016 CTP 3.1, so if RTM comes along, and something here is different, that's why. Of course, backwards scans are probably close to 15 years old, so don't sit on your thumbs waiting for them to get parallel support.

Backwards scan!

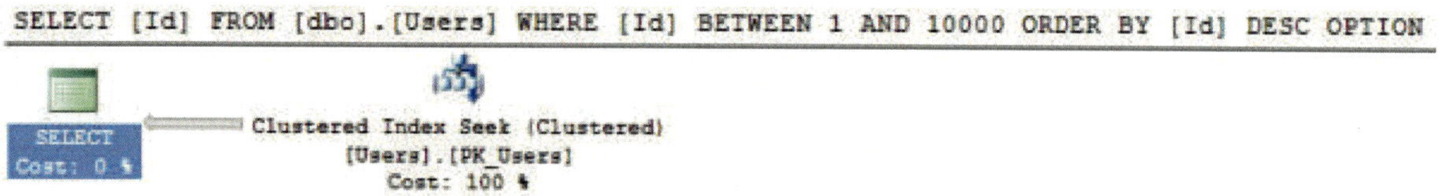

This is what happens when your ORDER BY is the opposite of your index.

Scalar!

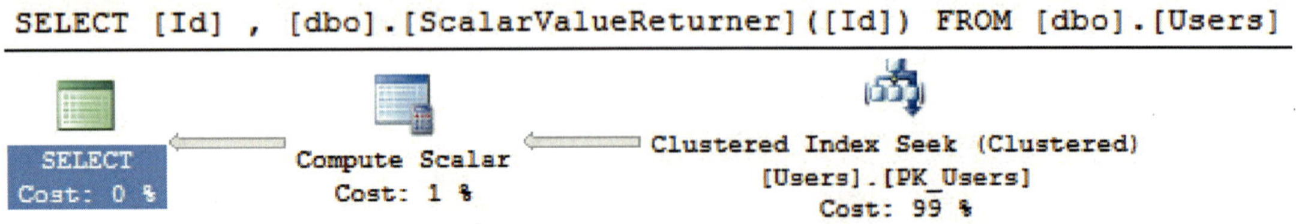

Not only do they run serial, but they run once for every row returned. Have a nice day!

Table with computed column

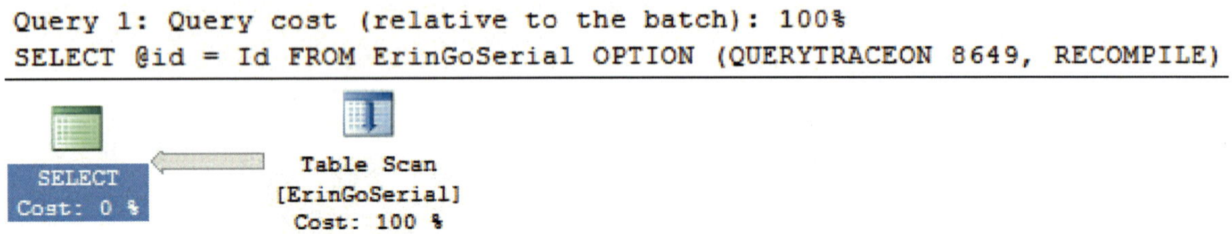

Hint: the Id column isn't the computed one.

MSTVF

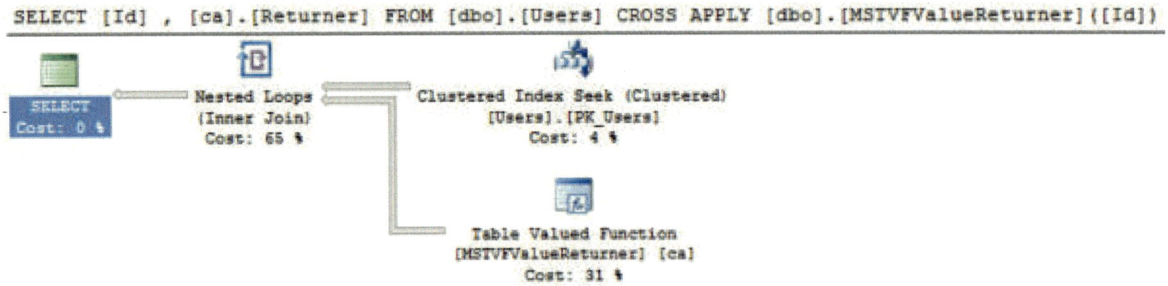

Multi-statement Table Valued Garbage

For the links, code, and comments, go here:
https://www.brentozar.com/archive/2016/01/still-serial-after-all-these-years/

Table Variable Insert

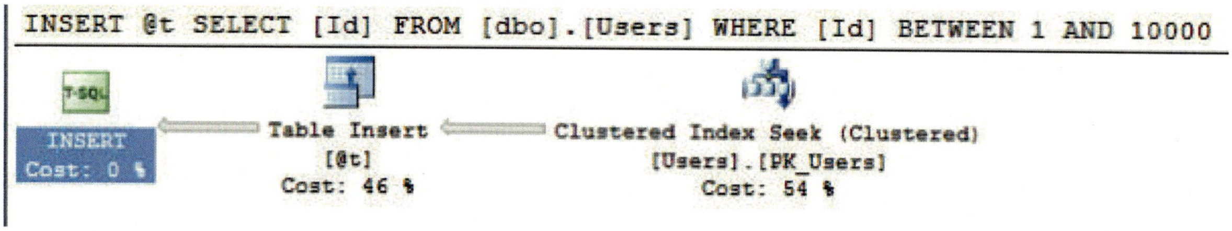

You probably can't name one good reason to use a table variable.

Top

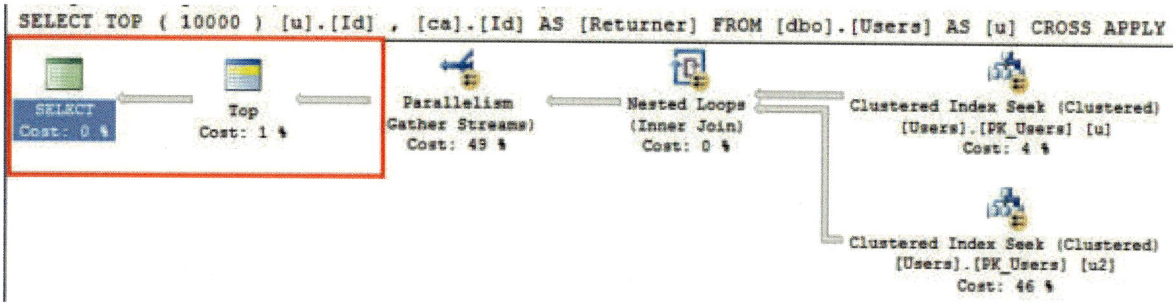

Top o' the nothin!

Aggregating

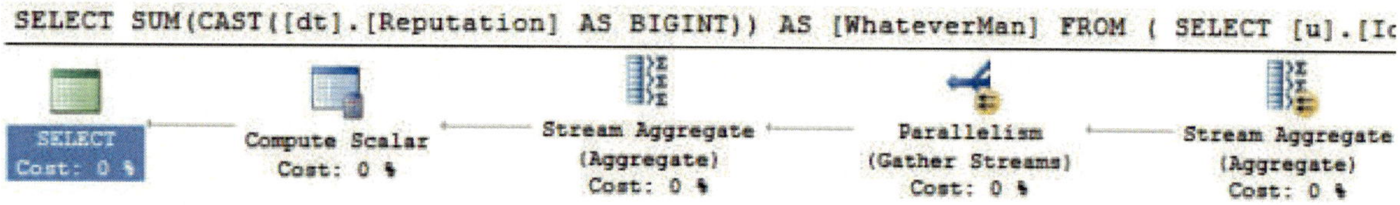

You're making me wanna use Excel, here.

Row Number (or any windowing/ranking function)

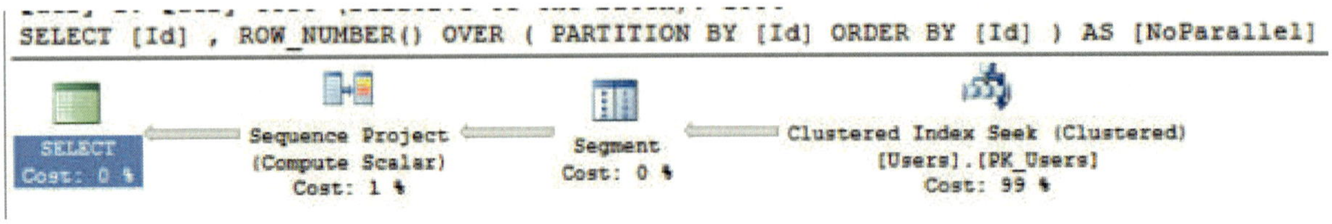

You're gonna get all those row numbers one by one.

Accessing System Tables

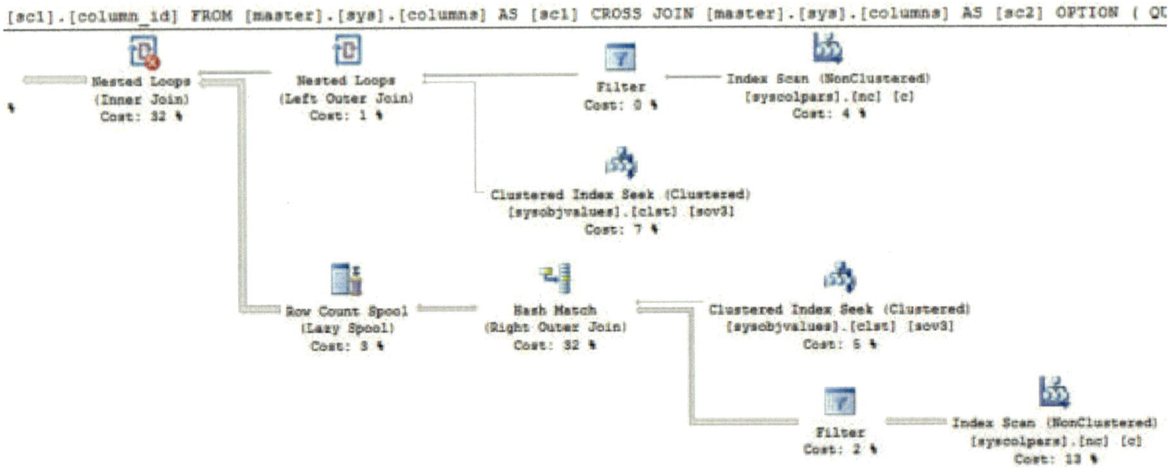

Twisted SYS-ter

The recursive part of a recursive CTE

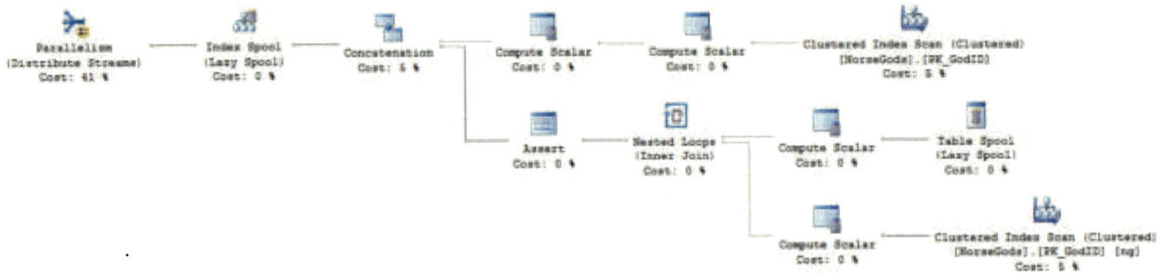

This part was fun. I liked this part.

For the links, code, and comments, go here:
https://www.brentozar.com/archive/2016/01/still-serial-after-all-these-years/

Picture time is over

Now you get to listen to me prattle on and on about how much money you're wasting on licensing by having all your queries run serially. Unless you have a SharePoint server; then you have... many other problems. If I had to pick a top three list that I see people falling victim to regularly, it would be:

1. Scalar functions
2. Table variables
3. Unsupported ORDER BYs

They're all relatively easy items to fix, and by the looks of it, we'll be fixing them on SQL Server 2016 as well. Maybe Query Store will make that easier.

Thanks for reading!

Das Code

```sql
USE StackOverflow;
SET NOCOUNT ON;
GO

/*Scalar*/
CREATE FUNCTION dbo.ScalarValueReturner ( @id INT )
RETURNS INT
WITH RETURNS NULL ON NULL INPUT, SCHEMABINDING
AS
    BEGIN
        RETURN @id * 1;
    END;
GO

/*MSTVF*/
CREATE FUNCTION dbo.MSTVFValueReturner ( @id INT )
RETURNS @Out TABLE ( Returner INT )
WITH SCHEMABINDING
AS
    BEGIN
        INSERT INTO @Out ( Returner )
        SELECT @id;
        RETURN;
    END;
GO

SELECT   Id
FROM     dbo.Users
WHERE    Id BETWEEN 1 AND 10000
ORDER BY Id DESC
OPTION ( QUERYTRACEON 8649, RECOMPILE );
```

```
SELECT Id, dbo.ScalarValueReturner(Id)
FROM   dbo.Users
WHERE  Id BETWEEN 1 AND 10000
OPTION ( QUERYTRACEON 8649, RECOMPILE );

SELECT      Id, ca.Returner
FROM        dbo.Users
CROSS APPLY dbo.MSTVFValueReturner(Id) AS ca
WHERE       Id BETWEEN 1 AND 10000
OPTION ( QUERYTRACEON 8649, RECOMPILE );

DECLARE @t TABLE ( Id INT );
INSERT @t
SELECT Id
FROM   dbo.Users
WHERE  Id BETWEEN 1 AND 10000
OPTION ( QUERYTRACEON 8649, RECOMPILE );

SELECT TOP ( 10000 )
       u.Id, ca.Id AS Returner
FROM   dbo.Users AS u
CROSS APPLY
       ( SELECT u2.Id FROM dbo.Users AS u2 WHERE u2.Id = u.Id ) AS ca
WHERE  u.Id BETWEEN 1 AND 10000
OPTION ( QUERYTRACEON 8649, RECOMPILE );

SELECT AVG(CAST(dt.Reputation AS BIGINT)) AS WhateverMan
FROM
       (   SELECT u.Id, u.Reputation
           FROM   dbo.Users AS u
           JOIN   dbo.Posts AS p
               ON u.Id = p.OwnerUserId
           WHERE  p.OwnerUserId > 0
           AND    u.Reputation > 0 ) AS dt
WHERE  dt.Id BETWEEN 1 AND 10000
OPTION ( QUERYTRACEON 8649, RECOMPILE );

SELECT Id, ROW_NUMBER() OVER ( PARTITION BY Id ORDER BY Id ) AS NoParallel
FROM   dbo.Users
WHERE  Id BETWEEN 1 AND 10000
OPTION ( QUERYTRACEON 8649, RECOMPILE );


SELECT     TOP ( 10000 )
           sc1.column_id
FROM       master.sys.columns AS sc1
CROSS JOIN master.sys.columns AS sc2
CROSS JOIN master.sys.columns AS sc3
CROSS JOIN master.sys.columns AS sc4
CROSS JOIN master.sys.columns AS sc5
OPTION ( QUERYTRACEON 8649, RECOMPILE );

CREATE TABLE dbo.NorseGods
     (
         GodID INT NOT NULL,
         GodName NVARCHAR(30) NOT NULL,
         Title NVARCHAR(100) NOT NULL,
         ManagerID INT NULL,
         CONSTRAINT PK_GodID
             PRIMARY KEY CLUSTERED ( GodID )
     );
```


For the links, code, and comments, go here:
https://www.brentozar.com/archive/2016/01/still-serial-after-all-these-years/

```
INSERT INTO dbo.NorseGods ( GodID, GodName, Title, ManagerID )
VALUES ( 1, N'Odin', N'War and stuff', NULL ),
       ( 2, N'Thor', N'Thunder, etc.', 1 ),
       ( 3, N'Hel', N'Underworld!', 2 ),
       ( 4, N'Loki', N'Tricksy', 3 ),
       ( 5, N'Vali', N'Payback', 3 ),
       ( 6, N'Freyja', N'Making babies', 2 ),
       ( 7, N'Hoenir', N'Quiet time', 6 ),
       ( 8, N'Eir', N'Feeling good', 2 ),
       ( 9, N'Magni', N'Weightlifting', 8 );

WITH Valhalla
    AS
     (
        SELECT ManagerID, GodID, GodName, Title, 0 AS MidgardLevel
        FROM   dbo.NorseGods
        WHERE  ManagerID IS NULL
        UNION ALL
        SELECT     ng.ManagerID, ng.GodID, ng.GodName, ng.Title, v.MidgardLevel + 1
        FROM       dbo.NorseGods AS ng
        INNER JOIN Valhalla AS v
            ON ng.ManagerID = v.GodID
     )
SELECT   Valhalla.ManagerID, Valhalla.GodID, Valhalla.GodName, Valhalla.Title, Valhalla.MidgardLevel
FROM     Valhalla
ORDER BY Valhalla.ManagerID
OPTION ( QUERYTRACEON 8649, RECOMPILE );
```

Another reason why scalar functions in computed columns is a bad idea

As if there weren't enough reasons

In my last blog post I talked about different things that cause plans, or zones of plans, to execute serially. One of the items I covered was computed columns that reference scalar functions. We know that they'll make queries go serial, but what about other SQL stuff?

Oh no my index is fragmented

If you're running Expensive Edition, index rebuilds can be both online and parallel. That's pretty cool, because it keeps all your gadgets and gizmos mostly available during the whole operation, and the parallel bit usually makes things faster.

That is, unless you have a computed column in there that references a scalar function. I decided to write my test function to not perform any data access so it could be persisted. It's dead simple, and I'm tacking it on to a column in the PostLinks table of the Stack Overflow database.

```
CREATE FUNCTION dbo.PIDMultiplier (@pid int)
RETURNS INT
    WITH RETURNS NULL ON NULL INPUT,
         SCHEMABINDING
AS
    BEGIN
        DECLARE @Out BIGINT;
        SELECT  @Out = @pid * 2
        RETURN @Out;
    END;
GO

ALTER TABLE dbo.PostLinks
ADD Multiplied AS dbo.PIDMultiplier(PostId) PERSISTED;
```

For this one, all we have to do is turn on actual execution plans and rebuild the index, then drop the column and rebuild again.

```sql
ALTER TABLE dbo.PostLinks REBUILD WITH ( ONLINE = ON );

ALTER TABLE dbo.PostLinks DROP COLUMN Multiplied;
```

Here are my execution plans. The rebuild I ran when the table had my computed column in it stayed serial.

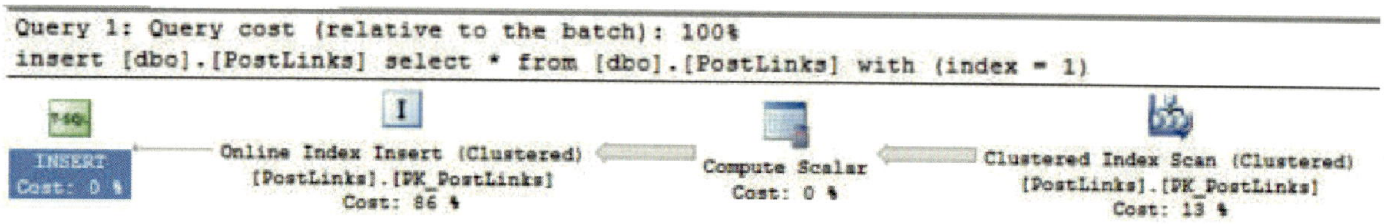

Hi, I'm garbage.

Parallel, sans computed column:

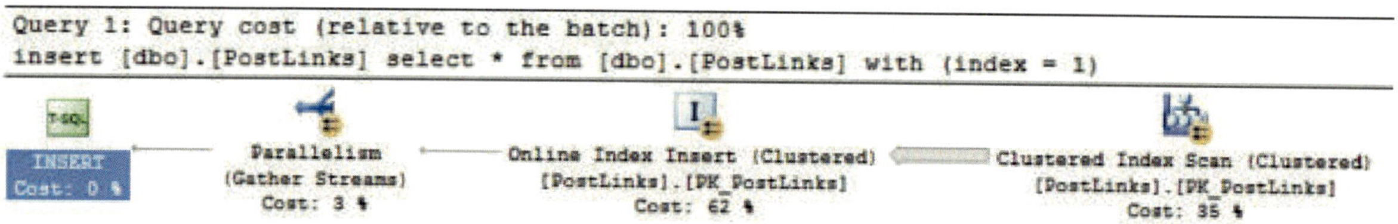

Dude, you're getting a parallel.

But there's a bigger fish in the pond

Probably the most important maintenance item you should be doing, aside from backups, is running DBCC CHECKDB. Seriously, if you're not doing them both, start today. Ola Hallengren has basically done all the work for you. Back when I had a real job, I used his scripts everywhere.

Before we were so rudely interrupted by a soap box, we were talking about parallelism. This part was a little bit more complicated, but don't worry, you don't have to follow along. Just look at the pretty pictures. Sleep now. Yes. Sleep.

The first couple times I tried, the DBCC check never went parallel. Since I'm on my laptop, and not a production server, I can set Cost Threshold for Parallelism to 0. You read that right, ZE-RO! Hold onto your drool dish.

With that set, I fire up Ye Olde Oaken sp_BlitzTrace so I can capture everything with Extended Events. You'll need all three commands, but you'll probably have to change @SessionId, and you may have to change @TargetPath. Run the first command to start your session up.

```sql
EXEC dbo.sp_BlitzTrace @SessionId = 61 , @Action = 'start' , @TargetPath = 'c:\temp\' , @TraceParallelism = 1 , @TraceExecutionPlansAndKillMyPerformance = 1

EXEC dbo.sp_BlitzTrace @Action = 'stop'

EXEC dbo.sp_BlitzTrace @Action = 'read'
```

With that running, toss in your DBCC command. I'm only using DBCC CHECKTABLE here to simplify. Rest assured, if you run DBCC CHECKDB, the CHECKTABLE part is included. The only checks that DBCC CHECKDB doesn't run are CHECKIDENT and CHECKCONSTRAINT. Everything else is included.

```sql
DBCC CHECKTABLE('dbo.PostLinks') WITH NO_INFOMSGS, ALL_ERRORMSGS

ALTER TABLE dbo.PostLinks
ADD Multiplied AS dbo.PIDMultiplier(PostId) PERSISTED;
```

Run DBCC CHECKTABLE, add the computed column back, and then run it again. When those finish, run the sp_BlitzTrace commands to stop and read session data. You should see execution plans for each run, and they should be way different.

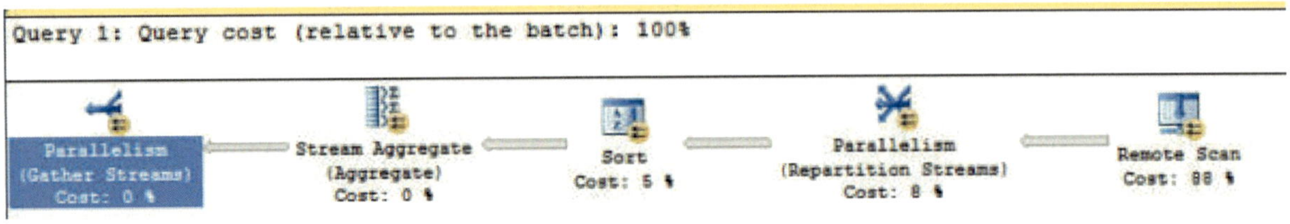

Hell Yeah.

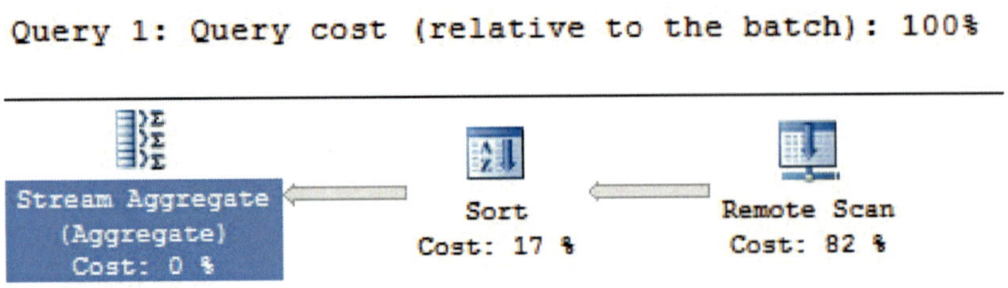

Hell No.

So even DBCC checks are serialized. Crazy, right? I'd been hearing about performance hits to varying degrees when running DBCC checks against tables with computed columns for a while, but never knew why. There may be a separate reason for regular computed columns vs. ones that reference scalar functions. When I took the equivalent SQL out of a function, the DBCC check ran parallel.

```
ALTER TABLE dbo.PostLinks ADD Multiplied AS PostId * 2 PERSISTED;
```

Of course, those online index rebuilds running single threaded might be a blessing in disguise, if you haven't patched SQL recently.

I don't have much of a grand closing paragraph here. These things can seriously mess you up for a lot of reasons. If you're a vendor, please get away from using scalar functions, and please please don't use them in computed columns.

Thanks for reading!

Another Hidden Parallelism Killer: Scalar UDFs In Check Constraints

Every single time

Really. Every single time. It started off kind of funny. Scalar functions in queries: no parallelism. Scalar functions in computed columns: no parallelism, even if you're not selecting the computed column. Every time I think of a place where someone could stick a scalar function into some SQL, it ends up killing parallelism. Now it's just sad.

This is (hopefully. HOPEFULLY.) a less common scenario, since uh... I know most of you aren't actually using any constraints. So there's that! Developer laziness might be a saving grace here. But if you read the title, you know what's coming. Here's a quick example.

Transact-SQL

```sql
USE tempdb;
SET NOCOUNT ON;

SELECT TOP 10000
        ROW_NUMBER() OVER ( ORDER BY ( SELECT NULL )) AS ID,
        DATEADD(MINUTE, m.message_id, SYSDATETIME()) AS SomeDate
INTO    dbo.constraint_test
FROM    sys.messages AS m, sys.messages AS m2;
GO

CREATE FUNCTION dbo.DateCheck ( @d DATETIME2(7))
RETURNS BIT
WITH RETURNS NULL ON NULL INPUT
AS
    BEGIN
        DECLARE @Out BIT;
        SELECT @Out = CASE WHEN @d < DATEADD(DAY, 30, SYSDATETIME()) THEN 1 ELSE 0 END;
        RETURN @Out;
    END;
GO

ALTER TABLE dbo.constraint_test
ADD CONSTRAINT ck_cc_dt CHECK ( dbo.DateCheck(SomeDate) = 1 );

SELECT *
FROM   dbo.constraint_test
OPTION ( QUERYTRACEON 8649, MAXDOP 0, RECOMPILE );
```

Parallelism appears to be rejected for maintenance operations as well as queries, just like with computed columns.

Interestingly, if we look in the plan XML (the execution plan itself just confirms that the query didn't go parallel) we can see SQL tried to get a parallel plan, but couldn't.

```
<StatementSetOptions ANSI_NULLS="true" ANSI_PADDING="true" ANSI_WARNINGS="true" ARITHABORT="true"
<QueryPlan DegreeOfParallelism="0" NonParallelPlanReason="CouldNotGenerateValidParallelPlan" Cac
    <MemoryGrantInfo SerialRequiredMemory="0" SerialDesiredMemory="0" />
```

Garbagio

There's a short list of possible reasons for plans not going parallel here from a while back. A quick search didn't turn up a newer or more complete list.

Check yourself, etc. and so forth

How do you know if this is happening to you? Here's a simple query to look at constraint definitions and search them for function names. This query is dumb and ugly, but my wife is staring at me because it's 5:30 on a Saturday and I'm supposed to be getting ready. If you have a better idea, feel free to share in the comments.

Transact-SQL

```sql
WITH c1
    AS
     (
         SELECT name, definition
         FROM   sys.check_constraints
         UNION ALL
         SELECT name, definition
         FROM   sys.default_constraints
     )
SELECT *
FROM   c1, sys.objects AS o
WHERE  o.type IN ( 'FN', 'TF' )
AND    c1.definition LIKE '%' + o.name + '%';
```

Thanks for reading!

Scalar Functions In Views: Where's The Overhead?

Short winded

Quite often people will inherit and rely on views written back in the dark ages, before people were aware of the deleterious effects that scalar valued functions can have on performance.

Of course, for some people, it's still the dark ages.

Sorry, you people.

Questions and answers

So what are the side effects of relying on an old view that has scalar valued functions in it? Well, it depends a little bit on how the view is called.

We all know that scalar valued functions are executed once per row, because we all read my blog posts. Well, maybe. I think the CIA uses them instead of waterboarding. Not sure how much they make it out to people not classified as enemy combatants.

But what about if you call the view without referencing the function?

It turns out, it's a lot like when you use a scalar valued function in a computed column. Let's look at how.

We're gonna need a function

```
CREATE FUNCTION dbo.ScalarID ( @Id INT )
RETURNS INT
        WITH RETURNS NULL ON NULL INPUT, SCHEMABINDING
  AS
      BEGIN
         RETURN 2147483647
      END;
```

This function doesn't touch data, and doesn't even return anything of value. But it can still mess things up.

Let's stick it in a view, and watch what happens next.

```
Transact-SQL
CREATE VIEW dbo.FunctionView
AS
SELECT TOP 1000
*, dbo.ScalarID(u.Id) AS [DumbFunction]
FROM dbo.Users AS u
```

There's a difference when we avoid selecting the column that references the scalar valued function.

```
Transact-SQL
SELECT fv.Id --No function reference
FROM dbo.FunctionView AS fv

SELECT fv.Id, fv.DumbFunction --Function reference
FROM dbo.FunctionView AS fv

EXEC master.dbo.sp_BlitzCache @DatabaseName = 'StackOverflow' --A Blitz of Caches
```

So what's the difference?

Database	Cost	Query Text	Query Type	Warnings	# Executions
StackOverflow	0.0157111	SELECT fv.Id, fv.DumbFunction FROM dbo.FunctionView AS fv	Statement	Forced Serialization, Calls 1 function(s), Plan created last 4hrs	1
StackOverflow	0	CREATE FUNCTION dbo.ScalarID (@Id INT) RETURNS INT ...	Procedure or Function: ScalarID	Plan created last 4hrs	1000
StackOverflow	0.0156111	SELECT fv.Id FROM dbo.FunctionView AS fv	Statement	Forced Serialization, Calls 1 function(s), Plan created last 4hrs	1

Crud and Crap

Well, both queries are forced to run serially because of the scalar valued function. That warning is surfaced in sp_BlizCache in not-decade-old versions of SQL Server.

But only the query that referenced the scalar valued function directly picked up the overhead of the row-by-row execution of the function. This is proven out in the '# Executions' column.

The function was called 1000 times, not 2000 times. Our TOP 1000 view ran twice, so if the function had run for both, it would show 2000 executions.

There's still a problem here

Both queries are forced to run serially. If you have a big bad view that does a lot of work, and performance is important to you, you probably won't want it to run single-threaded because of a silly function.

This doesn't give scalar valued functions (in general, or in views) a pass, but you can avoid some of the overhead by not referencing them when you don't need to.

Thanks for reading!

2017 Stuff

Around here, we celebrate every new SQL Server release with champagne. Major versions, Service Packs, Cumulative Updates, Hot Fixes -- heck sometimes we just speculate about new releases to pour a glass.

BRENT OZAR UNLIMITED®

Look Ma, Adaptive Joins

This probably won't seem like a big deal soon

But I just got the optimizer to pick an Adaptive Join! It took a few tries to figure out what would cause some guesswork to happen, but here it is.

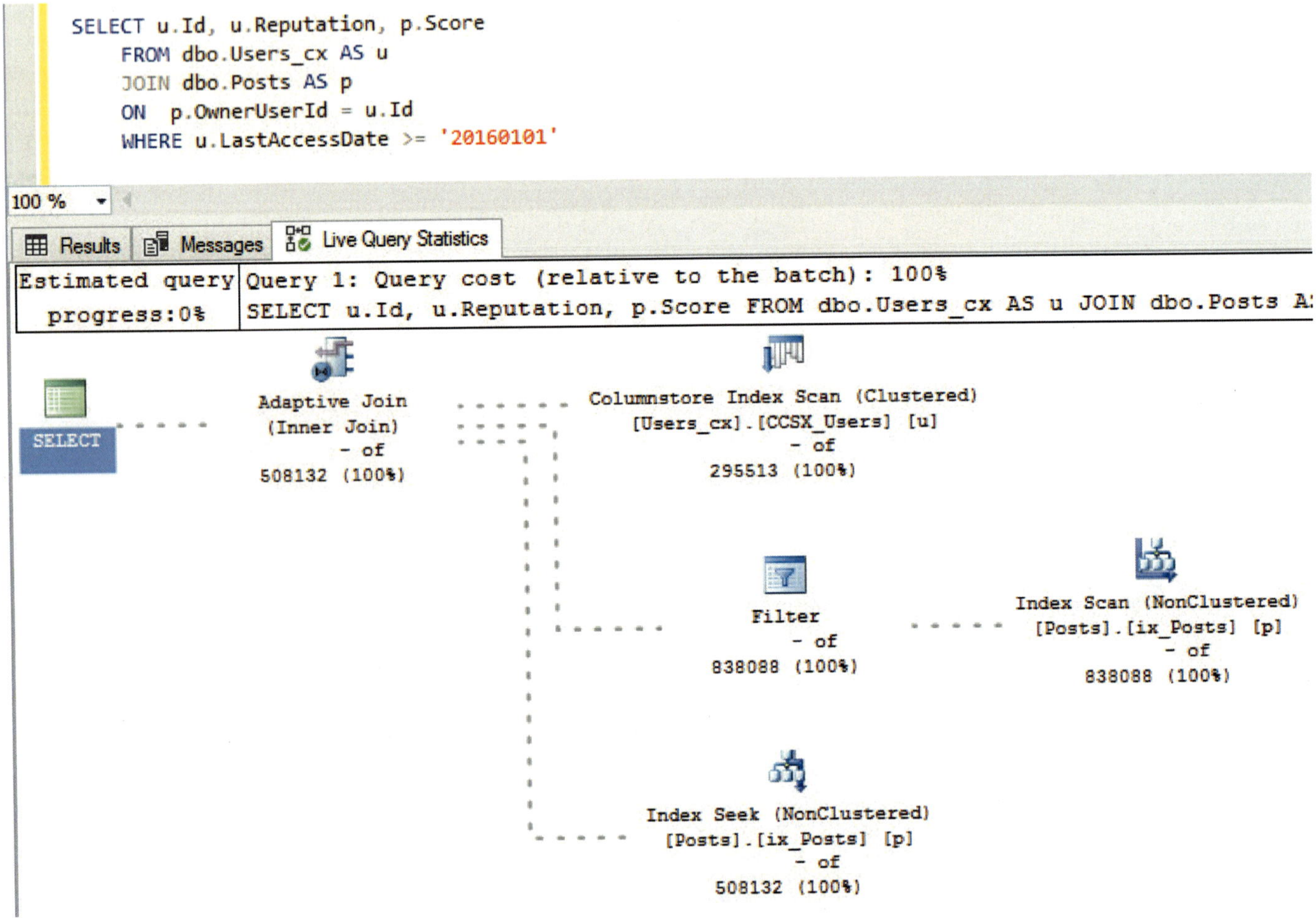

I hope Joe Sack has strong ribs.

For the links, code, and comments, go here:
https://www.brentozar.com/archive/2017/04/look-ma-adaptive-joins/

And here's the tool tip info!

Adaptive Join

Chooses dynamically between hash join and nested loops.

Physical Operation	Adaptive Join
Logical Operation	Inner Join
Actual Join Type	AdaptiveJoin
Actual Execution Mode	Batch
Adaptive Threshold Rows	18902.2
Is Adaptive	True
Estimated Execution Mode	Batch
Estimated Join Type	HashMatch
Actual Number of Rows	622961
Actual Number of Batches	1809
Estimated I/O Cost	0
Estimated Operator Cost	0 (0%)
Estimated Subtree Cost	4.26179
Estimated CPU Cost	0.0101626
Estimated Number of Executions	1
Number of Executions	1
Estimated Number of Rows	508132
Estimated Row Size	19 B
Actual Rebinds	0
Actual Rewinds	0
Node ID	0

Output List

[SUPERUSER].[dbo].[Users_cx].Id, [SUPERUSER].[dbo].[Users_cx].Reputation, [SUPERUSER].[dbo].[Posts].Score

Hash Keys Probe

[SUPERUSER].[dbo].[Posts].OwnerUserId

Probe Residual

[SUPERUSER].[dbo].[Users_cx].[Id] as [u].[Id]=[SUPERUSER].[dbo].[Posts].[OwnerUserId] as [p].[OwnerUserId]

Outer References

[SUPERUSER].[dbo].[Users_cx].Id

Dynamic Duo

This is so cool! Now I can start picking apart the XML to add stuff to sp_BlitzCache.

In the XML, we have this information.

```
PhysicalOp="Adaptive Join" IsAdaptive="true" AdaptiveThresholdRows="18902.2"
```

Papers, please

There also appears to be a whole XML path dedicated to the AdaptiveJoin, but I'm still working out what all goes on in there.

Remember that you need at least CTP2 of SQL Server 2017, and SSMS 2017 to see the new operators.

Thanks for reading!

Anatomy Of An Adaptive Join

I don't like it unless it's brand new

When new features drop, not everyone has time to jump on top of them and start looking at stuff. That's what consultants with nothing better to do are for.

I've been excited about this feature since talking to The Honorable Joseph Q. Sack, Esq. about it at PASS last October. My pupils dilated like I just found the bottom of a bottle of Laphroaig 18.

Let's look at the Adaptive Join process in a way that most of you will eventually see it: in a query plan. Query Plan. Should I capitalize that? The jury is out.

The Operator

This is what the operator itself looks like:

Greased Lightning

And as of CTP2 of 2017, this is the information available in the Adaptive Join operator itself.

Adaptive Join

Chooses dynamically between hash join and nested loops.

Estimated operator progress: 100%

Physical Operation	Adaptive Join
Logical Operation	Inner Join
Actual Join Type	AdaptiveJoin
Actual Execution Mode	Batch
Estimated Join Type	HashMatch
Adaptive Threshold Rows	9845.36
Is Adaptive	True
Estimated Execution Mode	Batch
Actual Number of Rows	324886
Actual Number of Batches	361
Estimated I/O Cost	0
Estimated Operator Cost	0 (0%)
Estimated Subtree Cost	3.31066
Estimated CPU Cost	0.0048717
Estimated Number of Executions	1
Number of Executions	1
Estimated Number of Rows	243583
Estimated Row Size	15 B
Actual Rebinds	0
Actual Rewinds	0
Node ID	0

Output List

[SUPERUSER].[dbo].[Users_cx].Id, [SUPERUSER].[dbo].[Posts].Score

Hash Keys Probe

[SUPERUSER].[dbo].[Posts].OwnerUserId

Probe Residual

[SUPERUSER].[dbo].[Users_cx].[Id] as [u].[Id]=[SUPERUSER].[dbo].[Posts].[OwnerUserId] as [p].[OwnerUserId]

Outer References

[SUPERUSER].[dbo].[Users_cx].Id

Evolution

For the links, code, and comments, go here: https://www.brentozar.com/archive/2017/05/anatomy-adaptive-join/

Some points of interest:

- Actual Join Type: doesn't tell you whether it chose Hash or Nested Loops
- Estimated Join Type: Probably does
- Adaptive Threshold Rows: If the number of rows crosses this boundary, Join choice will change. Over will be Hash, under will be Nested Loops.

The rest is fairly self-explanatory and is the usual stuff in query plans.

The Plan

Each Adaptive Join plan will have a branch for each path the optimizer can choose.

In our case, the Index Scan/Hash Join plan is the first path, and the Index Seek/Nested Loops Join is the second path.

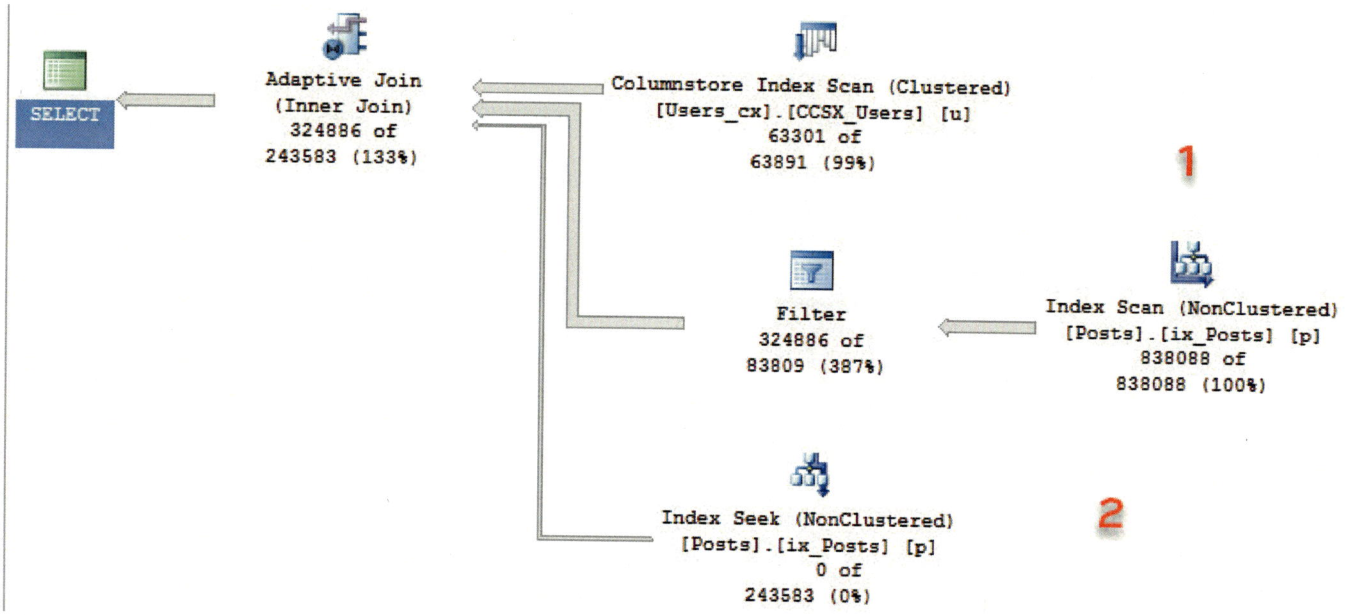

Hekaton doesn't even have query plans

Inside the plan, there are a couple visual cues that let you know which path the query took.

1. The width of the lines: the wider line likely had data flow through it
2. The number of executions line in the tool tip for the index access: So far as I've seen, the path the query chooses will have > 0, and the path the query didn't choose will have 0 here.

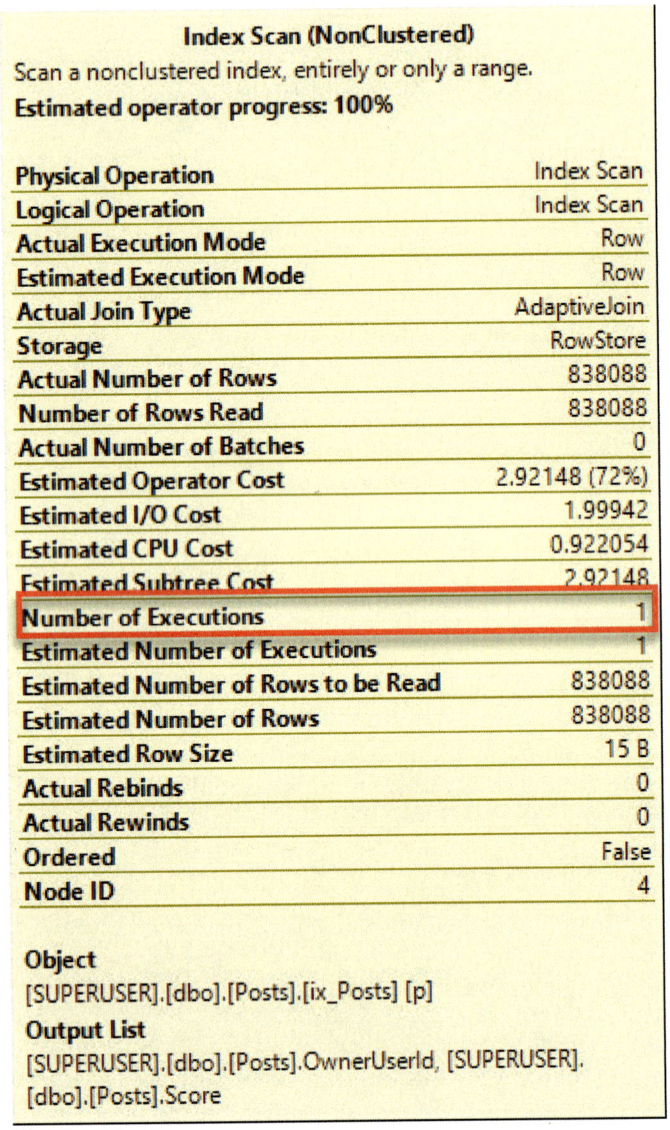

Best Execution Ever.

Misc

In other posts I've mentioned stuff! And things. I'm going to bring it all together here.

1. You need CTP2 of SQL Server 2017 to use Adaptive Joins (for now)
2. At least one table has to use a ColumnStore index (for now)
3. Database compatibility has to be 140 (for now)
4. You need to be using SSMS 2017 to see the Adaptive Join operator in graphical query plans (you can see it in SET STATISTICS XML ON otherwise, it's text only)

5. Right now, only Nested Loops and Hash Join are supported (my best guess is that Merge Join was left out because of the potential cost of having to inject a Sort operator into the plan)

Whew. Hey. That's it. Go home.

Thanks for reading!

Brent says: *this has interesting implications for index-tracking DMVs like sys.dm_db_index_usage_stats. In the past, I've explained that DMV as "counting the number of times a plan with that index in it has executed," but I'm going to have to dig deeper now that it shows the same index twice here with two different operations (a seek and a scan.)*

Adaptive Joins And Local Variables

With new features

I really love kicking the tires to see how they work with existing features, and if they fix existing performance troubleshooting scenarios.

One issue that I see frequently is with local variables. I'm not going to get into Cardinality Estimator math here, we're just going to look at Adaptive Join plan choice for one scenario.

Understanding local variables

When you use local variables, SQL Server doesn't look at statistics histograms to come up with cardinality estimates. It uses some magical math based on rows and density.

This magical math is complicated by multiple predicates and ranges.

It's further complicated by Adaptive Joins. Sort of.

A simple example

The easiest way to look at this is to compare Adaptive Joins with literal values to the same ones using local variables. The results are a little... complicated.

Here are three queries with three literal values. In my copy of the Super User database (the largest Stack Overflow sub-site), I've made copies of all the tables and added Clustered ColumnStore indexes to them. That's the only way to get Adaptive Joins at this point — Column Store has to be involved somewhere along the line.

The last day of data in this dump is from December 11. When I query the data, I'm looking at the last 11 days of data, the last day of data, and then a day where there isn't any data.

For the links, code, and comments, go here:
https://www.brentozar.com/archive/2017/05/adaptive-joins-local-variables/

Transact-SQL

```sql
SELECT u.Id, p.Score
  FROM dbo.Users_cx AS u
  JOIN dbo.Posts AS p
  ON  p.OwnerUserId = u.Id
WHERE u.LastAccessDate >= '2016-12-01'
GO

SELECT u.Id, p.Score
  FROM dbo.Users_cx AS u
  JOIN dbo.Posts AS p
  ON  p.OwnerUserId = u.Id
WHERE u.LastAccessDate >= '2016-12-11'
GO

SELECT u.Id, p.Score
  FROM dbo.Users_cx AS u
  JOIN dbo.Posts AS p
  ON  p.OwnerUserId = u.Id
WHERE u.LastAccessDate >= '2016-12-12'
GO
```

I get Adaptive Join plans back for all of these, with accurate estimates. I'm looking at the Live Query Statistics for all these so you can see the row counts on the Users table. You can see this stuff just fine in Actual and Estimated plans, too.

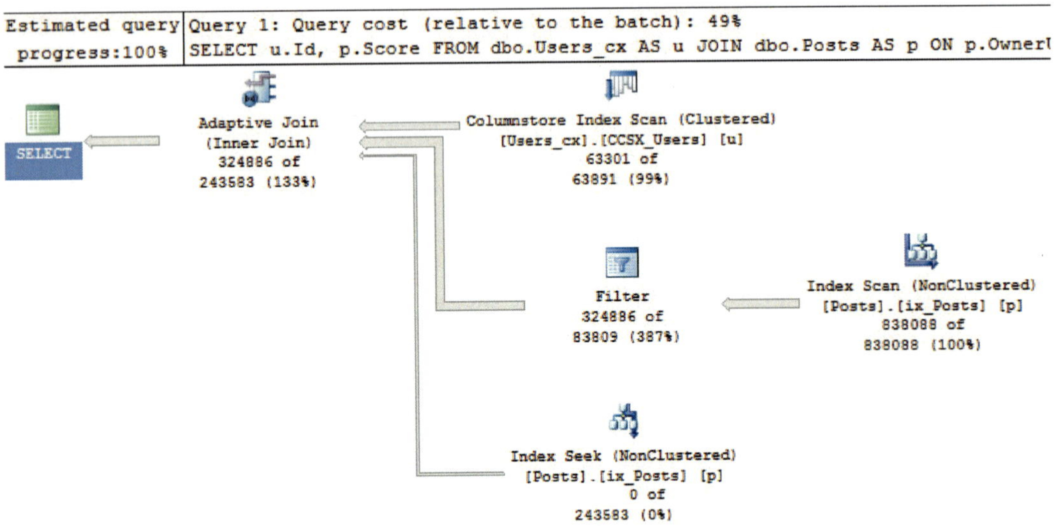

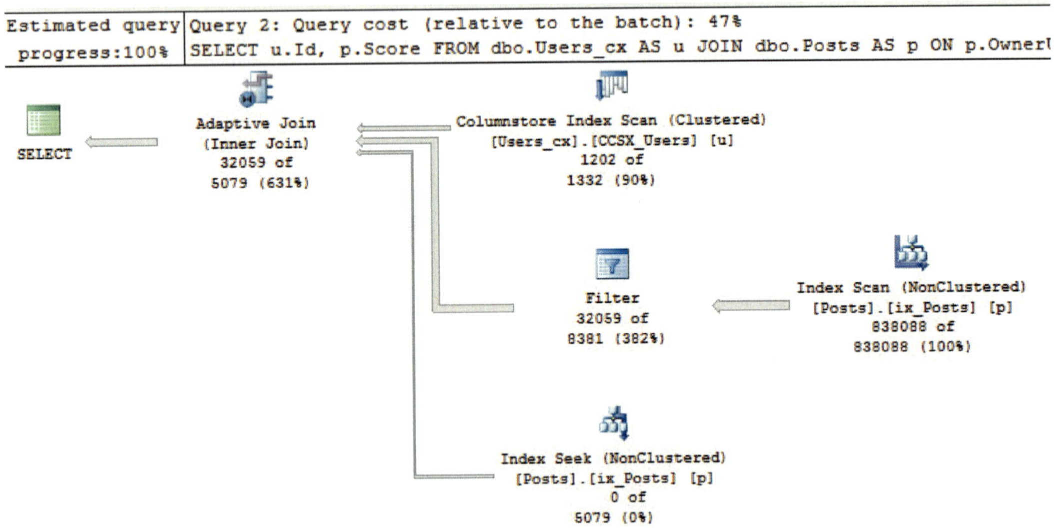

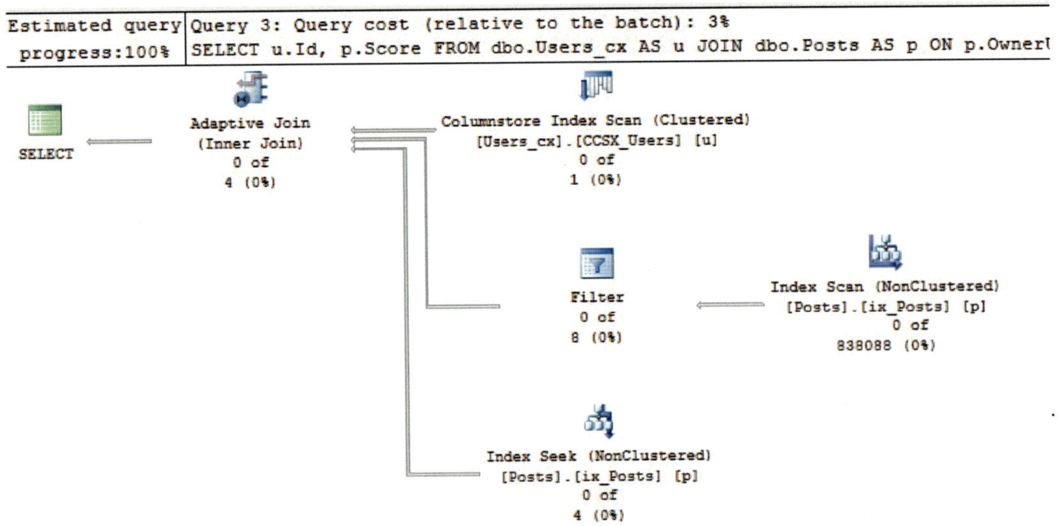

Just trust me

The first two queries that actually return rows estimate that they'll use a Hash Join, and both choose the Index Scan of the Posts table branch of the plan to execute. The last query chooses the Index Seek branch, and doesn't end up needing to execute either branch because no rows come out of the Users table. It also estimates that it will use a Nested Loops Join rather than a Hash Join because of the lower number of rows.

Think Locally, Act Mediocrely

If I flip the query around to use local variables, some things change. I'm using all the same dates, here.

Transact-SQL

```
DECLARE @MyLeftFoot DATETIME = '2016-12-01'

SELECT u.Id, p.Score
  FROM dbo.Users_cx AS u
  JOIN dbo.Posts AS p
  ON  p.OwnerUserId = u.Id
WHERE u.LastAccessDate >= @MyLeftFoot
GO

DECLARE @MyLeftFoot DATETIME = '2016-12-11'

SELECT u.Id, p.Score
  FROM dbo.Users_cx AS u
  JOIN dbo.Posts AS p
  ON  p.OwnerUserId = u.Id
WHERE u.LastAccessDate >= @MyLeftFoot
GO

DECLARE @MyLeftFoot DATETIME = '2016-12-12'

SELECT u.Id, p.Score
  FROM dbo.Users_cx AS u
  JOIN dbo.Posts AS p
  ON  p.OwnerUserId = u.Id
WHERE u.LastAccessDate >= @MyLeftFoot
GO
```

A bunch of stuff changed, mainly with estimates from the Users table. Which makes sense. That's where u.LastAccessDate is.

Most importantly: they're all the same now! All three estimated 143,495 rows would match from the Users. And this is where things get interesting.

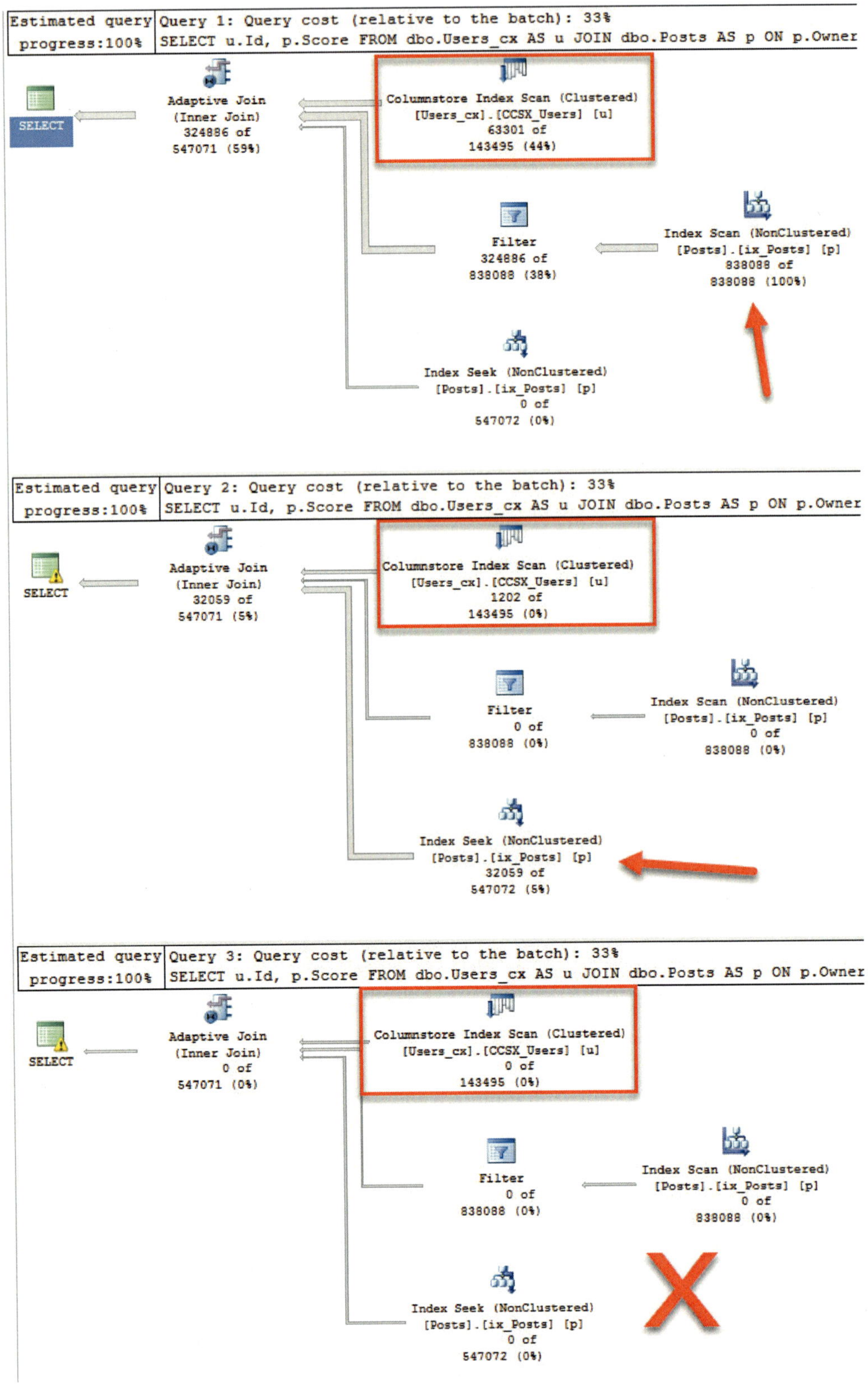

HEH HEH HEH

The second query chooses a different index, but with the same estimated join type (Hash), and the third query bails on the Nested Loops Join it estimated when it gets no rows back.

They both have unused memory grant warnings — only the first query asked for and used its entire grant.

Lesson: Adaptive Plans can still get wonky memory grants with local variables.

But what actually happened?

Exactly what was supposed to happen. The secret is in the thresholds.

In the local variable plan, the threshold for Join choice is MUCH higher than in the plan for the literal. When the actual rows (1202) doesn't hit that threshold, the Join type switches to Nested Loops, and likely abandons the memory grant that it asked for when it estimated a Hash Join.

Adaptive Join

Chooses dynamically between hash join and nested loops.

Physical Operation	Adaptive Join
Logical Operation	Inner Join
Actual Join Type	AdaptiveJoin
Actual Execution Mode	Batch
Estimated Join Type	HashMatch
Adaptive Threshold Rows	15623.9
Is Adaptive	True
Estimated Execution Mode	Batch
Actual Number of Rows	32059
Actual Number of Batches	36
Estimated I/O Cost	0
Estimated Operator Cost	0 (0%)
Estimated Subtree Cost	4.05613
Estimated CPU Cost	0.0109414
Estimated Number of Executions	1
Number of Executions	1
Estimated Number of Rows	547071
Estimated Row Size	15 B
Actual Rebinds	0
Actual Rewinds	0
Node ID	0

Output List

[SUPERUSER].[dbo].[Users_cx].Id, [SUPERUSER].[dbo].[Posts].Score

Hash Keys Probe

[SUPERUSER].[dbo].[Posts].OwnerUserId

Probe Residual

[SUPERUSER].[dbo].[Users_cx].[Id] as [u].[Id]=[SUPERUSER].[dbo].[Posts].[OwnerUserId] as [p].[OwnerUserId]

Outer References

[SUPERUSER].[dbo].[Users_cx].Id

30 KAZILLION

The plan with the literal values has a threshold of 1116 rows for Join choices. We hit 1202 rows, so we get the Hash Join plan.

Adaptive Join

Chooses dynamically between hash join and nested loops.

Physical Operation	Adaptive Join
Logical Operation	Inner Join
Actual Join Type	AdaptiveJoin
Actual Execution Mode	Batch
Estimated Join Type	HashMatch
Adaptive Threshold Rows	1116.58
Is Adaptive	True
Estimated Execution Mode	Batch
Actual Number of Rows	32059
Actual Number of Batches	36
Estimated I/O Cost	0
Estimated Operator Cost	0 (0%)
Estimated Subtree Cost	3.16345
Estimated CPU Cost	0.0001016
Estimated Number of Executions	1
Number of Executions	1
Estimated Number of Rows	5079.08
Estimated Row Size	15 B
Actual Rebinds	0
Actual Rewinds	0
Node ID	0

Output List

[SUPERUSER].[dbo].[Users_cx].Id, [SUPERUSER].[dbo].[Posts].Score

Hash Keys Probe

[SUPERUSER].[dbo].[Posts].OwnerUserId

Probe Residual

[SUPERUSER].[dbo].[Users_cx].[Id] as [u].[Id]= [SUPERUSER].[dbo].[Posts].[OwnerUserId] as [p].[OwnerUserId]

Outer References

[SUPERUSER].[dbo].[Users_cx].Id

Yeah that's what adaptive means, knucklehead.

Is that better or worse?

Well, the real lesson here is that local variables still aren't a great choice. The Adaptive Join process figures that out now, at least.

I'm not sure if it gives the memory grant back immediately when it figures out it doesn't need it. That'll take some digging. Or someone from Microsoft to comment.

Thanks for reading!

Brent says: *In the last year, Microsoft has been generous with backporting memory grant info all the way to 2012 via cumulative updates. However, it's still a relatively new topic for a lot of performance tuners. To learn more about that, check out our past post on An Introduction to Query Memory, and check out sp_BlitzCache's @SortOrder = 'memory grant'.*

For the links, code, and comments, go here:
https://www.brentozar.com/archive/2017/05/adaptive-joins-local-variables/

Adaptive Joins And SARGability

There's a famous saying

Non-SARGable predicates don't get missing index requests.

And that's true! But can they also stifle my favorite thing to happen to SQL Server since, well, last week?

You betcha!©

One Sided

I'm going to paste in some queries, each with something non-SARGable.

There are two tables involved: Users and Posts. Only one table will have a non-SARGable predicate in each query.

```
SELECT u.Id, p.Score
FROM dbo.Users_cx AS u
JOIN dbo.Posts AS p
ON LTRIM(RTRIM(p.OwnerUserId)) = u.Id --I'm icky and gross to Posts
WHERE u.LastAccessDate >= '20160101';

SELECT u.Id, p.Score
FROM dbo.Users_cx AS u
JOIN dbo.Posts AS p
ON p.OwnerUserId = LTRIM(RTRIM(u.Id)) --I'm a loser to Users
WHERE u.LastAccessDate >= '20160101';

SELECT u.Id, p.Score
FROM dbo.Users_cx AS u
JOIN dbo.Posts AS p
ON p.OwnerUserId = u.Id
WHERE YEAR(p.LastActivityDate) >= 2016; --I'm antiPostial

SELECT u.Id, p.Score
FROM dbo.Users_cx AS u
JOIN dbo.Posts AS p
ON p.OwnerUserId = u.Id
WHERE YEAR(u.LastAccessDate) >= 2016; --Sacre bleUser!
```

What do you think will happen?

Will all of them use Adaptive Joins?

Will some of them use Adaptive Joins?

Will none of them use Adaptive Joins?

Will you stop asking me these questions to fill space before the picture?

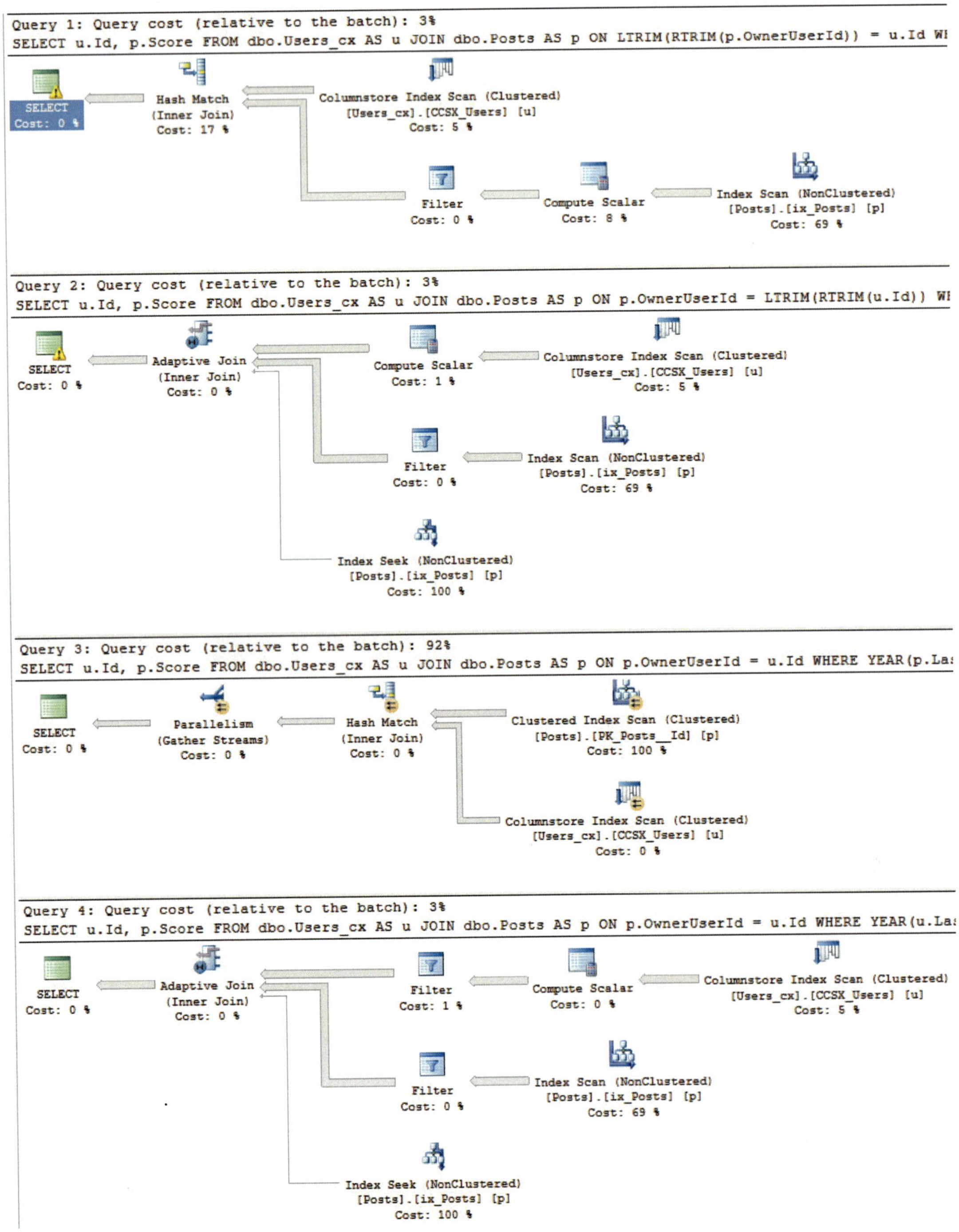

Half and half

For the links, code, and comments, go here:
https://www.brentozar.com/archive/2017/05/adaptive-joins-sargability/

I told you something would happen

The queries with non-SARGable predicates on the Users table used Adaptive Joins.

The queries with non-SARGable predicates on the Posts table did not.

Now, there is an Extended Events... er... event to track this, called adaptive_join_skipped, however it didn't seem to log any information for the queries that didn't get Adaptive Joins.

Bummer! But, if I had to wager a guess, it would be that this happens because there's no alternative Index Seek plan for the Posts table with those predicates. Their non-SARGableness takes that choice away from the optimizer, and so Adaptive Joins aren't a choice. The Users table is going to get scanned either way — that's the nature of ColumnStore indexes, so it can withstand the misery of non-SARGable predicates in this case and use the Adaptive Join.

Thanks for reading!

Brent says: *when you see stuff like this, it's tempting to slather columnstore indexes all over your tables, including OLTP ones. Before you do that, read Niko's post on using UPDATEs with columnstore, and watch his GroupBy session, Worst Practices and Lesser-Known Limitations of Columnstore Indexes. Yes, you can still get excited about adaptive joins, but they're not quite a solution to bad OLTP queries – yet.*

Adaptive Joins And Scalar Valued Functions

I know, I know

Here we are in 2017, which means we're about two years away from the next Ska revival effort, if my watch is correct.

I hope it isn't, but since Brent sent it to me with a note that says "please stop blogging" and it starts shocking me every time I open a new blog post, I'm pretty sure it's accurate.

You're probably sick of hearing about Adaptive Joins by now. "Dead horse!" you're screaming, about a feature in a product that hasn't been released yet.

God these shocks hurt.

Function Friction

If you're not aware of the performance problems scalar valued functions can (and often do) cause, well, uh... click here. We'll talk in a few days.

If you are, and you're worried about them crapping on Adaptive Joins, follow along.

The big question I had is if various uses of scalar valued functions would inhibit Adaptive Joins, and it turns out they're a lot like non-SARGable queries.

Starting with a simple function that doesn't touch anything.

```
Transact-SQL
  CREATE FUNCTION [dbo].[ScalarID] ( @Id INT )
RETURNS INT
  AS
      BEGIN

          RETURN 2147483647

      END;
```


For the links, code, and comments, go here:
https://www.brentozar.com/archive/2017/05/adaptive-joins-scalar-valued-functions/

We can all agree that it doesn't access any data and just returns the INT max. Now some queries that call it!

```
SELECT u.Id, p.Score, dbo.ScalarID(u.Id) --In the SELECT on the Users table
  FROM dbo.Users_cx AS u
  JOIN dbo.Posts AS p
  ON  p.OwnerUserId = u.Id
WHERE u.LastAccessDate >= '2016-12-01'

SELECT u.Id, p.Score
  FROM dbo.Users_cx AS u
  JOIN dbo.Posts AS p
  ON  p.OwnerUserId = u.Id
WHERE dbo.ScalarID(u.Id) = u.Id --In the WHERE clause on the Users table

SELECT u.Id, p.Score, dbo.ScalarID(p.Id) --In the SELECT on the Posts table
  FROM dbo.Users_cx AS u
  JOIN dbo.Posts AS p
  ON  p.OwnerUserId = u.Id
WHERE u.LastAccessDate >= '2016-12-01'

SELECT u.Id, p.Score
  FROM dbo.Users_cx AS u
  JOIN dbo.Posts AS p
  ON  p.OwnerUserId = u.Id
WHERE dbo.ScalarID(p.Id) = p.Id --In the WHERE clause on the Posts table
```

If you're the kind of monster who puts scalar functions in WHERE clauses, you deserve whatever you get. That's like squatting in high heels.

Not that I've ever squatted in high heels.

Alright look, what's that Brent says? I was young and I needed the money?

Let's forget about last week.

Query Plans!

By this point, you've seen enough pictures of Adaptive Join plans. I'll skip right to the plan that doesn't use one.

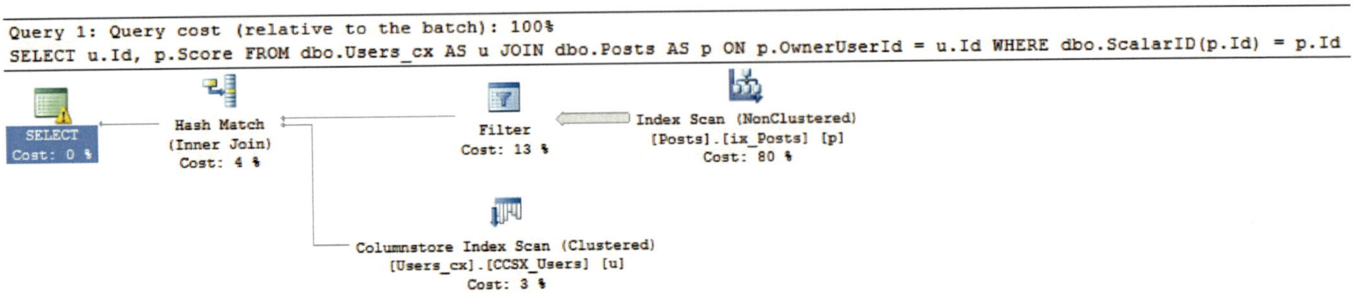

Ew

It's for the last query we ran, with the scalar function in the WHERE clause with a predicate on the Posts table.

See, this isn't SARGable either (and no, SCHEMABINDING doesn't change this). When a predicate isn't SARGable, you take away an index seek as an access choice. You don't see too many Nested Loops with an index scan on the other end, do you?

No.

So there you go. It's not the function itself that bops our Adaptive Join on the head, but the lack of SARGability.

Thanks for reading!

Do SQL Server 2017's Adaptive Joins Work with Cross Apply or Exists?

I think I've mentioned that the most fun part of new features is testing them with old ideas to see how they react.

It occurred to me that if Adaptive Joins didn't work with APPLY, I might cry.

So, here goes nothin'!

Cross

Simple Cross Apply…ies can use Adaptive Joins, though at first glance there's nothing special or different about this plan from the regular Inner Join version.

```
Transact-SQL
SELECT u.Id, ca.Score
  FROM dbo.Users_cx AS u
CROSS APPLY (
  SELECT p.Score
  FROM dbo.Posts AS p
  WHERE  p.OwnerUserId = u.Id
  AND u.LastAccessDate >= '2016-12-11'
) ca
```

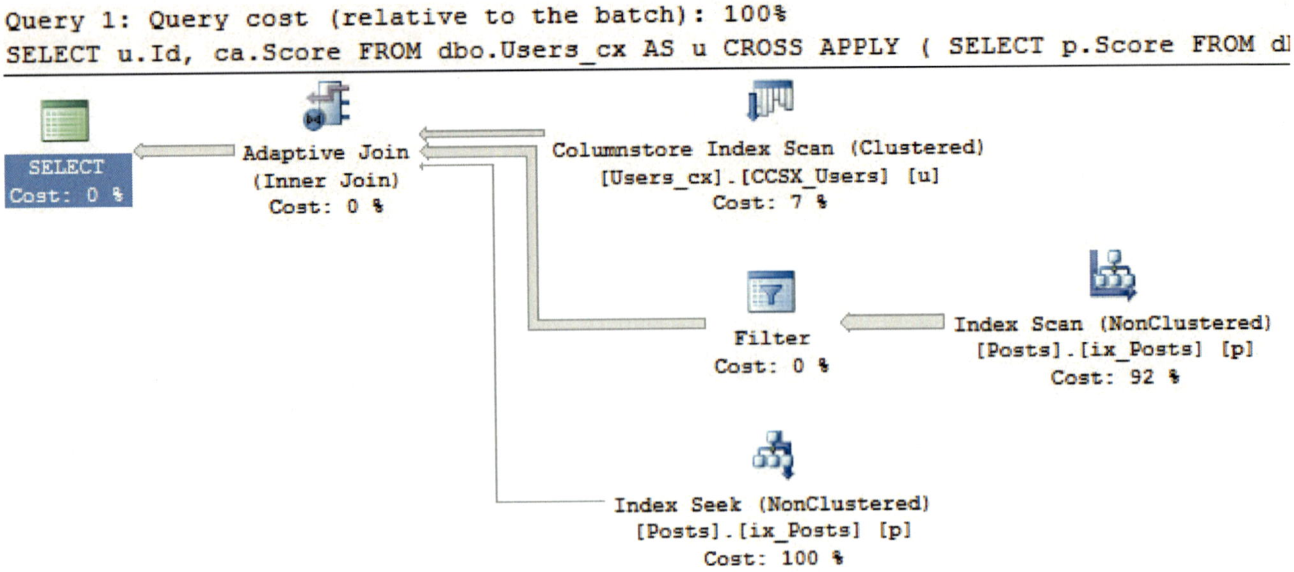

Backwards pants

I do have to point out that Cross Apply used to only be implemented as a Nested Loops Join. I learned that many years ago from one of the best articles written about Cross Apply by Paul White. That changed recently — it's possible to see it implemented with a Hash Join in at least 2016. I've seen it crop up in Cross Apply queries without a TOP operator.

It may have been in previous versions, but... Yeah. ColumnStore before 2016.

Anyway, the Cross Apply with a TOP operator does appear to skip the Adaptive Join and favor Parallel Nested Loops, as you can see in this particularly Machanic-y query.

```sql
SELECT u.Id, ca.Score
  FROM dbo.Users_cx AS u
CROSS APPLY (
  SELECT TOP 2147483647 p.Score
  FROM dbo.Posts AS p
  WHERE  p.OwnerUserId = u.Id
  AND u.LastAccessDate >= '2016-12-01'
) ca
```

PNL4LYFE

For the links, code, and comments, go here:
https://www.brentozar.com/archive/2017/05/adaptive-joins-cross-apply/

Outer

Outer Apply suffers a rather gruesome fate, where neither implementation gets an Adaptive Join.

```sql
SELECT u.Id, ca.Score
  FROM dbo.Users_cx AS u
OUTER APPLY (
  SELECT p.Score
  FROM dbo.Posts AS p
  WHERE  p.OwnerUserId = u.Id
  AND u.LastAccessDate >= '2016-12-11'
) ca

SELECT u.Id, ca.Score
  FROM dbo.Users_cx AS u
OUTER APPLY (
  SELECT TOP 2147483647 p.Score
  FROM dbo.Posts AS p
  WHERE  p.OwnerUserId = u.Id
  AND u.LastAccessDate >= '2016-12-11'
) ca
```

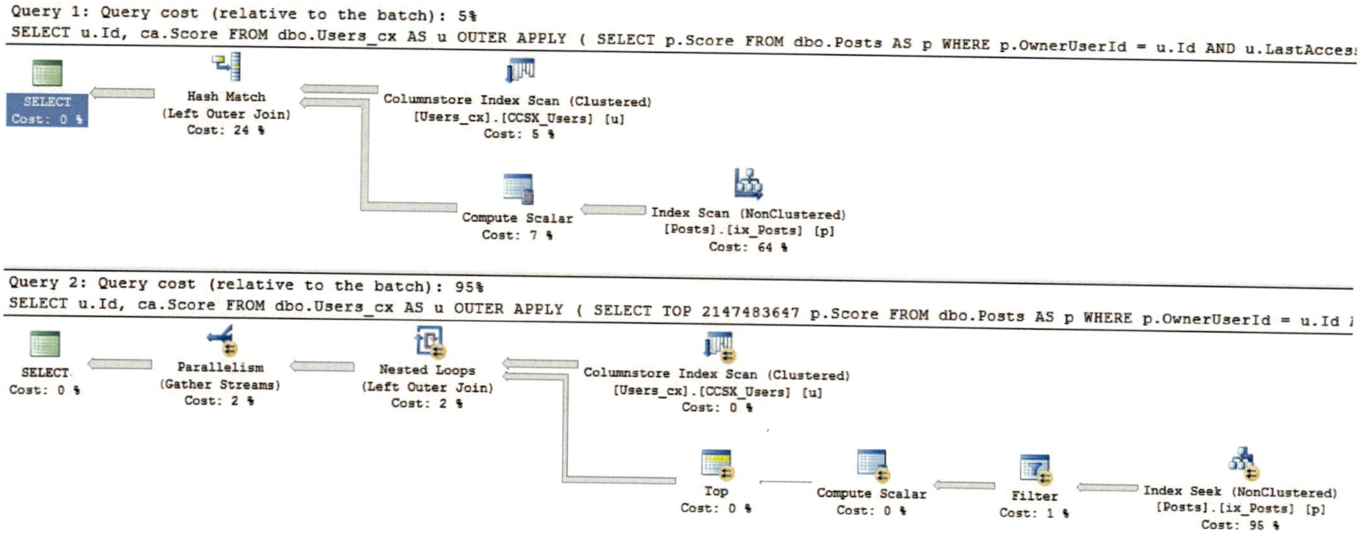

No one likes you anyway

Sad face. I still haven't gotten anything to show up in my Extended Events session for why Adaptive Joins were skipped for certain queries.

Exists

Exists not only doesn't get an Adaptive Join, but... MY EXTENDED EVENTS SESSION FINALLY SORT OF TELLS ME WHY!

I mean, it doesn't make any sense, but it's there.

Like your alcoholic aunt.

```sql
SELECT u.Id
  FROM dbo.Users_cx AS u
WHERE EXISTS (
  SELECT 1
  FROM dbo.Posts AS p
  WHERE  p.OwnerUserId = u.Id
  AND u.LastAccessDate >= '2016-01-01'
)
```

I'm going to skip showing you a non-Adaptive plan, because you've seen enough of those.

Here's what the Extended Events session shows. The query in the XE session and the query I ran are slightly different because I was testing different permutations (I paid like $7 for that word) to see if it made any difference.

Field	Value
database_name	SUPERUSER
reason	eajsrUnMatchedOuter
sql_text	SELECT u.Id FROM dbo.Users_cx AS u WHERE EXISTS (SELECT 1 FROM dbo.Posts AS p WHERE p.OwnerUserId = u.Id) AND u.LastAccessDate >= '2016-01-01'

Ho hum.

Got that? eajsrUnMatchedOuter.

I'm going to say that the next time a bartender tries to cut me off.

Not Exists

Would you believe that Not Exists gets an Adaptive Join, but Exists doesn't?

```sql
SELECT u.Id
  FROM dbo.Users_cx AS u
WHERE NOT EXISTS (
  SELECT 1
  FROM dbo.Posts AS p
  WHERE  p.OwnerUserId = u.Id
  AND u.LastAccessDate >= '2016-12-01'
)
```

And... would you believe that there's a bug in the query plan that makes the lines all woogy?

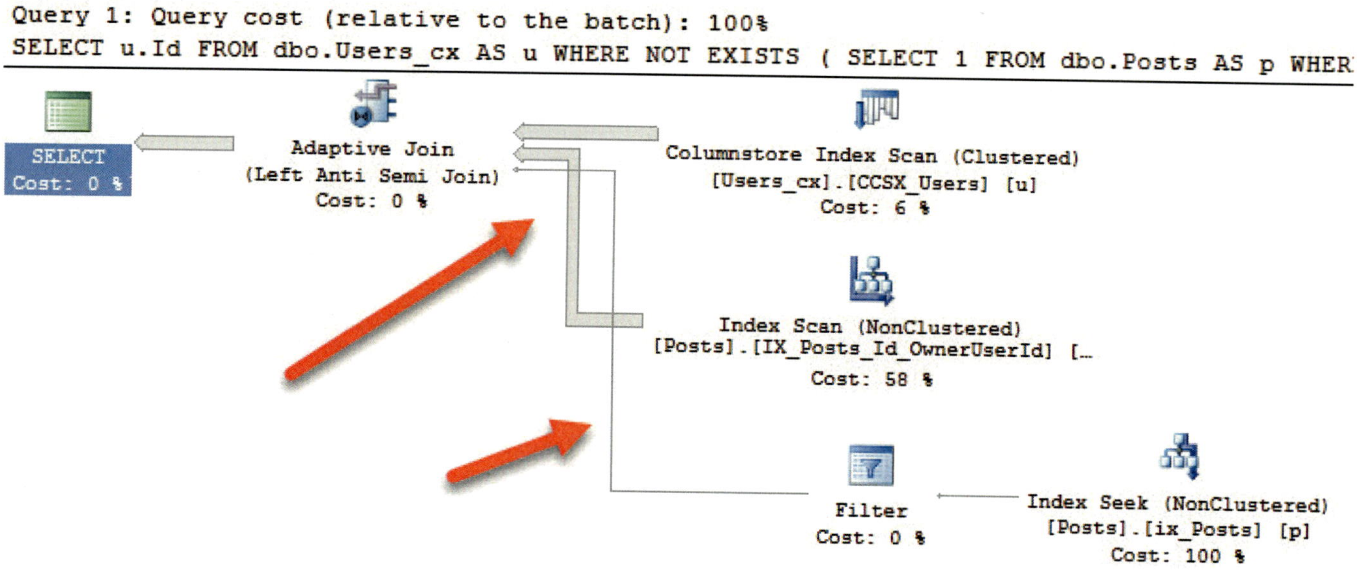

Fire Hydrant

Sir, I'm going to need you to step out of the vehicle.

Territory

I just love looking at and experimenting with this stuff! I hope you've been enjoying reading about it.

Thanks for still doing that!

Adaptive Blog Posts

It turns out I can be dumb

In a previous blog post about Adaptive Joins, I thought that EXISTS wasn't supported by the new feature. It turns out that EXISTS is totally 100% supported, as long as your indexes support EXISTS.

To show this, I need to show you a query that gets an Adaptive Join plan. After I show you a query that can't get one.

```sql
SELECT uc.Id, uc.Reputation, p.Score
FROM   dbo.Users_cx AS uc
JOIN   dbo.Posts AS p
ON p.OwnerUserId = uc.Id
WHERE  uc.CreationDate >= '20160101';
```

Forget about the Users table. With no index on the Posts table that has OwnerUserId as the leading column, there's no join choice.

There is no Dana, there is only hash join.

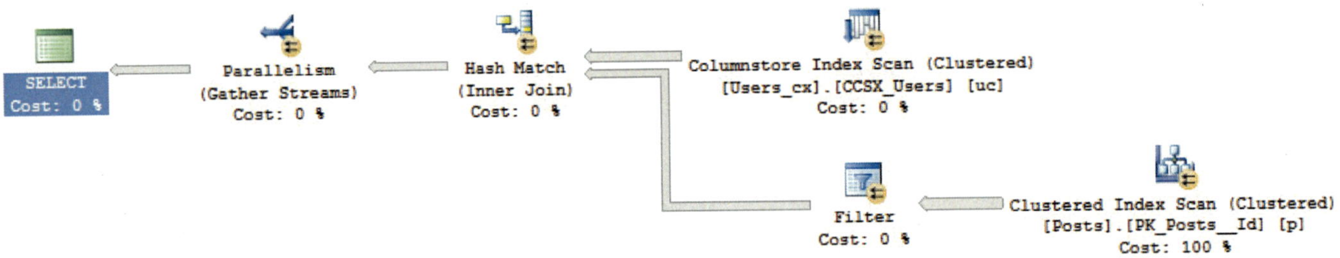

Probably more Canadian regulations

If I add an index that makes join choices possible, I get an Adaptive Join plan.

```sql
CREATE INDEX ix_ADAPT_THIS_JOIN ON dbo.Posts (OwnerUserId) INCLUDE (Score)
```

Re-running the same query, I get El Adaptivo Plana.

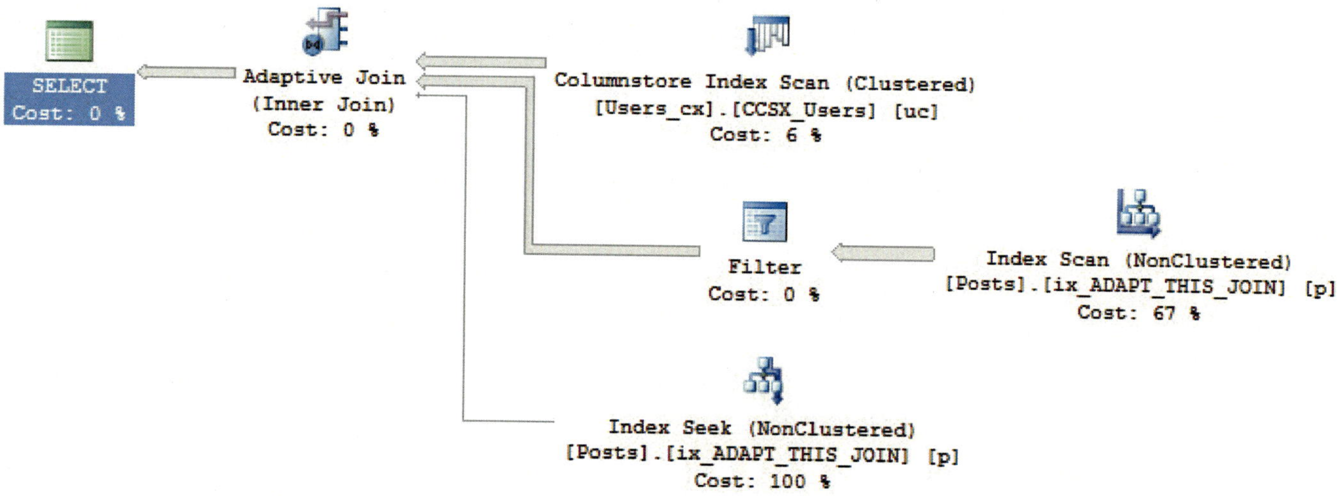

Ain't It Fun?

Now, I'm going to run two slightly different queries. The main difference is that I'm now selecting PostTypeId. The where clause date changes a bit to show different types of plans with the new column.

```sql
SELECT uc.Id, uc.Reputation, p.Score, p.PostTypeId
FROM dbo.Users_cx AS uc
JOIN dbo.Posts AS p
ON p.OwnerUserId = uc.Id
WHERE uc.CreationDate >= '20160101'


SELECT uc.Id, uc.Reputation, p.Score, p.PostTypeId
FROM dbo.Users_cx AS uc
JOIN dbo.Posts AS p
ON p.OwnerUserId = uc.Id
WHERE uc.CreationDate >= '20161201'
```

The two plans that result from these two queries aren't Adaptive at all.

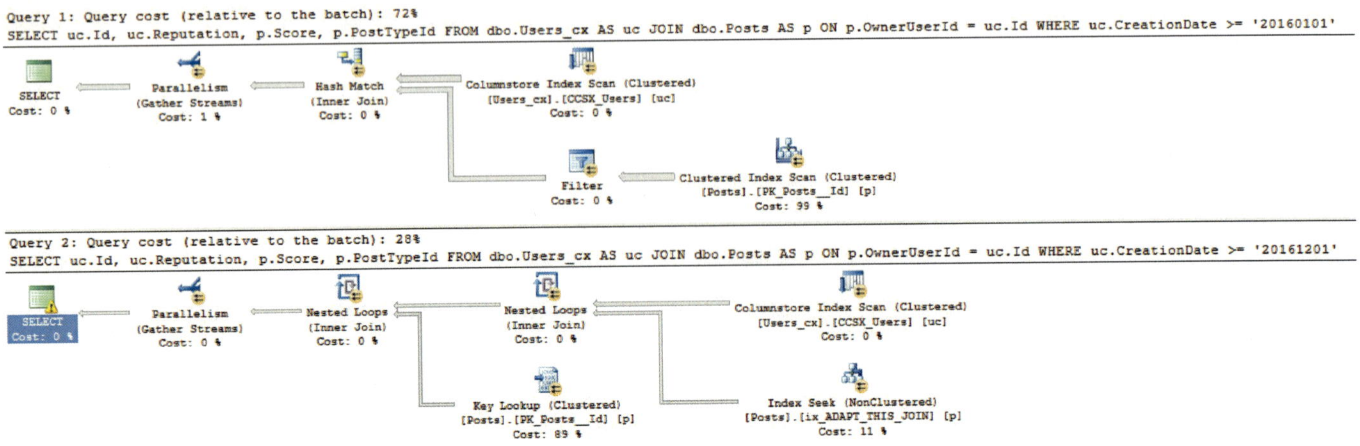

Human Being

What Happened?

Well, that first plan looks just like the original plan. It uses an index where OwnerUserId isn't the leading column, so no other plan choice is available. It has to hash.

That second plan, though. It uses the right index to give us an Adaptive Join, but it seems like the Key Lookup and downstream Nested Loops join does the whole caper in.

Since I decided to stop being dumb, I started up my Extended Events session to capture reasons why Adaptive Joins aren't used.

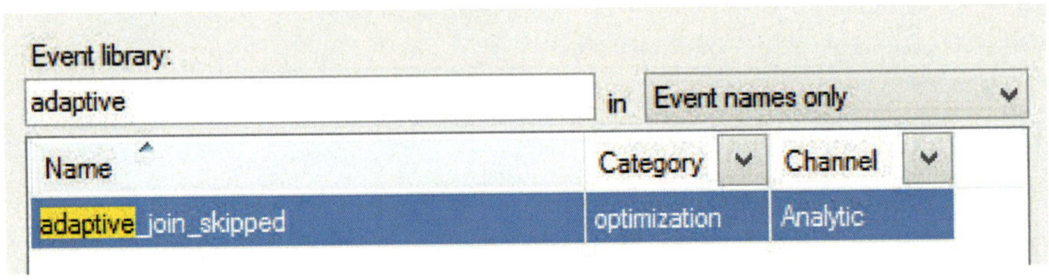

Cryptic Walk

The reason it shows for that is eajsrUnMatchedOuter.

There are a number of reasons listed in that XE session for why Adaptive Joins might be skipped:

- eajsrExchangeTypeNotSupported
- eajsrHJorNLJNotFound
- eajsrInvalidAdaptiveThreshold
- eajsrMultiConsumerSpool
- eajsrOuterCardMaxOne
- eajsrOuterSideParallelMarked
- eajsrUnMatchedOuter

I've tried some other methods to trigger other reasons, like hinting Merge Joins, generating Eager Spools, and joining to one row tables. So far nothing else has made something pop up.

Oh well. At least I'm less dumb now.

Thanks for reading!

Adaptive Joins, Memory Grant Feedback, and Stored Procedures

Not Exactly The Catchiest Name

There's a TL;DR here, in case you don't feel like reading the whole darn thing.

- Batch mode memory grant feedback works with stored procedures
- It takes several runs to adjust upwards to a final number
- It seems to only adjust downwards once (in this case by about 40%)

This isn't perfectly scientific. It's just one example that I came up with, and may behave differently both in the future, on other systems, and for other code.

But you gotta start somewhere, eh?

The Rest Of The Thing

I have a pretty simple stored procedure here, that qualifies both for Batch Mode Memory Grant Feedback and Batch Mode Adaptive Joins.

And I thought I had a hard time naming things.

Transact-SQL

```
CREATE OR ALTER PROCEDURE dbo.UsersByLastAccessDate
    (
        @LastAccessDate DATETIME
    )
AS
    BEGIN
        SELECT  uc.Id, uc.Reputation, p.Score
        FROM    dbo.Users_cx AS uc
        JOIN    dbo.Posts AS p
        ON p.OwnerUserId = uc.Id
        WHERE   uc.LastAccessDate >= @LastAccessDate;
    END;
```

For different values passed to Last Access Date, the Adaptive join changes.

This returns 622,961 rows:

```sql
EXEC dbo.UsersByLastAccessDate @LastAccessDate = '20160101'
```

This returns 24,803 rows:

```sql
EXEC dbo.UsersByLastAccessDate @LastAccessDate = '20161211 01:00:00.003'
```

Clearly processing these different amounts of data requires different amounts of memory.

It's not clear from the plan which operator consumes the memory (there are no Memory Fraction indicators), but we can assume that it's the Adaptive Join operator. In Adaptive Join plans, both the join types have a startup memory cost. This is a safety net to support the runtime decision.

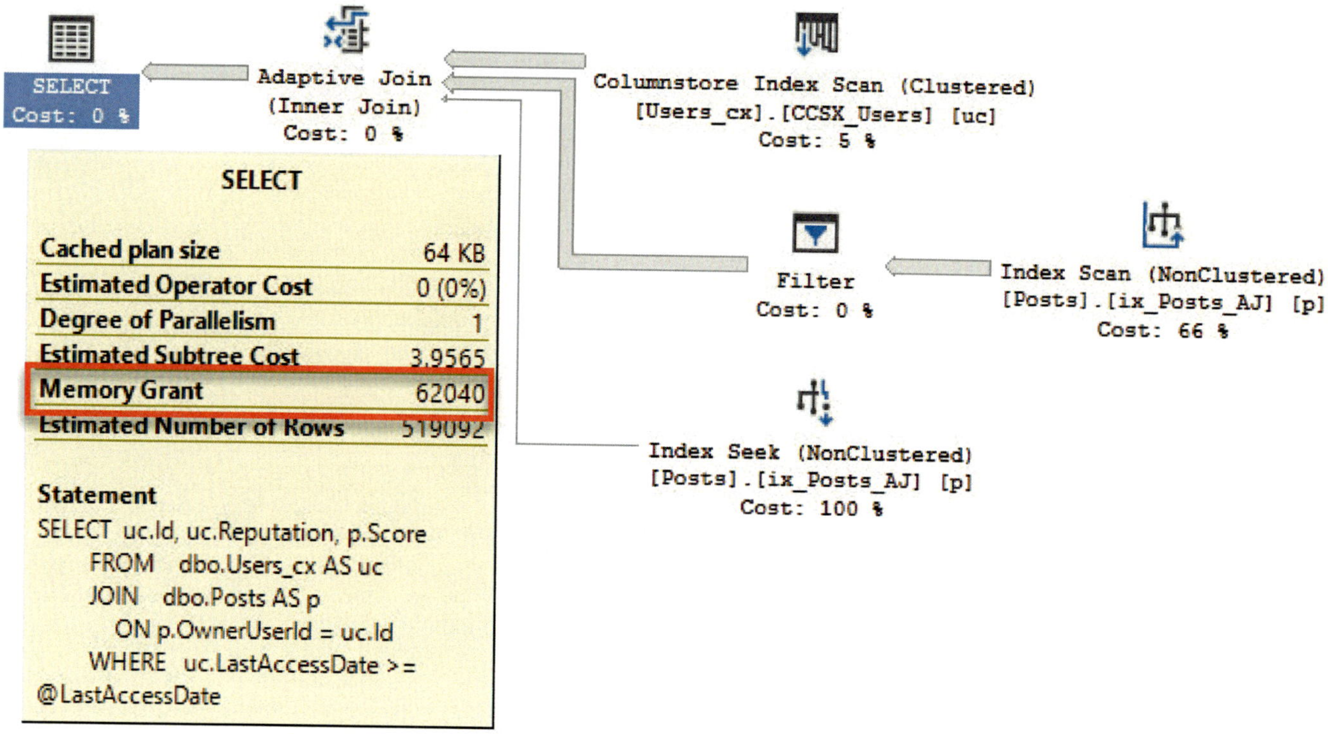

Bird Trouble

Little Plan First

When we execute the proc with the small value first, we start off with a small memory grant, that over five iterations adjusts upwards to 14,000KB, and stops there.

timestamp	name	sql_text	granted_memory_kb	ideal_memory_kb
2018-02-09 17:30:20.5324703	query_memory_grant_usage	EXEC dbo.UsersByLastAccessDate @LastAccessDate = '20161211 01:00:00.003'	1504	1504
2018-02-09 17:30:22.5800598	additional_memory_grant	EXEC dbo.UsersByLastAccessDate @LastAccessDate = '20160101'	1024	NULL
2018-02-09 17:30:23.8903947	query_memory_grant_usage	EXEC dbo.UsersByLastAccessDate @LastAccessDate = '20160101'	2528	1504
2018-02-09 17:30:26.3042960	additional_memory_grant	EXEC dbo.UsersByLastAccessDate @LastAccessDate = '20160101'	1024	NULL
2018-02-09 17:30:26.3853417	additional_memory_grant	EXEC dbo.UsersByLastAccessDate @LastAccessDate = '20160101'	1024	NULL
2018-02-09 17:30:27.1166061	query_memory_grant_usage	EXEC dbo.UsersByLastAccessDate @LastAccessDate = '20160101'	7672	5624
2018-02-09 17:30:29.4897439	additional_memory_grant	EXEC dbo.UsersByLastAccessDate @LastAccessDate = '20160101'	1024	NULL
2018-02-09 17:30:29.9332990	query_memory_grant_usage	EXEC dbo.UsersByLastAccessDate @LastAccessDate = '20160101'	10808	9784
2018-02-09 17:30:32.8788565	query_memory_grant_usage	EXEC dbo.UsersByLastAccessDate @LastAccessDate = '20160101'	14000	14000
2018-02-09 17:30:35.8755288	query_memory_grant_usage	EXEC dbo.UsersByLastAccessDate @LastAccessDate = '20160101'	14000	14000

I Hate Extended Events

In between each run, it fires off a request for more memory next time. Feedback, and all that.

I cast a pretty wide net with the stuff I was collecting while running this. Some of it caught stuff, some of it didn't. I'm just showing you the interesting bits.

Name		
additional_memory_grant	1	✓
excessive_non_grant_memory_used	1	✓
hash_spill_details	1	✓
memory_grant_feedback_loop_dis...	1	✓
memory_grant_updated_by_feedb...	1	✓
query_execution_batch_hash_join...	1	✓
query_execution_batch_spill_started	1	✓
query_memory_grant_info_sampling	1	✓
query_memory_grant_usage	1	✓
spilling_report_to_memory_grant_f...	1	✓

More naming problems

For instance, there were a bunch of rows for the spill event, but everything was NULL for them, and the spill details aren't really pertinent here.

Whatever.

Make Profiler Great Again.

Big Plan First

When the large plan fires first, something a bit odd happens.

It asks for a much larger grant up front than it it adjusted to last time — 14MB vs 62MB:

name	sql_text	granted_memory_kb	ideal_memory_kb
query_memory_grant_usage	EXEC dbo.UsersByLastAccessDate @LastAccessDate = '20160101'	62040	62040
query_memory_grant_usage	EXEC dbo.UsersByLastAccessDate @LastAccessDate = '20161211 01:00:00.003'	38512	38512
query_memory_grant_usage	EXEC dbo.UsersByLastAccessDate @LastAccessDate = '20161211 01:00:00.003'	38512	38512
query_memory_grant_usage	EXEC dbo.UsersByLastAccessDate @LastAccessDate = '20161211 01:00:00.003'	38512	38512

LITTLE PIG, LITTLE PIG

When the smaller plans run, the memory grant cuts down by 23.5MB, and stops adjusting from there.

On each subsequent execution, there's a plan warning about excessive memory.

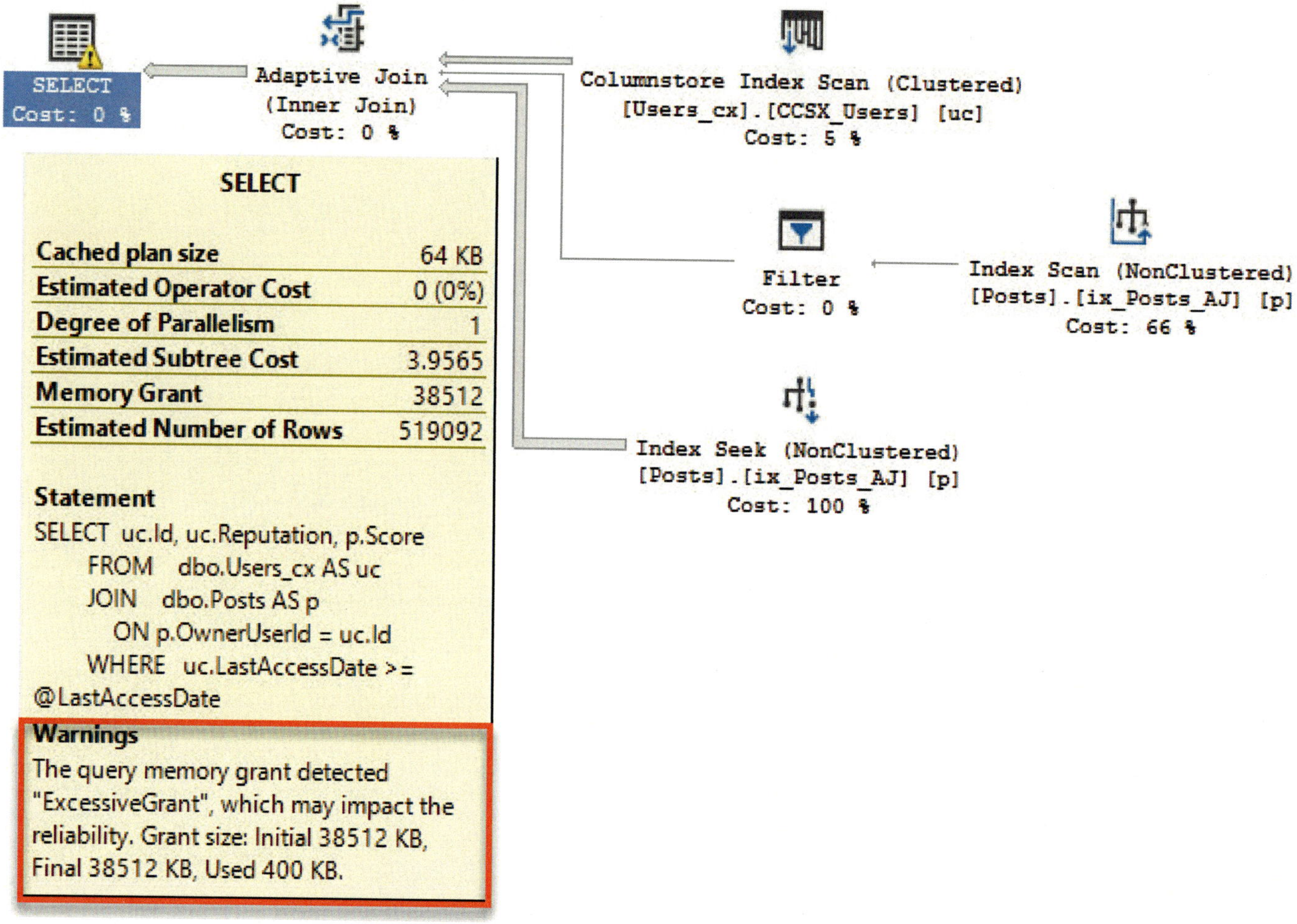

You Can't Put Your Arms Around A Memory Grant

Further executions of the large plan don't increase the memory grant. Ticking the Last Access Date back to 2010 also doesn't cause the grant to increase upwards.

Which Is Better?

Well, if the memory needs of the query truly are 14MB of memory overall, it would seem like starting low and ticking up is ideal. I mean, unless something awful happens and your next few runs just spill and take forever and everyone hates you.

If the grant of 38MB isn't harming concurrency, and sets a safe bound for larger values, it might not be bad if you end up there after just one run.

In either situation, you're much better off than you are on earlier versions of SQL that can't swap joins at run time, or adjust memory grants between runs.

Those are two of the many things that make dealing with parameter sniffing difficult.

I really hope that (JOE SACK RULES) the QO team at Microsoft keep at this stuff. Right now, it only helps for queries running in Batch Mode, which requires the Scent Of A Column Store.

Making features like this available in Row Mode, or making aspects of Batch Mode accessible to Row Mode queries...

One can dream.

Thanks for reading!

Brent says: *I feel for people out there who don't have the luxury of spare time to read blogs. You, dear reader, are going to be able to recognize these symptoms when they show up in your server, but other folks are going to be even more mystified about why their query performance is all over the place when they swear haven't changed the queries. Don't get me wrong, I love this feature – but in these early iterations of it, it'll catch people by surprise.*

SQL Server 2017: Interleaved Execution for MSTVFs

What I don't want you to take away from this

Is that I want you to start using Multi Statement Table Valued Functions all over the place. There are still problems with them.

- Backed by table variables
- Lots of hidden I/O cost
- Number of executions may surprise you

One important current limitation (May-ish of 2017) is that Interleaved Execution doesn't happen when you use MSTVFs with Cross Apply. It's only for direct Joins to MSTVFs as far as I can see.

But does it improve anything?

Well, kinda.

Let's get physical

I've got this stinker over here. It stinks. But it gets me where I'm going.

Transact-SQL

```
CREATE FUNCTION [dbo].[MultiStatementTVF_Join] (@h BIGINT)
RETURNS @Out TABLE (UserId INT, BadgeCount BIGINT )
AS
    BEGIN
        INSERT  INTO @Out
                (UserId, BadgeCount)
        SELECT  UserId, COUNT_BIG(*) AS BadgeCount
        FROM    dbo.Badges AS b
        GROUP BY b.UserId
        HAVING COUNT_BIG(*) > @h;
        RETURN;
    END;
```

I wanted to run different kinds of queries to test things, because, well Adaptive Joins require Batch mode processing which right now is limited to ColumnStore indexes.

"Good" news: Interleaved Execution doesn't require a ColumnStore index.

Confusing news: They still get called Adaptive Joins.

Yeah. Words. More pictures.

Old plans

I lied. More words first.

Dropping compatibility levels down to 130 (I know, down to 130, what a savage) pulls Interleaved Execution out of the mix.

Running against both a ColumnStore index version of Users and a Row Store version…

Transact-SQL

```
ALTER DATABASE SUPERUSER SET COMPATIBILITY_LEVEL = 130
GO

  SELECT u.Id, mj.*
    FROM dbo.Users_cx AS u --ColumnStore!
    JOIN dbo.MultiStatementTVF_Join(0) mj
    ON  mj.UserId = u.Id
  WHERE u.LastAccessDate >= '2016-12-01'

  SELECT u.Id, mj.*
    FROM dbo.Users AS u --RowStore!
    JOIN dbo.MultiStatementTVF_Join(0) mj
    ON  mj.UserId = u.Id
  WHERE u.LastAccessDate >= '2016-12-01'
GO
```

Here's the stats time and IO results.

Table 'Users_cx'. Scan count 1, logical reads 0, physical reads 0, read-ahead reads 0, lob logical reads 626, lob physical reads 0, lob read-ahead reads 0.

Table 'Users_cx'. Segment reads 1, segment skipped 0.

Table '#AC8B865E'. Scan count 1, logical reads 754, physical reads 0, read-ahead reads 0, lob logical reads 0, lob physical reads 0, lob read-ahead reads 0.

SQL Server Execution Times:

CPU time = 1250 ms, elapsed time = 1996 ms.

Table 'Users'. Scan count 0, logical reads 888887, physical reads 0, read-ahead reads 6, lob logical reads 0, lob physical reads 0, lob read-ahead reads 0.

Table '#AC8B865E'. Scan count 1, logical reads 754, physical reads 0, read-ahead reads 0, lob logical reads 0, lob physical reads 0, lob read-ahead reads 0.

SQL Server Execution Times:

CPU time = 2344 ms, elapsed time = 2742 ms.

Alright, pictures.

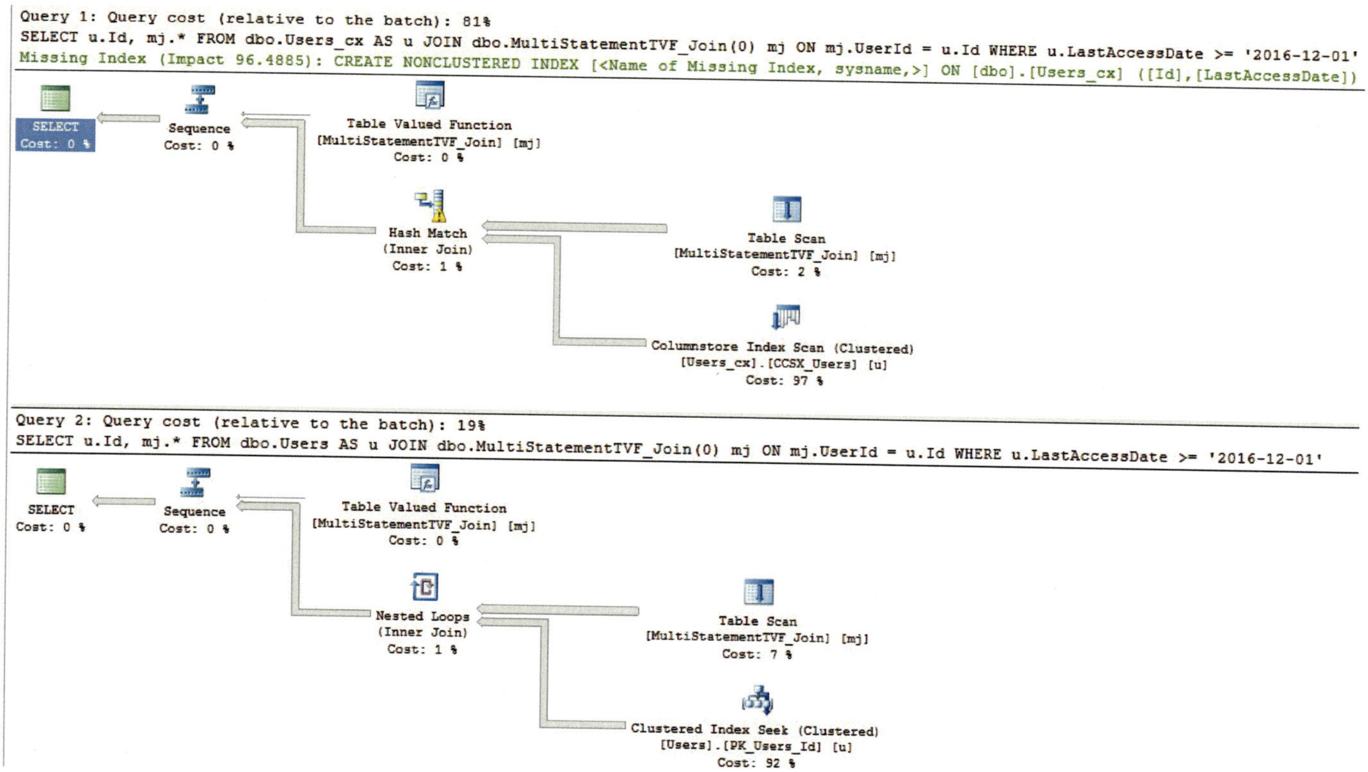

But you say he's just a friend.

Isn't it weird and confusing when you get these missing index requests on queries that use ColumnStore indexes? I can't figure out who's wrong.

Are my queries that bad? Does the optimizer not have a rule about this? Did it break the rule because my query is so bad?

Why... why do you wanna have a different index, here, SQL? What's on your mind?

What if I add the index?

EVERYTHING GETS WORSE

The plan looks just like the Row Store plan from before, and has the same stats time and IO pattern.

Lesson learned: Stop listening to missing index requests when you're using ColumnStore.

New Plans

Calgon, take me away.

```sql
ALTER DATABASE SUPERUSER SET COMPATIBILITY_LEVEL = 140
GO

  SELECT u.Id, mj.*
    FROM dbo.Users_cx AS u --UltraVox!
    JOIN dbo.MultiStatementTVF_Join(0) mj
    ON  mj.UserId = u.Id
  WHERE u.LastAccessDate >= '2016-12-01'

  SELECT u.Id, mj.*
    FROM dbo.Users AS u --RegularVox!
    JOIN dbo.MultiStatementTVF_Join(0) mj
    ON  mj.UserId = u.Id
  WHERE u.LastAccessDate >= '2016-12-01'

GO
```

Table 'Users_cx'. Scan count 1, logical reads 0, physical reads 0, read-ahead reads 0, lob logical reads 626, lob physical reads 0, lob read-ahead reads 0.

Table 'Users_cx'. Segment reads 1, segment skipped 0.

Table '#B1503B7B'. Scan count 1, logical reads 754, physical reads 0, read-ahead reads 0, lob logical reads 0, lob physical reads 0, lob read-ahead reads 0.

SQL Server Execution Times:

CPU time = 1488 ms, elapsed time = 1633 ms.

For the links, code, and comments, go here:
https://www.brentozar.com/archive/2017/05/sql-server-2017-interleaved-execution-mstvfs/

Table 'Workfile'. Scan count 0, logical reads 0, physical reads 0, read-ahead reads 0, lob logical reads 0, lob physical reads 0, lob read-ahead reads 0.

Table 'Worktable'. Scan count 0, logical reads 0, physical reads 0, read-ahead reads 0, lob logical reads 0, lob physical reads 0, lob read-ahead reads 0.

Table '#B1503B7B'. Scan count 1, logical reads 754, physical reads 0, read-ahead reads 0, lob logical reads 0, lob physical reads 0, lob read-ahead reads 0.

Table 'Users'. Scan count 1, logical reads 145, physical reads 0, read-ahead reads 0, lob logical reads 0, lob physical reads 0, lob read-ahead reads 0.

SQL Server Execution Times:

CPU time = 1530 ms, elapsed time = 1592 ms.

Exciting already! The ColumnStore index is right about in the same place, but the RowStore index is much faster.

But why?

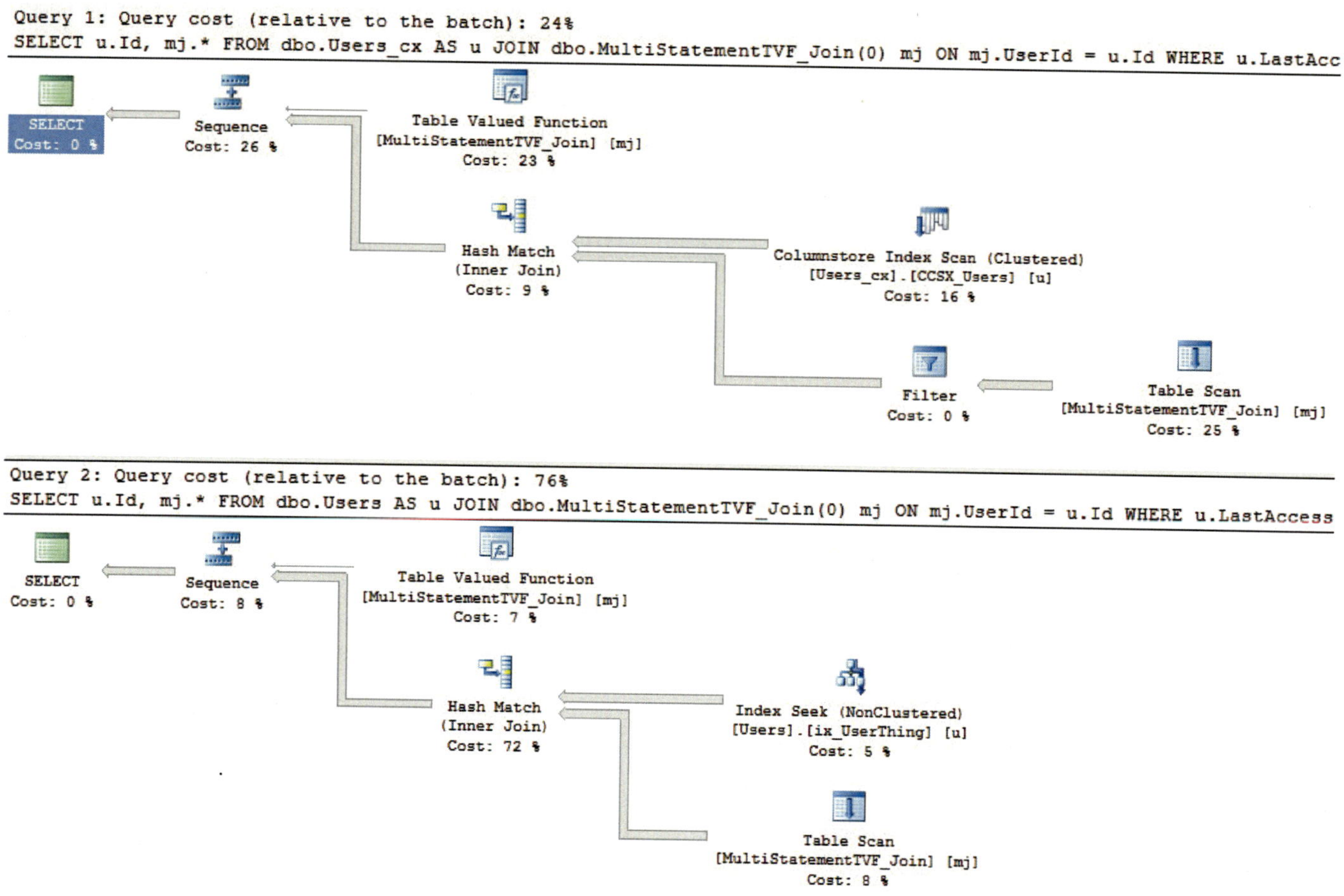

Choices, choices

This part is pretty cool!

In the first plan, the optimizer chooses the ColumnStore index over the nonclustered index that it chose in compat level 130.

This plan is back to where it was before, and I'm totally cool with that. Avoiding bad choices is just as good as making good choices.

I think. I never took an ethics class, so whatever.

In the second plan, there's yet another new index choice, and the cpu and IO profile is down to being competitive with the ColumnStore index query.

The optimizer realized that with more than 100 rows coming out of the MSTVF, it might be a good idea to use a more efficient index than the PK/CX. Another good move. Way to go, optimizer. Exactly how many rows did it estimate?

The Operators

An Interleaved Execution plan doesn't have any special operators, but it does have special operator properties.

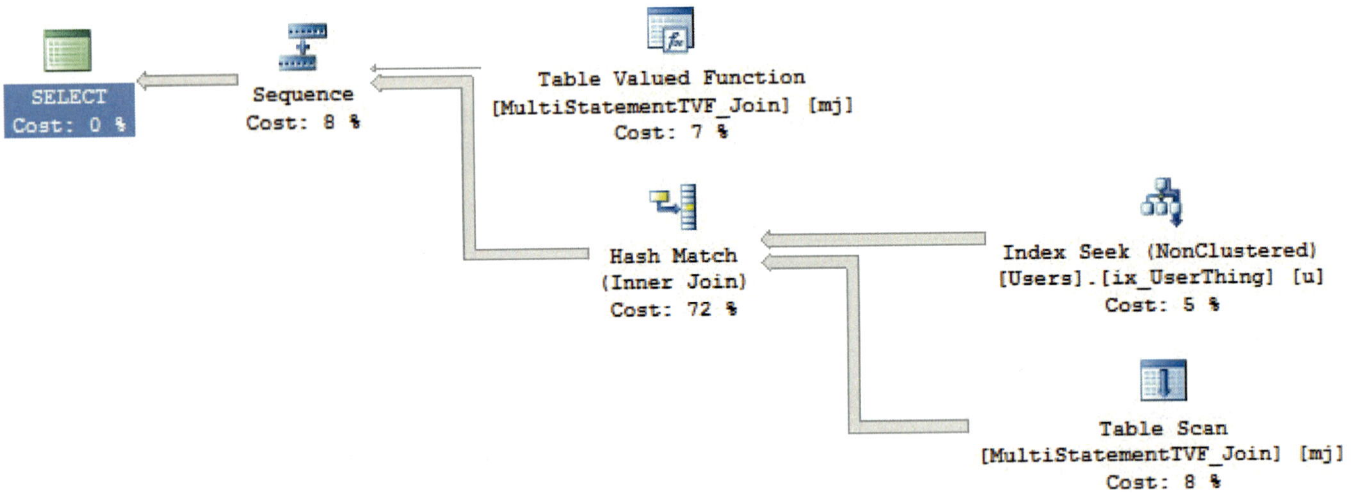

Ain't nothin special

Hovering over the topmost Table Valued Function operator, that's where some of the new properties live.

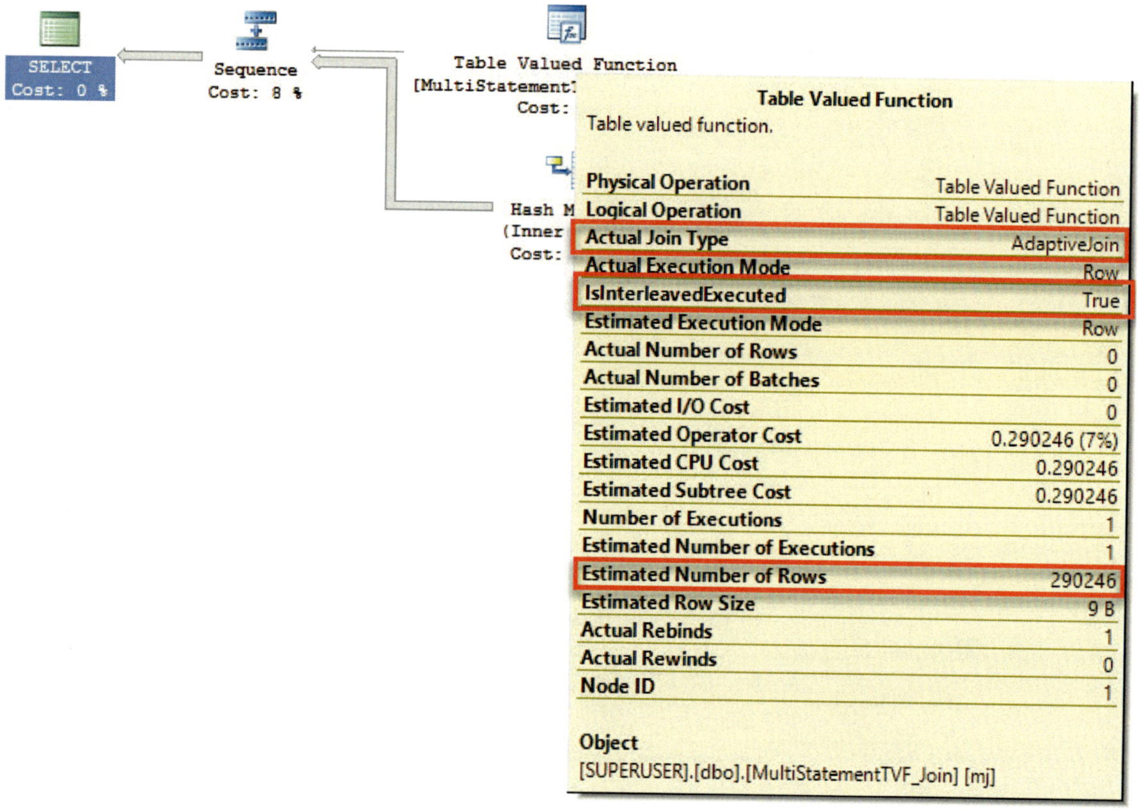

I promise this will be in sp_BlitzCache

Even though this is all in Row mode, the Join type is Adaptive. I'm guessing that Adaptive Join is going to be an umbrella term for new reactive optimizations.

Maybe. I'm guessing.

One thing you want to pay extra attention to here is the estimated number of rows.

It's not 100 anymore.

It's the actual number of rows that end up in the table variable.

Ain't that somethin?

The bottom Table Valued Function operator doesn't have the Interleaved property, but it does show that it's an Adaptive Join, and we have the correct estimate again.

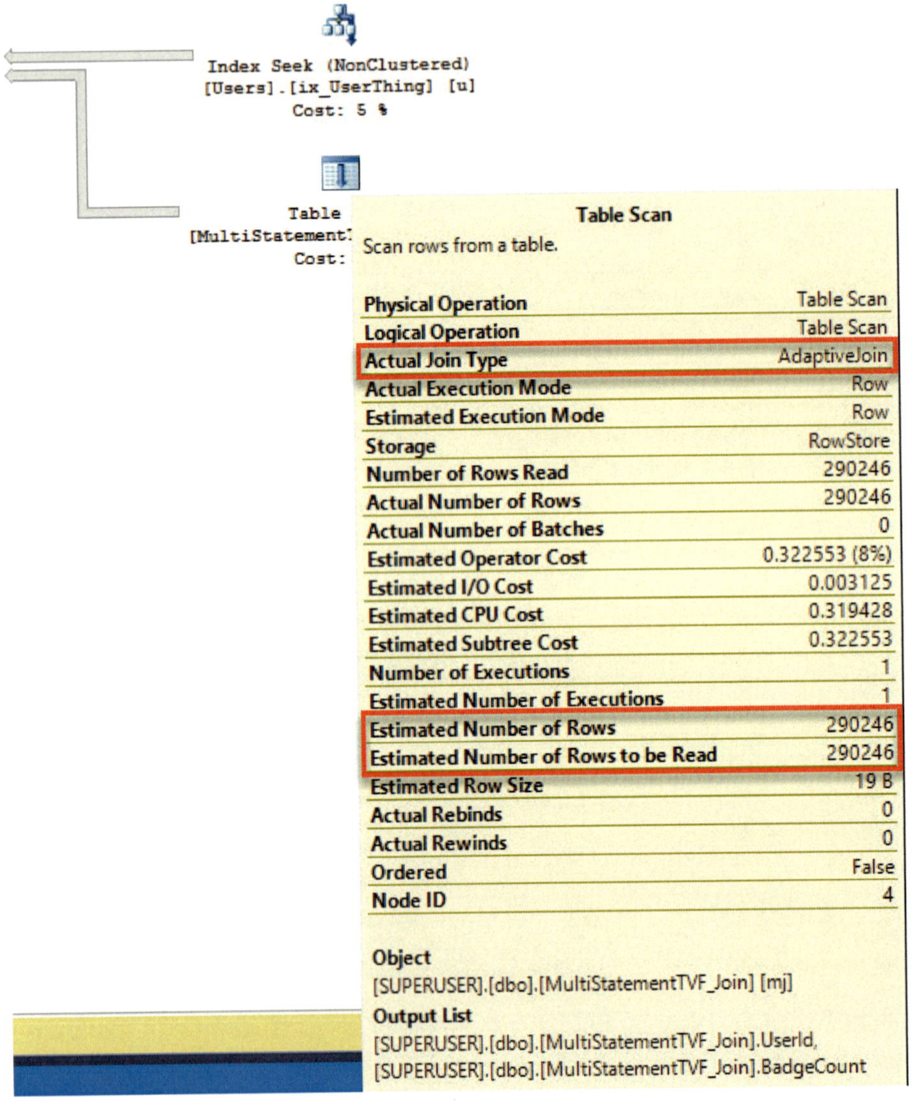

ooh barracuda

Not bad

If you have a lot of MSTVFs in legacy code that you don't have time to untangle, SQL Server 2017 could save you a ton of time.

This is a huge improvement over what you used to get out of MSTVFs — I wonder if something similar might be coming to regular old Table Variables in the near future?

UPDATE: Them's bugs! Calling interleaved execution joins Adaptive Joins is an error, and will be fixed in a future version of SSMS.

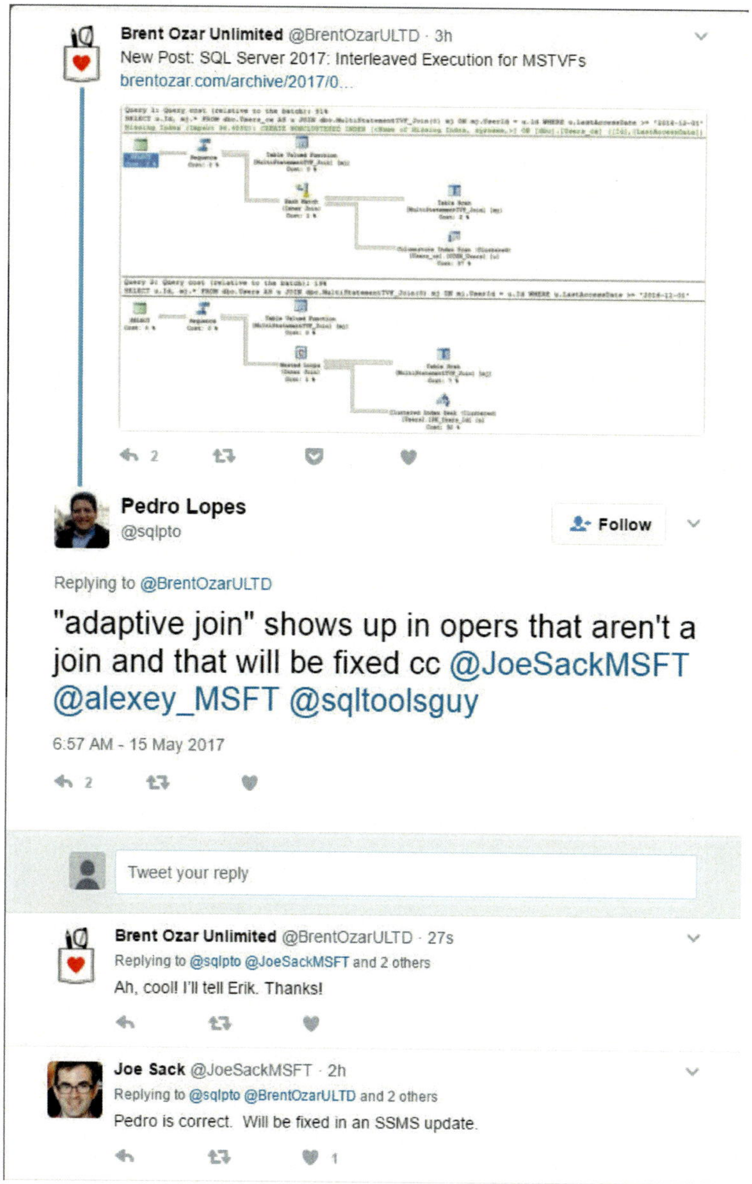

Twitter is for work.

Thanks for reading!

SQL Server 2017: Interleaved MSTVFs Vs Inline Table Valued Functions

But is it faster?

Now, I know. There are very few "always" things out there in SQL Server. This is also true for functions.

A lot of the time — I might even say most of the time, inline table valued functions are going to be faster that scalar and multi statement table valued functions.

Before you huff and puff, I've seen cases where a scalar valued function was faster than either other kind of function.

Of course, Jeff Moden was involved, so there is clearly black magic at play here. Or maybe just some more beer popsicles.

Unfortunately... Or, I don't know, maybe fortunately, Microsoft doesn't seem to have been putting much development time into improving the performance characteristics of scalar valued functions. Just little bits.

Us vs Them

Let's get back to the point at hand, though. MSTVFs have been improved in certain circumstances. Inline table valued functions are the reigning champions.

How do they stack up?

I'm going to take my best-timed MSTVF with Interleaved Execution, and put it up against an inline table valued function.

Here are my functions.

```
CREATE FUNCTION [dbo].[MultiStatementTVF_Join] (@h BIGINT)
RETURNS @Out TABLE (UserId INT, BadgeCount BIGINT )
AS
    BEGIN
        INSERT  INTO @Out
                (UserId, BadgeCount)
        SELECT  UserId, COUNT_BIG(*) AS BadgeCount
        FROM    dbo.Badges AS b
        GROUP BY b.UserId
        HAVING COUNT_BIG(*) > @h
        RETURN;
    END;

CREATE FUNCTION [dbo].[ITVF_Join] (@h BIGINT)
RETURNS TABLE
AS
    RETURN
        SELECT  UserId, COUNT_BIG(*) AS BadgeCount
        FROM    dbo.Badges AS b
        GROUP BY b.UserId
        HAVING COUNT_BIG(*) > @h;
```

Here are my queries.

```
SELECT u.Id, mj.*
  FROM dbo.Users_cx AS u
  JOIN dbo.MultiStatementTVF_Join(0) mj
  ON  mj.UserId = u.Id
WHERE u.LastAccessDate >= '2016-12-01'

SELECT u.Id, mj.*
  FROM dbo.Users_cx AS u
  JOIN dbo.ITVF_Join(0) mj
  ON  mj.UserId = u.Id
WHERE u.LastAccessDate >= '2016-12-01'
```

Start your (relational) engines

First, here's are the stats on my MSTVF

Table 'Users_cx'. Scan count 1, logical reads 0, physical reads 0, read-ahead reads 0, lob logical reads 626, lob physical reads 0, lob read-ahead reads 0.

Table 'Users_cx'. Segment reads 1, segment skipped 0.

Table '#B42CA826'. Scan count 1, logical reads 754, physical reads 0, read-ahead reads 0, lob logical reads 0, lob physical reads 0, lob read-ahead reads 0.

SQL Server Execution Times:

CPU time = 1117 ms, elapsed time = 1122 ms.

Here's the execution plan (I collected this separately from getting the CPU timing).

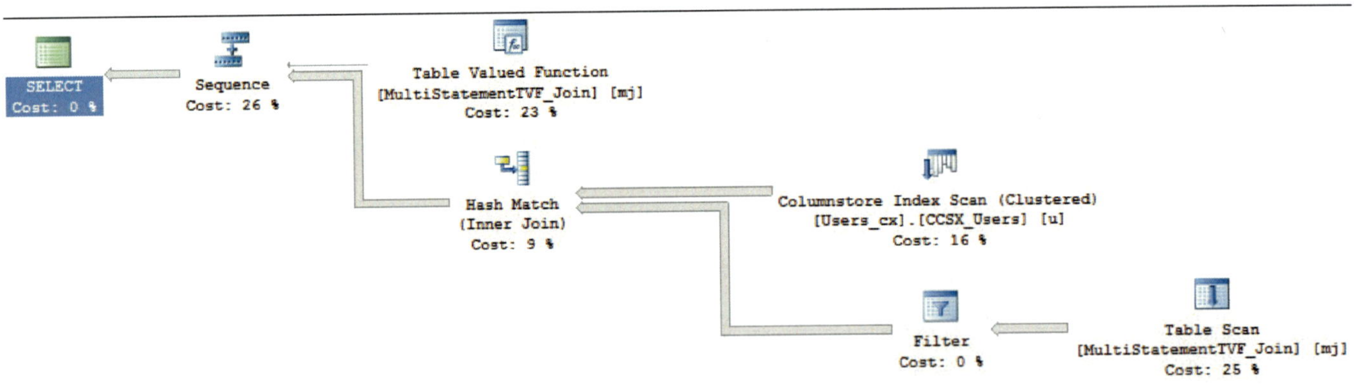

No funny business

Second, here are the stats on my inline table valued function.

Table 'Users_cx'. Scan count 1, logical reads 0, physical reads 0, read-ahead reads 0, lob logical reads 626, lob physical reads 0, lob read-ahead reads 0.

Table 'Users_cx'. Segment reads 1, segment skipped 0.

Table 'Badges'. Scan count 1, logical reads 1759, physical reads 0, read-ahead reads 0, lob logical reads 0, lob physical reads 0, lob read-ahead reads 0.

SQL Server Execution Times:

CPU time = 250 ms, elapsed time = 271 ms.

Here's the execution plan (again, collected this separately from getting the CPU timing).

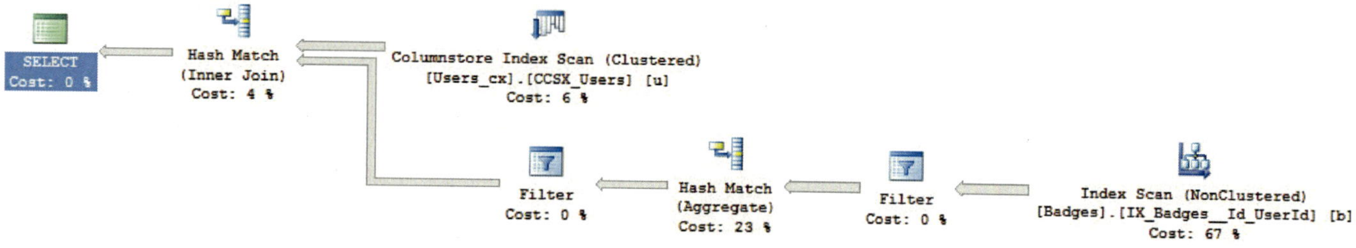

Double filtered for your pleasure

Well then

In this case, the inline table valued function wiped the floor with the MSTVF, even with Interleaved Execution.

Obviously there's overhead dumping that many rows into a table variable prior to performing the join, but hey, if you're dumping enough rows in a MSTVF to care about enhanced cardinality estimation...

Picture my eyebrows.

Picture them raising.

Thanks for reading!

Misc

We've reached the end. We've opened a lot of bottles, and had a lot of good times. To finish, take whatever you have leftover and pour it all into one glass. Maybe make sure your house is in order, first.

BRENT OZAR
UNLIMITED®

Spills SQL Server Doesn't Warn You About

Don't make me spill

Table variables get a lot of bad press, and they deserve it. They are to query performance what the TSA is to air travel. No one's sure what they're doing, but they've been taking forever to do it.

One particular thing that irks me about them (table variables, now) is that they'll spill their spaghetti all over your disks, and not warn you. Now, this gripe isn't misplaced. SQL Server will warn you when Sort and Hash operations spill to disk. And they should! Because spilling to disk usually means you had to slow down to do it. Disks are slow. Memory is fast. Squatting in the Smith Machine is cheating.

Wouldn't it be nice?

Why am I picking on table variables? Because people so frequently use them for the wrong reasons. They're in memory! They made my query faster! No one harbors delusions about temp tables, except that one guy who told me they're a security risk. Sure, we should get a warning if temp tables spill to disk, too. But I don't think that would surprise most people as much.

So let's see what hits the sneeze guard!

You've been here before

You know I'm going to use Stack Overflow. Here's the gist: I'm going to set max memory to 1 GB, and stick the Votes table, which is about 2.4 GB, into a table variable. While that goes on, I'm going to run sp_BlitzFirst for 60 seconds in Expert Mode to see which files get read from and written to. I'm also going to get STATISTICS IO information, and the query plan.

```sql
SET STATISTICS IO ON

DECLARE @Votes TABLE (Id INT NOT NULL, PostId INT NOT NULL, UserId INT NULL, BountyAmount INT NULL, VoteTypeId INT NOT NULL, CreationDate DATETIME NOT NULL)

INSERT @Votes
        ( Id, PostId, UserId, BountyAmount, VoteTypeId, CreationDate )
SELECT v.Id, v.PostId, v.UserId, v.BountyAmount, v.VoteTypeId, v.CreationDate
FROM dbo.Votes AS v

SELECT COUNT(*) FROM @Votes AS v
```

First, let's look at stats IO output. The first section shows us hitting the Votes table to insert data. The second section shows us getting the COUNT from our table variable. Wouldn't you know, we hit a temp object! Isn't that funny? I'm laughing.

```
Table 'Votes'. Scan count 1, logical reads 309027, physical reads 0, read-ahead reads 308527, lob logical reads 0, lob physical reads 0, lob read-ahead reads 0.

(67258370 row(s) affected)

Table '#ACD2BA14'. Scan count 1, logical reads 308525, physical reads 36, read-ahead reads 308077, lob logical reads 0, lob physical reads 0, lob read-ahead reads 0.
```

The query plan doesn't give us any warnings. No little yellow exclamation points. No red X. It's all just kind of bland. Even Paste The Plan doesn't make this any prettier.

The query plan doesn't warn us about anything.

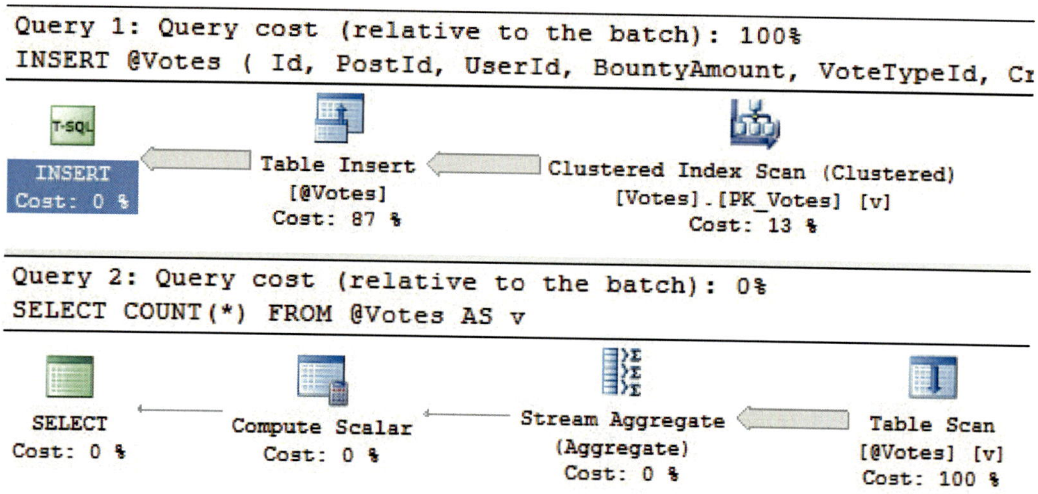

Oatmeal

Well, unless you really go looking at the plan...

Table Scan

Scan rows from a table.

Physical Operation	Table Scan
Logical Operation	Table Scan
Actual Execution Mode	Row
Estimated Execution Mode	Row
Storage	RowStore
Number of Rows Read	67258370
Actual Number of Rows	67258370
Actual Number of Batches	0
Estimated Operator Cost	0.0032831 (100%)
Estimated I/O Cost	0.0032035
Estimated CPU Cost	0.0000796
Estimated Subtree Cost	0.0032831
Number of Executions	1
Estimated Number of Executions	1
Estimated Number of Rows	1
Estimated Row Size	9 B
Actual Rebinds	0
Actual Rewinds	0
Ordered	False
Node ID	2

Object

[@Votes] [v]

Oh, that terrible estimate

Okay, that sucks

Let's look at sp_BlitzFirst. Only Young And Good Looking® people contribute code to it, so it must be awesome.

Pattern	Sample Time	Sample (seconds)	File Name	Drive	# Reads/Writes	MB Read/Written	Avg Stall (ms)	file physical name
PHYSICAL READS	2016-11-02 14:19:13.0341706 -04:00	60	tempdev3 [ROWS]	D:	2439	598.1	7	D:\tempdb2014\tempdb3.ndf
PHYSICAL READS	2016-11-02 14:19:13.0341706 -04:00	60	tempdev4 [ROWS]	D:	3364	596.4	6	D:\tempdb2014\tempdb4.ndf
PHYSICAL READS	2016-11-02 14:19:13.0341706 -04:00	60	tempdev [ROWS]	D:	2856	596.4	6	D:\tempdb2014\tempdb.mdf
PHYSICAL READS	2016-11-02 14:19:13.0341706 -04:00	60	tempdev2 [ROWS]	D:	2937	596.4	6	D:\tempdb2014\tempdb2.ndf
PHYSICAL WRITES	2016-11-02 14:19:13.0341706 -04:00	60	tempdev [ROWS]	D:	76662	598.9	1	D:\tempdb2014\tempdb.mdf
PHYSICAL WRITES	2016-11-02 14:19:13.0341706 -04:00	60	tempdev2 [ROWS]	D:	76651	598.8	1	D:\tempdb2014\tempdb2.ndf
PHYSICAL WRITES	2016-11-02 14:19:13.0341706 -04:00	60	tempdev3 [ROWS]	D:	76650	598.8	1	D:\tempdb2014\tempdb3.ndf
PHYSICAL WRITES	2016-11-02 14:19:13.0341706 -04:00	60	tempdev4 [ROWS]	D:	76594	598.4	1	D:\tempdb2014\tempdb4.ndf

Just too physical

For the links, code, and comments, go here:
https://www.brentozar.com/archive/2016/11/spills-sql-server-doesnt-warn/

Boy oh boy. Boy howdy. Look at all those physical writes. We spilled everything to disk. That's right at the 2.4 GB mark, which is the same size as the Votes table. We should probably know about that, right?

Is a temp table any better?

In short: kinda. There are some reasons! None of them are in stats IO. They're nearly identical.

For the insert, the scan could go parallel, but doesn't. Remember that modifying table variables forces query serialization, so that's never an option to us.

In SQL Server 2016, some INSERT operations can be fully parallelized, which is really cool. If it works. Much like minimal logging, it's a bit of a crapshoot.

The COUNT(*) query gets an accurate estimate and does go parallel. Hooray. Put those pricey cores to use. Unless you recompile the query, you're not going to get an accurate estimate out of your table variable. They're just built that way. It doesn't even matter if you put an index on them.

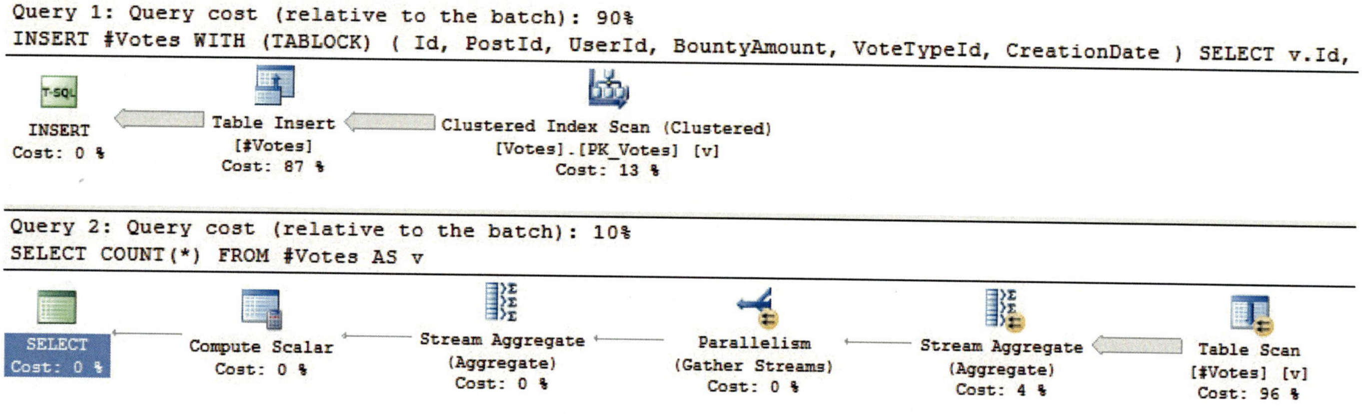

Promised Land

Does sp_BlitzFirst tell us anything different?

Pattern	Sample Time	Sample (seconds)	File Name	Drive	# Reads/Writes	MB Read/Written	Avg Stall (ms)	file physical name
PHYSICAL READS	2016-11-02 14:48:11.2853095 -04:00	60	tempdev2 [ROWS]	D:	1262	599.4	19	D:\tempdb2014\tempdb2.ndf
PHYSICAL READS	2016-11-02 14:48:11.2853095 -04:00	60	tempdev3 [ROWS]	D:	1261	600.2	19	D:\tempdb2014\tempdb3.ndf
PHYSICAL READS	2016-11-02 14:48:11.2853095 -04:00	60	tempdev4 [ROWS]	D:	1274	600.3	19	D:\tempdb2014\tempdb4.ndf
PHYSICAL READS	2016-11-02 14:48:11.2853095 -04:00	60	StackOverflow [...	D:	29612	2349.9	7	D:\Data\StackOverflow.mdf
PHYSICAL WRIT...	2016-11-02 14:48:11.2853095 -04:00	60	master [ROWS]	D:	42	0.3	7	D:\Program Files\Microsoft ...
PHYSICAL WRIT...	2016-11-02 14:48:11.2853095 -04:00	60	tempdev [ROWS]	D:	76995	601.5	2	D:\tempdb2014\tempdb.mdf
PHYSICAL WRIT...	2016-11-02 14:48:11.2853095 -04:00	60	tempdev2 [ROWS]	D:	76951	601.2	2	D:\tempdb2014\tempdb2.ndf
PHYSICAL WRIT...	2016-11-02 14:48:11.2853095 -04:00	60	tempdev3 [ROWS]	D:	76989	601.5	2	D:\tempdb2014\tempdb3.ndf

SCANDAL

For the links, code, and comments, go here:
https://www.brentozar.com/archive/2016/11/spills-sql-server-doesnt-warn/

Yeah! For some mystical magical reason, we only spilled out 1.8 GB, rather than the full 2.4 GB.

Party on, Us.

I still hate table variables

I mean, I guess they're okay if the # key on your keyboard is broken? But you should probably just buy a new keyboard and stop using Twitter.

Anyway, I think the point was that we should have some information at the plan level about spills to disk for table variables and (possibly) temp tables. It wouldn't help tools like sp_BlitzCache, because spill information isn't in cached plans, but it might help if you're doing live query tuning.

Thanks for reading!

Brent says: *OMG THESE ARE SPILLS TOO. I never thought of it that way.*

Memory Grants and Data Size

What does memory do?

In SQL Server, just about everything. We cache our data and execution plans in it (along with some other system stuff), it gets used as scratch space for temporary objects, and of course queries use it for certain operations, most notably sorting and hashing. And of course, now Hekaton comes along to eat up more of our RAM.

In general, not having enough of it means reading pages from disk all the time, but it can have RAMifications down the line (GET IT?!), like queries not having enough memory to compile or run, and your plan cache constantly being wiped out.

If you're struggling with the limits of Standard Edition, older hardware, bad hardware choices, or budget issues, you may not be able to adequately throw hardware at the problem. So you're left to have someone spend way more money on your time to try to mitigate issues. This of course means query and index tuning, perhaps Resource Governor if you've made some EXTRA BAD choices, and last but not least: cleaning up data types.

How can this help?

Leaving aside the chance to maybe make your storage admins happy, you can also cut down on large memory grants for some queries. Here's a quick example.

We'll create a simple table. In order to make Joe Celko happy, it has a PK/CX. We have an integer column that we'll use to ORDER BY. The reason for this is that if you order by a column that doesn't have a supporting index, SQL will need a memory grant. The VARCHAR columns are just to show you how memory grants increase to account for larger chunks of data.

Transact-SQL

```
CREATE TABLE dbo.MemoryGrants
(
  ID INT PRIMARY KEY CLUSTERED,
  Ordering INT,
  Crap1 VARCHAR(10),
  Crap2 VARCHAR(1000),
  Crap3 VARCHAR(8000)
);

INSERT dbo.MemoryGrants WITH (TABLOCK)
        ( ID, Ordering, Crap1, Crap2, Crap3 )
SELECT
    c,
  c % 1000,
  REPLICATE('X', c * 10 % 10),
  REPLICATE('Y', c * 1000 % 1000),
  REPLICATE('Z', c * 8000 % 8000)
FROM (
SELECT TOP (100000) ROW_NUMBER() OVER (ORDER BY (SELECT NULL)) AS c
FROM sys.messages AS m
CROSS JOIN sys.messages AS m2
) x

SELECT mg.ID --Returning one column
FROM dbo.MemoryGrants AS mg
ORDER BY mg.Ordering
GO

SELECT mg.ID, mg.Ordering --Returning a couple INTs
FROM dbo.MemoryGrants AS mg
ORDER BY mg.Ordering
GO

SELECT mg.ID, mg.Ordering, mg.Crap1 --Returning a VARCHAR(10)
FROM dbo.MemoryGrants AS mg
ORDER BY mg.Ordering
GO

SELECT mg.ID, mg.Ordering, mg.Crap2 --Returning a VARCHAR(1000)
FROM dbo.MemoryGrants AS mg
ORDER BY mg.Ordering
GO

SELECT mg.ID, mg.Ordering, mg.Crap3 --Returning a VARCHAR(8000)
FROM dbo.MemoryGrants AS mg
ORDER BY mg.Ordering
GO
```

```
SELECT mg.ID, mg.Ordering, mg.Crap1, mg.Crap2, mg.Crap3 --Returning all columns
FROM dbo.MemoryGrants AS mg
ORDER BY mg.Ordering
GO
```

Some test queries

When we run the queries above, we can see in the query plans, and thanks to fairly recent updates (2014 SP2, 2016 SP1), a warning in actual plans about memory grant issues.

To make this a little easier to visualize, we'll use an Extended Events session using a new event called query_memory_grant_usage. If you want to use this on one of your servers, you'll want to change or get rid of the filter on session ID — 55 just happens to be the session ID I have.

```
CREATE EVENT SESSION [QueryMemoryGrantUsage] ON SERVER
ADD EVENT sqlserver.query_memory_grant_usage(
    ACTION(sqlserver.sql_text)
    WHERE ([sqlserver].[session_id]=(55)))
WITH (MAX_MEMORY=4096 KB,EVENT_RETENTION_MODE=ALLOW_SINGLE_EVENT_LOSS,
MAX_DISPATCH_LATENCY=30 SECONDS,MAX_EVENT_SIZE=0 KB,MEMORY_PARTITION_MODE=NONE,
TRACK_CAUSALITY=OFF,STARTUP_STATE=OFF)
GO
```

Here's what we get from our XE session.

sql_text	granted_memory...	granted_percent	ideal_memory_kb	usage_percent	used_memory_kb
SELECT mg.ID FROM dbo.MemoryGrants AS mg ORDER BY mg.Ordering	7256	100	7256	73	5320
SELECT mg.ID, mg.Ordering FROM dbo.MemoryGrants AS mg ORDER BY mg.Ordering	7256	100	7256	73	5320
SELECT mg.ID, mg.Ordering, mg.Crap1 FROM dbo.MemoryGrants AS mg ORDER BY mg.Ordering	8352	100	8352	63	5320
SELECT mg.ID, mg.Ordering, mg.Crap2 FROM dbo.MemoryGrants AS mg ORDER BY mg.Ordering	68776	100	68776	7	5320
SELECT mg.ID, mg.Ordering, mg.Crap3 FROM dbo.MemoryGrants AS mg ORDER BY mg.Ordering	496032	100	496032	1	5320
SELECT mg.ID, mg.Ordering, mg.Crap1, mg.Crap2, mg.Crap3 FROM dbo.MemoryGrants AS mg ORDER BY mg.Ordering	558160	100	558160	0	5320

Does anyone have a calculator?

Our query memory grants range from around 8 MB to around 560 MB. This isn't even ordering BY the larger columns, this is just doing the work to sort results by them. Even if you're a smarty pants, and you don't use unnecessary ORDER BY clauses in your queries, SQL may inject them into your query plans to support operations that require sorted data. Things like stream aggregates, merge joins, and occasionally key lookups may still be considered a 'cheaper' option by the optimizer, even with a sort in the plan.

Of course, in our query plans, we have warnings on the last two queries, which had to order the VARCHAR(8000) column.

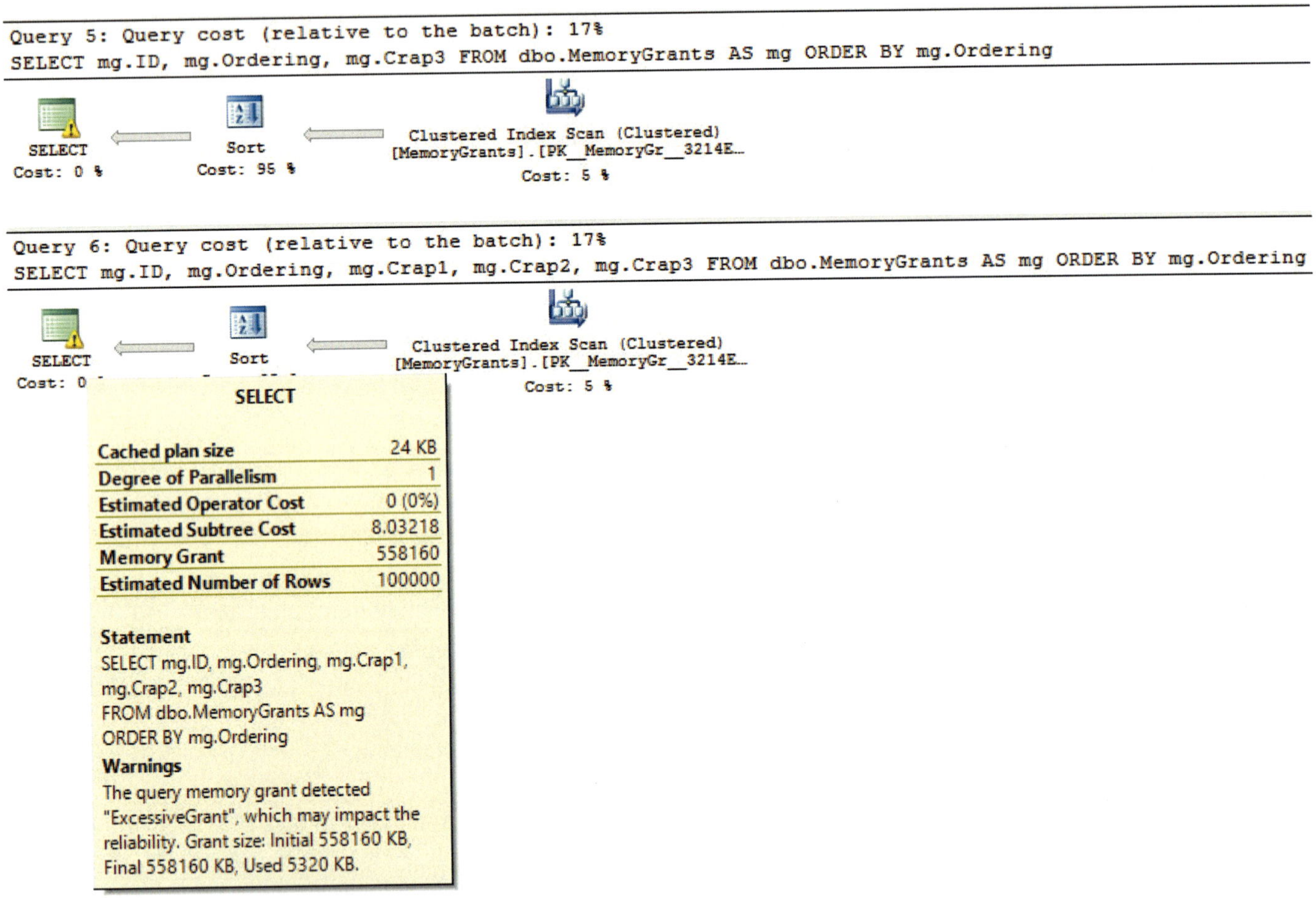

Barf

Sort it out

You may legitimately need large N/VARCHAR columns for certain things, but we frequently see pretty big columns being used to hold things that will just never approach the column size. I'm not going to sit here and chastise you for choosing datetime over date or bigint over int or whatever. Those are trivial in comparison. But especially when troubleshooting memory grant issues (or performance issues in general), foolishly wide columns can sometimes be an easy tuning win.

Thanks for reading!

Brent says: *whenever anybody asked me, "Why can't I just use VARCHAR(1000) for all my string fields?" I didn't really have a good answer. Now I do.*

Locking When There's Nothing To Lock

Demo Day

We use StackOverflow for demos a lot. For all the reasons Brent mentions in his Great Post, Brent©, it's pretty awesome.

Where things get tricky is with locking demos.

Sometimes the modifications can take a long time. This may be by design if you need to show long-held locks by sessions that aren't sleeping.

Sometimes rollbacks can take a long time. After all, they're single threaded, and you know how I feel about things that are single threaded.

The No-Row Update

To get around this, I decided to try some updates that didn't actually update any rows. The WHERE clause excludes everything in the Users table.

I thought that SQL would outsmart me here, but it didn't. It didn't even try.

Here are two queries, neither of which will have any qualifying rows in my 2016/03 copy of the database. (If you're using a more recent export, choose a more recent LastAccessDate.)

Transact-SQL

```
SELECT *
FROM dbo.Users AS u
WHERE u.LastAccessDate >= '20160307'

SELECT *
FROM dbo.Users AS u
WHERE u.Reputation >= 2147483647
```

The only index on the Users table is a PK/CX on Id. That means it's the one way in or out of the table for any queries, no matter what they're trying to do.

So if I run an update that will also hit 0 rows, it has to use that.

```
BEGIN TRAN

UPDATE dbo.Users
SET Reputation = Reputation + 100
WHERE Reputation >= 2147483647
```

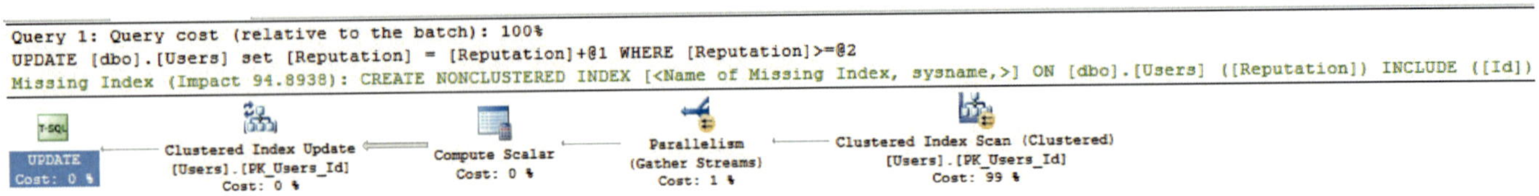

No Holds Barred

While that update is running, I'll try to run my query with the WHERE clause on LastAccessDate. It'll get blocked — and we can confirm that by running sp_BlitzWho.

session_id	database_name	wait_info	top_session_waits	status	query_text	query_plan	query_cost	blocking_session_id
83	StackOverflow	LCK_M_IS (63807)	CXPACKET (234 ms)	sleeping	BEGIN TRAN UPDATE dbo.Users SET Reputation = ...	NULL	NULL	NULL
81	StackOverflow	LCK_M_IS (63813 ms)	LCK_M_IS (55003 ms), CXPACKET (181 ms), IO_COMPLETION (83 ms)	running	SELECT * FROM [dbo].[Users] [u] WHERE [u].[LastAcc...	<ShowPlanXML xmlns="http://schemas.microsoft.com...	NULL	83

Low fiber diet

Rollback, Repeat

So look, clearly we need an index.

Maybe we need 75 indexes. If we do, we'll run DTA and then set our pants on fire in defiance of all humanity.

But in the meantime, let's try adding one.

```
CREATE UNIQUE NONCLUSTERED INDEX ix_helper_lad ON dbo.Users (LastAccessDate, Id)
```

This gives our select query a separate access path. Sort of. I know what you're thinking — that SELECT * is a trick! He's messing with us. The clustered index needs to get updated, so the key lookup will get blocked. Ha ha ha. Nice one, dummy. We're smarter than you.

So I'll do this instead.

```sql
SELECT u.Id, u.LastAccessDate
FROM dbo.Users AS u
WHERE u.LastAccessDate >= '20160307'
```

This query only needs columns in our nonclustered index, so it won't get blocked. Right?

Right?

session_id	database_name	wait_info	top_session_waits	status	query_text	query_plan	query_cost	blocking_session_id
83	StackOverflow	LCK_M_IS (4282)	CXPACKET (480 ms)	sleeping	BEGIN TRAN UPDATE dbo.Users SET Reputation = Reputation + 100 WHERE Reputation >= 2147483647	NULL	NULL	NULL
81	StackOverflow	LCK_M_IS (4287 ms)	LCK_M_IS (534881 ms), CXPACKET (10276 ms), LCK_M...	running	SELECT [u].[Id],[u].[LastAccessDate] FROM [dbo].[Users] [u] WHERE [u].[LastAccessDate]>=@1	<ShowPlanXML xmlns="http://schemas.microsoft.com...	NULL	83

Wrong.

The answer lies in sp_BlitzWho's much cooler older brother, sp_WhoIsActive.

```sql
EXEC dbo.sp_WhoIsActive @get_locks = 1
```

Our update query is locking the whole darn thing. Even though it changes 0 rows, and the query is done running (though it's in a BEGIN TRAN), we're still stuck with this lock.

```xml
<Database name="StackOverflow">
  <Locks>
    <Lock request_mode="S" request_status="GRANT" request_count="1" />
  </Locks>
  <Objects>
    <Object name="Users" schema_name="dbo">
      <Locks>
        <Lock resource_type="OBJECT" request_mode="X" request_status="GRANT" request_count="1" />
      </Locks>
    </Object>
  </Objects>
</Database>
```

I learned it from watching you!

So what to do?

Our clustered index doesn't help, and our nonclustered index doesn't either. Maybe our update needs an index?

It's simple enough. We're updating Reputation, and filtering on Reputation. Maybe we need an index on Reputation, too?

For the links, code, and comments, go here:
https://www.brentozar.com/archive/2017/08/locking-theres-nothing-lock/

We have some options.

A separate index that leads with Reputation, and index that leads with LastAccessDate, and an index that leads with Reputation.

```
CREATE UNIQUE NONCLUSTERED INDEX ix_helper_rep ON dbo.Users (Reputation, Id);

CREATE UNIQUE NONCLUSTERED INDEX ix_helper_lad_rep ON dbo.Users
(LastAccessDate, Reputation, Id);

CREATE UNIQUE NONCLUSTERED INDEX ix_helper_rep_lad ON dbo.Users
(Reputation, LastAccessDate, Id);
```

For the sake of blog post brevity: the index that leads with LastAccessDate doesn't fix our blocking scenario.

So what's better: Two separate indexes on (Reputation, Id) and (LastAccessDate, Id), or one index on (Reputation, LastAccessDate, Id)?

And then what if our UPDATE changes? What if we need to filter on LastAccessDate? Or something else? What if having LastAccessDate as the second key column makes our SELECT queries eat speed bumps?

```
UPDATE dbo.Users
SET Reputation = Reputation + 100
WHERE LastAccessDate >= '20160307'
```

You can't index for everything, and as we sort-of-glossed-over, leading index key columns seem necessary to get us out of locking jams.

Sure, you could get around things with NOLOCK hints, but if that makes you queasy, it's time to start looking into other Isolation Levels.

Indexes can be extra tricky. If you're lucky enough to be going to PASS, be sure to hit up Kendra's session on indexing.

I'll probably be there, making sure you don't start texting.

Partition Level Locking: Explanations From Outer Space

It's not that I don't like partitioning

It's just that most of my time talking about it is convincing people not to use it.

They always wanna use it for the wrong reasons, and I can sort of understand why.

Microsoft says you can partition for performance.

> Partitioning large tables or indexes can have the following manageability and performance benefits.

How?

> You may improve query performance, based on the types of queries you frequently run and on your hardware configuration. For example, the query optimizer can process equi-join queries between two or more partitioned tables faster when the partitioning columns in the tables are the same, because the partitions themselves can be joined.

Takeaway: PARTITION EVERYTHING

But...

> When SQL Server performs data sorting for I/O operations, it sorts the data first by partition. SQL Server accesses one drive at a time, and this might reduce performance. To improve data sorting performance, stripe the data files of your partitions across more than one disk by setting up a RAID. In this way, although SQL Server still sorts data by partition, it can access all the drives of each partition at the same time.

Takeaway: This was written before anyone had a SAN, I guess?

Ooh ooh but also!

> In addition, you can improve performance by enabling lock escalation at the partition level instead of a whole table. This can reduce lock contention on the table.

Takeaway: Except when it causes deadlocks

> HoBT-level locks usually increase concurrency, but introduce the potential for deadlocks when transactions that are locking different partitions each want to expand their exclusive locks to the other partitions. In rare instances, TABLE locking granularity might perform better.

Why tho?

Good question! In the Chicago perf class last month, we had a student ask if partition level locks would ever escalate to a table level lock. I wrote up a demo and everything, but we ran out of time before I could go over it.

Not that I'm complaining — partitioning, and especially partition level locking, can be pretty confusing to look at.

If you really wanna learn about it, you should talk to Kendra — after all, this post is where I usually send folks who don't believe me about the performance stuff.

Demo a la mode

To talk about this, I've partitioned the Votes table in the Stack Overflow database by CreationDate.

Transact-SQL

```
/*Partitioning*/
CREATE PARTITION FUNCTION VotesCreationDate ( DATE )
    AS RANGE RIGHT FOR VALUES ( '20070101',
                                '20080101',
                                '20090101',
                                '20100101',
                                '20110101',
                                '20120101',
                                '20130101',
                                '20140101',
                                '20150101',
                                '20160101',
                                '20170101' );

/*Scheming*/
CREATE PARTITION SCHEME VotesSchemeCreationDate
    AS PARTITION VotesCreationDate
    ALL TO ( [PRIMARY] );

```

```sql
/*Indexing*/
ALTER TABLE dbo.Votes
    ADD CONSTRAINT PK_Partition_CD_Id
    PRIMARY KEY CLUSTERED ( CreationDate, Id )
    ON VotesSchemeCreationDate(CreationDate);
```

Now, partition level locking isn't the default, you have to set it per-table. It's not the default because of the deadlock scenarios that are talked about in the BOL link up there.

```sql
/*This isn't the default, you need to set it*/
ALTER TABLE dbo.Votes SET ( LOCK_ESCALATION = AUTO );
```

Query that

Let's look at how updates work!

I'm going to use sp_WhoIsActive to look at the locks, with the command

EXEC dbo.sp_WhoIsActive @get_locks = 1.

This query will hit exactly one year, and one partition, of data.

```sql
/*What about one clean partition?*/
BEGIN TRAN;

UPDATE v
SET    v.BountyAmount = v.BountyAmount + 100
FROM   dbo.Votes AS v
WHERE  v.CreationDate >= '20090101'
       AND v.CreationDate < '20100101';

ROLLBACK;
```

What do locks look like?

```
<Database name="SUPERUSER_Partition">
  <Locks>
    <Lock request_mode="S" request_status="GRANT" request_count="1" />
  </Locks>
  <Objects>
    <Object name="Votes" schema_name="dbo">
      <Locks>
        <Lock resource_type="HOBT" index_name="PK_Partition_CD_Id" request_mode="X" request_status="GRANT" request_count="1" />
        <Lock resource_type="OBJECT" request_mode="IX" request_status="GRANT" request_count="1" />
      </Locks>
    </Object>
  </Objects>
</Database>
```

Confusing part, the first

We have an object lock, and a HOBT lock. Both have been granted, with a single request.

But the Object lock is only IX (intent exclusive), which means that other queries can still dance around it.

If I run a query that hits a different partition, say for the year 2014, it will finish without being blocked.

```
SELECT COUNT(v.BountyAmount) AS records
FROM   dbo.Votes AS v
WHERE  v.CreationDate >= '20140101'
       AND v.CreationDate < '20150101';
```

The X lock (exclusive), is just on the one partition for the year 2009. If I run a select query for that partition, it will be blocked.

Patterns

This basic pattern will continue if we cross a partitions, and hit two years of data

```sql
/*What if we cross partition boundaries?*/
BEGIN TRAN;

UPDATE v
SET    v.BountyAmount = v.BountyAmount + 100
FROM   dbo.Votes AS v
WHERE  v.CreationDate >= '20090101'
       AND v.CreationDate < '20110101';

ROLLBACK;
```

If we cross lots of partition boundaries

```sql
/*What if we cross lots of partition boundaries?*/
BEGIN TRAN;

UPDATE v
SET    v.BountyAmount = v.BountyAmount + 100
FROM   dbo.Votes AS v
WHERE  v.CreationDate >= '20090101'
       AND v.CreationDate < '20130101';

ROLLBACK;
```

Or if we cross all of them

```sql
/*What if we cross every partition boundaries?*/
BEGIN TRAN;

UPDATE v
SET    v.BountyAmount = v.BountyAmount + 100
FROM   dbo.Votes AS v
WHERE  v.CreationDate >= '20070101'
       AND v.CreationDate < '20170101';

ROLLBACK;
```

Confusing, part the second

When we cross a single partition boundary, this is what locks look like. I can deal with this. The HOBT X lock has two requests. One for each partition.

This'll happen for a few more partition crossing queries.

Transact-SQL

```
<Database name="SUPERUSER_Partition">
  <Locks>
    <Lock request_mode="S" request_status="GRANT" request_count="1" />
  </Locks>
  <Objects>
    <Object name="Votes" schema_name="dbo">
      <Locks>
        <Lock resource_type="HOBT" index_name="PK_Partition_CD_Id"
         request_mode="X" request_status="GRANT" request_count="2" />
        <Lock resource_type="OBJECT" request_mode="IX" request_status="GRANT"
         request_count="1" />
      </Locks>
    </Object>
  </Objects>
</Database>
```

Until we hit 2013, and then our locks change. Now we have three requests for X locks on HOBTs, and one IX. Huh. We have a bunch of X locks on pages now, too.

Transact-SQL

```
<Database name="SUPERUSER_Partition">
  <Locks>
    <Lock request_mode="S" request_status="GRANT" request_count="1" />
  </Locks>
  <Objects>
    <Object name="Votes" schema_name="dbo">
      <Locks>
        <Lock resource_type="HOBT" index_name="PK_Partition_CD_Id"
         request_mode="IX" request_status="GRANT" request_count="1" />
        <Lock resource_type="HOBT" index_name="PK_Partition_CD_Id"
         request_mode="X" request_status="GRANT" request_count="3" />
        <Lock resource_type="OBJECT" request_mode="IX" request_status=
         "GRANT" request_count="1" />
        <Lock resource_type="PAGE" page_type="*" index_name="PK_Partition_CD_Id"
          request_mode="X" request_status="GRANT" request_count
      </Locks>
    </Object>
  </Objects>
</Database>
```

When we cross every partition boundary, this is what the locks end up looking like. The HOBT locks went up, we have two kinds of Page locks, and now Key locks as well.

```
<Database name="SUPERUSER_Partition">
  <Locks>
    <Lock request_mode="S" request_status="GRANT" request_count="1" />
  </Locks>
  <Objects>
    <Object name="Votes" schema_name="dbo">
      <Locks>
        <Lock resource_type="HOBT" index_name="PK_Partition_CD_Id"
         request_mode="IX" request_status="GRANT" request_count="7" />
        <Lock resource_type="HOBT" index_name="PK_Partition_CD_Id"
         request_mode="X" request_status="GRANT" request_count="3" />
        <Lock resource_type="KEY" index_name="PK_Partition_CD_Id"
         request_mode="X" request_status="GRANT" request_count="3356" />
        <Lock resource_type="OBJECT" request_mode="IX" request_status="GRANT"
         request_count="1" />
        <Lock resource_type="PAGE" page_type="*" index_name="PK_Partition_CD_Id"
         request_mode="IX" request_status="GRANT" request_count="16" />
        <Lock resource_type="PAGE" page_type="*" index_name="PK_Partition_CD_Id"
         request_mode="X" request_status="GRANT" request_count="10866" />
      </Locks>
    </Object>
  </Objects>
</Database>
```

So what's going on with all that?

Remember that this setting changes lock escalation. Locks don't always escalate, and SQL Server can choose to lock different partitions with different granularity.

This becomes a little more obvious with a pretty simple query!

```sql
SELECT   OBJECT_NAME(p.object_id) AS table_name,
         p.index_id,
         p.partition_number,
         SUM(p.rows) AS sum_rows,
         dtl.resource_type,
         dtl.request_mode,
         dtl.request_type,
         dtl.request_status,
         COUNT(*) AS records
FROM     sys.dm_tran_locks AS dtl
JOIN     sys.partitions AS p
ON dtl.resource_associated_entity_id = p.partition_id
WHERE    dtl.request_session_id = 56
GROUP BY OBJECT_NAME(p.object_id),
         p.index_id,
         p.partition_number,
         dtl.resource_type,
         dtl.request_mode,
         dtl.request_type,
         dtl.request_status
ORDER BY p.partition_number;
```

table_name	index_id	partition_number	sum_rows	resource_type	request_mode	request_type	request_status	records
Votes	1	2	0	HOBT	IX	LOCK	GRANT	1
Votes	1	3	3356	HOBT	IX	LOCK	GRANT	1
Votes	1	3	11262736	KEY	X	LOCK	GRANT	3356
Votes	1	3	53696	PAGE	IX	LOCK	GRANT	16
Votes	1	4	198418	HOBT	X	LOCK	GRANT	1
Votes	1	5	238942	HOBT	X	LOCK	GRANT	1
Votes	1	6	347797	HOBT	X	LOCK	GRANT	1
Votes	1	7	435133	HOBT	IX	LOCK	GRANT	1
Votes	1	7	868960601	PAGE	X	LOCK	GRANT	1997
Votes	1	8	460090	HOBT	IX	LOCK	GRANT	1
Votes	1	8	971249990	PAGE	X	LOCK	GRANT	2111
Votes	1	9	452132	HOBT	IX	LOCK	GRANT	1
Votes	1	9	937721768	PAGE	X	LOCK	GRANT	2074
Votes	1	10	529509	HOBT	IX	LOCK	GRANT	1
Votes	1	10	1286177361	PAGE	X	LOCK	GRANT	2429
Votes	1	11	491560	HOBT	IX	LOCK	GRANT	1
Votes	1	11	1108467800	PAGE	X	LOCK	GRANT	2255

Different locks!

This makes the locking a bit more clear. Some partitions have different kinds of locks, different levels of locks, and different numbers of locks.

I'm not saying there's a flaw in Who Is Active — sys.partitions is per database, so unless We added a bunch of nasty, looping, dynamic SQL in here, we couldn't get partition-level information.

I know what you're thinking

These are all using the partitioning key. What happens if we change our where clause to something that doesn't? Say, where BountyAmount is NULL, instead. That column isn't even indexed.

/*So let's just update the NOT NULL ones*/

```
Transact-SQL
/*So let's just update the NOT NULL ones*/
BEGIN TRAN;

UPDATE v
SET     v.BountyAmount = v.BountyAmount + 100
FROM    dbo.Votes AS v
WHERE   v.BountyAmount IS NOT NULL;

ROLLBACK;
```

Heh heh heh

```
<Database name="SUPERUSER_Partition">
  <Locks>
    <Lock request_mode="S" request_status="GRANT" request_count="1" />
  </Locks>
  <Objects>
    <Object name="Votes" schema_name="dbo">
      <Locks>
        <Lock resource_type="HOBT" index_name="PK_Partition_CD_Id"
         request_mode="IX" request_status="GRANT" request_count="12" />
        <Lock resource_type="KEY" index_name="PK_Partition_CD_Id"
         request_mode="X" request_status="GRANT" request_count="3112" />
        <Lock resource_type="OBJECT" request_mode="IX" request_status="GRANT"
         request_count="1" />
        <Lock resource_type="PAGE" page_type="*" index_name="PK_Partition_CD_Id"
         request_mode="IX" request_status="GRANT" request_count="2014" />
        <Lock resource_type="PAGE" page_type="*" index_name="PK_Partition_CD_Id"
         request_mode="X" request_status="GRANT" request_count="5212" />
      </Locks>
    </Object>
  </Objects>
</Database>
```

Our X locks are still only on HOBTs and pages. Our object lock is still only IX!

This is exciting, because even using a non-partitioning key where clause doesn't lead to an X lock on the object.

We still lock different partitions with different granularity, too. We have a mix of HOBT, Key, and Page locks.

Thanks for reading!

Heaps, Deletes, and Optimistic Isolation Levels

The Humble Heap

If you don't know this by now, I'm going to shovel it at you:

If you have a table with no clustered index (a Heap), and you delete rows from it, the resulting empty pages may not be deallocated.

You'll have a table with a bunch of empty pages in it, and those pages will be read whenever the Heap is scanned.

Under "normal" circumstances, you can use a TABLOCK or TABLOCKX hint along with your delete to force the deallocation to happen.

Otherwise, you're left relying on your delete query possibly escalating to a table level lock, and releasing the pages on its own (absent a rebuild table command).

This is true under any pessimistic isolation level. This is not true under optimistic isolation levels (Snapshot, RCSI).

Demonstrate My Syntax

Here's some stuff:

```
Transact-SQL
USE Crap;
SET NOCOUNT ON;

ALTER DATABASE Crap SET ALLOW_SNAPSHOT_ISOLATION ON;

--Save this for a second test
--ALTER DATABASE Crap SET READ_COMMITTED_SNAPSHOT ON;

DROP TABLE IF EXISTS dbo.HeapMe;
CREATE TABLE dbo.HeapMe
(
    id INT PRIMARY KEY NONCLUSTERED,
    filler_bunny CHAR(1000) DEFAULT 'A'
);

INSERT dbo.HeapMe WITH(TABLOCKX) ( id )
SELECT x.n
FROM  (   SELECT TOP 100000 ROW_NUMBER() OVER ( ORDER BY @@DBTS ) AS n
          FROM   sys.messages AS m ) AS x;

ALTER TABLE dbo.HeapMe REBUILD;
```

We have a Heap with a nonclustered primary key. This sounds misleading, but it's not. A nonclustered PK is not a substitute for a clustered index.

It's there to speed up the delete that we'll run in a minute.

We have a couple ways to look at the Heap.

A query I kinda hate:

```
Transact-SQL
SELECT DB_NAME(ps.database_id) AS database_name,
       OBJECT_NAME(ps.object_id) AS table_name,
       ISNULL(i.name, 'EL HEAPO') AS index_name,
       ps.page_count,
       ps.avg_fragmentation_in_percent,
       ps.avg_page_space_used_in_percent,
       ps.index_id
FROM   sys.dm_db_index_physical_stats(DB_ID(N'Crap'), OBJECT_ID(N'dbo.HeapMe')
, NULL, NULL, 'SAMPLED') AS ps
JOIN   sys.indexes AS i
ON ps.object_id = i.object_id
   AND i.index_id = ps.index_id;
```

database_name	table_name	index_name	page_count	avg_fragmentation_in_percent	avg_page_space_used_in_percent	index_id
Crap	HeapMe	EL HEAPO	14200	0	88.7941685198913	0
Crap	HeapMe	PK__HeapMe__3213E83E79517A1F	223	0	99.7003829997529	2

Uch

And sp_BlitzIndex:

```sql
EXEC master.dbo.sp_BlitzIndex @DatabaseName = N'Crap',
                              @SchemaName = N'dbo',
                              @TableName = N'HeapMe';
```

Details: db_schema.table.index(indexid)	Definition: [Property] ColumnName {datatype maxbytes}	Secret Columns	Fillfactor	Usage Stats	Op Stats	Size
Database [Crap] as of 2017-12-15 13:59 (sp_BlitzInd...	http://FirstResponderKit.org	From Your Community Volunteers	NULL	NULL	NULL	NULL
dbo.HeapMe.Unknown (0)	[HEAP]	[RID]	0	Reads: 0 Writes:1	0 singleton lookups; 1 scans/seeks; 0 deletes; 0...	100,000 rows; 111.7MB
dbo.HeapMe.PK__HeapMe__3213E83E79517A1F (2)	[PK] [1 KEY] id {int 4}	[1 INCLUDE] [RID]	0	Reads: 0 Writes:1	0 singleton lookups; 0 scans/seeks; 0 deletes; 0...	100,000 rows; 1.8MB

Such Happy Days

What do we know from looking at these?

- The first query tells us that our heap has 14,200 pages in it, and the NC/PK has 223 pages in it, that there's no fragmentation (lol I know), and that the average space used for both is pretty high. Our pages are full, in other words.
- sp_BlitzIndex tells us that our Heap is ~111MB, and our NC/PK is 1.8MB. Both have 100k rows in them. It does not regale us with tales of fragmentation.

Deleting Many Singletons

If a delete comes along — alright, so it's a row-at-a-time delete (stick with me on this) — and deletes every row in the table, what happens?

```
--Quote this out to test RCSI
SET TRANSACTION ISOLATION LEVEL SNAPSHOT;

DECLARE @id INT = 1;
WHILE @id <= 100000
    BEGIN

        DELETE hm
        FROM   dbo.HeapMe AS hm WITH (TABLOCKX)
        WHERE  hm.id = @id;

        SET @id += 1;

    END;
```

I'm doing the delete like this because it will never escalate to a table level lock on its own, but I'm hinting a table level lock for EVERY delete.

You can do this in other ways to avoid them, but this is the path of least resistance.

What do our exploratory queries have to say?

database_name	table_name	index_name	page_count	avg_fragmentation_in_percent	avg_page_space_used_in_percent	index_id
Crap	HeapMe	EL HEAPO	14200	0	0.148257968865827	0
Crap	HeapMe	PK__HeapMe__3213E83E79517A1F	31	3.2258064516129	84.0710402767482	2

Details: db_schema.table.index(indexid)	Definition: [Property] ColumnName {datatype maxb...	Secret Columns	Fillfactor	Usage Stats	Op Stats	Size
Database [Crap] as of 2017-12-15 14:09 (sp_BlitzInd...	http://FirstResponderKit.org	From Your Community Volunteers	NULL	NULL	NULL	NULL
dbo.HeapMe.Unknown (0)	[HEAP]	[RID]	0	Reads: 0 Writes:100,001	100,000 singleton lookups; 1 scans/seeks; 100,0...	0 rows; 111.7MB
dbo.HeapMe.PK__HeapMe__3213E83E79517A1F (2)	[PK] [1 KEY] id {int 4}	[1 INCLUDE] [RID]	0	Reads: 100,000 (100,000 seek) Writes:100,001	100,000 singleton lookups; 0 scans/seeks; 0 dele...	0 rows; 0.4MB

Shruggy the Shrugger

We have 0 rows in the table, but pages are still allocated to it.

In the case of the Heap, all pages remain allocated, and it retains the same size.

In the case of the NC/PK, about 200 pages were deallocated, but not all of them were (yet — more on this later).

So that's... fun. I'm having fun.

You can get slightly different results without the loop.

If you just delete everything, the Heap will remain with all its pages in tact. The NC/PK will (as far as I can tell) be reduced to a single page.

```sql
SET TRANSACTION ISOLATION LEVEL SNAPSHOT;
    DELETE hm
    FROM   dbo.HeapMe AS hm WITH (TABLOCKX)
```

Oddball

Under both RCSI and SI, if we use a TABLOCK hint instead of TABLOCKX...

database_name	table_name	index_name	page_count	avg_fragmentation_in_percent	avg_page_space_used_in_percent	index_id
Crap	HeapMe	EL HEAPO	14200	0	1.44551519644181	0
Crap	HeapMe	PK__HeapMe__3213E83E30D24A89	446	99.3273542600897	88.6198171485051	2

Details: db_schema.table.index(indexid)	Definition: [Property] ColumnName {datatype maxbytes}	Secret Columns	Fillfactor	Usage Stats	Op Stats	Size
Database [Crap] as of 2017-12-15 14:36 (sp_BlitzInde...	http://FirstResponderKit.org	From Your Community Volunteers	NULL	NULL	NULL	NULL
dbo.HeapMe.Unknown (0)	[HEAP]	[RID]	0	Reads: 0 Writes:2	100,000 singleton lookups; 1 scans/seeks; 100,0...	0 rows; 111.7MB
dbo.HeapMe.PK__HeapMe__3213E83E30D24A89 (2)	[PK] [1 KEY] id {int 4}	[1 INCLUDE] [RID]	0	Reads: 1 (1 scan) Writes:2	0 singleton lookups; 1 scans/seeks; 0 deletes; 0 u...	0 rows; 3.5MB

U WOT?

The size of, and the number of pages in the NC/PK effectively DOUBLES.

DOUBLES.

>mfw

Repetition Is Everything

I left other code in there if you want to try it at home with other combinations.

You can also try it under Read Committed if you'd like, to see different results where pages are deallocated.

Now, you can fix this by running ALTER TABLE dbo.HeapMe REBUILD;, which will release all the empty pages back.

Deletes Mangle Scans

If we run a couple simple queries, things get awkward.

```
SET STATISTICS IO ON;

SELECT COUNT_BIG(DISTINCT h.filler_bunny)
FROM   dbo.HeapMe AS h;

SELECT COUNT_BIG(DISTINCT h.id)
FROM   dbo.HeapMe AS h;

SET STATISTICS IO OFF;
```

The first query, which needs to access data via the Heap, does a lot of extra work.

The query that hits the PK/NC does significantly less (comparatively)

```
Table 'HeapMe'. Scan count 1, logical reads 14287, physical reads 0, read-ahead reads 0,
lob logical reads 0, lob physical reads 0, lob read-ahead reads 0.
Table 'HeapMe'. Scan count 1, logical reads 2, physical reads 0, read-ahead reads 0,
lob logical reads 0, lob physical reads 0, lob read-ahead reads 0.
```

Q&A

Why does this happen?

My pedestrian explanation is that when the deletes happen, and rows get versioned out to tempdb, the pointers keep the pages allocated just in case.

Why don't they deallocate afterwards?

It looks like they do deallocate from the NC/PK the next time a CHECKPOINT/Ghost Record Cleanup process runs.

The Heap remains Heapy, with all the pages allocated to it though. It's as if the table level lock never happened.

Does query isolation level matter?

No, setting it to Serializable, Repeatable Read, or anything else results in the same mess.

Thanks for reading!

Msg 8948, Level 16, Line 1

Database error: Page (1:9) is marked with the wrong type in PFS page (1:8088). PFS status 0x40 expected 0x60.

SHUTDOWN WITH NOWAIT;

10968687R00205

Made in the USA
Lexington, KY
03 October 2018